AMERICAN CENTURIES

The Ideas, Issues, and Values That Shaped U.S. History

AMERICAN CENTURIES

The Ideas, Issues, and Values That Shaped U.S. History

Volume Three: 18th Century

Brendan McConville, Ph.D., Editor

Facts On File
An Infobase Learning Company

American Centuries: The Ideas, Issues, and Values That Shaped U.S. History

Facts On File, Inc.
An imprint of Infobase Learning
132 West 31st Street
New York, N.Y. 10001

Library of Congress Cataloging-in-Publication Data

American centuries : the ideas, issues, and values that shaped U.S. history / edited by Karen Ordahl Kupperman ... [et al].
p. cm.
Includes bibliographical references and index.
ISBN 978-0-8160-7518-8
1. United States—History—Encyclopedias. I. Kupperman, Karen Ordahl, 1939-

E174.A534 2011
973.03—dc22
2010049904

Facts On File books are available at special discounts when purchased in bulk quantities for businesses, associations, institutions, or sales promotions. Please call our Special Sales Department in New York at (212) 967-8800 or (800) 322-8755.

You can find Facts On File on the World Wide Web at http://www.factsonfile.com.

Developed and produced by MTM Publishing, Inc.
New York, New York
www.mtmpublishing.com

President: Valerie Tomaselli
Editor-in-Chief: Eleanora von Dehsen
Senior Project Editor: Tim Anderson
Production Associates: Zach Gajewski, Lavanya Narasimhan, and Abby Rugg
Design: Annemarie Redmond Design
Maps and Charts: Richard Garratt
Copyediting: Peter Jaskowiak and Glenn E. Novak
Fact Checking: Lavanya Narasimhan, Abby Rugg, and Min Jeong Yoon
Proofreading: Carol Holmes and Glenn E. Novak
Indexing: Stepping Stones Indexing Services

Cover design: Alicia Post

Printed in the United States of America.

10 9 8 7 6 5 4 3 2 1

This book is printed on acid-free paper.

CONTENTS

18th Century CHRONOLOGY

ca. 1700	The population of the English colonies on the mainland of North America numbers about 250,000, including free, indentured, and enslaved inhabitants.
ca. 1700	The American Indian population in what would eventually become the continental United States stands at about 987,000, according to some estimates, though others place it has high as two million.
1701	Adhering to ideals of Christian equality, Quakers open their schools to girls, admit poor children free of charge, and open schools for black children, the first in Philadelphia.
1701	Yale is founded as a college to train ministers.
1701-02	France establishes fortified settlements including Detroit (Michigan) in 1701 and Mobile (Alabama) in 1702.
1702	New Jersey becomes a royal colony, in continuing efforts by the English Crown to increase colonial control.
1702	Maryland legally establishes the Church of England; North and South Carolina—in forms that give a variety of rights to Protestants who dissent from the Anglican Church—do as well.
1702–13	Queen Anne's War takes place; known in Europe as the War of the Spanish Succession, the conflict inflames concerns about France's power as it enters a royal alliance with Spain; the English, Dutch, and Austrians respond in an alliance that leads to war; the greatest concentration of fighting in North America is in New England and French Canada.
1704	The first regular newspaper in the colonies, the *Boston News-Letter*, begins publication; it includes information that its publisher, John Campbell, gleans through his position as the Crown-appointed postmaster, all its material is cleared through the colonial governor's office.
1708	As early as this year, blacks reach 50 percent of South Carolina's population.
1710–29	As do other cities, Boston experiences riot during periods of food shortage in 1710, 1711, 1713, and 1729.

1711 The lower Tuscaroras and some of their coastal Algonquian allies, led by Chief Hancock, strike European settlements to protest their expansion on Indian lands and enslavement of Indian peoples; they are overmatched by the coalition of white settlers aligned against them.

1712 In a slave revolt in New York City, 23 blacks set a building on fire and kill 9 whites; the rebellion is halted and about 21 blacks are found guilty of revolt and executed by New York authorities.

1715 Pennsylvania formally recognizes the right of private and religious bodies to maintain schools and hold property for that purpose; Delaware follows suit in 1743.

1715 By this time, the American colonies are essential to the English navy's power, providing half of all Britain's naval stores—including white pines for ship masts.

1715–18 The Yamasee War occurs; it is the final effort of Native Americans to reverse the establishment of a colony along the British Atlantic coast.

1716–18 The Creeks, in a strategy to survive colonial encroachment, seek multiple alliances, permitting a French garrison at Fort Toulouse in 1716 and a Spanish Fort San Marcos on Apalachee Bay in 1718, even as they welcomed mule trains by English traders into their villages.

1716–19 The MacPheadris-Warner House in Portsmouth, New Hampshire, is built in the Georgian style of residential architecture; it is one of the only such structures existing in 2010.

1718 New Orleans is established; it will become mildly prosperous during the 18th century, but will not realize its prominence until later.

1718 The pueblo that becomes San Antonio is founded; it has a central plaza with a church, surrounded by square blocks of buildings.

1718-21 New England Congregationalists under the leadership of Cotton Mather, a Boston minister, run an evening school to instruct blacks and Indians in reading the scriptures.

1719 African slaves, mainly from Senegambia and West Central Africa, arrive in Louisiana as early as this year; some introduce rice to the riverbanks and bayous, and within two years plantations near New Orleans are producing thousands of pounds of it annually.

1719 Newspaper publication spreads from Boston to Philadelphia, the colonies' second-largest colonial city, when postmaster Andrew Bradford launches the *American Weekly Mercury.*

1719–29 In addition to other measures to shore up its power, the English Crown takes control of South Carolina in 1719, and purchases the proprietorships of both North and South Carolina in 1729.

1720 Trade up and down the East Coast develops due to the strength of the rum and molasses trade that flourishes between the mainland and Barbados after this year.

ca. 1720s–30s The expansion of the colonial population farther inland encourages, in some cases, continued diplomacy and cooperation between colonial governments and Native Americans, including the building of a post at Oswego on Lake Ontario in 1727.

ca. 1720s–30s Formal holidays celebrating the empire's national subgroups, particularly the English, Welsh, Scottish, and Irish peoples, are established in the American colonies as migrants from all areas of the British Isles poured into the provinces on the Atlantic's western shore.

ca. 1720s–50s During this time, colonial America experienced a series of religious revivals that historians come to refer to as the Great Awakening; this movement begins to awaken a pan-colonial popular culture.

1721 Inoculation against smallpox, proposed first proposed by Onesimus, an African slave in the household of the Reverend Cotton Mather of Boston, is successfully tried by the physician Zabdiel Boylston, though the efforts engender controversy.

1721 The Iroquois League—comprising the Mohawks, Oneidas, Onondagas, Cayugas, and Senecas—add the Tuscaroras to form the Six Nations; they adopt a multipronged strategy of warfare and diplomacy to preserve land and avoid the fate of their eastern Indian neighbors.

1721 The spirited *New England Courant* is published without oversight from authority by James Franklin, the elder brother of Benjamin Franklin; unlike the establishment papers, the *Courant* practices rebellious journalism with literary élan.

1722–25 Governor Dummer's War is fought along the New England frontier from Vermont to Maine; in it, Indians aim to establish boundaries of settlement between European powers and Native American allies.

1723–35 A new Anglican church is founded in Boston 1723, and another in 1735, despite its still being Congregationalist stronghold.

1724–62 The Associates of Dr. Thomas Bray is the first Anglican organization to actually create schools for northern blacks—in Philadelphia in 1758, New York City in 1760, and Newport, Rhode Island, in 1762.

1725–26 Pennsylvania's "Act for Better Regulation of Negroes" implements restrictions on manumissions (the formal freeing of slaves), and free blacks who appear to spend their time loitering risk temporary or lifelong enslavement.

1729 Benjamin Franklin takes over the *Pennsylvania Gazette*, started the previous year by Samuel Keimer; under Franklin's direction, it becomes the most widely read paper in the colonies and demonstrates that journalism can be a respectable and profitable occupation.

ca. 1730 After this time, the North American slave population experiences natural population growth, first in the Upper South, and later in the century in the Lower South; Creole slaves (slaves born in the New World) enjoy relatively lower mortality rates and have more balanced sex ratios.

ca. 1730 After this time, white Americans significantly enhance their living standard to include luxuries, due to rising colonial incomes and declining prices of English durable goods.

ca. 1730 Beginning at this time, immigration from Europe increases steadily, and roughly 36,000 Europeans arrived in the coming decade; during the same period, 40,000 Africans are brought to North America to meet the demand for labor in the southern colonies.

ca. 1730s–60s The middle of the 18th century witnesses outbreaks of unrest, relating mostly to land claims and landlord-tenant relations along the Pennsylvania-Maryland border, in northern New Jersey, the Hudson Valley, northeast Pennsylvania's Wyoming Valley, South Carolina's Rocky Mount district, and North Carolina's Granville district.

1731 Benjamin Franklin and his Junto club establishes the first social or subscription library the first time in Philadelphia; the social library spreads rapidly through America.

1732–52 The English Crown issues a proprietary grant for Georgia in 1732; it subsidizes the colony's settlement, and the colony's charter provides for a royal takeover in 1752.

1732–57 Benjamin Franklin publishes *Poor Richard's Almanack*, a best-selling book supposedly compiled by a character created by Franklin named Poor Richard.

1733 Savannah, Georgia, is founded; the city is designed as a rectangular grid of square wards with public buildings fronting the open squares.

1735 South Carolina passes legislation this year that stipulates what slaves can and cannot wear and determines that privately manumitted slaves must leave the colony within six months of their manumission, and are not allowed to return to the colony for at least seven years.

1738 Many of the African descendants in Florida, along with freed blacks from British colonies, settle in Gracia Real de Santa Teresa de Mose, or Fort Mose, a free black community that the Spanish governor founded in this year.

1738-42 The private residence, Drayton Hall, is constructed near Charleston, South Carolina, in the Georgian style of architecture, which is popular during the period.

1738–46 Elizabeth Timothy of South Carolina, who succeeds her husband in his printing enterprise, printed the *South Carolina Gazette* during this period; at least 17 women are counted among the ranks of printers in the colonial period.

1739 The slave revolt, known as the Stono Rebellion, occurs in South Carolina; white militias put down the rebellion, executing the rebels afterward, or selling them into slavery in the West Indies.

1739 Following the Stono Rebellion, the South Carolina assembly passes legislation outlawing the teaching of writing to slaves.

1739–44 The War of Jenkins' Ear takes place over Spanish restrictions on British trade in the West Indies and the violations against British ships committed by Spain, including the supposed cutting off of merchant captain Robert Jenkins's ear by a Spanish sailor during a boarding skirmish.

ca. 1740s By this time, blacks reach 40 percent of the population in some parts of Virginia, though they will never become a majority as they do in the Lowcountry of South Carolina and Georgia.

ca. 1740s By this time, Gullah or Geechee in the South Carolina and Georgia Sea Islands becomes the primary language for local blacks.

1740 The British Board of Trade applies the 1720 Bubble Act, regulating bank charters in the empire to the Massachusetts and Connecticut land banks.

1740 A seriously devastating fire level whole blocks of Charleston, South Carolina.

1740 South Carolina passes a law that prohibits anyone from educating slaves.

ca. 1740–70 In this time period, immigration increases to an average of 130,000 per decade, with half coming from Africa.

1744–48 King George's War is fought when Britain enters the War of the Austrian Succession against France in 1744 and helps New England forces gain control of the French stronghold of Louisbourg in Nova Scotia; Britain cedes Louisbourg in the treaty that ends the war.

1741 The colonies first magazines are published in Philadelphia, including Andrew Bradford's *American Magazine* and Benjamin Franklin's *General Magazine*; Franklin's survives the longest—for six months; by 1800, nearly 100 magazines are published.

1741–47 The arrival of navy "press gangs" who sweep up involuntary recruits spark riots in Boston in 1741, 1745, and 1747.

1743 The American Philosophical Society is founded in Philadelphia; it brings together countless scientists, artisans, and inventors, as well as statesmen, politicians, and others, to organize and enhance learning and public service.

1746 The Presbyterians inaugurate a new age of college building when they found the College of New Jersey (later Princeton); the Anglicans follow suit with King's College (later Columbia) in 1754, the Baptists with the College of Rhode Island (later Brown) in 1764, the Dutch Reformed Church with Queen's College (later Rutgers), and the Congregationalists with Dartmouth in 1769.

1746 France spends 54,000 livres (a significant sum) on Indian presents, an example indicating the importance the European powers—especially France and England—placed on Indian diplomacy.

ca. 1750s By this time, colonists, especially those who lived along the coast, are regularly enjoying access to food from other regions: Okra from South Carolina moves to Rhode Island, Virginian ham is sold in South Carolina, and New England cod goes to the middle colonies.

ca. 1750 Total population in colonial British North America is 1,186,000, with 934,000 white and 252,000 black; total population in what would become the continental United States is 1,956,000, with 770,000 Indians.

ca. 1750 By this time, blacks outnumber whites by nearly two to one in South Carolina and about 50 percent of Louisiana's population is of African descent.

ca. 1750 By this time, the King's Highway—later to be known as the Boston Post Road—connects all of the major coastal cities between Boston and Charleston.

1750 The Quakers, many of whom are committed to slave emancipation, establish their first school for blacks, when Anthony Benezet starts teaching slave children in his Philadelphia home at night.

1750 By this time, at least 12 newspapers are being published in the colonies, in Maryland, Virginia, South Carolina, Massachusetts, New York, and Pennsylvania.

1751 Parliament passes the Currency Act, which ends various New England efforts to print paper money.

1751 Benjamin Franklin's findings from his multi-year investigations into static electricity are published in *Experiments and Observations on Electricity*.

1751 Pennsylvania Hospital, the first institution dedicated solely to the care of the sick, is established in Philadelphia; it is dedicated to both medical services and training of physicians; the second such institution, New York Hospital, opens in 1791.

1754 *A Careful and Strict Inquiry into the Modern Prevailing Notions of That Freedom of the Will* is published; it is written by Jonathan Edwards, America's greatest religious philosopher of the time; he also pens *The Great Christian Doctrine of Original Sin Defended*, published four years later.

1754–63 Conflict among European powers erupts in 1754 primarily between France and Britain, who formally declare war in 1756; known as the Seven Years' War in Europe and the French and Indian War in America, it is won by Britain, who gains much land in North America as a result.

1755 The Georgia legislature passes a law in prohibiting teaching writing to slaves.

1755 The College of Philadelphia (later the University of Pennsylvania) is the only college established in the age of "college enthusiasm" that lacks denominational affiliation, although it soon comes under Anglican control.

1755 In *Some Account of the Fore Part of the Life of Elizabeth Ashbridge*, published in this year, Ashbridge recounts her conversion to Quakerism, which she once had rejected, as well as the challenges of practicing it in the face of her husband's resistance.

1758 At the annual meeting of the Society of Friends, the Quakers decide to prohibit its members from owning slaves.

1758-64 After the British victory during the Seven Years' War, the British rename Fort Duquesne as Pittsburgh in 1758 and begin to lay out a city there in 1764.

ca. 1760s	By this time, circulating libraries are set up in many areas; in contrast to social libraries, whose membership is limited, circulating libraries disseminate books to as many readers as are willing to pay a nominal fee.
ca. 1760s	After hovering around 70 percent for the period 1670–1710, the rate of male signing literacy rises to 85 percent by this time; the rate of female signature literacy increases to over 60 percent during the 1760s from 45 percent in 1710.
ca. 1760s–70s	In the South Carolina Regulation, frontier vigilantes battle bandits and vagrants and clamor for a more effective frontier judicial system.
1760	The Long Island writer and slave Jupiter Hammon pens "An Evening Thought: Salvation by Christ with Penitential Cries."
1760	In Boston, a devastating fire destroys massive sections of the city.
1760–61	A rebellion of Cherokees along the Carolina and Georgia frontiers arises from the changing nature of their relations with Britain; denied their customary grants of gunpowder by Britain, Cherokees villages unite against the British, who eventually nullifies initial Cherokee successes.
1763	Britain establishes the Proclamation Line of 1763 at the end of the French and Indian War; it runs along the Appalachian Mountains and restricts colonists from settling beyond it, on Indian lands, but causes anger in settlers and speculators who fought in the war primarily to gain access to new land.
1763	After this date, following the end of the French and Indian War, Indians in the Ohio River Valley, Great Lakes region, and interior Southeast face a growing Anglo-American population who are eager to seize Indian territory, particularly in the absence of the Indian's French allies.
1763–64	The Paxton Boys riots occur, when vigilantism against Indians turns into a protest against Pennsylvania's provincial government and ends with a march by armed rioters on Philadelphia; the arrival of royal troops and formation of a city militia turns back the rioters.
1763–65	Believing that a united Native American force could drive the British from the Great Lakes region, Ottawa chief Pontiac organizes a multitribal alliance against the British; after some initial success, he is forced into a peace treaty in 1765.
1764	France establishes a fortified settlement in Missouri, at St. Louis.
1764	By this year, mail is being carried by day and night between Philadelphia and New York, with plans to extend a similar level of more rapid service to Boston.

1764–65 Anti-impressment riots take place in New York and Newport, Rhode Island.

1764–65 In conjunction with renewed enforcement of the Navigation Acts passed a century earlier, Parliament passes the Sugar Act (1764) and Stamp Act (1765), aimed at increasing revenue from the colonies in order to retire the British national debt and pay for troops stationed in America, while also increasing control over the colonies as well.

1765 Representatives of nine colonies assemble the Stamp Act Congress and issue the Declaration of Rights and Grievances, which condemns the Stamp Act and claims for the colonists the inherent rights of all natural-born Englishmen, including trial by jury and taxation through representation.

1765 With the formation of a committee known as "the Loyal Nine" in Boston, who will be absorbed into the Sons of Liberty, a trend begins whereby extra-legal groups organize and defend the rights of the colonists against British oppression.

1765 In a riot involving protesters against the Stamp Act in Boston, a crowd tears down a building built by the newly appointed stamp distributor, Andrew Oliver and then ransacks Oliver's home.

1765–66 John Bartram, one of the most accomplished plant collectors in the colonies, researches extensively in eastern North America, including a trip at this time to the Southeast, after which he published the influential *Diary of a Journey through the Carolinas, Georgia, and Florida.*

1765–67 John Morgan and a group of prominent physicians establish a medical school as part of the College of Philadelphia (later the University of Pennsylvania); King's College (later Columbia University) opens its own medical school and becomes the first American school to award the MD degree.

1765–67 *The Prince of Parthia* by Thomas Godfrey is the first play written by an American to be staged in America.

1765–69 Sir William Blackstone publishes his famous *Commentaries on the Laws of England*, a four-volume summary of English common law; well into the 19th century, American lawyers use it for their legal education and main source for knowledge about English common law.

1766 The battle between tenant farmers and the Hudson Valley's manor lords reaches a climax with an uprising led by William Prendergast; British troops stationed in New York help to quell this disturbance; but resistance continues in the following decades.

1766-67 Parliament rescinds the Stamp Act in 1766 in the face of massive noncompliance and threats of mob violence, but also passes the Declaratory Act, stating that Parliament's authority is the same in America as in Britain, and that it retains lawmaking power over the colonies in all cases.

1767 Phillis Wheatley, a Senegambian woman who learned to read and write while the slave of a Boston merchant, publishes her poem, "An Address to the Atheist."

1767 Parliament enacts the Townshend Acts, a series of five acts primarily designed to assert parliamentary supremacy while raising revenue from the colonies for their own administration; the colonists protest and Parliament, fearing rebellion, repeals the taxes, except that on tea.

1767–78 John Dickinson's 12 "Letters from a Farmer in Pennsylvania" are first printed in the *Pennsylvania Chronicle*, and then widely reproduced in other colonies; read across America and in Europe, they call for colonial unity and urged peaceful resistance to British oppression.

1768 A group of 20 merchants organizes the first chamber of commerce in America in New York City.

1768 Boston's "Liberty Riot" occurs: Several thousand Bostonians take to the streets when sailors from the HMS *Romney*, who are also on an impressment run in the city, attempt to impound John Hancock's sloop *Liberty* for customs violations.

1768–69 The "Journal of Occurrences" is published in the *New York Journal* and papers from New England to Georgia; it is culled together by members of the Sons of Liberty, a group of patriots agitating for independence from Britain, from their contacts throughout the colonies

1769 Spanish evangelization of Native peoples in California begins in this year with the founding of San Diego; by 1804 there are 19 missions along the coast, including San Francisco and Santa Barbara.

1769-82 Spain expands its northern reaches in Mexico, by making inroads into California; it adds presidios, or forts, in San Diego in 1769, in Monterey in 1770, in San Francisco in 1776, and in Santa Barbara in 1782; to feed these garrisons, the governor of California established pueblos at San José in 1777 and in Los Angeles in 1781.

ca. 1770 By this time, a half-dozen cities feature permanent, purpose-built theaters, and another two dozen towns have hosted at least one professional touring company.

ca. 1770 By this time, the slave population in the North remains small:; close to 70,000 blacks live in the North, which is still less than 5 percent of the total population.

ca. 1770 By this time, African descendants constitute 50 percent of the population in Georgia.

ca. 1770 By this time, New York City and Philadelphia have grown to urban centers of about 25,000 and 32,000 people, respectively; Boston's growth, however, stagnates reaching approximately 16,000 by the 1740s and will remain at that level until the end of the century.

1770 The Georgia legislature passes a law in prohibiting the of teaching reading to slaves.

1770 The Quaker Anthony Benezet raises enough money to build a separate black school and hire a schoolmaster.

1770 In the Boston Massacre, crowds of colonists harass British soldiers, who open fire on the mob; Crispus Attucks, an African American believed to have been a runaway slave, is one of the five men killed and is considered to be the first person to die for the Revolutionary cause.

1771 In the North Carolina War of Regulation, frontier insurgents, who protest government corruption and forcefully shut down the county court system, are put down violently by provincial authorities at the Battle of Alamance.

1771 By this time, as Benjamin Carp notes in *Rebels Rising*, there is one tavern or liquor license for every 13 adult white men in New York City.

1773 Colonists—in protest against British taxes levied on tea and the tea monopoly granted the East India Company by Britain in this year—dump three shiploads of tea into the Boston Harbor; this incident comes to be known as the Boston Tea Party

1773 Phillis Wheatley's collection, *Poems on Various Subjects, Religious and Moral*, is published in London the year she is freed from slavery; she is the first black American to publish a book of poetry.

1773 James Rivington, begins publishing *Rivington's New York Gazetteer* in 1773; as editor, he tries to remain neutral, but after the 1775 fighting at Lexington and Concord, he abandons objectivity; during the Revolutionary War, he renames it the *Royal Gazette* and hews to Tory, or loyalist, ideals.

1774 Parliament enacts a series of punitive laws, known as the Intolerable Acts, in reaction to the Boston Tea Party; among other regulations, the measures close Boston's port, abolish the election of provincial councilors, and strengthen the powers of the royal governor while weakening those of town meetings.

1774 The First Continental Congress, which meets in Philadelphia, passes the Declaration of Rights and Resolves, which condemns Britain's imperial policy since 1763 and rejects Parliament's claims of sovereignty within the colonies.

1774 The Continental Association, formed out of the Continental Congress of 1774, issues a colonies-wide prohibition of British goods and other forms of "extravagance," but the embrace of imported goods and styles persists into the years of open conflict with Great Britain.

1774 Following a recommendation issued by the Continental Congress in 1774, every colony—and, later, state—explicitly outlaws theater, horse racing, cockfighting, and other activities affiliated with gambling and organized public entertainment.

1774 *The Journal of John Woolman*, a classic in the genre of spiritual autobiography, is published.

1775 The battles of Lexington and Concord are fought between British regulars and American militiamen; the skirmishes effectively launch the American Revolution.

1775 A crowd of New Yorkers tar and feather a shoemaker named Tweedy after he speaks out against the city's Revolutionary committee—an extra-legal group of Patriots who run the city's affairs following the breakdown of imperial authority in the colony.

1775 Virginia's royal governor, Lord Dunmore, promises freedom to those blacks who join the British forces, and by the end of the year, the British have enlisted 300 African Americans.

1775-83 The Revolutionary War takes place; the beginning of the war begins to establish American diplomatic independence, as the colonies attempt to align themselves with—and seek material support from—European powers other than Britain.

1775–83 During the Revolutionary War, most Native groups side with the British, including four of the six Iroquois nations, nearly all of the Ohio and Great Lakes tribes, and, for a time, the Cherokees; Native groups on both sides, however, suffer major losses in power, land, and numbers by the war's end.

1776 The Declaration of Independence, penned primarily by Thomas Jefferson, is signed; it is driven in part by the need to establish separation with Britain, as the imperial power, in order to parlay formally with European powers.

1776 Thomas Paine's pamphlet *Common Sense* is published; in it, Paine rejects the arguments for reconciliation with Great Britain and calls for "a final separation;" Paine will be one of the most important literary forces behind the Revolution.

1776–77 New republican constitutions based on popular sovereignty are created in most states and the fear of arbitrary power concentrated in the hands of one person lead constitution writers to diminish the power of governors.

1776–80 The third—and perhaps most ambitious—of James Cook's voyages, and the one that culminated in Cook's death in Hawaii, yields highly accurate navigational charts for the Northwest Coast of North America from Vancouver Sound to Alaska and the Aleutian Islands.

1777 By this time, the Continental forces more commonly accept both free and enslaved blacks.

1777–78 French monarch, Louis XVI, signs a treaty with the newly declared United States, shortly after the American victory at the Battle of Saratoga; a French declaration of war follows in 1778.

1778 A formal system of post riders is created by the Continental Congress, in which teams of mail riders every 25 to 30 miles or so will carry the mail—at least three times a week, day and night—until delivered to the next rider.

1779–80 Spain joins the Revolutionary War conflict against the British, and in 1780 the British, fearing Dutch intervention, declares war on the Netherlands.

ca. 1780 Slaves account for 40 percent of the total population of the southern colonies by this time.

ca. 1780 By this time, at least 260 private schoolmasters work in New York, and 283 in Philadelphia by 1783.

ca. 1780s In Carlisle, Pennsylvania; Albany, New York; and New York City, street processions by anti-Federalists and Federalists devolve into violence.

1781 The Articles of Confederation are ratified; the government they establish remains in place immediately after the Revolutionary War, but the Articles are weak; for instance, they providefor only one federal court, which hears appeals from states in cases involving shipping and the high seas.

1781 Mum Bett—later Elizabeth Freeman—succeeds in petitioning for her freedom by claiming that the preamble of Massachusetts's 1780 constitution, which states that "all men are born free and equal," should pertain to her; she is the first African American to gain freedom under the state's constitution.

1781–1804 The Massachusetts high court abolishes slavery in the state; other northern states pass acts for the gradual abolition of slavery, including Pennsylvania in 1780, Connecticut in 1784, New York in 1799, and New Jersey in 1804.

1782 *Letters from an American Farmer* by J. Hector St. John de Crèvecoeur is published; it is an explicit, often ecstatic, celebration of America as a land of opportunity.

1782 Farmers rise in protest against taxes and debt during Ely's Rebellion in Western Massachusetts and Connecticut.

1783 By the end of the Revolutionary War, 5,000 African Americans have served in the Continental Army, while the offer of freedom in exchange for military service have motivated about 15,000 to 20,000 black men and women to flee to the British lines, with almost a thousand of them serving in the army.

1783 The Chesapeake colonies abolish the importation of African slaves.

1784 America's first law school, Litchfield Law School, is opened in Litchfield, Connecticut; it operates as a private, for-profit school; its graduates will include 3 U.S. Supreme Court justices, 56 state supreme court justices, 129 federal legislators, 14 state governors, and 6 U.S. Cabinet members.

1784–87 The U.S. government under the Articles of Confederation passes a series of ordinances, culminating in the three Northwest Ordinances of 1784–87, that outline a method to establish new governments in the interior.

1785 The Virginia state legislature commissions the French sculptor Jean-Antoine Houdon to complete a full-length sculpture of Revolutionary War hero, George Washington, for the Virginia State Capitol; Houdon depicts Washington as a Roman senator.

1785-88 The Land Ordinance of 1785 specifies that the states that become the Midwest will be laid out in square townships; Ohio towns like Marietta and Cincinnati, both founded in 1788, reflected this grid pattern.

1785-89 The Virginia State Capitol, designed by Thomas Jefferson in the neo-classical style and based on a Roman temple, is built.

1786 Charles Wilson Peale creates one of the first museums in America; the Philadelphia Museum combines natural history specimens and curiosities, with paintings and portraits of founding fathers.

1786-87 Farmers rise up in rebellion against the state of Massachusetts during Shays's Rebellion, led by Daniel Shays; the rebels shut down the county courts in order to halt prosecution for debt and challenge authority of the state, which responds by raising a militia that puts down the rebels.

1787 One of the most significant plays of the era, Royall Tyler's *The Contrast* (1787), is published; it is a comedy of manners featuring a colonial army colonel named Manly and the prototype for the Yankee rustic in a character named Jonathan.

1787 Founding father and future president, Thomas Jefferson, writes in *Notes on the State of Virginia*, published in this year, that descendants of Africans are inferior to whites; Jefferson himself is a slaveholder.

1787 A constitutional convention in Philadelphia shapes a new government based on a new constitution, which provides for enhanced power of the central government over taxation, the military, and interstate commerce, as well as the creation of a complex federal judiciary, the establishment in theory of federal supremacy over state law.

1787–88 A series of 85 essays known as the Federalist Papers, written by Alexander Hamilton, James Madison, and John Jay write under the pen name "Publius," are published in the semiweekly *New York Independent Journal*; these pieces strongly advocate the ratification of the Constitution, and

1788 The Constitution, though bitterly debated, is adopted by the states; in addition to enhancing authority of the central government, it reinforces slavery with the "three-fifths compromise," which says that slaves count toward a state's population as three-fifths of a person.

1788 New Jersey passes a law mandating the teaching of slaves prior to their emancipation.

1789 The U.S. Post Office is established, becoming an important part of creating the new federal government; it becomes a permanent organ of government three years later.

1789 The autobiography of freed slave Olaudah Equiano, *The Interesting Narrative of the Life of Olaudah Equiano, or Gustavus Vassa, the African*, is published; it is the first notable example of an American genre called the slave narrative.

1789 In the Judiciary Act of 1789, Congress provides for a United States Supreme Court composed of six justices and for a system of lower federal courts; John Jay becomes the first chief justice of the United States.

1789 University legal education begins in America when a lawyer named George Wythe is appointed "Professor of Law and Police" at the College of William and Mary in Williamsburg, Virginia.

1789 William H. Brown pens a popular novel, *The Power of Sympathy*, which is usually identified as the first novel written by an American.

1789–93 John Fenno starts the *Gazette of the United States* in New York; it backs the Federalists in their support of a strong federal government and loose interpretation of the Constitution; other Federalist papers appear, including the *Minerva* in New York in 1793 edited by Noah Webster.

1789–97 George Washington, having led the country in the Revolution, serves as the new nation's first president.

ca. 1790 The rate of male signature literacy rises to 90 percent by this time.

ca. 1790 By this time, thousands of settlers are developing the resources of the Tennessee Valley, with thousands more on the Cumberland Plateau and in the eastern foothills of the Blue Ridge Mountains; the Appalachian region as a whole has at least 80,000 inhabitants.

1790 The Naturalization Act of 1790 offers naturalization to any "free white person" who has resided in the country for at least two years, proven his "good character," and taken an oath to "support the constitution of the United States."

1790 The first U.S. Census is taken; it counts a total black population of 757,208, of which 59,511 (7.9 percent) are free; blacks total 6.2 percent of the Mid-Atlantic population, 1.7 in New England population was; 32.6 in the Lower South, and 37.6 in the Upper South; almost 90 percent of the total African American population resides in the Upper or Lower South.

1791 The Bill of Rights, passed unopposed in the first Congress, becomes part of the Constitution; the individual amendments institute additional rights not in the original text of the Constitution, such as freedom of speech and the right not to be forced to testify against oneself in court.

1791 *Travels through North and South Carolina, Georgia, East and West Florida* is written by William Bartram, perhaps the greatest American science writer of the age, who describes the alligators, fish, flowers, and other animals and plants he encounters.

1791 The novel *Charlotte Temple, A Tale of Truth*, written by British-American novelist Susanna Rowson, is written; it is the most popular best seller in America at the end of the 18th century.

1792 Postal legislation expands the role of the postal service; it prevents government surveillance of personal letters, provides for low rates to mail newspapers, and passes control of new postal routes from the executive branch to Congress.

1792 As the country emerges from wartime recession, every state loosens its prohibition on leisure activities and by this time every state has legalized theater.

1792–1800 The Democratic-Republicans, or Republicans, organize in opposition to the Federalists, who are in power from 1789 to 1801; the Federalists support a strong central government, while the Republicans support states' rights; the conflict is diffused by a peaceful transfer of power to the Republicans when Thomas Jefferson's is elected president in 1800.

1793 Portrait painter Gilbert Stuart returns from Britain with the express intention of painting George Washington; by this time, he had become the most sought-after portraitist in the country.

1793 A yellow fever epidemic ravages Philadelphia.

1793 A party of trappers and Native guides, led by Scottish fur trader Alexander Mackenzie and funded by Montreal's Northwest Company in hopes of finding a route to the west coast, is the first to traverse the North America.

1793 Joel Barlow, one in a group of writers who came to be known as the Connecticut Wits, or Hartford Wits, adapts one of the era's favorite genres, the epic, for comic purposes in his poem *The Hasty-Pudding*.

1793 Philadelphia suffers a devastating yellow fever epidemic, in which between 3,000 and 5,000 of the city's 55,000 residents die; after the epidemic, the city founds a permanent public health committee.

1793–94 A diplomatic and constitutional crisis unfolds as French citizen Edmond Genêt recruits Americans supporters of the French Revolution to privateer against British vessels, following President George Washington demand for neutrality in Europe's War of the First Coalition.

1794 The Jay Treaty is signed, whereby Britain agrees to evacuate the Northwest Territories in 1796 and to end discrimination against American commercial interests.

1794 Collection of internal taxes leads to violent resistance, culminating in the Whiskey Rebellion, also known as the Pennsylvania Regulation; the unrest ends when the federal government sends a militia army of 13,000 troops into western Pennsylvania to restore order.

1794	The American Convention of Abolition Societies encourages members to instruct free black and slave children in "common literature."
1794	Congress creates the U.S. Navy to defend American ships from Barbary Coast piracy off the northern African coast, yet the federal government still pays ransoms two years later.
1795	Charles Pinckney, the American envoy to Spain, reports a treaty with Spain, which surrenders its ambitions in the trans-Appalachian Southwest.
1795	A new Naturalization Act is passed, increasing the length of residency, over the 1790 act, to five years before an individual can obtain citizenship.
1796	Tennessee joins the United States and settlement surges across the Appalachians; with negotiations for the Jay Treaty having established closer relations between the Britain and the United States, Britain withdraws its support for Indians living in the frontiers.
1797	President John Adams seeks to continue President Washington's policy of neutrality—a stance that leads to the undeclared Quasi-War with France from 1798 to 1800.
1798	The Alien and Sedition Acts, passed in this year and to remain in force for the next two, tighten naturalization requirements and mandate substantial fines and imprisonment for anyone who criticizes the government.
1799	Farmers in the eastern part of Pennsylvania challenge federal authority and taxes during Fries's Rebellion, but federal troops quell the protest
1799	With the Compromise Act of 1799, Pennsylvania makes provisions to provide northeast Pennsylvania's agrarian insurgents with land at prices they can afford; this eventually undermines rural resistance in the area.
ca. 1800	Total population in the United States is 5,308,000, with 4,306,000 white and 1,002,000 black; total population in what would become the continental United States is 5,908,000, with 600,000 Indians.
ca. 1800	By this time, log dwellings have become the most common form of housing in the new United States.
ca. 1800	By this time, the population of the early republic spreads beyond the Appalachian Mountains; about 500,000 are settled on land near the Ohio, Tennessee, and Cumberland rivers that drain into the Mississippi River.
1800	The census lists Philadelphia, New York City, Baltimore, Boston, and Charleston as the five largest cities, each with over 10,000 people.

18th Century INTRODUCTION

"Who was there," wrote the Connecticut minister Jabez Huntington in 1777, "twenty years past, that beheld the harmony that subsisted between Britain and her colonies—that saw the wide Atlantic full of vessels laden with effects from America, bound to our native country—who could have thought . . . that all the powers of earth and hell could have produced so sudden an alteration in the nature of things." America had become an independent nation, and Huntington noted that "the same ocean full of shipping from our mother country, bound to America, [is now] laden with soldiers, arms and ammunition, and all manner of instruments of death and cruelty, to destroy her own children!" "Who," he continued, "could have thought a little detestable tea, thrown into the ocean by a factious mob, should be the cause of an ocean of bloodshed, and for ever dissolve that union that was worth more tea than the East Indies produced."

Jabez Huntington's emotional words were shaped in a society locked in a terrible war on its own soil. And yet as upset and unsettled as he might have been, Huntington understood a central aspect of the 18th century: It was a period of profound changes, not only in political relationships, but in all realms of human activities. Religion, the arts, economic relationships, science, and literature—all were dramatically altered or reformed in a century punctuated by religious upheaval, imperial warfare, and the American Revolution. Great empires fell, republics formed, new religious sects emerged, and, by century's end, the steam engine was foreshadowing the rise of industrial capital. Subjects gave way to citizens; learned religious ministers gave way to evangelical enthusiasts; and the capitalist entrepreneur supplanted the colonial placeman bent on winning a position in one of the royal governments that controlled the American governments. New personalities and social identities came with these new times. People, and families, changed along with institutions and ideas as part of the broader struggle to create a working nation and a national identity.

Transformations

This massive transformation—or better yet, transformations—had roots deep in the 16th and 17th centuries, and was part of broader changes in European, Native American, and African societies sparked by contact, trade, and warfare on the three continents. The chronologies of these changes often do not fit our preconceived notion of events that led to the creation of the American republic. There were, though, some constants as forces of change in the period between 1700 and 1800: the dynamic growth of European and African populations, which by natural increase and immigration (forced immigration, in the case of African slaves) doubled every 25 years and encouraged the expansion of trade; warfare, and the threat of warfare, which was a constant part of life throughout the 18th century in North America among the European empires, against the European empires after the Revolution, and against the Native Americans; and the search for working cultural templates for these new societies.

In 1700, after a quarter century of turmoil in North America and the British Isles over who would rule was settled by the Glorious Revolution in England, a tendency toward the royalization of colonial government was visible—haphazard and incomplete though it was. The London government was in charge, and it wanted to bring the colonies into the empire. Political ceremonies that celebrated Britain's Protestant monarchy were introduced into American port towns and villages, the courts became more British in their appearance and function as professionally trained judges and lawyers appeared, and a print culture derived from or modeled on publications in England and Scotland, and carrying the views of the London government, became more visible in colonial towns.

The material and social life of many colonial Americans reflected this change. British consumer goods became more common in the mainland colonies, as well as in the British possessions in the West Indies. Anglicization, the remodeling of the colonies on the template provided by Britain and British society, predominated as a cultural tendency in the first four decades of the 18th century. London fashions became all the rage for the wealthy in the port towns of America, and British food and drink were the standard by which colonial fare was measured. Though imperial control remained loose institutionally due to the vast distances between the imperial center and the periphery in an era in which transportation was dominated by sailing ships, the American colonies were becoming part of the British Empire and taking their cues about government and culture from British models.

Colonial Society Remade

This powerful tendency toward identifying with Britain continued until the American Revolution, but long before those dramatic events, other changes in the society or societies of North America created new trajectories of development that made the colonies distinct from European societies. Because of massive forced migrations from Africa, most West Indian societies and South Carolina were predominantly populated by people of African descent by 1740. German-speaking people, Scots, and Scots-Irish arrived in North America from northern Europe by the thousands and tens of thousands and expanded their settlements into the interior and down the Appalachian Mountains into the Carolinas and Georgia, further diversifying the population and, in the process, creating immense new problems in the relationships with Native Americans. With immigration and natural increase doubling the population of British America every 25 years, towns and villages increased in number and size, becoming commercial and social hubs.

The increase in population encouraged the expansion of trade and commerce. Shipping carried goods within colonies, between them, and to outposts around the Atlantic Ocean. Timber, tobacco, and indigo, and sugar from the West Indies and rum from New England flowed outward, while European manufactured goods, wines from the Atlantic islands, tea from China, and slave labor from Africa flowed inward. Complex commercial interchanges increased dramatically between 1700 and 1750 as trade expanded, and the wealth visible in communities near the ocean or major rivers often increased markedly.

Trade and the movement of populations also encouraged new ideas and new forms of communication. Itinerant evangelical Protestant preachers appeared, some American-born and others hailing from England, Scotland, Northern Ireland, Germany, the Netherlands, and Switzerland, traveling from town to town in every colony and promising fire and brimstone to all who would not obey God's word as explained in the Bible, in what became known as a "Great Awakening" of religion. Ignoring parish and town boundaries, they preached wherever they could gather audiences, and they ultimately encouraged the appearance of new religious sects in the society. The ever-more-numerous newspapers, broadsides, and pamphlets published in the leading towns reported on these religious radicals and the controversies they created, as well as events in the colonies and in Europe. These publications reached more and more people as grammar schools and ultimately colleges (many with ties to the evangelical community) were established on the Eastern Seaboard of North America and encouraged a broad literacy.

Had these changes alone acted on British America and the American continent, the impact would have been dramatic but, in all likelihood, containable. The British Empire might have survived the 18th century, and the Atlantic might have become a British lake for centuries thereafter. Beginning in 1730s, however, the intensification of imperial warfare between Britain on one hand and France and Spain on the other entangled the colonists, and the Native American nations, in a series of conflicts that amplified the impact of all changes in the society and created other powerful, transformative social currents. The fighting, part of a long hundred years' war between the European powers that began in 1689 with the outbreak of King William's War (1689–97) and did not really end until Napoleon was defeated at Waterloo in 1815, encouraged new men in business who challenged old ways, led to the creation of paper money supplies in the colonies to finance the war effort and greatly expand available credit markets, and created massive new problems of imperial administration and control. With the British Empire's victory in the Seven Years' War in 1763, the French were expelled from most of North America, and millions of acres were brought under the control of the London administration.

Resistance and Revolution

This vast imperial war, which ran from 1756 to 1763, provided the immediate backdrop to the imperial crisis and the American Revolution, which proved so dramatic a rupture that many of the trends in government and culture that were

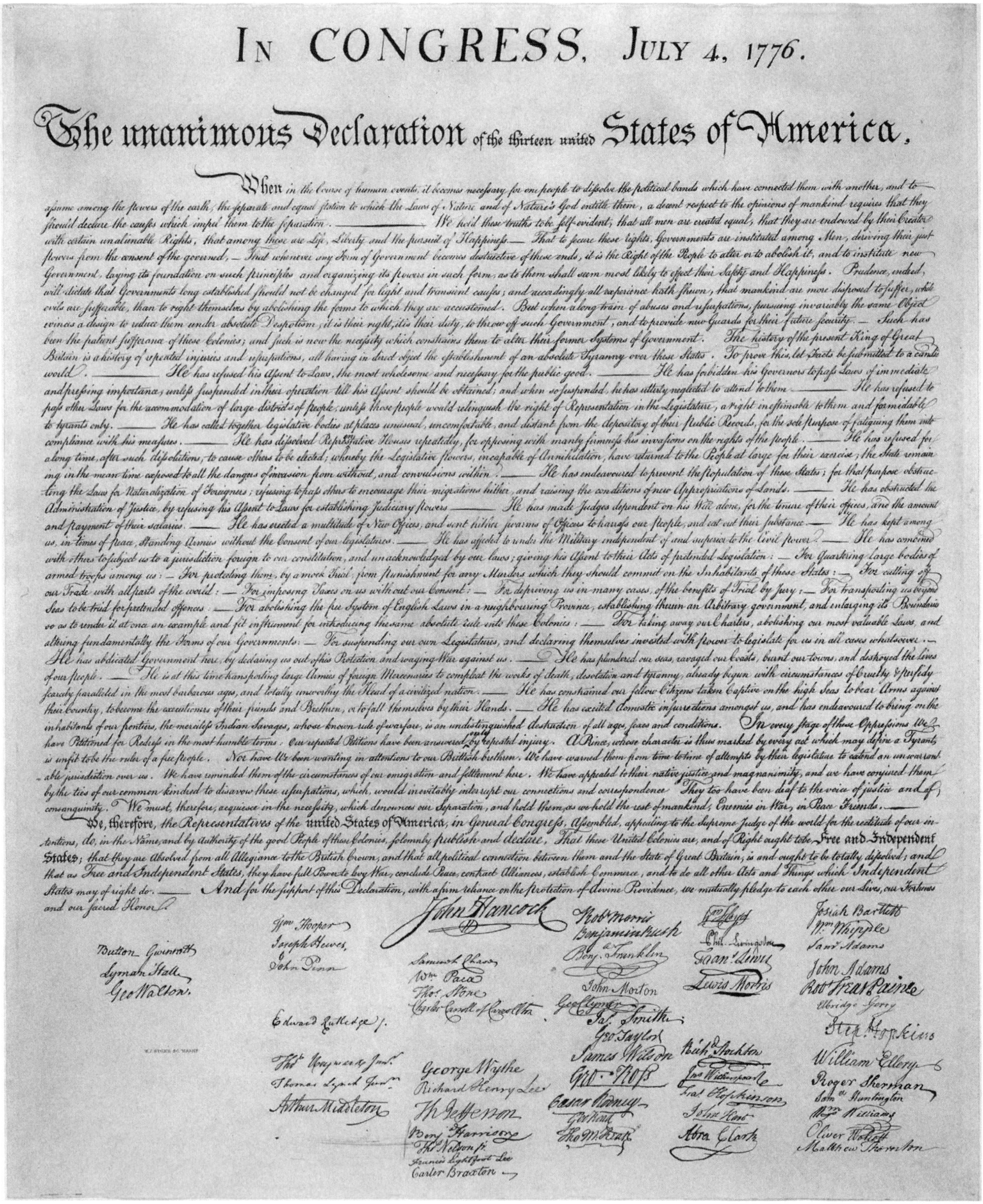
IN CONGRESS, JULY 4, 1776.

The unanimous Declaration of the thirteen united States of America,

When in the Course of human events, it becomes necessary for one people to dissolve the political bands which have connected them with another, and to assume among the powers of the earth, the separate and equal station to which the Laws of Nature and of Nature's God entitle them, a decent respect to the opinions of mankind requires that they should declare the causes which impel them to the separation. —— We hold these truths to be self-evident, that all men are created equal, that they are endowed by their Creator with certain unalienable Rights, that among these are Life, Liberty and the pursuit of Happiness. — That to secure these rights, Governments are instituted among Men, deriving their just powers from the consent of the governed, — That whenever any Form of Government becomes destructive of these ends, it is the Right of the People to alter or to abolish it, and to institute new Government, laying its foundation on such principles and organizing its powers in such form, as to them shall seem most likely to effect their Safety and Happiness. Prudence, indeed, will dictate that Governments long established should not be changed for light and transient causes; and accordingly all experience hath shewn, that mankind are more disposed to suffer, while evils are sufferable, than to right themselves by abolishing the forms to which they are accustomed. But when a long train of abuses and usurpations, pursuing invariably the same Object evinces a design to reduce them under absolute Despotism, it is their right, it is their duty, to throw off such Government, and to provide new Guards for their future security. — Such has been the patient sufferance of these Colonies; and such is now the necessity which constrains them to alter their former Systems of Government. The history of the present King of Great Britain is a history of repeated injuries and usurpations, all having in direct object the establishment of an absolute Tyranny over these States. To prove this, let Facts be submitted to a candid world. —— He has refused his Assent to Laws, the most wholesome and necessary for the public good. —— He has forbidden his Governors to pass Laws of immediate and pressing importance, unless suspended in their operation till his Assent should be obtained; and when so suspended, he has utterly neglected to attend to them. —— He has refused to pass other Laws for the accommodation of large districts of people, unless those people would relinquish the right of Representation in the Legislature, a right inestimable to them and formidable to tyrants only. —— He has called together legislative bodies at places unusual, uncomfortable, and distant from the depository of their public Records, for the sole purpose of fatiguing them into compliance with his measures. —— He has dissolved Representative Houses repeatedly, for opposing with manly firmness his invasions on the rights of the people. —— He has refused for a long time, after such dissolutions, to cause others to be elected; whereby the Legislative powers, incapable of Annihilation, have returned to the People at large for their exercise; the State remaining in the mean time exposed to all the dangers of invasion from without, and convulsions within. —— He has endeavoured to prevent the population of these States; for that purpose obstructing the Laws for Naturalization of Foreigners; refusing to pass others to encourage their migrations hither, and raising the conditions of new Appropriations of Lands. —— He has obstructed the Administration of Justice, by refusing his Assent to Laws for establishing Judiciary powers. —— He has made Judges dependent on his Will alone, for the tenure of their offices, and the amount and payment of their salaries. —— He has erected a multitude of New Offices, and sent hither swarms of Officers to harrass our people, and eat out their substance. —— He has kept among us, in times of peace, Standing Armies without the Consent of our legislatures. —— He has affected to render the Military independent of and superior to the Civil power. —— He has combined with others to subject us to a jurisdiction foreign to our constitution, and unacknowledged by our laws; giving his Assent to their Acts of pretended Legislation: — For Quartering large bodies of armed troops among us: — For protecting them, by a mock Trial, from punishment for any Murders which they should commit on the Inhabitants of these States: — For cutting off our Trade with all parts of the world: — For imposing Taxes on us without our Consent: — For depriving us in many cases, of the benefits of Trial by Jury: — For transporting us beyond Seas to be tried for pretended offences — For abolishing the free System of English Laws in a neighbouring Province, establishing therein an Arbitrary government, and enlarging its Boundaries so as to render it at once an example and fit instrument for introducing the same absolute rule into these Colonies: — For taking away our Charters, abolishing our most valuable Laws, and altering fundamentally the Forms of our Governments: — For suspending our own Legislatures, and declaring themselves invested with power to legislate for us in all cases whatsoever. — He has abdicated Government here, by declaring us out of his Protection and waging War against us. —— He has plundered our seas, ravaged our Coasts, burnt our towns, and destroyed the lives of our people. —— He is at this time transporting large Armies of foreign Mercenaries to compleat the works of death, desolation and tyranny, already begun with circumstances of Cruelty & perfidy scarcely paralleled in the most barbarous ages, and totally unworthy the Head of a civilized nation. —— He has constrained our fellow Citizens taken Captive on the high Seas to bear Arms against their Country, to become the executioners of their friends and Brethren, or to fall themselves by their Hands. —— He has excited domestic insurrections amongst us, and has endeavoured to bring on the inhabitants of our frontiers, the merciless Indian Savages, whose known rule of warfare, is an undistinguished destruction of all ages, sexes and conditions. In every stage of these Oppressions We have Petitioned for Redress in the most humble terms: Our repeated Petitions have been answered only by repeated injury. A Prince, whose character is thus marked by every act which may define a Tyrant, is unfit to be the ruler of a free people. Nor have We been wanting in attentions to our Brittish brethren. We have warned them from time to time of attempts by their legislature to extend an unwarrantable jurisdiction over us. We have reminded them of the circumstances of our emigration and settlement here. We have appealed to their native justice and magnanimity, and we have conjured them by the ties of our common kindred to disavow these usurpations, which, would inevitably interrupt our connections and correspondence. They too have been deaf to the voice of justice and of consanguinity. We must, therefore, acquiesce in the necessity, which denounces our Separation, and hold them, as we hold the rest of mankind, Enemies in War, in Peace Friends.

We, therefore, the Representatives of the united States of America, in General Congress, Assembled, appealing to the Supreme Judge of the world for the rectitude of our intentions, do, in the Name, and by Authority of the good People of these Colonies, solemnly publish and declare, That these United Colonies are, and of Right ought to be Free and Independent States; that they are Absolved from all Allegiance to the British Crown, and that all political connection between them and the State of Great Britain, is and ought to be totally dissolved; and that as Free and Independent States, they have full Power to levy War, conclude Peace, contract Alliances, establish Commerce, and to do all other Acts and Things which Independent States may of right do. —— And for the support of this Declaration, with a firm reliance on the protection of divine Providence, we mutually pledge to each other our Lives, our Fortunes and our sacred Honor.

John Hancock

Button Gwinnett, Lyman Hall, Geo Walton. Wm Hooper, Joseph Hewes, John Penn. Edward Rutledge. Thos Heyward Junr, Thomas Lynch Junr, Arthur Middleton. Samuel Chase, Wm Paca, Thos Stone, Charles Carroll of Carrollton. George Wythe, Richard Henry Lee, Th Jefferson, Benja Harrison, Thos Nelson jr, Francis Lightfoot Lee, Carter Braxton. Robt Morris, Benjamin Rush, Benja Franklin, John Morton, Geo Clymer, Jas Smith, Geo Taylor, James Wilson, Geo Ross. Caesar Rodney, Geo Read, Tho M:Kean. Wm Floyd, Phil Livingston, Frans Lewis, Lewis Morris. Richd Stockton, Jno Witherspoon, Fras Hopkinson, John Hart, Abra Clark. Josiah Bartlett, Wm Whipple, Saml Adams, John Adams, Robt Treat Paine, Elbridge Gerry, Step Hopkins, William Ellery, Roger Sherman, Samel Huntington, Wm Williams, Oliver Wolcott, Matthew Thornton.

The Declaration of Independence (above) was issued by the Second Continental Congress in July 1776. It enumerated the "causes" for rebellion against Britain and put forth a general theory of legitimate government. ***(National Archives)***

evident in the first half of the 18th century were reversed completely. What began as an aftershock to the Seven Years' War quickly became a constitutional and political crisis within the British Empire when colonists not only refused to pay taxes designed to retire Britain's extensive debt and pay for the garrisons the British believed were needed to control the vast territories won in the war, but also refused to pay on the grounds that they could not be taxed without actual representation in the governing body.

The resulting turmoil lasted a decade and politicized British American society as never before. Most major towns experienced rioting and social violence as the British ministry's real and imagined agents were confronted and often physically attacked. By 1775 there was an extensive network of Revolutionary committees and congresses throughout America that gradually usurped the role of the imperial governments and legal systems in the different colonies. From the ashes of the resulting imperial collapse, new republican governments formed in popular conventions, whose authority was based entirely on the sovereignty of the people, appeared in the 13 states. The Continental Congress assumed authority over the new states as a whole, and the society plunged into eight years of warfare on its own soil as Britain, assisted by German mercenaries, mounted a determined military effort to reclaim its rogue colonies, campaigning in New England, the Mid-Atlantic, and the South, in turn, in an effort to break the rebellion. The intervention of France and the determination of Americans to hold together and fight for every state and region allowed them to wear the British Empire down until the 1781 victory at Yorktown, Virginia, ultimately forced the London government to acknowledge American independence in 1783 with the Treaty of Paris.

A New Order

Victory in the war did not resolve all problems in the society, and in fact created a host of new ones. A constitution for the new nation, the Articles of Confederation, was ratified in 1781, but financial and political instability throughout the society led to its being abandoned in 1787 for the federal Constitution (the government we now enjoy), which passed into being after a bitter ratification struggle in the states between the Federalists, who favored a strong central government as necessary to the republic's survival, and the Anti-Federalists, who feared such a government. Ten years of political struggle followed as America's first more or less formal political parties, the Federalists and the Jeffersonian Republicans (or Democratic-Republicans), battled to define the new society's political order and foreign policy until the election of 1800 established the Jeffersonian hegemony for two decades and enshrined in American consciousness the idea of limiting government's interference in people's lives.

The struggle to settle the political order of the new society was paralleled by, and part of, a broader discussion about what America, and Americans, would be as an independent nation and culture. As the Revolution had been so unexpected, so sudden in its rupture of the empire, there had been little, if any, long-term social or even political planning. Republican political ideology and the desire to reject all things British led to reconsiderations of architecture, dress, entertainment, family and gender relations, legal practices and procedures, language, education, and community structure. The last two decades of the century saw broad, even utopian, efforts to remake human nature in a republican template, educate children in republican citizenship, ease the often harsh rule of fathers over families, and create a culture that was distinctively American in character and feel. Slavery was gradually abolished in the states north of Maryland even as it continued in those to the south, and African American family life became more stable in areas where there were free people of color. Building design began, haltingly, to reflect republican values, painting increasingly expressed patriotic themes; new words expressive of American experiences were put to traditional music tunes; and clothing styles changed as Americans adopted European finery, but with an American twist.

By 1800 this transformation was far from complete. It would take the generation born during and after the Revolution to carry on the process, which, paradoxically, never seems to end. Indeed, the process of creating an American national identity as a republican, and inclusive, society continues to this day.

Even those changes not tied directly to the efforts to create a republican society were transformative breaks with the colonial past. Victory in the war gave Americans claim to all the lands up to the Mississippi River, and after 1783, European and African populations began to pour into Kentucky, Tennessee, and the Ohio country, establishing new towns and villages, creating new roads and new trade networks, and pushing (often by means of warfare) Native American tribes from their traditional homelands farther and farther west, or onto reservations. The physical expansion of the European population encouraged the creation of new modes of transportation as canals were dug throughout the country and entrepreneurs experimented with primitive steamboats. Such advances were attributed to national independence and republicanism, even when their connection to political developments was tenuous.

In this social environment, the evangelical tendencies within colonial society blossomed into a full-blown force of spiritual and social transformation as new (or newly popular) Protestant religious groups, especially the Baptists and Methodists, drew tens and then hundreds of thousands of converts to massive open-air revival meetings with the promise of spiritual rebirth and eternal salvation. The older established churches remained important, but these new groups, and indeed wholly new and previously unknown religious sects, appeared and placed an indelible mark on American society and culture.

Twenty-first-century Americans are heirs to the society that was emerging in that later period, during and after the war, with trends that would lead to our own world historically visible in 1800. That familiarity, however, has obscured how different the world was in 1700, and how jarring the changes were that ripped colonial society from its moorings and made the world anew between 1700 and 1800.

—*Brendan McConville*

18th Century AFRICAN AMERICANS

The African American experience in 18th-century North America was multifaceted. Though African Americans came from various African ethnic origins and social backgrounds, either they or their ancestors all shared the traumatic experience of the transatlantic slave trade. Once in North America, they endured slavery differently, depending on the region where they were slaves. Virtually all African descendants, both enslaved and free, developed communities and cultures that provided survival mechanisms in their trying circumstances, while enslaved Africans used resistance and rebellion to fight the institution of slavery.

In early 18th-century North America, new laws codified slavery and racism, as large plantations became increasingly important to the colonies' economies. White colonists imported increasing numbers of African slaves, and in some regions blacks outnumbered whites by three to one. While most African Americans spent their lives toiling in the fields, on the docks, or in the houses of their white masters, they still managed to leave a lasting imprint on American society and culture as they helped build American communities, fought on both sides in the Revolution, and greatly influenced American culture.

African Origins and the Slave Trade

European or American slave traders usually stopped at only one or two ports on the west coast of Africa before they shipped their newly bought slaves to the Americas. At these ports, African middlemen sold Africans from the surrounding regions who had been enslaved in various ways, including captured in warfare or slave raids, or enslaved to pay off debt or as punishment for a crime. Though many of these ships first stopped at Caribbean transshipment points, such as Jamaica or Curaçao, before continuing on to North America, most of the slaves that reached the North American shores were Africa-born, or "saltwater slaves," as white traders often called them. These men and women were sold at any of the North American slave markets that could be found in Boston, Philadelphia, New York, Newport, Savannah, New Orleans, and Charles Town (Charleston), the last of which emerged as the principal slave-trading port.

The men and women who arrived from Africa had survived a harrowing journey across the Atlantic, usually referred to as the Middle Passage. Most slave traders filled their ships with as many slaves as they possibly could. Because these slaves had only limited space, with poor sanitary conditions and only little food and water, they struggled to survive the voyage that lasted at least three weeks and often much longer. As a result, about 10 percent of them died from either disease or suicide, while the others usually arrived in the Americas in poor health.

Though the specific ethnic origins of slaves are hard to determine, shipping records demonstrate that of the approximately 348,400 Africans that were imported into North America from 1700 to 1820, the majority came from West Central Africa (currently Angola and Congo), the Bight of Biafra (southeastern Nigeria, Cameroon, and Gabon), Sierra Leone (present-day Sierra Leone, Guinea-Bissau, Guinea, Liberia, and Ivory Coast), Senegambia (roughly the area that is now Senegal, Gambia, and western Mali), Gold Coast (Ghana), and the Bight of Benin (present-day Togo, Benin, and southwestern Nigeria). In America, slaveholders often selected slaves based on then-popular ethnic stereotypes: Gambians were tall, strong, and trustworthy; Ibos, from Nigeria, were more likely to commit suicide; Gold Coast Coromantees were rebels; and Angolans were treacherous and prone to run away. Moreover, planters favored certain ethnicities because of their specific skills. South Carolinian rice planters, for example, had a preference for Senegambian and Sierra Leonean slaves because of their expertise in rice cultivation.

Slavery in North America

Regional differences in climate, settlement patterns, race relations, colonial government, culture, and main cash crop all affected the institution of slavery and consequently the lives of slaves. To some extent, however, slavery was similar everywhere: Black slave labor was used for the benefit of white colonists.

The North

Slavery in the northern colonies was as much a part of society as it was in the South, and during most of the 18th century the institution did not find much opposition in the North. Overall, however, the slave population in this region remained small: By 1770, close to 70,000 blacks lived in the North, which was still less than 5 percent of the total population. Most slaveholders in New England and the middle colonies owned only one or two slaves, who usually lived and worked closely with their masters. These slaves slept in basements, attics, closets, or toolsheds. While slaves in rural areas frequently labored in agriculture or as domestics, slaves in urban areas often worked as skilled laborers, dockworkers, or sailors. In New York and Rhode Island, where many slaves worked on small commercial plantations, slavery was particularly prevalent, and in some areas slaves made up 50 percent or more of the local population.

The Chesapeake

Most 18th-century Chesapeake slaves worked on tobacco plantations, though by the later part of the century many planters had diversified, cultivating additional crops such as corn and wheat. Tobacco production required gang labor, which meant that a white overseer closely supervised the slaves, leaving them little independence. While by the 1740s blacks reached 40 percent of the population in some parts of Virginia, they never became a majority as they did in the Lowcountry of South Carolina and Georgia. Chesapeake slaves lived and worked relatively close to whites; as a result, their cultures and ways of life were influenced significantly by that of their masters. The rather personal relationship these slaves often had with their masters also softened the cruelty of slavery slightly. As a result, much like their counterparts to the north, Chesapeake slaves developed a self-sustaining population by the 1740s, and in 1783 the Chesapeake colonies actually abolished importation of African slaves.

The Southern Lowcountry

Slavery in the Lowcountry did not develop until Barbados planters with their slaves first moved to Carolina in the 1670s, while in Georgia slavery was prohibited until 1750. Even though slavery in the Lowcountry was still at its infancy in the early 18th century, by the late 1700s the region's economy was sustained primarily through slave labor. As early as 1708, blacks reached 50 percent of South Carolina's population, and by 1750 they outnumbered whites by nearly two to one. In Georgia, African descendants constituted 50 percent of the population in 1770. A black majority as it existed in these southern regions was not seen in any of the other colonies.

Whereas South Carolina's early economy depended on small farms, in the early 18th century it transformed into a plantation economy, with rice as its main cash crop. Georgia followed this example when slavery became legal and planters from the Carolinas moved into the area. Rice cultivation demanded hard labor in swampy rice fields, where disease spread easily. African slaves who dealt with these health hazards on a daily basis were more likely to die at a young age; consequently, slave populations in the Lowcountry were usually not self-sustaining, which meant that planters continually had to import slaves from Africa and the Caribbean to replenish the slave population. While rice cultivation was especially demanding and dangerous, slaves on the rice plantations did have one advantage: They usually worked according to a task system under which slaves had to complete an assigned set of tasks that they could finish at a time and pace of their own choosing. This system allowed slaves relative independence, as they experienced little white supervision, and once they completed their tasks they often had the opportunity to work on their own small plots of land.

Louisiana and Florida

Because of French and Spanish rule, Louisiana and Florida developed differently from the English colonies culturally,

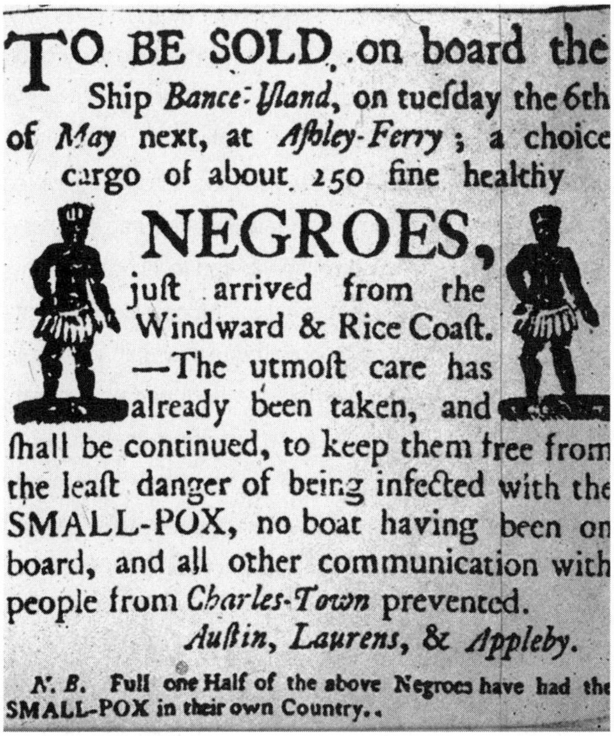
TO BE SOLD on board the
Ship Bance-Iſland, on tueſday the 6th
of May next, at Aſhley-Ferry; a choice
cargo of about 250 fine healthy
NEGROES,
juſt arrived from the
Windward & Rice Coaſt.
—The utmoſt care has
already been taken, and
ſhall be continued, to keep them free from
the leaſt danger of being infected with the
SMALL-POX, no boat having been on
board, and all other communication with
people from Charles-Town prevented.
Auſtin, Laurens, & Appleby.
N. B. Full one Half of the above Negroes have had the
SMALL-POX in their own Country.

African Americans comprised roughly half of the population of South Carolina in 1708, but by the middle of the century they outnumbered whites by two to one, most of them living as slaves in the state's plantation economy. Above is a newspaper advertisement from the 1780s announcing the sale of slaves at Ashley Ferry outside of Charleston, South Carolina. ***(Library of Congress)***

politically, and economically. In neither of these regions did an extensive plantation economy exist until the early 19th century. Nevertheless, African slaves, mainly from Senegambia and West Central Africa, arrived in Louisiana as early as 1719, while in Florida blacks had been part of its settlements from the earliest beginnings. In Louisiana, African slaves played an important role in building the region's infrastructure and securing the settlers' safety. In addition, many of the slaves labored in tobacco, indigo, and rice production on the relatively small plantations owned by German and French planters. By 1750, about 50 percent of Louisiana's population was of African descent. Compared to slaves in the English colonies, Louisiana's blacks had more rights and freedoms, as stipulated in the Code Noir (1685). For example, the Code Noir specified that enslaved mothers and children could not be separated. Moreover, African descendants had more opportunities to obtain their freedom and advance socially and economically.

Florida's slaves also had certain rights, as well as ample opportunities to buy their own freedom. Moreover, they had relative independence as a result of the frequent use of the task system in this colony. Because the Spanish settlements in Florida and the Southwest were small, relatively few African slaves lived in these colonies. In Florida this changed, however, when during British rule over the region from 1763 to 1783 slaves lost many of their rights while planters established increasing numbers of large plantations.

Slavery, Racism, and the Law

Initially, the legalities of slavery and racism in North America were somewhat ambiguous, but in the late 17th and early 18th century white colonists instituted laws that secured their supposed racial, social, political, and economic superiority. By 1700 most colonies had determined that the status of black children should be the same as that of the mother, and slavery was now a lifelong condition. Using Caribbean slave codes as a model, Chesapeake whites first implemented their version of these laws, which soon were adapted across the North American colonies. These codes regulated the institution of slavery and slaves' lives, taking away their rights to bear arms, own property, use the courts, assemble in large groups (more than five), and marry legally, among other things.

African American Communities and Cultures

Even though they came from significantly different backgrounds, slaves were able to forge an African American identity and community through their common experience of slavery and racism. Most slaves had trouble forming families: Because most African slaves were captured male warriors, and slaveholders often preferred male slaves, men frequently outnumbered women. Moreover, marriage was usually discouraged or even prohibited; and because slaves lived under poor conditions, their average life expectancy was low. Flexible understandings of kinship, which were widespread in African societies, allowed blacks to construct new and extended kinship ties in the Americas.

On large plantations, blacks were able to create close-knit communities because they lived relatively separated from whites. Enslaved Africans on the large plantations often worked from sunrise to long after sunset, but because they usually lived closely together, they could gather in the evenings for dancing, music making, and storytelling, which allowed them to preserve parts of their African cultures. Their small log cabins were often poorly constructed, letting in rain and wind, with only basic furnishings. The average slave lived off a very basic diet, while some were able to supplement the foods allotted to them with foods they had cultivated on their own little plots of land—a practice that was particularly prevalent in the Lowcountry, Florida, and Louisiana. Sundays and holidays they used to visit friends, join in celebration, or meet at markets to exchange goods. With whites spending much of the day in church, Sunday provided an excellent opportunity for blacks to congregate without white supervision, even for those slaves who lived in northern and urban communities.

Because most northern slaves lived in proximity to their masters, European ways of life strongly influenced these slaves' cultures. Consequently, it was challenging for them to build African American communities or retain specific African practices and traditions. Only on some evenings, Sundays, and holidays, which were usually limited to Christmas, Easter, and Whitsuntide, were they able to meet with other blacks. As a result, some of these holidays became elaborate African American festivals—such as Pinkster in New York and New Jersey and Election Day in New England—with African-influenced dances, parades, and fairs.

Free Blacks

Although most 18th-century African Americans were slaves, some blacks either obtained their freedom or descended from free black Americans. Yet regardless of their free status, they too faced insurmountable hardships and constant racism. In particular, their opportunities decreased significantly as most colonies codified laws that legalized racial discrimination in the late 17th and early 18th century. Free blacks now had only few legal rights, and they often struggled to secure an income. In addition, many of the southern states tried to expel free blacks from their territory, afraid that they would instigate rebellion among slaves; as a result, free African American families who had lived in a region for generations were often forced to relocate.

In both Louisiana and Florida, African descendants had more opportunities to obtain and maintain their freedom. Free blacks in these regions held certain property and legal rights that were taken away from their counterparts in the British colonies. The free black community in Florida grew steadily, because slaves in this Spanish colony had various opportunities to obtain their freedom; moreover, some slaves from Georgia and the Carolinas fled to Florida because its authorities promised these runaway slaves their freedom. Many of these African descendants settled in Gracia Real de Santa Teresa de Mose (or Fort Mose), a free black community that the Spanish governor founded in 1738. Here, African Americans had the possibility to develop their own, independent community.

Religion

Traditional African religions as well as Christianity and Islam played an important role in the lives of Africans in Africa and in the Americas. Those aspects that were integral parts of all Atlantic African religions were most likely to survive the Middle Passage: Most Africans believed in spirits of various sorts and considered music and dance an integral part of their religions. As a result, Africans across North America sought to maintain good relationships with the ancestors and other spirits, and they used dance and music as part of their religious worship, as is evident in the "ring shout," a counterclockwise ritual dance practiced by African descendants throughout the Americas. Many Africans considered themselves either Muslim or Christian, but this did not mean that they had discarded their traditional African beliefs; rather, they maintained both belief systems either as parallel religions or in a syncretized form. African Americans reshaped the religions of their homelands to fit the realities of life in America.

Even though most 18th-century colonial governments ruled that slaves' conversion to Christianity did not alter their slave status, many slaveholders did not allow their slaves to become Christians, because they were fearful that these slaves would then be more likely to demand their freedom. Certain denominations did actively proselytize blacks, as was the case in New York, where Elias Neau of the Society for the Propagation of the Gospel spent countless days among African Americans in an effort to teach them the Gospel, while Moravians in North Carolina and Pennsylvania converted most of their slaves and accepted them as equals before God. The emotional aspects and egalitarian message of the First Great Awakening of the mid-18th century resonated with many of America's blacks. Throughout the North in particular, growing numbers of African Americans joined the religious revivals. But because many slaveholders prevented their slaves' conversion, no great number of blacks became Christians until the Second Great Awakening in the 19th century. When blacks did attend Christian churches, they were usually segregated from the white congregants, being assigned places in the back of the church or in the balcony. This discrimination led the black Methodist minister Richard Allen to open his own black church in Philadelphia in 1794 and eventually found the African Methodist Episcopal Church in 1816. Soon after, other African Americans followed his example, establishing African churches across the young nation.

Language and Folklore

Language and folklore helped African slaves to retain parts of their cultures, adapt to already existing American cultures, develop a distinct African American identity, and demonstrate their intellectual capabilities. Most slaves learned to speak the language of their masters, whether that was English, Dutch, German, French, or Spanish. In the predominantly black regions, however, African slaves developed Creole languages that combined African and European languages to allow communication with each other as well as their white masters. By the 1740s Gullah or Geechee in the South Carolina and Georgia Sea Islands became the primary language for local blacks. This and similar languages and dialects influenced the language of their white masters with words like *juke*, *okra*, *gumbo*, *goober*, and *tote*.

As in most African cultures, folktales that were passed on from generation to generation played an important role in African American culture. In particular, the trickster tales of Br'er Rabbit and Compair Lapin, which revolved around a trickster rabbit that was able to overcome any difficulties it encountered through wits and deceit, were popular among slaves, as these stories served as cultural tools to endure slavery: The rabbit represented the slave who had to outsmart his or her master. The tales resemble West Central African and Senegambian folktales, and they also show significant similarities to the Gold Coast folktales that revolve around the spider Anansi.

While some black Muslims were literate before they were brought to America, most slaves never learned how to read or write. In fact, in some of the colonies, such as South Carolina in 1740, laws prohibited anyone from educating slaves. Masters were afraid that literacy would empower blacks; moreover, black literacy would belie claims of black inferiority. Nevertheless, numerous blacks did learn to read and write, and some of them became well-respected authors: Phillis Wheatley, a Senegambian woman who learned to read and write while the slave of a Boston merchant, published many of her poems, such as "An Address to the Atheist" (1767); the Long Island writer and slave Jupiter Hammon penned, among other things, "An Evening Thought: Salvation by Christ with Penitential Cries" (1760); and Olaudah Equiano, who obtained his freedom in the 1760s, became an important figure in England's abolitionist movement, and wrote his autobiography in support of this cause.

Slave Resistance and Rebellion

Enslaved Africans did not accept their bondage without struggle, as they fought slavery in various ways. Most commonly this resistance was subtle. For example, to obstruct the slave system, slaves would slow down the work pace, withdraw labor, or break tools. Running away was a particularly popular form of resistance among young men, most of whom were either captured and returned to their master or decided to return independently after struggling to stay alive as a runaway

Most slaves never learned how to read and write, and some colonies and states even had laws prohibiting the education of slaves. Even in the face of such restriction, numerous blacks did learn to read and write, and some even became revered authors. The poet Phillis Wheatley (left) published a book in 1773 and later won emancipation from her owner. Olaudah Equiano (right) bought his freedom in 1766 and wrote his autobiography, *The Interesting Narrative of the Life of Olaudah Equiano, or Gustavus Vassa, the African*, which was published in 1789. *(Library of Congress)*

slave. Some, however, found refuge in the cities, in free black communities, among Native Americans, such as the Seminoles in Florida, or on ships that left from the North American ports. A more dramatic form of slave resistance was suicide or murder. For those who committed suicide, death allowed their return to the African homeland. Murder was least common, but in rare cases an enslaved mother would kill her child so that it would not have to live a life in bondage.

To the white colonists, the most threatening form of slave resistance was rebellion. Even though only a few slave rebellions actually occurred in North America, slaveholders had good reason to fear them: Numerous slave revolts were foiled—Chesapeake in 1709, 1710, 1722, and 1729–32, New York in 1741, and Pointe Coupee, Louisiana, in 1795—and individual slaves did occasionally kill their masters or commit arson. Nevertheless, only a few slave conspiracies actually turned into revolt, such as the New York slave revolt of 1712 and the Stono Rebellion in 1739. A group of about 20 predominantly West Central African slaves instigated the Stono Rebellion in South Carolina, but soon the group reached about 80 blacks. They were on their way to St. Augustine, Florida, where slaves who ran away from the English colonies were promised freedom by the Spanish authorities. On their way south, the rebels burned down several plantations and killed at least 20 whites. Eventually, white militias stopped the rebels, who were either killed in the resulting battles, executed afterward, or sold into slavery in the West Indies. In the New York slave revolt, 23 blacks set a building on fire and then killed 9 whites. The rebellion was halted quickly, however, and about 21 blacks were found guilty of revolt and executed by New York authorities. These revolts led authorities to impose stricter slave codes and respond aggressively to any rumor of slave conspiracy, often preempting slave revolts by executing those suspected of plotting.

The American Revolution

In some ways, the American Revolution was the ultimate North American slave rebellion, as countless enslaved blacks across the 13 colonies sought opportunities of freedom by joining either the Continental or the British forces. In fact, the first person to die for the Revolutionary cause was Crispus Attucks, an African American believed to have been a runaway slave, who was one of the five men killed in the Boston Massacre of 1770. By the end of the war, 5,000 African Americans had served in the Continental Army, while the offer of freedom in exchange for military service had motivated about 15,000 to 20,000 black men and women to flee to the British lines, with almost a thousand serving in the army. Many of these black Loyalists resettled in England, Canada, the West Indies, or West Africa after the war.

The Continental forces at first hesitated to accept African Americans, as armed black men were still a threatening sight to whites who were fearful of slave rebellions. While the Revolutionary forces began to accept free blacks, they were not yet ready to arm slaves. The British, on the other hand, were more willing to recruit slaves, because it strengthened their forces and crippled the Revolutionary cause. In November 1775, Virginia's royal governor, Lord Dunmore, promised freedom to those blacks who joined the British forces, and by December 1775 the British had enlisted 300 African Americans. These men formed the British Ethiopian Regiment, wearing military uniforms with sashes that read "Liberty to Slaves." Whereas the promise of freedom was a useful tool to attract slaves to join the king's forces, the Revolutionaries could not give such a promise, as many of them depended on slave labor.

When British forces launched raids in Georgia and South Carolina, the Continental Congress urged those states to recruit 3,000 slaves to aid in their defense, and by 1777 the Continental forces more commonly accepted both free and enslaved blacks. Most of these African Americans signed up as a way out of poverty, or because they hoped it would help them obtain their freedom; others joined, either willingly or by force, on behalf of their masters, an accepted practice in most northern states by 1781. Blacks in the forces were usually assigned the most grueling or dangerous tasks, and many of them served as bodyguards or orderlies. The African American William Lee, for example, was General Washington's orderly, and Agrippa Hull assisted General William Paterson and later Thaddeus Kosciuszko.

The language of the white Revolutionaries of "freedom from tyranny" and "all men are created equal" brought about significant challenges to the slave system, and in the northern states in particular, where slavery was least beneficial to the economy, blacks as well as increasing numbers of whites began to challenge the institution. As early as 1773, a group of black slaves from Boston and surrounding areas had petitioned for their freedom, but without success. Several other attempts were rejected, until an enslaved black woman from western Massachusetts by the name of Mum Bett, which she later changed to Elizabeth Freeman, succeeded by claiming that the preamble of Massachusetts's 1780 constitution, which stated that "all men are born free and equal," should also pertain to her. She won the case in 1781, making her the first African American to receive freedom under the state's constitution. Her case set a precedent, and two years later the Massachusetts high court abolished slavery in the state. Other northern states passed acts for gradual abolition of slavery: Pennsylvania in 1780, Connecticut in 1784, New York in 1799, and New Jersey in 1804. In the southern states, however, it took another war to bring an end the institution of slavery.

—Andrea C. Mosterman

Further Reading

Berlin, Ira. *Generations of Captivity: A History of African American Slaves*. Cambridge, Mass.: Belknap Press of Harvard University Press, 2003.

———. *Many Thousands Gone: The First Two Centuries of Slavery in North America.* Cambridge, Mass.: Belknap Press of Harvard University Press, 1998.

Carney, Judith A. *Black Rice: The African Origins of Rice Cultivation in the Americas.* Cambridge, Mass.: Harvard University Press, 2001.

Eltis, David. *The Rise of African Slavery in the Americas.* Cambridge, U.K.: Cambridge University Press, 2000.

Gomez, Michael. *Exchanging Our Country Marks: The Transformation of African Identities in the Colonial and Antebellum South*. Chapel Hill: University of North Carolina Press, 1998.

Hall, Gwendolyn Midlo. *Africans in Colonial Louisiana: The Development of Afro-Creole Culture in the Eighteenth Century*. Baton Rouge: Louisiana State University Press, 1992.

———. *Slavery and African Ethnicities in the Americas: Restoring the Links.*Chapel Hill: University of North Carolina Press, 2005.

Harris, Leslie M. *In the Shadow of Slavery: African Americans in New York City, 1626–1863.* Chicago: University of Chicago Press, 2003.

Hodges, Graham Russell. *Root & Branch: African Americans in New York and East Jersey, 1613–1863.* Chapel Hill: University of North Carolina Press, 1999.

Holloway, Joseph E. *Africanisms in American Culture.* Bloomington: Indiana University Press, 1990.

Horton, James Oliver, and Lois E. Horton. *In Hope of Liberty: Culture, Community and Protest Among Northern Free Blacks, 1700–1860.* New York: Oxford University Press, 1997.

Landers, Jane L. *Black Society in Spanish Florida.* Urbana: University of Illinois Press, 1999.

Lepore, Jill. *New York Burning: Liberty, Slavery, and Conspiracy in Eighteenth-Century Manhattan.* New York: Alfred A. Knopf, 2005.

Morgan, Philip D. *Slave Counterpoint: Black Culture in the Eighteenth-Century Chesapeake and Lowcountry.* Chapel Hill: University of North Carolina Press, 1998.

Nash, Gary B. *The Forgotten Fifth: African Americans in the Age of Revolution.* Cambridge, Mass.: Harvard University Press, 2006.

Parent, Anthony S. *Foul Means: The Formation of a Slave Society in Virginia, 1660–1740.* Chapel Hill: University of North Carolina Press, 2003.

Piersen, William D. *Black Yankees: The Development of an Afro-American Subculture in Eighteenth-Century New England.* Amherst: University of Massachusetts Press, 1988.

Rucker, Walter C. *The River Flows On: Black Resistance, Culture, and Identity Formation in Early America.* Baton Rouge: Louisiana State University Press, 2006.

Schama, Simon. *Rough Crossings: Britain, the Slaves, and the American Revolution*. New York: HarperCollins, 2006.

Sensbach, Jon. *A Separate Canaan: The Making of an Afro-Moravian World in North Carolina, 1763–1840.* Chapel Hill: University of North Carolina Press, 1998.

Sobel, Mechal. *The World They Made Together: Black and White Values in Eighteenth-Century Virginia.* Princeton, N.J.: Princeton University Press, 1987.

Thornton, John K. *Africa and Africans in the Making of the Atlantic World.* Cambridge, U.K.: Cambridge University Press, 1992.

Wood, Gordon. *Black Majority: Negroes in Colonial South Carolina.* New York: W. W. Norton, 1974.

18th Century AGRICULTURE

Life in 18th-century British North America revolved around agriculture. Almost all colonists lived and worked on the farm, and most of those who did not made their living serving the agricultural population by supplying its needs or processing or exporting its products. Immigration, too, was largely driven by the desire for land and profitable farming. Throughout the century, struggles over existing or potential farmland and farm labor divided the colonies along racial lines, while state regulation of the land market and the export trade in farm produce dominated political life.

Old Patterns, New Markets

Farming during the second century of British colonization of North America continued many patterns of the first. Until the Revolution, the American colonies remained within the British Empire and commercial system, a fact that still defined the farm economy. Except in the South, where the plantation system had taken root, isolation and lack of internal markets limited cash-crop agriculture, but 18th-century colonists still exported farm products to earn credit for manufactured goods. By the beginning of the century, European demand and the American environment had already created strong regional patterns in agricultural production. Farmers throughout the colonies produced subsistence staples like corn, beef, and pork, but the colder climate of the New England and middle colonies was forcing farmers there to specialize in northern European cereal grains like wheat, oats, and rye. Farther south, farmers were able to grow subtropical cash crops—tobacco in the Chesapeake and indigo, rice, and cotton along the coast of South Carolina and the newly founded colony of Georgia.

The first two-thirds of the century witnessed important developments in the colonies' agricultural economy. American merchants opened new markets outside Britain, including the sugar islands of the Caribbean; formerly small urban markets steadily grew in towns like Boston, New York, Philadelphia, and Baltimore, and, along with them, a burgeoning coastal trade. Later in the century, growing consumer markets developed in southern Europe. All these new markets' demand for foodstuffs pushed American farmers further into commercial grain and meat production, increasing the wealth of the northern colonies. Processing and shipping flour, in particular, created economic linkages that diversified their economies. But many of these new markets were either heavily taxed or off limits under British mercantile law, a fact that would force increasingly prosperous American farmers and merchants into conflict with imperial lawmakers and customs agents.

Agriculture and Immigration

British North America's growing farm economy kept attracting immigrants during the 18th century. Improving economic conditions slowed departures from England, but troubles on the fringes of Great Britain and on the European continent still pushed colonists to the Americas. Landlords extorted exorbitant rents from tenant farmers on estates in Scotland and Northern Ireland, while the princes of German states persecuted radical Protestant sects. Consequently, Scots, Scots-Irish, and Germans all saw opportunity in the cheap land and tolerant diversity of British North America. During the mid-18th century, these migrants headed for the booming port of Philadelphia. Finding southeastern Pennsylvania's farmlands occupied by the descendants of the original Quaker colonists, they headed inland to find land. Faced with poor soils in the Pennsylvania mountains and hostility from the Ohio Indians, many turned south, buying land and establishing farms in Virginia's Shenandoah Valley. Others continued into the piedmont backcountry of the Carolinas, or west into the valleys of Appalachian Tennessee and Kentucky. Until cut off by the Revolution, this stream of farm colonists continued to swell, pushing westward expansion and upsetting colonial politics and diplomacy.

With European immigrants heading west to acquire their own farms, wealthy planters had to look elsewhere for the labor they needed to work their estates. Between 1690 and 1710, Virginia and Maryland's leading tobacco planters turned away from indentured servants and started buying large numbers of enslaved Africans. As rice, cotton, and indigo farming took hold in South Carolina and Georgia, planters there imported large numbers of slaves, leaving the southern colonies dominated by the twin institutions of plantation agriculture and race slavery. The African and African American population of British North America grew nearly tenfold between 1700 and the Revolution, and slaves accounted for 40 percent of the total population of the southern colonies by 1780. During the second half of the century, wealthy Virginia planters, worried about rebellion and hoping to force higher prices, tried to restrict the importation of slaves. They were thwarted by imperial opposition and by the ambitions of smaller planters who hoped to buy cheap slaves and move into the planter aristocracy. The demand of southern plantations for bound labor continued to draw slave ships to the United States until Congress banned the trade in 1808.

Planters in South Carolina and Georgia turned away from indentured servants and adopted a system of permanent racial slavery once rice, cotton, and indigo farming took hold in those colonies. Above is a watercolor by Bernarda Bryson showing slaves disembarking a ship at a slave auction in Charleston, South Carolina. *(Library of Congress)*

Agriculture and Social Relations

Many immigrants to British North America had left Europe to escape feudalism. The aristocracy's control of Europe's agricultural land trapped most of the Continent's people in the peasantry—impoverished tenant farmers without political rights or social respect. Worse, it left them vulnerable to the greed of their landlords, who raised rents and expelled unprofitable tenants. In contrast, the open land market of British North America offered security and status to settlers who could acquire farm property. The desire to keep feudalism out of America was a driving political, economic, and social force during the 18th century. Colonial elites may have brought Old World social attitudes and economic ambitions with them from Europe, but they were unable to establish themselves as a true landed aristocracy. A few holders of old Dutch manors in the Hudson Valley of New York maintained a feudal system, but American land markets forced them to give their tenants more favorable terms. Outside the Hudson Valley, tenancy reverted to short-term arrangements between owners of undeveloped land and small farmers looking to turn a quick profit on their labor.

Instead of building feudal estates, most large-scale landowners turned to land speculation. They used political influence to grab large tracts of backcountry forest before selling it on credit to small farmers. Even then, farmers were suspicious of the power, profits, and aristocratic airs of these speculators and resisted this system when it thwarted their ambitions. Many settlers embraced John Locke's theory of property, declaring that their own labor in "improving" the land gave them a claim superior to government grants. Farmers squatted on lands where contested colonial and land grant boundaries made ownership dubious. Indeed, speculator-politicians who failed to deliver cheap property to small farmers, whether because of lack of local government (South Carolina), corrupt local government (North Carolina), passive Indian diplomacy (Pennsylvania), or high prices (northern New York and Vermont), faced armed rebellion on the frontiers in the years before the Revolution. After 1780, the unwillingness of small farmers to defer to their "betters" was reflected in the land policies of the new republic. The government worked to dump large amounts of land on the market, and after the turn of the century, farmers threw their votes to Thomas Jefferson's Republican Party with the demand that the federal Land Office bypass speculators and sell public lands in the trans-Appalachian West directly to cultivators. By the early 19th century, the landowning small farmer had become the model for citizenship and social status in America's democratic republic.

Agriculture and Race

The failure of feudalism in the colonies also intensified racism during the 18th century, dividing the people of British North America into three groups—red, white, and black—who struggled over farmland and farm labor. Speculators and settlers might fight over who should profit from land and its development into working farms, but they agreed on who should not—Native Americans. Followers of Locke's theory of property argued that since Indian men hunted for a living, they had failed to "improve" the land into European-style farms and thus forfeited any property rights they might have had. Speculators and settlers congratulated themselves on the defeat and dispossession of the "savages," believing that turning Native hunting grounds into privately owned farms established America as a civilized country. White Indian agents and missionaries were prepared to find a place for Native peoples in American society, but only if the Indians adopted settled agriculture and private property. But most whites were increasingly unwilling to wait for this process of "civilizing" to occur. During the Seven Years' War (1756–63), frontier farmers rejected "friendly" Indians, Christian converts, and mission settlements in favor of violent removal—a policy that was embraced by the American republic early in the next century.

Racism also reconciled many settlers to the emergence of a new kind of agricultural aristocracy in rural America, the plantation gentry. During the 17th century, the use of white indentured servants as bound farm laborers had created social strife in Virginia, culminating in Bacon's Rebellion in 1675–76. But the adoption of race slavery had allowed wealthy men to profit from bound labor while preserving status and opportunity for poor whites. White small farmers could accept the wealth and status of the planter class, if they retained the property, personal independence, political rights, and social prestige denied to enslaved Africans. At the same time, the growing market in slaves and the lack of real economies of scale in tobacco, indigo, and cotton farming all allowed many white farmers to purchase a few slaves while dreaming of moving up into the planter class.

Agriculture and the Environment

During the 18th century, the adaptation of European farming to British North America transformed the region's natural environment. Compared to western Europe, land in America was abundant and cheap, while labor was scarce and therefore expensive. Faced with these economics, farmers continued 17th-century patterns of extensive resource use that maximized the productivity of their labor. Rather than going to the effort of penning and feeding livestock, American farmers let their cattle and hogs run loose in the woods, feeding off undergrowth and mast (fallen nuts). Colonists encouraged this growth by adopting the Indian practice of burning off the forest understory every year. Free-ranging, semiferal European livestock took over the forests, particularly in the southern backcountry, where drovers turned the open range into a commercial undertaking. Cattle and hogs drove the deer from Native hunting grounds, undermining the Indian trade and further increasing hostility between settlers and Indians. Rather than working to clear permanent fields and preserve soil fertility, many farmers continued to practice slash-and-burn cultivation. They girdled trees, burned the underbrush, hoed up the soil, and then farmed these "fields" until they were worn out, before attacking the forest again. This kind of agriculture turned much of rural America into a patchwork landscape of forests, old fields, and small farms surrounded by zigzag, cross-rail fences. If farmers did not own enough land to practice forest fallowing (abandoning old fields for decades to allow tree growth to restore the soil), they just moved to fresh lands on the frontier.

During the second half of the 18th century, this pattern was challenged, however. Imperial and Indian wars penned farmers into long-settled communities in New England and other areas, forcing them to adopt a more intensive, sustainable kind of farming. At the same time, though, the growing demands of domestic and foreign markets encouraged more commercial production. To improve the marketability of their livestock, ambitious husbandmen started controlling breeding, clearing pasture, and penning their animals. Grain farmers improved yields by rotating crops, manuring fields, and using commercial fertilizers like gypsum. When soils began eroding from heavy plowing, better-educated farmers looked across the Atlantic to English farm reformers like Arthur Young and began importing their techniques of "scientific" farming. Military and diplomatic successes of the United States opened lands in Kentucky, Ohio, and Tennessee during the 1790s, however, and cheap, uncleared western land continued to tempt American farmers well into the 19th century.

Agriculture and Politics

Eighteeenth-century American politics was dominated by agricultural interests. In England, the right to vote was restricted on the basis of a property requirement, typically the "40 shilling freehold"; such measures were quite effective at reducing the electorate in a country where landownership was dominated by the upper classes. In British North America, on the other hand, widespread small-farm ownership led to a much larger body of voters. In some regions as much as 40 percent of the adult white male population qualified as "freeholders" eligible for the franchise. The voting strength of the "middling sort" did little to exacerbate class politics, however. Instead, a largely unified farming interest set the unspoken terms of American politics. By the end of the 17th century, merchants and officials involved in the Indian trade had been pushed to the margins by this interest. Small farmers who worked their own land had little cause to fight with wealthy planters—all were landowners, all were crop exporters, and all were white Christians. In the 18th-century Chesapeake, for instance, the word *planter* was used to describe all free tobacco farmers, regardless of economic status. Although sometimes violent, the tension between frontier migrants and land speculators was muted by their common belief that land seized from the Indians would eventually become privately owned farms.

The agricultural interest's dominance of American politics was not challenged until after the Seven Years' War. When the British government began taking more interest in colonial administration, American farmers quickly discovered their powerlessness in Parliament. Although American resistance to new taxes and trade regulations centered on the major towns, it was the ministry's attempt to restrict the markets for colonial farm products and cut off cash and credit to American farmers that attracted the most ire. The colonial Committees of Correspondence found an eager audience for patriot propaganda in the hinterlands, and rural communities strongly supported the nonimportation and nonexportation plans of the Continental Association. Southern colonies also supported the resistance, as planters worried about markets for their crops. On the frontier, when the imperial administration's agents took control of Indian diplomacy away from the colonies, speculators and settlers overcame their differences to support the Revolution.

Agriculture after the American Revolution

One downside of independence for American farmers was expulsion from the British mercantile system. As the new nation's merchants and diplomats struggled to find markets for the nation's farm produce, the country's agricultural sector entered a depression that lasted more than a decade. As farmers fell into debt, bankruptcy proceedings multiplied and rural discontent increased. American farmers returned to pre-Revolutionary protest traditions, forming mobs that harassed sheriffs, disrupted tax auctions, chased surveyors off speculative tracts, and closed bankruptcy courts. These uprisings reached their peak during the winter of 1786–87 in western Massachusetts, where impoverished farmers demanded debt relief from the General Court. When Boston's merchant-politicians refused, farmers banded together under the leadership of Daniel Shays and marched on the federal arsenal in Springfield, threatening to overthrow the government of the commonwealth. Although they were defeated by eastern militia units, Shays's rebels frightened the delegates to the Constitutional Convention into forming a strong national government—both to suppress future revolts like the rebellion against the whiskey excise in western Pennsylvania (1794) and to negotiate better terms for American shippers, as in the Jay Treaty with Great Britain (1794).

The depression ended with the outbreak of the wars of the French Revolution, which created a demand for American agricultural products in Europe that did not subside until the Panic of 1819. In the later 1790s, the spread of cheap cotton gins revived both slavery and the internal market in foodstuffs. But under the leadership of Jefferson and Madison, the farming interest still overturned the power of eastern Federalists. After Jefferson's victory in the election of 1800, the national state committed itself to westward expansion, an agrarian economy, and a citizenry of white, landowning small farmers.

—*Lynn A. Nelson*

Further Reading

Anderson, Virginia DeJohn. *Creatures of Empire: How Domestic Animals Transformed Early America*. New York: Oxford University Press, 2006.

Bidwell, Percy, and John Falconer. *History of Agriculture in the Northern United States, 1620–1860*. Washington, D.C.: Carnegie Institution, 1941.

Chaplin, Joyce. *An Anxious Pursuit: Agricultural Innovation and Modernity in the Lower South, 1730–1815*. Chapel Hill: University of North Carolina Press for the Omohundro Institute of Early American History and Culture, 1996.

Clemens, Paul. *The Atlantic Economy and Colonial Maryland's Eastern Shore: From Tobacco to Grain*. Ithaca, N.Y.: Cornell University Press, 1980.

Donahue, Brian. *The Great Meadow: Farmers and the Land in Colonial Concord*. New Haven, Conn.: Yale University Press, 2000.

Gray, Lewis Cecil. *History of Agriculture in the Southern United States to 1860*. Washington, D.C.: Carnegie Institution, 1933.

Hofstra, Warren. *The Planting of New Virginia: Settlement and Landscape in the Shenandoah Valley*. Baltimore, Md.: Johns Hopkins University Press, 2005.

Kelsey, Darwin, ed. *Farming in the New Nation: Interpreting American Agriculture, 1790–1840*. Washington, D.C.: Agricultural History Society, 1972.

Kim, Sung Bok. *Landlord and Tenant in Colonial New York: Manorial Society, 1664–1775*. Chapel Hill: University of North Carolina Press for the Omohundro Institute of Early American History and Culture, 1987.

Kulikoff, Allan. *From British Peasants to Colonial American Farmers*. Chapel Hill: University of North Carolina Press for the Omohundro Institute of Early American History and Culture, 2000.

———. *Tobacco and Slaves: The Development of Southern Cultures in the Chesapeake, 1680–1800*. Chapel Hill: University of North Carolina Press for the Omohundro Institute of Early American History and Culture, 1986.

McCusker, John, and Russell Menard. *The Economy of British America, 1607–1789*. Chapel Hill: University of North Carolina Press for the Omohundro Institute of Early American History and Culture, 1991.

Merchant, Carolyn. *Ecological Revolutions: Nature, Gender, and Science in New England*. Chapel Hill: University of North Carolina Press, 1989.

Morgan, Philip. *Slave Counterpoint: Black Culture in the Eighteenth-Century Chesapeake and Lowcountry*. Chapel Hill: University of North Carolina Press for the Omohundro Institute of Early American History and Culture, 1998.

Rohrbaugh, Malcolm. *The Land Office Business: The Settlement and Administration of American Public Lands, 1789–1837*. New York: Oxford University Press, 1968.

Taylor, Alan. *Liberty Men and Great Proprietors: The Revolutionary Settlement on the Maine Frontier, 1760–1820*. Chapel Hill: University of North Carolina Press for the Omohundro Institute of Early American History and Culture, 1990.

18th Century ART AND ARCHITECTURE

While people migrated to North America from across northern Europe and Africa, the key factor in determining America's artistic and architectural development was the colonists' changing relationship with the culture of Great Britain. In particular, two events had a significant impact upon Americans' visual and material culture: the "consumer revolution," which occurred when new types and numbers of British manufactured goods became available to a greater percentage of colonial consumers; and the American Revolution, when colonists declared their political independence from the mother country. Despite America's new nationhood, however, its art and architecture remained closely tied to British artistic developments and to larger European styles.

Portraiture, 1700-1776

The portrait was the predominant art form in colonial America. The limited opportunities for artistic training in the colonies meant that few painters were proficient in those art forms that demanded the greatest skill, namely sculpture or history painting, which required the artist to depict the nude human body. Moreover, most colonial consumers were interested only in buying likenesses of themselves or their family members.

Colonial portraits reflect changes in British and European artistic styles. During the opening decades of the century, portraits followed the relatively dark and severe Baroque style. Beginning around 1750, however, traveling British artists, particularly Joseph Blackburn and John Wollaston, introduced the Rococo style to America. This style embraced a brighter palette and showed sitters with more pleasant expressions. With very few teachers in the colonies, American portrait painters also relied heavily on English examples for sitters' poses and costumes, which often circulated through mezzotint engravings.

Many of the artists who made their living painting portraits in the colonies had direct ties to Great Britain. For example, John Smibert, who was born in Edinburgh, Scotland, studied in Italy and worked in London before immigrating to America as part of a failed venture to open a college in Bermuda. In addition to painting portraits, Smibert operated a color shop in Boston where he sold artist's materials and British prints. Several American-born artists trained or permanently relocated to London for better artistic opportunities. Benjamin West, who was born near Philadelphia, moved to London in 1763 after traveling in Italy and quickly rose to success, becoming the historical painter to King George II. West later welcomed many American-born artists to his studio for training, including the Marylander Charles Willson Peale.

John Singleton Copley was the preeminent portraitist of the colonial period. The son of a Boston tobacconist, Copley painted over 300 portraits during his American career. His clientele included Boston's wealthy mercantile elites, including John Hancock, as well as the silversmith Paul Revere. Like Benjamin West, Copley eventually moved to London. He left the colonies shortly before the Revolutionary War and settled in England after a period of study in Italy. Even before he relocated, Copley had garnered interest in England for his portrait *Boy with a Squirrel*, painted in 1765 and exhibited at the Society of Artists in London the next year. Since there were no venues for public exhibition in the colonies, London's art scene offered colonial artists such as Copley and West unparalleled avenues for advancement.

The "Consumer Revolution" and Anglicization, 1720-1760

Beginning around 1720, portraiture was influenced by what scholars have called the "consumer revolution." In the 18th century, colonial consumers from most sectors of society began buying British manufactured goods in quantities and types that would have been unimaginable previously. Colonial consumers used these new wares to express their social status and to communicate their identities, or a sense of who they were. Portraiture reflected this trend. It communicated wealth and culture by illustrating the sitter's possession of luxury goods and displaying his or her familiarity with the newest London artistic styles.

These new purchasing patterns in the colonies were spurred by significant cultural changes, known collectively as Anglicization. In the period between 1660 and 1720, colonists had developed distinctive local subcultures that varied by town and by region. For example, techniques for framing the roofs of houses and for constructing furniture differed in the northern and southern colonies. Vernacular traditions developed incrementally as colonial builders and craftsmen recombined local English and European cultures in isolated communities. Starting around 1720, these regional variations began to disappear as colonists more closely adhered to styles that came from England. As colonists' wealth increased, and as they enjoyed heightened access to British goods, they once again turned to British art and architecture for inspiration. The sum result was that by the start of the American Revolution, colonial culture resembled English culture more than it had at any other time since the 1660s.

Georgian Architecture, 1740–1780

The process of Anglicization is most visible in the style of architecture known as Georgian. Named after King George I, who reigned from 1714 to 1727, the Georgian style became popular in Great Britain beginning around 1720 and appeared in the American colonies soon thereafter. It peaked in popularity in America between 1740 and 1770. Derived from and inspired by the work of the 16th-century Venetian architect Andrea Palladio, it is a loosely Classical style. Based upon Greek and Roman architecture, it exemplifies the ideals of symmetry and rationality.

Unlike vernacular styles, which developed organically through the constant negotiation between builders' knowledge and their patrons' social requirements, the Georgian was the first popular or academic style, meaning that it was uniform across space and could be learned from consulting books rather than by practice. Colonial patrons, amateur architects, or local builders could consult pattern books to select overall building plans or individual elements, such as pedimented doorways. For example, when the English-born amateur architect Peter Harrison built the Redwood Library in Newport, Rhode Island, in 1748–50, he relied on a plate included in Edward Hoppus's *Andrea Palladio's Architecture*, published in 1735.

As it developed in the colonies, the Georgian style was characterized by several features: the use of permanent materials (usually brick or stone, although wood painted in imitation of stone was also used); symmetrical window and door openings; and Classical ornament, including fanlights over doorways, belts or stringcourses to delineate stories, and columns and pediments on building facades. Commonly used for public buildings and churches, the Georgian style was also fashionable for elite private residences such as Drayton Hall, constructed near Charleston, South Carolina, between 1738 and 1742, and probably designed by the plantation owner, John Drayton.

By the 1770s, colonists with less social standing had also adopted elements of Georgian architecture. The typical Georgian house plan was a double-pile building (two rooms deep) that measured two stories. The first floor was bisected by a central hall (which contained the main doorway and a staircase) and featured two rooms (front to back) on either side. This design answered the social needs created by the "consumer revolution" and Anglicization. Colonists required places to display and use their new goods that were separated from the daily activities of family life. Whereas the hall and parlor plan popular in the 17th century grouped together areas for cooking and household work with those for social gathering, the Georgian plan divided spaces into increasingly specific activities, and spaces for polite entertainment were separated from kitchen work.

This spatial division mirrored the trend occurring in consumer goods and furniture design as objects became more individualized and differentiated. In the 17th century, decorative arts were overwhelmingly communal. Even in elite households, diners ate from shared wooden trenchers and sat on wooden benches, with only the most important family member meriting a chair. Over the course of the 18th century, however, elites began to use individual plates (earthenware or porcelain), and each expected to have his or her own glass and chair. Moreover, colonists purchased matching sets of ceramics, glassware, and seating furniture, so that their interiors were increasingly uniform and harmonious. Cabinetmakers invented types of furniture to meet consumers' need to store and display manufactured goods. Like the Georgian house, these new forms, such as the high chest, dressing table, and chest of drawers, enabled greater categorization. Individual drawers contained one person's clothing or one type of textile, replacing the simple 17th-century chest that held all of an elite family's textiles in common, with smaller compartments intended for certain functions.

Art and Revolution, 1770–1783

In the 1760s and 1770s, tensions between the colonies and the mother country escalated over trade restrictions and the new taxes Great Britain levied against Americans. Art played an important role in generating public support for the Patriots'

One of the most celebrated pieces of art from the Revolutionary era, Paul Revere's *The Bloody Massacre* depicts the violent skirmish of March 5, 1770, known as the Boston Massacre, in which British regulars opened fire on a group of unarmed Boston colonists. The piece is one of Revere's most famous engravings and was one of the first colonially manufactured engravings to memorialize an American event. *(Library of Congress)*

cause. Colonists in Boston were particularly vociferous in their resistance, and as a result they were targeted by British authorities, who dissolved the Massachusetts Assembly and stationed troops in the city. The Boston Massacre of March 5, 1770, had the greatest artistic impact. In response to British troops firing upon a crowd of Bostonians, the silversmith and engraver Paul Revere created an emotionally powerful print titled *The Bloody Massacre*. The engraving portrays a group of unarmed colonists being brutally attacked by British regulars. Prior to the Revolutionary period, printmaking was virtually unknown in America, as most colonial engravers lacked the skills and equipment to complete complex engravings. As a result, colonists overwhelmingly purchased their prints from London print sellers. Revere's work broke from this trend and was one of the first colonially manufactured engravings to commemorate an American event.

For the most part, however, art making stopped during the Revolution, for there was little demand for portraits among private citizens during this period. Likewise, during the uncertain economic times caused by the political turmoil, few inhabitants commissioned buildings. Once the war had begun, many structures were destroyed by cannon fire or burned by the British army, which needed fuel during the winters the soldiers were garrisoned in colonial cities, including Boston and Philadelphia. Colonists even practiced acts of iconoclasm, the deliberate destruction of art works. On July 9, 1776, in New York City, for example, Patriots pulled down an equestrian monument of King George III on the Bowling Green and cut off the statue's head before parading its body through the city.

Making an American Art, 1776-1800

When the colonies became an independent nation, Americans were faced with the challenge of how to represent themselves. Which people and what events would best define the characteristics and ideals of the fledgling nation? With the abolition of the monarchy and the creation of a republican government, Americans now relied on fellow citizens for the success of their country. Artists and architects were called upon to create emblems of the new United States that would celebrate republican ideals of equality and virtue. One of the most popular subjects for art produced during and after the Revolutionary War was George Washington. Washington initially became a symbol for the heroism and accomplishments of the new nation because of his military leadership as general of the Continental Army. After colonists had won their independence, Washington retained his tremendous popularity as the first president of the United States.

The artist Charles Willson Peale, who served in the Continental Army, spearheaded efforts to promote republicanism through art. Peale was one of the first artists to complete public portraits of Washington that showed him as a military hero. Such depictions were commissioned during the war by local governments, such as the Executive Council of Pennsylvania, and they were placed in public settings in an effort to bolster the Patriots' cause. After the Revolution, Peale created one of the first museums in America. His Philadelphia Museum first opened in 1786, and it expanded to the second story of Independence Hall in 1794. A joint effort by Peale and several of his children, the museum combined natural history specimens and curiosities, such as the skeleton of a mammoth, with paintings and portraits of republican worthies, including George Washington, Benjamin Franklin, and John Adams. Peale believed these portraits provided examples of virtuous citizenship for visitors to emulate in order to help them become better Americans.

The most popular depictions of George Washington came from the portrait painter Gilbert Stuart. Stuart was born in Newport, Rhode Island, and trained in London. He worked both in London and in Dublin, Ireland, before returning to America in 1793. Stuart came back to America with the express intention of painting Washington. In the meantime, he became the most sought after portraitist in the United States, painting elite sitters first in New York City and then in Philadelphia, Washington, D.C., and Boston. In his portraits of Washington, Stuart successfully captured the new president as a civil leader rather than a military hero. He painted more than 60 replicas of his original portrait to meet the demands of eager American consumers, who wished to share in his heralding of Washington as the "Father of the Country."

History Painting and Sculpture, 1768–1800

With the conclusion of the war, the new demands of creating a national identity inspired a desire for fine arts that extended beyond portraiture. The expatriates Benjamin West and John Singleton Copley were at the forefront of artistic change in London, and their innovations influenced those in the United States. West, along with several English artists, including Joshua Reynolds, sought to popularize a form of painting known as "Grand Manner" history painting. For these large-scale works, artists selected biblical or Classical scenes that had a didactic function. They wanted their paintings to inspire self-sacrifice and devotion to the state in the viewer. West and his contemporaries were heavily influenced by Classical (Greco-Roman) painting and sculpture, and their canvases embody the ideals of the Neoclassical movement, a larger European style that spanned painting, architecture, and the decorative arts, in which artists and architects looked back to the Classical past for inspiration.

In the 1770s, Benjamin West and John Singleton Copley revolutionized Grand Manner painting by introducing recent events (rather than historical themes) and showing subjects wearing contemporary clothing. In *The Death of General Wolfe* (1770), West depicted the noble self-sacrifice

John Singleton Copley was the preeminent portraitist of the colonial period, but he also excelled at the more highly regarded genre of historical painting. *Watson and the Shark* (1778) was his first important work in this sphere and it highlighted what would become a signature theme of 19th-century Romantic art: the struggle of man against nature. *(Library of Congress)*

of the British general who died in the Battle of Quebec in 1759. In the painting, West celebrated the British victory in the most important conflict of the Seven Years' War, during which France and England battled for control over the North American colonies. Upon his death, Wolfe became an immediate hero because of his importance in the conflict. John Singleton Copley followed suit with works such as *Watson and the Shark* (1778). In this painting, Copley monumentalized the dramatic incident in which his patron, Brook Watson, lost his leg in a shark attack in Havana Harbor.

John Trumbull, an American student of Benjamin West, applied this style of history painting to subjects taken from the recent American Revolution and the creation of the new nation. Painting first in London and then briefly in Paris, Trumbull undertook a series of American battle and political scenes that he hoped to have engraved. Unfortunately, he could not interest enough patrons and his project remained incomplete, even after his return to the United States and his careers as a portraitist and diplomat. Approximately 30 years after he began his initial paintings, however, the U.S. Congress commissioned several large canvases from Trumbull as decoration for the newly rebuilt United States Capitol Building, including *The Declaration of Independence, 4 July 1776*, painted between 1786 and 1820.

The Neoclassical style also had an impact upon sculptural depictions of American heroes, especially George Washington. In 1785 the Virginia state legislature commissioned the French sculptor Jean-Antoine Houdon to complete a full-length statue of George Washington for the Virginia State Capitol. Houdon, selected by Thomas Jefferson and

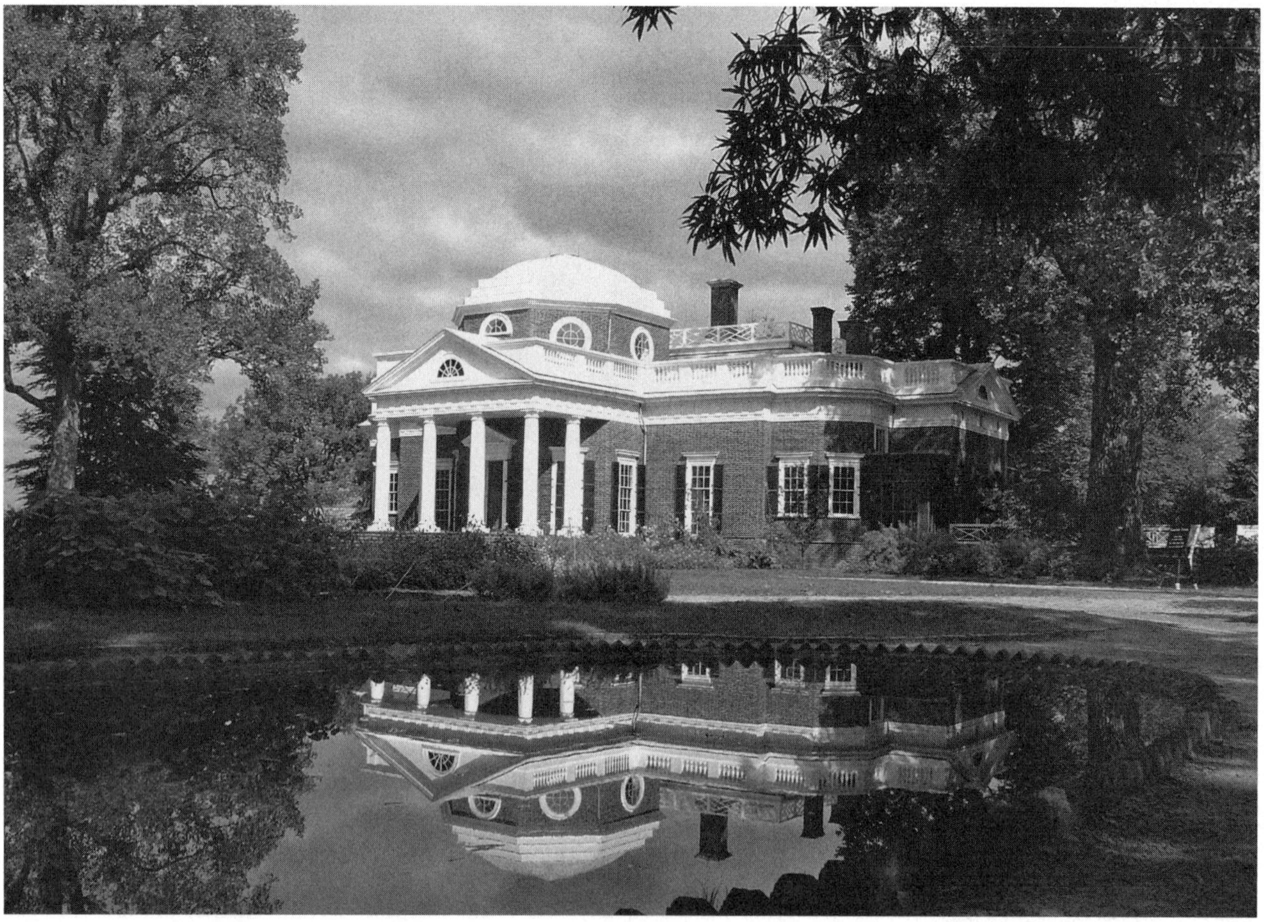

Thomas Jefferson's home, Monticello, located near Charlottesville, Virginia, was built according to his own design and is a prominent example of the Neoclassical style so popular in Revolutionary-era America. Harking back to Greco-Roman structures, such as the Pantheon in Rome, the house features a dome in the center and four frontal columns topped by a pediment. ***(Matt Kozlowski)***

Benjamin Franklin, represented Washington in the style of a Roman senator, standing in an oratorical pose favored by Roman sculptors, with his left arm resting on a bundle of fasces (rods) a reference to the Roman Republic. Rather than show him in antique costume, however, Houdon followed Washington's directions to show him in contemporary costume, in the manner of a Benjamin West history painting.

Neoclassical Architecture, 1776-1800

Beginning in the 1770s, Americans embraced a stricter Neoclassical style of architecture than that inspired by Palladio. As it evolved across Europe, the Neoclassical style entailed a greater attention to historical accuracy and a more archaeological understanding of Greco-Roman buildings. Spurred by the recent excavations of the Roman cities of Pompeii and Herculaneum, which had been preserved by volcanic ash in 79 C.E., Neoclassical architects and designers extolled a more blatant and exuberant classicism.

Thomas Jefferson was one of the strongest proponents of the Neoclassical style in America. He was inspired in part by his own travels in France and England as the American ambassador to France. Both in designing his home, Monticello, as well as the Virginia State Capitol, built between 1785 and 1789, Jefferson turned to Classical precedents. Monticello includes a dome (a feature of Roman structures such as the Pantheon), and both buildings feature columns topped by a pediment (a design taken from Greek temple façades). For the Virginia State Capitol, Jefferson looked to one ancient building in particular, the Maison Carrée, a Roman temple he visited in the south of France.

Jefferson played a critical role in forging the association of Neoclassical architecture with the American government, a connection still common today. Beyond the buildings he designed, Jefferson also selected the British-born architect Benjamin Henry Latrobe to design the U.S. Capitol Building in a Classically inspired style. For those trying to build a new government, Neoclassical architecture pronounced America's political status as a republic like the first Roman Republic, and instilled civic virtue and patriotism in its citizens.

—Jennifer Van Horn

Further Reading

Barratt, Carrie Rebora, and Ellen G. Miles. *Gilbert Stuart*. New Haven, Conn.: Yale University Press for the Metropolitan Museum of Art, 2004.

Barratt, Carrie Rebora, and Paul Staiti. *John Singleton Copley in America.* New York: Harry N. Abrams for the Metropolitan Museum of Art, 1995.

Breen, T. H. *The Marketplace of Revolution: How Consumer Politics Shaped American Independence*. Oxford, U.K.: Oxford University Press, 2004.

Bushman, Richard L. *The Refinement of America: Persons, Houses, Cities.* New York: Alfred A. Knopf, 1992.

Calo, Mary Ann, ed. *Critical Issues in American Art: A Book of Readings*. Boulder, Colo.: Westview Press, 1998.

Craven, Wayne. *American Art: History and Culture*. New York: Harry N. Abrams, 1994.

———. *Colonial American Portraiture: The Economic, Religious, Social, Cultural, Philosophical, Scientific, and Aesthetic Foundations*. Cambridge, U.K.: Cambridge University Press, 1986.

Deetz, James. *In Small Things Forgotten: The Archaeology of Early American Life*. Garden City, N.Y.: Anchor/Doubleday, 1977.

Doezema, Marianne, and Elizabeth Milroy, eds. *Reading American Art*. New Haven, Conn.: Yale University Press, 1998.

Lovell, Margaretta M. *Art in a Season of Revolution: Painters, Artisans, and Patrons in Early America.* Philadelphia: University of Pennsylvania Press, 2005.

McCoubrey, John W., ed. *American Art 1700–1960: Sources and Documents.* Englewood Cliffs, N.J.: Prentice-Hall, 1965.

Pohl, Francis K. *Framing America: A Social History of American Art*. New York: Thames & Hudson, 2002.

Saunders, Richard H., and Ellen G. Miles. *American Colonial Portraits, 1700–1776*. Washington, D.C.: Smithsonian Institution Press for the National Portrait Gallery, 1987.

Upton, Dell. *Architecture in the United States*. New York: Oxford University Press, 1998.

Upton, Dell, and John Michael Vlach, eds. *Common Places: Readings in American Vernacular Architecture*. Athens: University of Georgia Press, 1986.

18th Century CITIES, TOWNS, AND SETTLEMENTS

As the American economy developed during the 18th century, European colonists continued to organize themselves into towns and cities. Towns afforded security and sociability, encouraging economic exchange and communal worship. Larger cities fostered even more sophisticated pursuits in commerce and finance, as well as a wider variety of entertainments and institutions. Over the course of the 18th century, American cities and towns developed into flourishing outposts of the British Empire. After the American Revolution, these cities would become the economic engines of the United States.

Urbanization

Europeans believed that towns were crucial for bringing their civilization to the Americas. Yet America in 1700 was far from urbanized, and no city in British North America held more than 7,000 people. During the 18th century, the percentage of Americans living in towns of 2,500 people or more never rose above 5 percent. Nevertheless, as the centers of politics, economy, society, and culture, the cities had an influence on American history that went far beyond mere numbers.

Urban development and growth varied by region. Since British merchants controlled trade in fish, fur, sugar, and tobacco, Americans had little incentive to build urban networks in the regions of Newfoundland, Hudson Bay, the West Indies, or the Chesapeake Bay. By contrast, the middle colonies, the New England colonies, and the wheat-growing areas in the South built networks of rural villages connected to several larger towns—particularly Boston, New York, and Philadelphia, followed by Newport, Rhode Island, and later by Norfolk, Virginia, and Baltimore, which was first laid out in 1729. Charleston, South Carolina, which offered protection from disease and raids, was the largest city in the American South, trading initially in skins and furs, and later slaves, naval stores, lumber, and especially rice and indigo.

During the 17th century, Anglo settlers in America had laid their towns in a variety of patterns. Variations in elevation and soil, water routes, and the changing needs of growing towns had created haphazard street patterns in places like Boston and New York. Yet regularized, gridded patterns prevailed in many other locations. The planning of Savannah, Georgia (founded in 1733), was particularly striking: The city was designed as a rectangular grid of square wards with public buildings fronting the open squares. Beyond the British settlements, one could find town plans as varied as the pallisaded villages of Iroquois longhouses and the circular groupings of domed houses on the Great Plains.

The Spanish Empire had been following a particular, codified pattern as it established missions (for converting Native Americans), presidios (fortified towns), and pueblos (civil settlements). The pueblo that became San Antonio, Texas (1718), for instance, had a central plaza with a church, surrounded by square blocks. During the late 18th century, Spain added presidios in San Diego (1769), Monterey (1770), San Francisco (1776), and Santa Barbara (1782). To feed these garrisons and add to Spain's reach, the governor of California established pueblos at San José (1777) and Los Angeles (1781). These were isolated places during the 18th century, at the northern reaches of Spain's holdings in Mexico.

New France also expanded its reach during the 18th century. Louisbourg (1712) fell twice to English forces (who built Halifax, Nova Scotia, in 1749 as its counterpart), and never rivaled more important towns like Quebec and Montreal. New Orleans (1718) was mildly prosperous during the 18th century, but it would not realize its prominence until later. Other fortified French settlements that also lay in waiting included Detroit (1701), Mobile (1702), Vincennes (1732), and St. Louis (1764). A British victory during the Seven Years' War (1756–63) allowed the British to rename Fort Duquesne as Pittsburgh in 1758 and to begin laying out a city there in 1764.

Economy

A network of small towns served as ports for the Atlantic coastal trade or as inland trading centers for local farms. In North America, only the largest eastern cities became important centers for imports, exports, and re-exports of goods from afar. American ports sent a variety of foodstuffs to southern Europe and the West Indies, which was in turn a source of rum, sugar, and molasses. A few towns in the Chesapeake region collected tobacco for Scottish ports and other destinations. American cities imported a wide variety of goods from English ports in exchange for lumber, furs and skins, naval stores, and whale oil. American markets also witnessed the exchange of bound laborers brought by slavers from African ports. Customs enforcement was lax for much of the 18th century, but it tightened after the Seven Years' War, and American smugglers responded with illegal voyages from the Caribbean and Continental Europe.

Townspeople employed themselves in a variety of occupations in the 18th century. Overseas traders brought a rich supply of goods to American wharves, especially after 1740, including Chinese tea, Indonesian spices, Caribbean sugar, Madeira wine, Indian textiles, and a variety of manufactured goods from England, such as glass, ironware, ceramics, woolens, and much more. The New England fisheries and the coastal trade among towns were other vibrant sources of economic activity. To keep commerce flowing, merchants employed ship captains and their crews, coopers, shipbuilders, and laborers. Retailers provided customers with medicine, books, clothing, tableware, and other imports. Bakers and butchers supplied food, while cobblers and tailors kept people shod and clothed. Distilleries, refineries, and tanneries produced rum, sugar, and leather, three of the earliest forms of American processing. The building trades kept the cities growing, and a number of furniture makers and metalworkers provided luxury goods, from clocks to teapots. The largest cities also nurtured a class of professionals, particularly government officials, doctors, lawyers, schoolmasters, and clergymen.

The century's numerous wars had a strong impact on the cities' populations. On the one hand, privateering (state-licensed piracy) and military contracts fueled economic growth. At the same time, conflict could disrupt trade, and military casualties sometimes hobbled the male population, leaving widows struggling to make ends meet. By midcentury, New York City and Philadelphia had become success stories, growing to populations of about 25,000 and 32,000, respectively, by the eve of the American Revolution. Boston, by contrast, fell on hard times. New England men suffered particularly severe casualties during the northern military campaigns of midcentury, and these losses, combined with competition from other ports (and the rockiness of the soil surrounding Boston) led the city's economy to falter. As a result, while the town's population reached 16,000 in the 1740s, it remained stagnant at that level until the end of the century. At the same time, America's fertile population was fueling the growth of smaller cities of 4,000 to 5,000, such as Salem, Newport, New Haven, Norfolk, and others.

Society and Culture

The cities, though small, held a broad cross-section of society. At the bottom were bound laborers—slaves and indentured servants. Although slavery was largely a rural institution, slaves were substantial parts of the urban labor force in Charleston, Savannah, Newport, New Orleans, and New York City. In addition to unskilled labor and domestic work, many blacks were skilled craftspeople, weavers, retailers, and boatmen. Cities also provided unique opportunities for blacks to socialize, trade, hire out their labor, and worship. Fears of slave revolts were constantly on the minds of white civic leaders, from Charleston to New Brunswick, New Jersey. Particularly intense scares troubled New York City in 1712 and 1741.

Deaths at sea and at war meant that in some cities, particularly in New England, women outnumbered men. In Boston, for instance, perhaps one of every four women was a widow. In late 18th-century Newport, women were at the head of one out of every five households, though among African Americans and other nonwhites, men outnumbered women. Cities gave women some

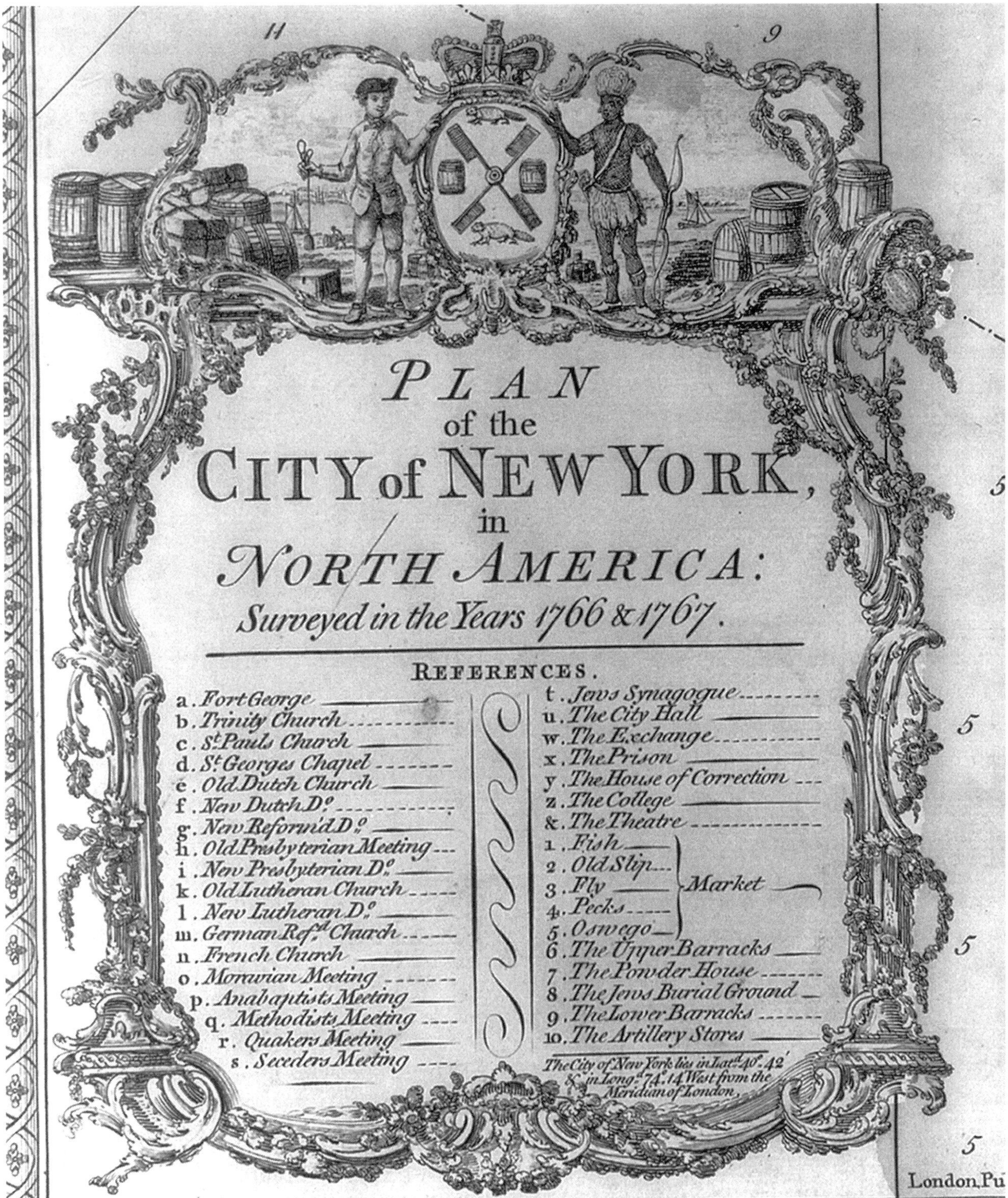

By midcentury, New York City was a major port city. A group of 20 merchants organized the first chamber of commerce in 1768, and by the eve of the American Revolution the city had grown to a population of about 25,000. Above is a cartouche, titled *Plan of the City of New York in North America: Surveyed in the Years 1766 & 1767*, showing an allegorical scene of an English trader and a Native American standing on the shore among barrels and bundles of merchandise. *(Library of Congress)*

opportunities they would not have had in the countryside, including work as retailers and tavernkeepers, greater access to education and female sociability, and a variety of other jobs. Urban women in New England initially had a voice in church affairs, greater economic opportunity, and more leverage within the legal system, but these privileges were in decline during the 18th century.

Even as urban society relied upon the labor of women, children, bound laborers, and poor men, the cities also had men of great wealth—planters, merchants, and some professionals. Especially after 1740, their conspicuous display of consumer goods in fine, symmetrical Georgian townhouses helped lend the cities a gloss of refinement. Some of the principal American churches were based on designs by the London architect Christopher Wren, lending further metropolitan elegance to these provincial towns.

Men of humbler or middling means, like the Boston chandler's son Benjamin Franklin, hoped to rise to a wealthier station during their lifetimes. Franklin, of course, would become a Philadelphia printer and then a leading scientist and statesman. But this sort of upward mobility was often extremely difficult to achieve, if not impossible. During the course of the 18th century, although there were always "middling" city dwellers among the merchants, retailers, and artisans, the extremes of urban wealth and poverty widened even further. From the turn of the century to the eve of the Revolution, the wealthiest 5 percent of colonial Philadelphians who drew up wills raised their share of the city's inherited wealth from 21.7 percent to 55.8 percent, according to Gary Nash's *Urban Crucible*.

Society was more strictly hierarchical in French and Spanish colonial cities such as Montreal, Quebec, St. Augustine, and Santa Fe, where royal officials had much more control than they did in the British colonies, and where social contact tended to be limited to people of the same social rank. Even after the British took over French Canada, the presence of the British military discouraged the more open sociability of the cities in the 13 colonies.

As urban centers grew, so did urban problems such as vice, poverty, crime, epidemic disease, and fire. It also became more difficult to supply sufficient fuel, water, market stalls, streets, and sewage systems for large populations. Particularly devastating fires leveled whole blocks of Charleston in 1740 and Boston in 1760. Cities developed public charity systems, and later workhouses, to stave off poverty. They also organized volunteer fire companies and increased the size of the town watch to keep an eye out for malefactors.

Yet the cities' chaotic nature could also yield creative entertainments and opportunities. In the household, men and women made the rounds for tea or meals. Merchants heard news and did business at coffeehouses, while public houses and taverns allowed men (in clubs or in informal groups) a place to exchange news and jokes over a bowl of punch. By 1771, as Benjamin Carp notes in *Rebels Rising*, there was one tavern or liquor license for every 13 adult white men in New York City. Cities tried to discourage "disorderly houses," or unlicensed taverns, which invited illicit drinking among blacks and servants, brawls, and prostitution. The upper crust had more refined pastimes, such as horse racing, ballroom dancing, and strolling in public gardens. In addition, music societies, stage plays, portrait painters, and subscription libraries enlivened elite society in the most cosmopolitan of the cities, which did their best to catch snatches of European culture from across the Atlantic. Children came together for schooling, which was more commonly available in the dense towns of the North than in the South.

Newspapers provided commercial societies with important information, such as shipping news, advertisements for goods and runaways, and stories of international importance. The printing presses that churned out books, pamphlets, and almanacs also helped to transmit cultural cues, political ideas, and intellectual advancements. Religious tracts and printed sermons were particularly popular, and they extended the networks of various Christian denominations throughout the colonies.

Cities attracted a great deal of ethnic and religious diversity. The Dutch were already present in New York City, and new immigrants arrived from Northern Ireland, the Rhineland, and other areas of Europe. Native Americans visited (and sometimes resided) in the cities. African Americans were a significant presence in all the major cities. Even Boston, which was considered relatively homogeneous, had Quakers, French Huguenots, and Baptists. Such diversity sometimes caused conflicts: between Congregationalists and Anglicans in Boston, between Presbyterians and Quakers in Philadelphia, and between Presbyterians and Anglicans in New York. But for the most part, British American city dwellers were united in their pursuit of material gain, committed to an uneasy pluralism that accepted people of different faiths, including nonbelievers, Jews, and occasional heretics. The evangelical preacher George Whitefield attracted large audiences when he came to the cities to preach. Meanwhile, many small towns experienced painful schisms as a result of the religious revivals that swept through colonial America around midcentury.

Politics

Towns might serve as important administrative centers for the settlement of legal disputes. The colonial capitals had even greater responsibilities: the enactment of legislation and the governance of the province. In Massachusetts, New York, and other colonies, the provincial capital was also the principal commercial center. Yet not every colony had a large, central capital. Williamsburg, Virginia, for instance, was much smaller than nearby Norfolk, and Connecticut and Rhode Island had seats of government that circulated from one town to another.

Town governance varied from region to region. In New England, the town meeting embodied the community's decisions in surprisingly democratic fashion. Although in practice residents deferred to the town's most eminent leaders, the town meeting system proved relatively responsive and efficient. In the South, the largest landowners generally controlled local affairs through the courthouse and vestry. In the middle colonies, chartered corporations governed the largest cities, as in England, while smaller towns had a variety of forms of local government.

Colonial American cities became laboratories for political experimentation during the 18th century. Traditional

This etching from 1789, published in *The Massachusetts Magazine, or, Monthly Museum of Knowledge and Rational Entertainment*, shows a view of Faneuil Hall in Boston. This and other buildings served as meeting places for formal gatherings and mass meetings to protest the encroachments of the British Empire. *(Library of Congress)*

English (and American) societies expected deference to local magistrates and officials. Yet factious conflicts arose, and less-privileged town dwellers refused to consistently obey their so-called betters. In Virginia and New England, religious schisms led vocal minorities to wring new demands from local governments. In the South Carolina backcountry, it was the lack of organized town government that led to widespread protests. Currency schemes, military policy, and party politics made for lively disputes in the cities. The Anglo-American tradition had long tolerated the occasional riot or public celebration. In Boston, for instance, November 5 was known as "Pope's Day," a day of parading the pope in effigy, which often resulted in violent clashes among the laborers and boys of the North End and South End. Boys, seamen, laborers, artisans, blacks, women, and other disadvantaged groups were able to draw upon a variety of festive traditions to make their voices heard. Sometimes this had an impact—white men were particularly successful in gaining a greater voice in politics—but in other cases this outdoor organizing could only lay the groundwork for future gains.

Cities and towns became particularly important during the political protests that arose after 1763. Merchants met to discuss new laws from Parliament and to organize boycotts. Printers fired off angry pamphlets and newspaper articles. Protestors took to the streets, igniting bonfires and riots. Urban networks allowed Patriot leaders to transmit information—through print, mail, or word of mouth—and to mobilize people throughout the town and countryside. While riots brought troops to Boston from late 1768 to early 1770, American towns and cities were largely free of the military presence that dominated cities in Canada or the Caribbean. As a result the cities of the 13 colonies became crucial flashpoints for the cries against British encroachment. Buildings like Faneuil Hall or the Old South Meeting House in Boston, or the State House (later Independence Hall) in Philadelphia hosted formal gatherings as well as mass meetings to protest the encroachments of the British Empire. The Sons of Liberty might also rally at outdoor spaces such as beneath a "Liberty Tree" or liberty pole. Events such as the Stamp Act riots of 1765, the Boston Massacre in 1770, and the Boston Tea Party of 1773 attained iconic status, in part because influential city dwellers were reporting urban protests far and wide.

Revolution and Beyond

The Revolutionary War (1775–83) was devastating to American cities, beginning with the closing of the port of Boston in 1774. Vulnerable to the British Navy, the largest ports were all abandoned at one time or another by Patriot governments (along with much of the civilian population) and occupied by the British armed forces. Indeed, it was Americans' willingness to abandon their cities that frustrated British military strategy, for there was no one port that the British could capture and thereby declare victory. Norfolk, Virginia, was burned almost entirely to the ground (mostly by Patriot militias), and several towns, especially in Connecticut and New Jersey, also suffered fiery fates. Newport, Rhode Island, was ravaged by British occupation and never recovered its former prominence. Towns relatively unscathed by the British presence, meanwhile, such as Baltimore and Providence, surged ahead when the war ended. Meanwhile, because they had supported the losing side, Loyalists from the 13 colonies were forced to resettle in the regions that became Canada and Florida, along with other parts of the British Empire.

By the century's end, the cities of the United States could look forward to a bright economic future. The 1800 census listed Philadelphia (including Southwark and the Northern Liberties), New York City, Baltimore, Boston, and Charleston as the five largest cities, each with over 10,000 people, and New York's population would shortly surpass that of Philadelphia, Southwark, and the Northern Liberties combined. Entrepreneurs took advantage of new trade and whaling opportunities to explore distant oceans and trade goods with the Caribbean, Europe, and Asia. During the Federalist era, Alexander Hamilton argued for banks, a centralized government, the federal assumption of debt, and the formation of the mint—all with the idea of lending credit and stability to urban merchants and financiers. Banks, insurance companies, speculation in land and securities, and canal companies developed as more sophisticated urban instruments for raising capital in the early republic. Manufacturing societies sprang up from Baltimore to Boston, although full-scale industrialization eluded 18th-century America.

Meanwhile, the American interior was also beginning to boast larger towns, including Camden, South Carolina (1758), Lynchburg, Virginia (1757), and Lancaster, Pennsylvania (1729). Even before the Revolution, New Englanders and New Yorkers were pushing north and west, and other Americans also began settling across the Appalachians in search of more land to carve into farms. After the Revolution, American military forces began displacing Native Americans in the Old Northwest and Old Southwest, and the federal government carved new tracts out of what became Kentucky, Tennessee, and Ohio. The Land Ordinance of 1785 specified that the states that became the Midwest would be laid out in square townships. Towns like Marietta (1788) and Cincinnati (1788) reflected this grid pattern; while others—like Cleveland (1796)—reflected the designs of their New England forebears. Roads linked the coastal settlements to Rutland, Vermont (1761); Utica, New York (1773); Pittsburgh; Louisville, Kentucky (1778); and Nashville, Tennessee (1779).

Within the cities and towns of the newly independent nation, Americans set about building an urban civil society without the underpinnings of the British Empire, the Revolutionary protest movement, or wartime military mobilization. The Constitution was ratified with strong artisan support in the major cities, as urban newspapers and urban festivals helped knit the nation together. New York and Philadelphia each hosted the American government for a brief period in the 1790s.

Yet leaders such as Alexander Hamilton and George Washington warned about the influence of radical artisans over the decisions of government. A number of Democratic-Republican societies began abandoning the Federalists in the early 1790s to support the French Revolution in defiance of Federalist policy. This grassroots politicking (which often included women as well as men) shocked many Federalists as improper, factious dissent. Still, urban artisans had won political acceptance in the new nation, and they would not surrender it lightly. Other urban groups, meanwhile, still struggled to attain a political role in the American republic. Women battled to be accepted as thinkers and writers in urban salons, theaters, and schools. African Americans in the cities, both free and enslaved, pursued what freedom and opportunity they had in churches and associations, in seafaring life and grogshops, at work and in school.

A few other urban problems seemed worrisome to the elite. Strikes, new immigrants, sexual license, and poor sanitation appeared to make cities into unsavory, riotous places. Meanwhile, Boston's Federal Street Theatre burned in 1798, a financial panic gripped New York City in 1792, and a yellow fever epidemic ravaged Philadelphia in 1793. All these incidents spoke to the continuing dangers presented by the cities' concentration of wealth and people. State legislators began moving their capitals away from coastal port cities to more centrally located towns such as Raleigh, North Carolina, or Columbia, South Carolina.

A century that had begun less than a generation after the surveying of Philadelphia in 1682 ended with the establishment of the United States capital at a sparsely populated bend in the Potomac River in 1801. In the West at the time, the center of government was separate from the principal economic hubs only in Russia and the United States. Yet this was deliberate: Many of the Founding Fathers had distrusted cities. Washington wrote that their "tumultuous populace . . . are ever to be dreaded," while Thomas Jefferson agreed that "the mobs of great cities" were "sores" on the body politic. The location of Washington, D.C., was a concession to the South and its rural, pastoral notions of a classical republican society. The new city was designed to stave off fears that it would become a center of centralized power, corruption, and privilege, like the cities of Europe. The capital city thus disdained urban values, urban vices, and urban commercial ventures, and it remained moribund as a city for a hundred years.

—Benjamin L. Carp

Further Reading

Branson, Susan. *These Fiery Frenchified Dames: Women and Political Culture in Early National Philadelphia*. Philadelphia: University of Pennsylvania Press, 2001.

Bridenbaugh, Carl. *Cities in Revolt: Urban Life in America, 1743–1776*. New York: Alfred A. Knopf, 1955.

———. *Cities in the Wilderness: The First Century of Urban Life in America, 1625–1742*. 2d ed. 1938; New York: Alfred A. Knopf, 1955.

Burrows, Edwin G., and Mike Wallace. *Gotham: A History of New York City to 1898*. New York: Oxford University Press, 1999.

Carp, Benjamin L. *Rebels Rising: Cities and the American Revolution*. New York: Oxford University Press, 2007.

Carr, Jacqueline Barbara. *After the Siege: A Social History of Boston 1775–1800*. Boston: Northeastern University Press, 2005.

Crane, Elaine Forman. *Ebb Tide in New England: Women, Seaports, and Social Change, 1630–1800*. Boston: Northeastern University Press, 1998.

Doerflinger, Thomas M. *A Vigorous Spirit of Enterprise: Merchants and Economic Development in Revolutionary Philadelphia*. Chapel Hill: University of North Carolina Press, 1986.

Hornsby, Stephen. *British Atlantic, American Frontier: Spaces of Power in Early Modern British America*. Hanover, N.H.: University Press of New England, 2005.

Lyons, Clare A. *Sex Among the Rabble: An Intimate History of Gender and Power in the Age of Revolution, Philadelphia, 1730–1830*. Chapel Hill: University of North Carolina Press, 2006.

Meinig, D. W. *Atlantic America, 1492–1800*. Vol. 1 of *The Shaping of America: A Geographical Perspective on 500 Years of History*. New Haven, Conn.: Yale University Press, 1986.

Nash, Gary B. *Forging Freedom: The Formation of Philadelphia's Black Community, 1720–1840*. Cambridge, Mass: Harvard University Press, 1988.

———. *The Urban Crucible: Social Change, Political Consciousness, and the Origins of the American Revolution*. Cambridge, Mass.: Harvard University Press, 1979.

Newman, Simon P. *Parades and the Politics of the Street: Festive Culture in the Early American Republic*. Philadelphia: University of Pennsylvania Press, 1997.

Onuf, Peter S. *Statehood and Union: A History of the Northwest Ordinance*. Bloomington: Indiana University Press, 1987.

Reps, John William. *The Making of Urban America: A History of City Planning in the United States*. Princeton, N.J.: Princeton University Press, 1965.

Wade, Richard C. *The Urban Frontier: The Rise of Western Cities, 1790–1830*. 1959. Reprint, Urbana: University of Illinois Press, 1996.

Waldstreicher, David. *In the Midst of Perpetual Fetes: The Making of American Nationalism, 1776–1820*. Chapel Hill: University of North Carolina Press, 1997.

Weigley, Russell F., ed. *Philadelphia: A 300-Year History*. New York: W. W. Norton, 1982.

18th Century CLOTHING AND FASHION

Over the course of the 18th century, clothing and fashion were central to many economic, social, political, and cultural developments in the British Atlantic world. As changes in production and consumption in England influenced Britain's North American colonies, the expanding colonial markets for cloth and clothing also shaped British political economy. From colonies that were economically, and somewhat culturally, dependent on Great Britain, to an American nation and its inhabitants struggling to define the terms of their personal and political independence, clothing and fashion responded to and helped produce some of the period's dramatic changes. The material reality of clothing, combined with its powerful symbolic qualities, meant that it served as a vehicle for contests over those transformations.

The English Background

Beginning in the late 17th century, the availability of cloth—the literal stuff of clothing—expanded in England due to innovations in production and supply. The beginnings of mechanization and factory production increased the volume of woolen fabrics produced, while new business ventures such as the East India Company began to import cotton cloth from India. These inexpensive cotton fabrics, known as calico and chintz, became wildly popular among a populace moving into towns and cities such as London—and thus away from home or local production of cloth. Out of necessity as well as desire, an emerging consumer public participated in a nascent consumer culture stimulated by both supply and demand. The basic items of dress changed little over the course of the 18th century: shirt, breeches, and coat for men; shift, petticoat, and gown or skirt and jacket for women. Yet changing styles and patterns of fabrics made for variety in dress and were part of a fashion cycle that relied on novelty. Indeed, in a period in which the forms of dress changed somewhat slowly compared with today, fabric was the chief indicator of fashionability. So popular were India-style cottons that some felt that they threatened the viability of the domestic cloth industry. This competition spurred riots by English weavers and finally resulted in a prohibition on the consumption of cottons that lasted from 1720 until 1774. The ban, however, did not apply to Britain's overseas colonies, which became important export markets for calico and chintz.

The 1720 law banning calicos was a form of economic protectionism but also a sumptuary regulation. Many complained that the donning of colorful cottons across ranks resulted in social confusion, particularly when it came to distinguishing among classes of women. Thus, the social anxiety generated by increasing access to consumer goods, clothing chief among them, contained a gendered component. Consumption itself, as well as the "exotic" consumer spoils of an emerging commercial empire, became feminized, associated with and projected onto women and effeminate men. The tension between economic expansion and the maintenance of social order grew as clothing became more varied, less expensive, and more accessible across social ranks, and as its production and consumption became increasingly critical to the health of the English nation. Once considered a clear marker of status, dress ceased to be a reliable indicator of where a person stood on the social ladder, although attire could still designate a person's occupation and geographic location. Although consumer goods reached into provincial England, the dress of farmers and small-scale artisans changed little across the century.

The North American Context

The same might be said of the most rural inhabitants of England's North American colonies, although they were not wholly isolated from the transatlantic trade in cloth, the linchpin of an expanding British commercial empire that produced social consequences. The colonies, designed to be markets for manufactured goods and prohibited from engaging in production on any scale that might compete with English items, grew increasingly dependent on those goods. Although some colonists produced cloth and clothes of their own making into the 18th century, imported fabric became cheaper and easier to acquire—more economical, in fact, than homespun. An emerging planter class in the slave societies of the Chesapeake and Lower South found that *osnabrug*, an inexpensive, rough cloth carried from Germany, was the cheapest way to clothe slaves. However, enslaved African Americans found ways to acquire other attire, through barter, purchase, or pilfer. As the consumption of fabric spread "down" the social ladder, the cloth trade also reached into backcountry communities and structured frontier diplomacy, as Native American groups engaged in networks of exchange of and dependency on manufactured goods. British cloth and garments joined traditional Native attire composed of animal skins, producing a hybrid style of dress adopted by both Native Americans and frontier inhabitants of European descent.

But perhaps nowhere were the economic and social changes stimulated by the importation and consumption of clothing more apparent than in the growing towns and cities of British North America. An increasingly wealthy and powerful merchant class imported boatfuls of fabric in an ever-expanding array of colors, patterns, textures, and prices, passing them along to shopkeeping retailers. The variety of cloth available to urban consumers was impressive, and city streets evolved into venues in which sartorial distinction took many forms, from Quaker plainness and workingmen's garb in Philadelphia, to the sumptuous appearance of Charleston's elites and the mix of high and low styles worn by that city's enslaved residents. Although some ready-made garments were available, the creation of attire generally relied on the skills of those in the fashion trades—tailors and dressmakers. As immigration from Europe increased in the middle decades of the 18th century, the ranks of craftspeople, touting their European training and experience, swelled. More colonists could acquire finely tailored garments, yet the elite tended to have at least some of their clothes made in England as a mark of fashionability and social distinction.

In addition to the purchase of cloth and clothing, sometimes quite inexpensively at public sales or auctions, an underground or informal economy of theft and pawning existed in the major port cities of British North America. These networks of illicit exchange were fueled by self-emancipated slaves and servants, who had taken clothing from their former masters, as well as by petty criminals. Clothing was valuable as a form of currency to be exchanged for other goods and services, it possessed social currency in its capacity to alter one's perceived identity, and it might be sold to obtain actual currency. Thus, the informal economy could increase social mobility. It undoubtedly expanded access to fine clothes, making colonists more anxious about the ability to "know" someone by his or her dress, especially among diverse and transient port city populations. However, other markers of social rank and identity, such as speech and manners, emerged in order to distinguish the genuinely genteel from those who merely counterfeited gentility through attire.

By the middle of the 18th century, the colonies were flush with consumer goods and practices. Colonists embraced many of these in imitation of England, but some, such as the calico cloth that found a market in North America after the 1720 prohibition, had become distinctively colonial. Europe was the acknowledged center of fashion, the seat of *la mode*, but residents of British North America displayed their own sartorial sensibilities, whether out of necessity or choice. Yet there was no denying colonists' economic as well as cultural reliance on imported cloth.

Imperial Crisis and Revolution

Such dependency became the basis of political resistance during the imperial crisis of the 1760s and 1770s. When Parliament passed the Revenue Act of 1764 and followed it a year later with the Stamp Act, which taxed all paper goods and transactions, many colonists were outraged. In pamphlet literature, they framed arguments about the need for consent to taxation and other traditional liberties under the British constitution. But resisters also advocated the renunciation of British goods as a form of resistance to the acts, beginning with mourning dress, which they deemed extravagant and unnecessary. Merchants in the northern port cities, Boston first among them, agreed not to import goods until the Stamp Act was repealed, and a corresponding campaign promoting the production of homespun cloth (to replace imported fabric) by women of sense and virtue filled colonial newspapers. When Parliament rescinded the Stamp Act in 1766, rejoicing ensued and colonists returned to their prior consumer habits.

But nonimportation and nonconsumption cranked up again with the passage of new taxes in 1767, as the rhetoric of resistance grew increasingly heated. The rejection of goods was a form of political action in which many residents of British North America could and did participate. Yet the promotions of the boycotts relied on hierarchies of status and gender in which men and women of the "best families"—people "of fashion"—joined the cause by donning homespun instead of imported finery. The colonial resistance movement displayed an ambivalent relationship toward the idea of fashion. On the one hand, resisters associated fashion in dress with England and advocated its rejection; on the other, they attempted to create new, distinctly American modes, making a fashion of antifashion. Still, the appeal of imports continued, as evidenced by the resumption of consumption after each round of boycotts. The Continental Association, formed out of the Continental Congress of 1774, issued a colonies-wide proscription of British goods and other forms of "extravagance," but the embrace of imported goods and styles persisted into the years of open conflict with Great Britain. While some, such as militiamen and Benjamin Franklin, who sported a beaver hat at the French court, adopted a look of frontier rusticity to signify American identity, not all Americans were swayed by calls for sacrifice, asceticism, and "homespun" virtue. Thus, fashion in dress was a crucible of contests over various forms of power and

Two famous American statesmen model wares that emphasize the "homespun" style of American dress in the second half of the 18th century. The beaver hat worn by Benjamin Franklin (left) suggested a frontier rusticity while the suit George Washington (right) wore to his 1789 inauguration as president was made from domestically produced broadcloth that was trumpeted as being equal in style and quality to that produced abroad. ***(Library of Congress)***

authority in a period of imperial crisis, war, and nation-making, processes that concerned gender, social, and economic relationships as well as political order.

The New American Nation

The fact that fabric was an essential component of 18th-century fashion linked the cloth trade to the fashion cycle, connecting cultural practices to political economy, and linking the personal and the political. In the period following the conclusion of the War for Independence, Americans debated how the new nation, and its citizens, should "look," as well as how it should behave economically. The 1780s saw a resumption of trade with England. Goods flooded into American ports, driving down their costs to the benefit of American consumers. Yet many critics felt that the absence of a unified national commercial policy, the notable imbalance of trade, and continued appetites for European goods and styles, did not befit an independent republic. In particular, "slavish" devotion to fashion was deemed antithetical to the independence and virtue required of a newly empowered citizenry, "the people."

Even after the adoption of the Constitution in 1788, the public prints, or newspapers, brimmed with competing visions of the nation's political economy. They all promoted and hoped to secure the United States' independence, but advocated different methods. Some thought that the nation should generate its own supply of goods—cloth in particular—through an expansion of industrial projects. Others feared industrialization in the English model and promoted the nation's agricultural destiny and small-scale "cottage" production of cloth. On some level, both visions sought to wean the nation from dependence on foreign products. Demonstrating the symbolic, cultural importance of this agenda of independence, George Washington wore a suit made of domestically produced broadcloth, publicly praised as equal in fineness and quality as imported, when he was inaugurated in 1789. For his second inauguration, however, he donned imported black velvet. Fashion in the European mode retained its social currency, and thus its political capital in venues at home and abroad. Americans were caught between the need to appear appropriately republican and the compulsion to appear legitimate in the eyes of a watchful Western world, as well as by the desire to distinguish themselves sartorially from one another.

To an extent, the dilemma between republican virtue and fashionability was resolved by changing modes themselves over the final third of the 18th century. Beginning in the 1750s, the look of the "country" (rather than the high styles of the court) gained favor in England and its colonies. A certain refined rusticity came into vogue, and pastoral styles had particular resonance in British America, as they were more associated with nature than with the mother country. Prevailing fashions in dress both produced and responded to the imperatives of the Age of Revolutions, with their emphasis on Enlightenment rationality, virtue, and sensibility. In particular, elite men's dress evolved from the periwigs and long-skirted coats of bright, sumptuous fabrics of the early 18th century, moving toward natural hair and closely cut suits in somber colors. Such sartorial understatements became the new indicators of masculine power, depicting certain men as rational, republican political actors embracing a new, national political economy. Yet the style itself, as well as the cloth, remained an import, much like the women's formal gowns that retained their splendor.

As it had been during the American Revolution, fashion in dress was a flashpoint of political conflict as parties emerged in the 1790s. Federalists and Democratic-Republicans alike used the language of personal style to attack one another in the public prints. The French Revolution, one of the issues around which the partisan binary formed, further politicized attire—the color of one's cockade, whether black or tricolor, signified party loyalty.

Beginning as early as the 1770s—but flowering in the late 1790s along with transatlantic republicanism—neoclassicism, particularly in women's high fashion, recalled the ancient republics of Greece and Rome. As debates over rights flourished, elite and middling women used dress as a means of participating in the public sphere of politics and signifying their knowledge of and importance to matters of state. The balls and salons to which elite women were essential, and at which fashion was very much on display, helped to form a political and social elite.

Yet as the 18th century became the 19th, the realm of popular politics and the exercise of the franchise were defined as exclusively male and, eventually, white. Fashion's conceptual feminization, unchanged from the late 17th century, gained a new use as part of a rationale underpinning the exclusion of ostensibly dependent, irrational bodies, such as all women and men of color, from the formal, republican body politic.

—*Kate Haulman*

Further Reading

Baumgarten, Linda. *What Clothes Reveal: The Language of Clothing in Colonial and Federal America.* Williamsburg, Va.: Colonial Williamsburg Foundation in association with Yale University Press, 2002.

Branson, Susan. *These Fiery Frenchified Dames: Women and Political Culture in Early National Philadelphia.* Philadelphia: University of Pennsylvania Press, 2001.

Breen, Timothy H. *The Marketplace of Revolution: How Consumer Politics Shaped American Independence.* New York: Oxford University Press, 2004.

Bushman, Richard L. *The Refinement of America: Persons, Houses, Cities*. New York: Alfred A. Knopf, 1992.

Calvert, Karin. "The Function of Fashion in Eighteenth-Century America." In *Of Consuming Interests: The Style of Life in the Eighteenth Century*, edited by Cary Carson, Ronald Hoffman, and Peter J. Albert, 252–283. Charlottesville: Published for the United States Capitol Historical Society by the University of Virginia Press, 1994.

Haulman, Kate. "Fashion and the Culture Wars of Revolutionary Philadelphia." *William and Mary Quarterly* 62, no. 4 (2005): 625–662.

Kuchta, David. *The Three-Piece Suit and Modern Masculinity: England, 1550–1850*. Berkeley: University of California Press, 2002.

Lemire, Beverly. *Fashion's Favourite: The Cotton Trade and the Consumer in Britain, 1660–1800*. Oxford, U.K.: Oxford University Press, 1991.

Mackie, Erin. *Market a la Mode: Fashion, Commodity, and Gender in* The Tatler *and* The Spectator. Baltimore, Md.: Johns Hopkins University Press, 1997.

Shannon, Timothy J. "Dressing for Success on the Mohawk Frontier: Hendrick, William Johnson, and the Indian Fashion." *William and Mary Quarterly* 53, no. 1 (1996): 13–42.

Shields, David S. *Civil Tongues and Polite Letters in British America*. Chapel Hill: University of North Carolina Press, 1997.

Styles, John. *The Dress of the People: Everyday Fashion in Eighteenth-Century England*. New Haven, Conn.: Yale University Press, 2007.

Waldstreicher, David. "Federalism, the Styles of Politics, and the Politics of Style." In *Federalists Reconsidered*, edited by Doron Ben-Atar and Barbara B. Oberg, 99–117. Charlottesville: University Press of Virginia, 1998.

Zabin, Serena R. *Dangerous Economies: Status and Commerce in Imperial New York.* Philadelphia: University of Pennsylvania Press, 2009.

18th Century COMMUNICATION

Methods of communicating within and among the American colonies and, after 1783, the new United States were little different from those that had been used for centuries. Nevertheless, America and Europe were very different places, and they had different communication needs. The colonies had a decentralized population spread over numerous middle-size towns and rural areas. Throughout the century, the colonies, and later the states, lacked a single, predominant metropolitan center such as London or Paris. Thus, effective means of communication were vital to Americans as a way of holding the separate colonies and the new nation together. The addition of three new states (Vermont, Kentucky, and Tennessee) in the 1790s increased the decentralization and further emphasized the growing importance of what today might be called an information marketplace.

The competition that developed in the second half of the 18th century—among states, cities, and towns, religious groups, political parties, fledgling newspapers, and businesses such as printing—played a crucial role in shaping the country's early years. For example, Boston, Philadelphia, and New York competed as printing and newspaper centers, with Boston and Philadelphia dominating. Their publications competed and circulated in numerous states. As the country's population grew, pressure for public education and the literacy it created also grew, as did the demand for information. Yet aside from providing a vital postal delivery service, the government stayed largely in the background for most Americans throughout the century.

During the 18th century, communication over any distance at all was measured not in minutes or hours, but in days and weeks. Indeed, there was little difference between the pace of transportation and communication, and the two were often one and the same. A man traveling by horse from New York to Philadelphia, for example, was doing both: He was being transported, and he was also taking the latest news and gossip from one place to the other. And that trip, which might take days in good spring or summer weather, often took far longer in the fall or winter.

Eighteenth-century business and government, both very small in scale by modern standards, operated in full knowledge of how long it took to communicate over any distance beyond a local community. News from Europe took weeks to reach America, leaving colonists always feeling out of date and behind the times. But so, too, news from Georgia might take weeks to finally reach New York or Boston. Such slow communication hindered effective business and government transactions, as decisions made in one place often no longer applied to changing conditions elsewhere.

Postal Mail

Other than individuals traveling from place to place, the distribution and delivery of mail was the single most important mode of communication in North America throughout the 18th century, though it was first organized over the whole area only in the 1770s. It was also the single mode of communication available over any distance, other than those individual travelers. Yet mail service was slow throughout this century, especially farther away from the coastal cities that were served by regular passing vessels carrying mail. Inland communication was far more difficult over the few developed routes available, and also slower and more costly. Thus, sending even a simple letter was rarely a simple process, nor was it inexpensive. For decades, there was no standard system of paying for carriage, as different communities and colonies used different systems. Demonstrating the system's inefficiencies, postal rates were often high, even by present-day standards, limiting the sending of most letters to businesses or the wealthy. Relatively low literacy rates also limited widespread writing of letters. Due to a lack of widespread public education, literacy rates varied at midcentury from about 10 percent in rural areas to an average of 25 percent across the colonies, with a high of better than 60 percent in Massachusetts.

For decades, primarily for reasons of safety, the transport of mail between towns and cities was limited to daylight hours. Indeed, only by 1764 were the mails being carried by day and night between Philadelphia and New York, with plans to extend a similar level of more rapid service to Boston. A more formal system of post riders was created by the Continental Congress a dozen years later. Teams of mail riders were established every 25 to 30 miles or so, with mail to be carried at least three times a week—day and night—until delivered to the next rider. The American Revolution interfered with these plans, however, as it disrupted most communication channels, especially those close to scenes of actual fighting.

As an important part of creating the new federal government, in 1789 the U.S. Post Office was established, and it became a permanent organ of government three years later. Building on the postal delivery service formed in the 1770s by the Continental Congress, the department took over the operation of some 75 post offices in the 13 original states, along with maintenance of about 2,000 miles of post road routes. Indeed, the only interaction most Americans had with their new government was with the post office.

Postal legislation of 1792 expanded the role and importance of postal service. It prevented government surveillance of personal letters, provided for low rates to mail newspapers, and passed control of new postal routes from the executive branch to Congress. These changes underpinned the long-range centrality of the mails in the nation's coming expansion. Yet as an indicator of the postal system's scope, the country's first postmaster general had a support staff of two. And in 1800, just two wagons were needed to carry the whole department and all of its records and other materials from Philadelphia to the new national capital in Washington.

Paul Revere's "midnight ride," which took place on the night of April 18, 1775, in advance of the battles at Lexington and Concord, is one of the iconic events of the American Revolution and one of the most famous 18th-century examples of military communications. *(National Archives)*

Military Communication

As with civilian communication, methods of military and naval communication also varied little during the 18th century. Modes in use for hundreds of years continued to be called upon, including couriers, fire for nighttime messages, smoke, signal lamps, the occasional use of horns or drums, and the like. Colonial militias also sometimes adopted modes of communication used by Native Americans. Messages carried by couriers often used simple codes to hide their real content, or the messenger simply memorized the signal. But, as often happened in colonial wars, couriers could all too easily be intercepted and messages lost.

Perhaps the best-known 18th-century example of military communications is Paul Revere's 1775 use of signal lanterns, which were hung high in the steeple of a church in Boston's North End. They signaled how British troops were advancing ("one if by land and two if by sea"), so that colonial militia forces west of the city could be forewarned. But that message was then disseminated by Revere and others galloping by horseback and simply shouting the news ("the regulars are coming!"). Even in such moments of crisis, communication and transportation were one and the same.

With the outbreak of fighting in 1775, George Washington created a communications network. During the fighting for New York in the summer of 1776, Washington used couriers between Long Island and New York City to provide warning of when and where British troops might land. Numerous battles to follow were sometimes lost for lack of standardized means of communicating battle plans amid the confusion, poor visibility, and noise of the battlefield. After training under Major General Baron von Steuben during their hard winter at Valley Forge in 1777, however, American forces began to use drummers (and sometimes the location of their battle flags) to signal calls for advance or retreat on the battlefield.

Later improvements in military communications developed in a Europe riven by continued conflicts between England and France. Those innovations would reach America early in the next century. Standardized naval flag signaling systems were developed for use in Britain's Royal Navy (similar systems would be soon be utilized by the fledgling American navy). By the 1790s, early mechanical semaphore telegraphs were appearing across France, able to transmit simple messages from one specially built tower to another over hundreds of miles in a matter of hours. Versions of these would also soon appear in America.

—Christopher H. Sterling

Further Reading

Burlingame, Roger. *March of the Iron Men: A Social History of Union through Invention.* New York: Charles Scribner's Sons, 1938.

John, Richard R. *Spreading the News: The American Postal System from Franklin to Morse.* Cambridge, Mass.: Harvard University Press, 1995.

Lacy, Dan. *From Grunts to Gigabytes: Communications and Society.* Urbana: University of Illinois Press, 1996.

Meadow, Charles T. *Making Connections: Communication through the Ages.* Lanham, Md.: Scarecrow Press, 2002.

Sterling, Christopher H., ed. *Military Communications: From Ancient Times to the 21st Century*. Santa Barbara, Calif.: ABC-CLIO, 2008.

Wood, Kenneth A. *Post Dates: A Chronology of Intriguing Events in the Mails and Philately.* Albany, Ore.: Van Dahl, 1998.

18th Century **DEMOGRAPHY**

The population of the English colonies on the mainland of North America numbered about 250,000 at the beginning of the 18th century, including free, indentured, and enslaved inhabitants. A century later, the second U.S. Census counted over 5.3 million individuals. This phenomenal growth was widely observed and, from the perspective of the population descended from Europeans, positively viewed. In 1751, Benjamin Franklin estimated that the British North American population doubled every 20 years—the result, he believed, of inexpensive and plentiful land, which encouraged early marriage and large families. In his famous 1798 essay on population, the Reverend Thomas Robert Malthus cited the American demographic experience as a model of maximum human population growth. Malthus emphasized America's exceptionally light constraints on this growth, noting that its cheap land, ample means of subsistence, and liberty and equality resulted in a "rapidity of increase probably without parallel in history."

There was, of course, another trend running counter to the rapidly growing colonial population. The aboriginal population of North America declined almost as rapidly as the colonial population grew. Although numbers are difficult to estimate, the American Indian population undoubtedly suffered substantial decline from the late 16th century. It is estimated that the American Indian population in what would eventually become the continental United States stood at 987,000 in 1700, though other estimates place it has high as 2 million. By 1800 the total had fallen to about 600,000. All reasons for the decline stem in part from European contact and colonization, including introduced disease, warfare and genocide, geographical removal and relocation, and destruction of Native ways of life. Diseases introduced from the Eastern Hemisphere were the overwhelming cause. Qualitative evidence suggests there were at least 9 epidemics of smallpox among American Indians (including the extremely destructive 1779–83 pandemic), as well as 11 major epidemics of other infectious diseases, including measles, influenza, typhus, and bubonic plague.

Racial and Ethnic Composition

The table below shows estimates of the population by race in each decade of the 18th century. The rapid expansion of the colonial white and black populations pushed eastern Indian tribes west, disrupting traditional subsistence economies and causing conflicts with interior tribes. Although there was a small overlap between the colonial/early republic and Indian populations on the frontier of colonial settlement and in a few other areas—some Indians, such as the Natick Indians of Massachusetts, continued to live in the East and some whites and blacks lived near or among the various Indian groups well beyond the frontier—the numbers were small relative to the overall size of the populations. For practical purposes, the combined white and black populations can be considered the population of colonial British North America and the early United States, and the Indian population can be considered the population in the remainder of the continent. The black share of the colonial population grew from 11 percent in 1700 to over 21 percent in 1750, and it remained at approximately 20 percent for the remainder of the century. In 1700 the continental American Indian population was nearly four times the size of the population in the British North American colonies. By the end of the century, it was only about one-tenth the size of the U.S. population. The 18th century thus represents a substantial shift in the racial composition of the population.

Each of the three population groups shown in the table was characterized by substantial ethnic, cultural, and linguistic diversity. Although the majority of the 18th-century white population was of English origin, there were substantial numbers of individuals with Irish, Scottish, and German ancestry. In the first two-thirds of the century, most white inmigrants were English. There was increasing ethnic diversity in the late 18th century, however, with large numbers of migrants coming from Scotland, Germany, and other places in Europe. New research on the slave trade suggests that while there was less diversity in local slave populations

Population by Race (in thousands)

	BRITISH NORTH AMERICA/UNITED STATES			CONTINENTAL UNITED STATES*	
Year	Total	White	Black	Indian	Total
1700	251	223	28	987	1,238
1710	327	285	43	939	1,266
1720	467	399	69	893	1,360
1730	636	538	98	850	1,486
1740	915	756	159	809	1,722
1750	1,186	934	252	770	1,956
1760	1,594	1,268	326	732	2,326
1770	2,165	1,696	469	697	2,862
1780	2,798	2,210	588	663	3,461
1790	3,930	3,172	757	631	4,561
1800	5,308	4,306	1,002	600	5,908

Note: Due to rounding, the total population on the left may not equal the total white plus the total black population.
* Area eventually representing the current United States, excluding Alaska and Hawaii
Sources: Data from McCusker 2006, 651; Haines and Steckel 2000, 691, 702.

than has been commonly supposed—specialized trading routes tended to bring slaves sharing similar cultures and languages to the same destination ports—the overall black population was far from uniform. Although the vast majority of slaves came from West Africa—especially from the lower Niger River "Slave Coast" area, the Congo, and Angola—there were more than a hundred distinct peoples living in the primary slave-originating region between Cape Verde and Angola. Perhaps the greatest intraracial diversity was among the Native American peoples. The precontact Indian population included hundreds of tribes and unique languages. Although population decline led to the eventual destruction of some groups and the merging of others, the federal government of the United States still recognizes over 300 unique tribes in the early 21st century.

Components of White Population Growth

Population growth or decline over a period of time is the net result of the numbers of births, deaths, in-migrants, and out-migrants. The number of births less the number of deaths constitutes "natural" population growth, while the number of in-migrants less the number of out-migrants represents net migration. The table indicates that overall colonial population growth ranged between 29 and 44 percent each decade. Annual population growth averaged a little over 3 percent, equivalent to the population doubling every 22 to 23 years, very close to Franklin's 20-year estimate.

Franklin and Malthus both emphasized the critical role of natural population growth over immigration in explaining the rapid increase in the American population. Franklin emphasized that of the "upwards of one million English souls" thought to be present in the mid-18th century, "scarce eighty thousand had been brought over sea." Unfortunately, there is not adequate vital registration data to estimate the number of births, deaths, and migrants in each decade for the colonies as a whole, making it impossible to determine the precise contribution of each to overall population growth. Community-based studies, however, indicate that high fertility played a major role. Birth rates for the 17th and early 18th centuries were very high, approximately 45–55 per 1,000 people, among the highest sustained birth rates ever observed for a large population. By comparison, birth rates in 18th-century rural parishes in England averaged 30–40 per 1,000.

High birth rates were in turn the result of low ages at first marriage and low proportions of men and women who remained single. Franklin called explicit attention to the role of marriage patterns in fueling the rapid growth of the colonial population. "People increase in Proportion to the Number of Marriages," he observed. "When families can be easily supported, more Persons marry, and earlier in Life. . . . Land being thus plenty in *America*, and so cheap as that a labouring Man, that understands Husbandry, can in a short Time save Money enough to purchase a Piece of new Land sufficient for a Plantation, whereon he may subsist a Family."

Franklin's focus on farm building makes sense given the overwhelming importance of agriculture to the 18th-century economy and cultural patterns of family formation. Colonial Americans followed what demographic historians have called a "northwestern European" pattern of family formation. Young men and women who married were expected to leave their parents' homes and set up a new household. This "neolocal" pattern required couples to either save or inherit adequate resources before they could marry. First- and second-generation settlers typically had large estates they could bequeath to their children, which sustained and contributed to the pattern of early and near universal marriage. Although there is some evidence that land was becoming more scarce and expensive in more densely settled areas by the end of the 18th century—thus inhibiting parents from bequeathing adequate farms in the local area for each surviving child—the existence of a western frontier with a ready availability of inexpensive land ensured that marriage remained relatively early for most men and women.

With the exception of women serving indentures, white women in the colonies typically married between the ages of 19 and 22, approximately five years earlier than English brides. When combined with the higher proportions who eventually married, the average woman surviving her childbearing years in 18th-century America bore seven to eight children, two more than her counterpart in England. Marriage timing for men varied depending on the local balance between the two sexes. Where men outnumbered women—as they did in many parts of the 18th-century South—they were forced to delay marriage. Despite greatly outnumbering women overall, however, men tended to marry at about the same age or at a slightly younger age than men in England.

Death rates in British North America varied by region. In healthy areas, such as in rural New England, death rates were approximately half of the 40-per-1,000 rate characteristic in rural areas of England. In other areas, such as the cities of Boston and Philadelphia and the malarial areas of the Upper and Lower South, mortality rates were much higher and probably exceeded typical mortality rates in Europe. The underrecording of infant and child deaths makes accurate assessment of life expectancy at birth impossible. As with other premodern populations, however, it is likely that infant mortality rates were very high, perhaps between 150 and 200 deaths per 1,000 live births. Given the high rates of childbearing, most 18th-century parents experienced the death of one or more children. Age-specific death rates and life expectancy improved after early childhood. In New England and the Mid-Atlantic colonies, average life expectancy at age 20 was approximately 40 additional years. Adult life expectancies in the southern colonies were approximately ten years lower.

Mortality was especially high among recent immigrants living in malarial areas. As a result, colonists in the Upper and Lower South experienced higher rates of widowhood and orphanhood and were much more likely to live in a household that contained stepchildren and unrelated individuals. Life expectancies increased in the latter part of the century as southerners drained swamps and moved into healthier interior regions. By the end of the century, the large regional differences in life expectancy had narrowed significantly. In contrast to the much higher life expectancies women enjoy compared to men today, men and women in the 18th century had approximately equal life expectancies. Females suffered higher mortality rates during their childbearing years, reflecting a higher risk of death from pulmonary tuberculosis, other respiratory diseases, and maternal causes, but they enjoyed lower mortality rates at other ages.

Overall, the colonial population was comparatively healthy. Lower population densities inhibited the spread of infectious disease, and most colonists and early citizens of the United States benefited from abundant land and food. Recent research has shown that the heights of American men in the 18th century were approximately 7 centimeters higher than that of 18th-century Europeans, suggesting a more nutritious diet and a lower disease burden.

Although demographic research has shown that Franklin and Malthus were correct to focus on natural population growth, Franklin underestimated the number of immigrants to British North America. A small but significant portion of population growth in the 18th century was the result of net migration. Approximately 850,000 immigrants are believed to have arrived in British North America and the early republic during the 18th century (roughly 350,000 slaves from western Africa and 500,000 free or indentured whites from Europe). Although some in-migrants failed to reproduce and some white migrants returned to Europe, migration is estimated to have accounted for about one-fifth of the population growth at the end of the 18th century.

Settlement Patterns of the White Population

In 1700 the white population of British North America was sparsely distributed in colonies from Atlantic Canada in the North to the British West Indies in the South. With the exception of the population descended from 17th-century Dutch settlers near Albany, New York, the vast majority of the white population lived on farms or in settlements on or near the coast. Approximately one in three white colonists lived in the New England colonies of Massachusetts, Connecticut, Rhode Island, and New Hampshire, and another one in three in the Chesapeake colonies of Maryland and Virginia. About one in five white colonists lived in the Mid-Atlantic colonies of New York, New Jersey, Pennsylvania, and Delaware, and just one in twenty lived in the Lower South.

Immigration, natural population growth, and intra-regional migration patterns dramatically altered the geographic distribution of the population. Early 18th-century immigrants tended to be young, male, skilled only in agriculture, bound for a five- or seven-year term of indentured labor, and destined for the richer agricultural areas of the Chesapeake, South Carolina, Georgia, or the British West Indies. Although the flow of indentured servants from Europe to America continued into the first few decades of the 19th century, the plantation colonies of the Upper and Lower South increasingly turned to slave labor to satisfy their labor needs. As the century progressed, increasing proportions of white immigrants paid for their own passage and a growing proportion was female. Indentured servants were increasingly trained in skilled occupations and destined for the Mid-Atlantic colonies. Few white migrants, whether free or serving an indenture, went to New England, where poor soil and a shorter growing season limited the economic returns from agriculture.

In both the North and the South, increased population densities in long-settled regions, a growing shortage of viable farmland, and the ready availability of inexpensive land on the frontier pushed the population inland. By 1800 the population of the early republic had spread beyond the Appalachian Mountains—about 500,000 people were settled on land near the Ohio, Tennessee, and Cumberland rivers that drained into the Mississippi River—and the trans-Appalachian states of Kentucky and Tennessee had been added to the Union. Significant internal migration within and between regions further altered the distribution of the white population. New England experienced a negative net migration rate as more migrants left the region than the number of new immigrants who arrived from overseas or other regions. Many migrants headed for regions sparsely populated at the beginning of the century. Pennsylvania, New York, North Carolina, South Carolina, and Georgia experienced significant population growth, increasing the proportion of the white population living in the Mid-Atlantic and Lower South regions relative to the proportion living in New England and the Upper South at the beginning of the century.

African American Population Growth and Geographic Distribution

The demand for servants and slaves was driven by the growing market for colonial staple crops, particularly tobacco in the Upper South, rice and indigo in the Lower South, and sugar in the British West Indies. Although white indentured servants represented the majority of the unfree migrants in the 17th century, black slaves made up the majority of unfree migrants in the 18th century. The transition from white indentured servants to slaves coincided with improved labor markets in late 17th-century England, decreasing the potential supply of indentured servants, and the ending of the London-based Royal African Company's monopoly of the slave trade in 1698, which opened the trade to independent merchants and increased the supply of African slaves.

Initially, slaves were unable or unwilling to reproduce. Many recently arrived slaves died in the new American disease environment, female slaves were often well advanced in their childbearing years when purchased, and male slaves greatly outnumbered female slaves. Small holdings, the reluctance of some owners to allow slaves to seek partners in neighboring slaveholdings, the lack of legal recognition of marriage, and the potential of sale and removal limited the ability of slaves to form lasting sexual unions. After 1730, however, the North American slave population experienced natural population growth, first in the Upper South, and later in the century in the Lower South. Creole slaves (slaves born in the New World) enjoyed relatively lower mortality rates and had more balanced sex ratios. A trend toward larger slave holdings increased the ability of slaves to form strong unions. Creole women began to bear children in their late teens and continued to bear children every two to three years, obtaining a total of six to eight children. Creoles made up a majority of the North American slave population by 1740. By the last decade of the century just one out of five slaves in the United States was African born. Despite an increase in the rate of manumission after the Revolution, the vast majority of slaves spent their lives in servitude. In 1790, the first U.S. Census counted a total black population of 757,208, of which only 59,511 (7.9 percent) were free.

Although most slaves obtained from West Africa by the British in the transatlantic slave trade were taken to sugar producing islands in the British West Indies, particularly Barbados and Jamaica, enough were imported to the mainland colonies to make the population in some areas, such as the lowland rice-producing parishes of South Carolina, black majority populations early in the 18th century. The close association of slave imports with the production of staple crops resulted in large regional differences in the proportion of the population that was African American. In 1790, 6.2 percent of the Mid-Atlantic population was African American, while a mere 1.7 percent of the New England population was. The percentage in the Lower South, in contrast, was 32.6 percent, and in the Upper South it was 37.6 percent. Almost 90 percent of the total African American population resided in the Upper or Lower South.

The rapid natural population growth of the American slave population stood in sharp contrast to the negative natural population growth among slaves in the British West Indies. West Indian planters were forced to purchase new slaves to keep their workforces from declining. Despite the fact that the number of slave imports to the mainland colonies was approximately one-fifth of the number imported to the British West Indies, the slave population of British North America in 1770 was slightly larger than that in the West Indies. These different demographic regimes are largely explained by the heavy concentration of West Indian slaves in sugar production, and by the lack of sugar production in the North American colonies. Sugar proved to be an extraordinarily deleterious crop for slave populations. The more intensive gang labor system employed by sugar growers favored male over female laborers, leading to an unbalanced sex ratio. In addition, tropical diseases were responsible for a heavier death toll among the slaves in the British West Indies.

Research Opportunities in 18th-Century Demography

Scholarly interest in the demography of the 18th century peaked in the 1980s. Many questions remain understudied or unexplored, while more research is needed on how migration, ethnic and racial diversity, and population growth affected society, economics, and politics. Rapid growth and expansion, the most defining characteristics of the 18th-century population, placed enormous strain on institutions, led to conflict with declining Indian populations, and contributed to the growing rift between England and its American colonies. It is little surprise that the first significant legislation passed by Congress, the Northwest Ordinance of 1787, created an institutional framework for the orderly settlement and government of territories filled by a rapidly expanding population.

—J. David Hacker

Further Reading

Gemery, Henry A. "The White Population of the Colonial United States, 1607–1790." In *A Population History of North America*, edited by Michael R. Haines and Richard H. Steckel, 143–190. Cambridge, U.K.: Cambridge University Press, 2000.

Haines, Michael R., and Richard H. Steckel. *A Population History of North America*. Cambridge, U.K.: Cambridge University Press, 2000.

Klein, Herbert S. *A Population History of the United States.* Cambridge, U.K.: Cambridge University Press, 2004.

McCusker, John J. "Population." In *Historical Statistics of the United States: Earliest Times to the Present.* Vol.5 (Part E), *Governance and International Relations*, edited by Susan B. Carter, Scott Sigmund Gartner, Michael R. Haines, Alan L. Olmstead, Richard Sutch, and Gavin Wright. Millennial ed. Cambridge, U.K.: Cambridge University Press, 2006.

McCusker, John J., and Russell R. Menard. *The Economy of British America, 1607–1789.* Chapel Hill: University of North Carolina Press, 1985.

Thornton, Russell. *American Indian Holocaust and Survival: A Population History since 1492*. Norman: University of Oklahoma Press, 1987.

Walsh, Lorena S. "The African American Population of the Colonial United States." In *A Population History of North America*, edited by Michael R. Haines and Richard H. Steckel, 191–240. Cambridge, U.K.: Cambridge University Press, 2000.

Wells, Robert V. "The Population of England's Colonies in America: Old English or New Americans?" *Population Studies* 46, no. 1 (1992): 85–102.

18th Century ECONOMY

Historians of colonial British North America agree that through most of the 17th and 18th centuries white colonists enjoyed better living conditions and greater economic growth than a large majority of the population in Europe. What historians do not agree on, however, are the sources of that prosperity. Overall, two interpretations have dominated this discussion: the Malthusian and the "staples" theories of economic growth. Malthusian-school historians argue that increases in population through immigration and increased fertility fueled the economic growth of the mainland British colonies. The "staples" theorists argue that staples exports, such as tobacco, grains, furs, and fish, led colonial economic expansion. Often ignored in these debates are colonists' appropriation and commoditization of vast expanses of land, colonial America's unique position in a worldwide imperial system, and the advantages derived from the combination of these interdependent factors. Demographic increase and staples exports were both clearly important to the economic growth of the British mainland economies, but neither development would have been possible without the opening up of millions of fertile acres to land-hungry European immigrants and their descendants, and the colonies' privileged position within the British Empire.

Population Growth

Demographic analysis confirms that population growth was critical to the economic vitality of the British mainland colonies. The population of the mainland colonies grew at a rate of 3 percent a year over the 18th century. At that rate, the population doubled every 25 years and increased from just over two hundred thousand in 1700 to 2.6 million on the eve of the American Revolution. Most of this increase was in the white population, which in the 1760s numbered 2.1 million, compared with half a million African American slaves.

This growth was fueled both by immigration and colonists' fecundity. Benjamin Franklin first noted the reasons for white colonists' extraordinary natural increase relative to their European counterparts: Younger marriages, higher birth rates, and lower infant mortality rates combined with longer life expectancy and lower death rates to fuel colonial demographic expansion. Colonial Americans typically married in their twenties, and two to three years earlier than the average marriage age of Europeans. Having married younger, they had more children than comparable Europeans; the annual colonial birth rate was 40 to 50 per 1,000, compared to 30 to 40 per 1,000 in Europe. Colonists also had lower infant mortality rates than Europeans. In England, approximately 20 percent of all children died in their first year; in the colonies, the comparable figure was 12 to 15 percent.

Colonists further enjoyed lower death rates as adults. In England the annual death rate was 40 per 1,000 people; in the 13 colonies the annual death rate was 15 to 25 per 1,000. Even in the deadly-disease-infested Chesapeake, which buried as much as 80 percent of its population in the early years, death rates eventually declined to 5 percent per annum by the late 17th century and approximated rates in the northern colonies in the 18th century. Historians attribute the lower colonial death rates to superior nutrition, wood for fuel, and dispersed living conditions that lowered the morbidity and mortality associated with 18th-century life in Europe.

For African American slaves, the story was similar in only some respects. Slaves married early relative to Europeans, and an average slave woman gave birth to seven to nine children over her lifetime. Slaves, however, suffered much higher infant mortality rates than white colonists or even whites in Europe. Approximately half of all slave children succumbed to disease in their first five years. Historians examining this phenomenon have generally blamed the poor diet that masters assigned their nonworking or nonproductive slaves.

Both free and forced immigration were also important to colonial population growth. From 1700 to the first decade of the 19th century more than 950,000 forced and free migrants arrived in the British mainland colonies. This included more than 400,000 slaves, close to 175,000 indentured servants, and just over 400,000 free migrants. With the important exception of slaves, however, the significance of immigration relative to the overall population declined in the 18th century. As late as the 1760s the slave trade accounted for 40 percent of African American population growth. Overall, however, in the second half of the 18th century 70 percent of all population growth derived from natural increase.

Agriculture

The "staples" theory of economic growth depends largely on agricultural production. Throughout this period agriculture was the mainstay of the colonial economy and central to the unprecedented prosperity enjoyed by free white men and their families. In the northern colonies, widespread land ownership, combined with demographic growth, seeded the land with thousands of relatively large farms producing for both home consumption and domestic and international markets. Agricultural and forest products from the northern colonies played a key role in trade with the West Indies, southern Europe, and the British Isles. In the Chesapeake and Lower South, a bound-labor system dominated the capitalist production of New World commodities for an international market; tobacco, rice, and indigo were key products driving 18th-century colonial trade networks and economic prosperity. Historians estimate that farmers in the north and the south grew sufficient crops to provide amply for their families and bring to market 25 to 50 percent of their harvest.

In New England and the middle colonies, farms were typically from 75 to 125 acres, and farmers harvested timber resources and grew a variety of grains, poultry, and livestock. Farmers maintained 35 or so acres in cultivation, including several acres of orchards, with the rest lying fallow or as woods for fuel. Corn and wheat were the most common crops. Farmers preferred pork as livestock because it was both a more efficient converter of corn and grain to protein and more easily and safely preserved. Cows were raised both for dairy and meat but most often slaughtered to eat fresh and thus infrequently. Sheep were raised for wool. Poultry was raised for both meat and eggs. A productive farm would have also included oxen for plowing and horses for transportation. Northern colonists' grain and livestock exports were key to the 18th century's Atlantic trade patterns; exports to the West Indies were particularly important in the development of the sugar islands' slave-driven monoculture.

Freehold farmers maintained this mixed farming system through a family and kinship labor network supplemented by indentured servants. In Europe, servants in husbandry on annual contracts, along with permanently landless agricultural workers, supplied a labor force. In the northern colonies, agricultural wage labor tended to be part of the development pattern of people's lives. Young men and women might work for wages before purchasing their own land or establishing their households. Most, however, contributed to the family farm and began their households with their family's assistance. Indentured servitude, an innovation begotten by the exigencies of transatlantic migration, made up deficits in this kinship labor system. Ship captains and merchants in effect loaned would-be-immigrant workers the passage money and other start-up costs in exchange for a fixed term of labor, typically seven years, purchased by colonial farmers and planters. Prior to the American Revolution almost 200,000 European indentured servants migrated to the colonies. In the 17th century the majority of these servants flocked to the southern tobacco plantations; in the 18th century they preferred the middle colonies. Many German migrants came over as "redemptioners"—a hybrid indenture contract by which immigrants with some resources accepted a loan for the passage and upon arrival entered into a shortened indenture that "redeemed" the loan. Approximately 50,000 British criminals were also sold off as indentured servants in the colonies.

Immigrant wanderlust and colonial fecundity were both fueled by readily available cheap productive land in "fee simple"—owned outright without feudal obligations. Tenancy and the semifeudal obligations common to this European land-tenure practice were known in the colonies but were not widespread or egregious. Tenants and would-be buyers benefited from land surpluses and labor shortages and could dictate favorable leases and sales from landlords and speculators. Repeated efforts through the colonial period into the 19th century to establish semi-feudal obligations in various proprietary colonies ultimately failed; land was plentiful and cheap and labor dear, and colonists exploited these conditions.

In the Chesapeake and Lower South, mixed-crop farms with a few slaves were numerically dominant, and corn and wheat were always important, if not the main crops. On the larger and more economically significant plantations, however, monoculture dominated; these planters grew tobacco in the Chesapeake, and rice and indigo in the Lower South. On these plantations slaves made up the largest part of the labor force.

Tobacco was the first significant crop grown in the Chesapeake colonies. When cultivation of tobacco began in the 17th century, it was a boom crop that produced enormous profits and fabulous fortunes in short periods. As production increased, tobacco prices declined, but tobacco remained the single most important colonial export through the 18th century. Its labor demands also shaped southern life in ways that transcend economic analysis.

Tobacco was a labor-intensive crop, and in the colonies labor was a commodity far more precious than land. In the Chesapeake, indentured servants first filled this need. However, several factors pushed planters to adopt a system of permanent racial slavery by the late 17th century. Indentured servants who survived their term became a class of free white men, often landless, that challenged the planter elite for hegemony. At the same time, declining sugar prices in Europe lowered the demand and prices for slaves in the Caribbean. Entrepreneurial slave traders thus sought to expand their markets and ventured to the Chesapeake and Carolinas with their human goods. Finally, the price of indentured servants rose relative to that of slaves as wages in England reversed a long period of decline.

Slavery also dominated the Carolinas and, eventually, Georgia. These Lower South colonies began as auxiliaries of the plantation system in the West Indies. South Carolina in particular began as a colony of Barbados. Servants reaching the end of their indentures, as well as the younger sons of established planters, and others unable to gain a foothold in the crowded island, moved northwest to the mainland and worked to make their fortune by provisioning their former home. Their first products were naval stores: tar, pitch, timber, and salt pork and other provisions. The search for a crop suitable to the marshy tidewater regions led them to rice and thus to immense fortunes. Historians still debate the origins of this innovation. Did slaves familiar with rice cultivation introduce this profitable crop to South Carolina? Or did planters experimenting with a variety of crops stumble across this bonanza? Regardless of origins, it is very clear that some Africans were certainly familiar with the cultivation of rice and contributed the labor and expertise necessary to its growth, making tidewater rice planters among the wealthiest men in the British mainland colonies. This prosperity was further increased by the cultivation of indigo, a dye used in the processing of textiles. The British Empire paid a bounty on indigo, and planters in the Lower South prospered from indigo production up until the American Revolution.

Trade

The creation of a colonial agricultural surplus invited merchant activity that seated the colonies in a worldwide imperial system of trade. Tobacco alone accounted for a quarter of all exports in the 18th century; food grains, including wheat, corn, and rice, were a third of all exports; other significant exports included fish, wood products, and indigo, each approximately 5 percent of the total. But trade was not just about transporting tobacco, wheat, or other staples; it sustained other economic factors, such as voluntary and forced immigration. Further, shipping, also known as the "carrying trade," provided "invisible" credits in services to balance trade with the empire. Finally, the carrying trade also maintained the West Indies plantation system and thus was again tied into larger imperial slave and staples markets.

The northern colonies' production and trade patterns were divided among Britain, southern Europe, and the West Indies. Northern colonists' main exports to the mother country consisted of furs, masts, whaling products, potash, and flaxseed. The fur trade was critical to the early development of the northern colonies and sustained itself into the 18th century. Lumber was too heavy and thus costly to transport profitably to wood-starved Britain, but the massive white pines of America's old-growth forests provided strong, tall masts for British ships and thus were strategically important to the empire. Colonists also exported wooden boards, shingles, and staves. Whaling provided significant revenues into the 19th century, as the oil derived from whales made excellent candles and lamp fuel. Potash, derived from burning hardwood forests by way of clearing the land for farming, was a valuable northern export. Finally, flaxseed, exported to England to be crushed into valuable oil and to Ireland as seed stock for the linen industry, proved important to colonial trade from the 17th and into the 18th century. Overall, however, the northern colonies ran a trade deficit with Britain, importing more manufactured goods than exporting raw materials

Northern colonists also traded at a deficit with the West Indies. New England and the middle colonies exported bread, flour, wheat, salted meat, salt fish, horses, livestock, spermaceti candles, and pine boards to the West Indies plantations. Returning ship captains filled up on molasses and rum. The molasses fueled a thriving distilling industry in cities like Boston, New York, and Philadelphia. The rum produced and imported was sold locally for domestic consumption and exported to Europe and Africa.

Colonists diminished these trade deficits by a trade surplus with southern Europe that created credits for payments in Britain. Salt fish and grains were the main northern exports to southern Europe. Wine and olive oil filled empty hulls for the return trip to the colonies by way of the British Isles. Also very important in terms of the trade balance, however, was the so-called invisible carrying trade. This trade was made up of shipping services, including transportation, insurance, and merchant commissions. In the late 18th century the value of these services exceeded the value of tobacco exports and contributed important credits to help balance colonial-imperial trade. New England dominated the shipping industry through this period. American ships held the majority of the West Indies trade and large parts of the trade between the mainland colonies and the British Isles.

In the southern colonies, tobacco, rice, indigo, and food grains were all export products that had European and West Indian markets and provided the basis for the slave plantation economy. These products were transported on American ships but bought and sold by Scottish and English factors. In the 18th century, tobacco was the single most important crop, making up nearly 25 percent of all exports and 70 percent of all southern exports. Rice accounted for more than 10 percent of exports. Indigo represented just less than 5 percent. More than two-thirds of the rice crop and all the indigo went to Britain. Southern agricultural products were key exports in and of themselves but also played a disproportionate role in the balance of payments, effectively subsidizing the importation of British manufactured goods and fueling the importation of African slaves.

Money

Regardless of whether the early American economy relied on trade or demographic growth for its expansion, the economy at all times and all places needed money in order to function. Farmers exchanging goods and services through barter kept their books in monetary sums; traders shipping goods to distant markets negotiated intricate monetary exchanges; ordinary colonists buying and selling products and services or paying their taxes used some form of money. How then did the colonial financial system work? What precisely did the colonists use as money? How did the international system of exchange work? Finally, how did the credit markets essential to economic growth work during the 18th century?

Strictly speaking, money in the colonial era was gold and silver coin. Most of this coin was Spanish, and the single most widely circulated coin was the Spanish piece of eight. These and other Spanish and Portuguese gold and silver coins invariably found their way into British colonial markets through the West Indies and served as the main circulating medium for the colonies. British or English specie was scarce in large part because of an imperial ban on the private exportation of specie from the kingdom. Further, the Board of Trade, the British government agency that governed the colonies, prevented colonial Americans from establishing their own mint. As a result, only in extraordinary circumstances, primarily in wartime, did large flows of British coins make their way to the colonies.

These constraints on the domestic money supply did not necessarily impede trade with the empire. Overseas trade in the colonies and Britain worked through financial instruments known as "bills of exchange." Basically, a colonist trying to import goods from London would use specie to purchase a draft or check drawn on a London bank or merchant house. An agent, merchant, or ship captain would then use the "bill of exchange" to complete the transaction in London. Often the seller was a colonial merchant who had accrued export credits with a British firm. Given the volume of imperial trade, bills of exchange circulated widely, and this system worked fairly well to facilitate commerce without transferring large volumes of specie. Problems arose, however, when trade deficits pushed up the price of bills of exchange and led to specie exports from the colonies. On these occasions, the colonists' perennial complaint that they suffered from a specie deficit was real.

Colonists reacted to shortages in the domestic money supply (real and perceived) with "commodity money," private credit networks, so-called land banks, and paper money. Commodity money thrived in monocultures such as Virginia, Maryland, and the Carolinas. Typically the system worked through legislative authority and involvement. The colonial assemblies warehoused commodities like tobacco and issued "tobacco notes" to be used for the payment of taxes and private debts. Colonists also created an elaborate system of private credit by bartering goods and services and maintaining the records of such exchanges in monetary sums. Finally, they used their legislative prerogative to create land banks and emit paper money. Specie-reserve banks such as existed in England and Scotland through the 18th century were eventually created in America during and after the American Revolution but did not exist in the colonial period. Parliament restricted the creation of banks in the empire, save for those Scottish institutions grandfathered by the 1707 Act of Union. In part with the intent of avoiding this legislation, colonists created land banks, or loan offices, that issued reverse mortgages on land. A landowner could mortgage half the value of his property and was issued private "notes"—backed by the value of the land—that circulated as money. Individual colonial legislatures also issued "fiat" money—paper money not backed by specie or land, that derived its value from legislative authority and its utility for the payment of special taxes scheduled to retire the money from circulation. Often, however, legislatures succumbed to popular pressure and ignored retirement schedules. In these circumstances, the value of the paper money deteriorated over time and acted as a tax on note-holders.

Colonists developed these innovations in the midst of wartime financial crises with little interference from imperial authorities. When they extended these efforts beyond war, however, British merchants resisted efforts to force them to accept nonspecie-based financial instruments as "money." Their collective pressure resulted in a variety of laws designed to stifle colonial innovations. As early as 1717 the Privy Council repealed tobacco note legislation, though colonists continued issuing tobacco and commodity money into the 1760s. In 1740 the Board of Trade applied the 1720 Bubble Act (regulating bank charters in the empire) to the Massachusetts and Connecticut land banks. In 1751 the Currency Act ended various New England efforts to print paper money. Subsequent efforts in 1764 to apply these laws across the colonies proved unsuccessful, and into the American Revolution individual colonies continued to experiment with land banks and paper money.

Manufacturing

Manufacturing was clearly the weakest sector of the colonial economy. The British Empire believed in mercantilism, an economic system designed to strengthen the "mother" country at the expense of its colonial "dependents." This meant that imperial trade regulations tried to stifle colonial manufacturing and promote the export of raw products. Burdened with the mercantilist yoke, the colonists could not compete with British manufacturers and could not export enumerated items to continental Europe. Nevertheless, several key industries stand out as regional pockets interconnected to other industries and thus to larger economic development. Specially important were iron and its relationship to the lumber industry; the distilleries with their multiple connections to the West Indies

Iron Exports in the Colonial Economy, 1770

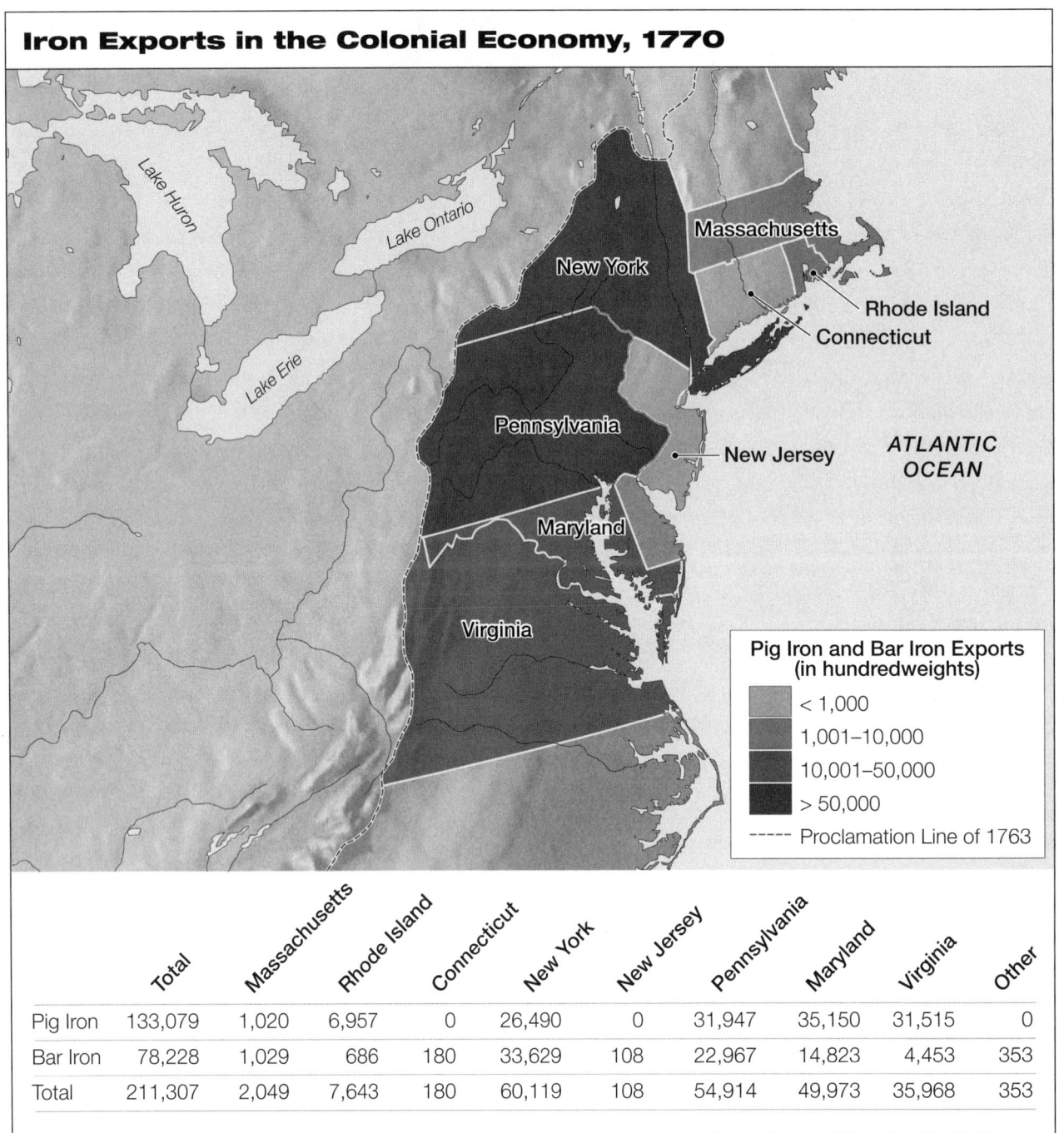

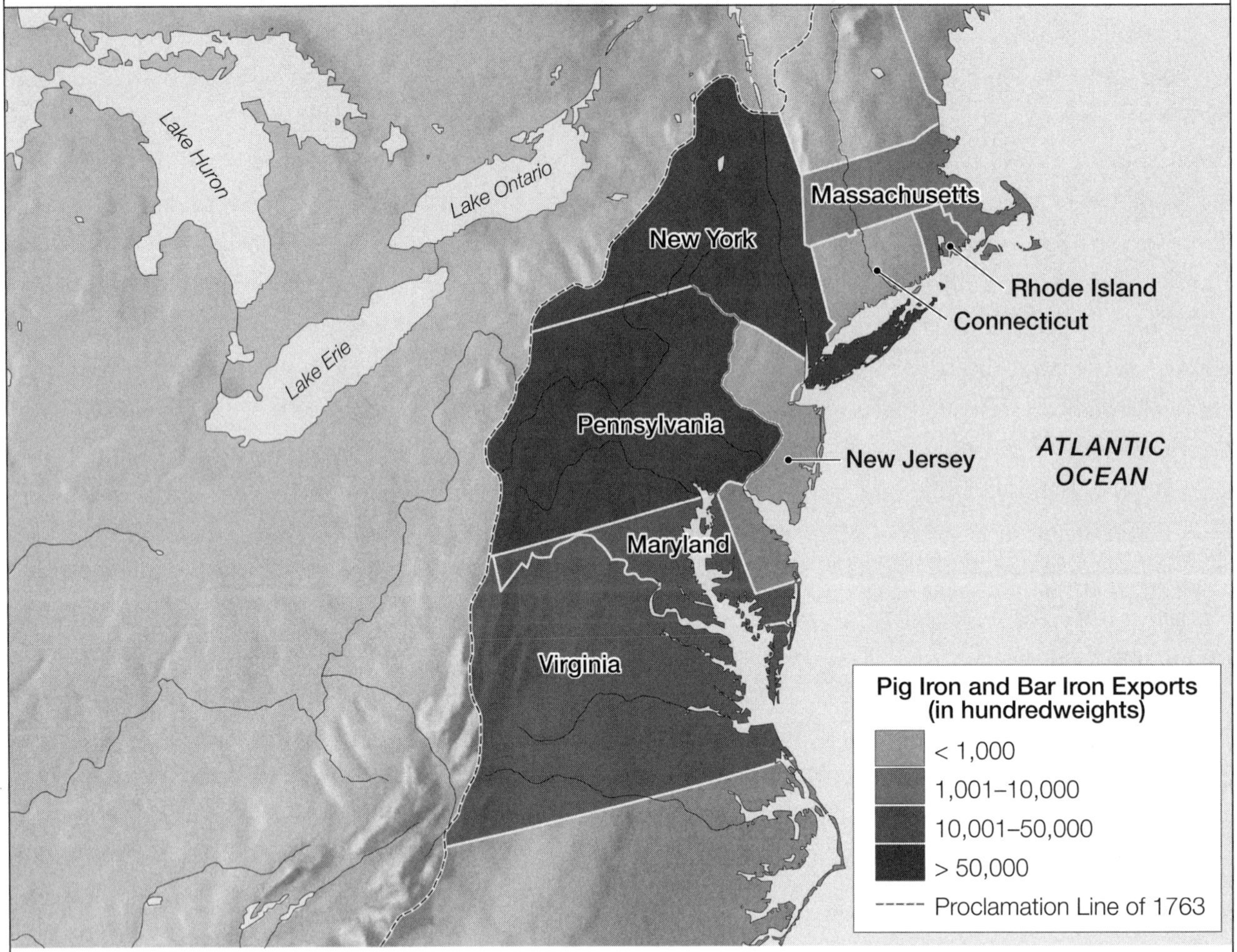

	Total	Massachusetts	Rhode Island	Connecticut	New York	New Jersey	Pennsylvania	Maryland	Virginia	Other
Pig Iron	133,079	1,020	6,957	0	26,490	0	31,947	35,150	31,515	0
Bar Iron	78,228	1,029	686	180	33,629	108	22,967	14,823	4,453	353
Total	211,307	2,049	7,643	180	60,119	108	54,914	49,973	35,968	353

Source: U.S. Department of Commerce, Bureau of the Census, *Historical Statistics of the United States: Colonial Times to 1970*, 1185, 1187 (Washington, D.C.: Bureau of the Census, 1975).
Notes: The exports figures include shipments to other colonies on the continent, as well as Great Britain, Ireland, and the West Indies. The "other" column for pig iron includes minor amounts from colonies not listed. The Proclamation Line of 1763, which Britain issued to control westward settlement, is shown here as the official boundary line of the existing colonies.

While manufacturing was a relatively small part of the colonial economy, iron production was by far one of the most important industries in the manufacturing sector. The high level of fuel resources—available from the plentiful forests in the new colonies—spurred the growth of the iron export trade.

trade; shipbuilding and its relationships to the timber industry, the carrying trade, export markets, and fishing and whaling; and finally artisan production and its connection to regional agricultural systems.

Iron manufacturing consumed a great deal of fuel and was relegated to those regions with abundant lumber supplies: Sweden, Russia, and the colonies. As early as the mid-17th century, iron furnaces were established in the British mainland colonies and accounted for perhaps as much as 2 percent of the world output. On the eve of the Revolution there were as many as 80 iron furnaces in the colonies. They employed approximately 8,000 workers and produced 15 percent of the world's iron. Most of this iron was exported to Britain. Mercantilist restrictions, although never completely successful, limited attempts to establish enterprises dedicated to the local manufacturing of iron goods.

As many as 150 colonial distilleries produced around 5 million gallons of rum in the 18th century. The molasses processed into rum derived from the West Indies and was a critical part of the West Indies grain, livestock, and fish trade. Overall, colonial alcohol consumption was historically high, and much of the rum produced in the colonies and imported from the West Indies was for domestic consumption.

Shipbuilding was an important industry that helped diminish mainland British colonies' trade deficits with the British Isles and the West Indies. Colonial shipyards benefited from lower lumber costs and more-efficient labor systems. They thus soon dominated shipping in British North America, the West Indies, and even held a significant portion of the British Isles market. By the 18th century as many as a third of all British ships were built in the colonies. Further, most of the ships engaged in the West Indian trade were built in the mainland British colonies.

Artisan production for local markets was also a significant manufacturing enterprise in the colonies. Blacksmiths and coppersmiths dominated the production of local hardware and other items such as pots. But the 18th-century colonial city was filled with men working in the clothing trades, metals, food production, the building trades, clock making, the printing trades, and other crafts.

Resource Extraction on Land and Sea

Though never as profitable as agriculture, resource extraction industries were key to specific regions and were often tied to larger manufacturing interests. New England, for example, prospered in part due to the fishing and whaling industries. Cod played a key role in the West Indies trade and was thus tied into imperial trade patterns. Whaling interests were also tied to the manufacture of candles and lamp oil sold the world over. The timber industry served maritime shipbuilding in the Northeast but also promoted the early growth of North and South Carolina, which prior to the establishment of rice and indigo cultivation started off with naval stores. Iron production relied on the ore and timber widely available in colonial America. Finally, potash and flaxseeds were also important exports related to agriculture and resource extraction.

Demographic growth and an abundance of readily harvestable staple commodities clearly facilitated economic success in the mainland British colonies. But these factors were themselves contingent on readily available land and an imperial institutional structure that promoted colonists' endeavors.

—Jose R. Torre

Further Reading

Bailyn, Bernard. *The Peopling of British North America: An Introduction*. New York: Alfred A. Knopf, 1986.

Brock, Leslie. *The Currency System of the American Colonies*. New York: Arno Press, 1975.

Davis, Ralph. *The Rise of the Atlantic Economies*. Ithaca, N.Y.: Cornell University Press, 1973.

Engerman, Stanley L., and Robert E. Gallman. *The Cambridge Economic History of the United States*. 3 vols. New York: Cambridge University Press, 1998.

Galenson, David W. *White Servitude in Colonial America: An Economic Analysis*. New York: Cambridge University Press, 1984.

Genovese, Elizabeth Fox, and Eugene Genovese. *Fruits of Merchant Capital: Slavery and Bourgeois Property in the Rise and Expansion of Capitalism*. New York: Oxford University Press, 1983.

Greene, Jack P. *Pursuits of Happiness: The Social Development of Early Modern British Colonies and the Formation of American Culture*. Chapel Hill: University of North Carolina Press, 1983.

Innes, Stephen E. *Work and Labor in Early America*. Chapel Hill: University of North Carolina Press, 1988.

Kolchin, Peter. *American Slavery, 1619–1877*. New York: Hill & Wang, 1994.

Matson, Cathy. *Merchants and Empire: Trading in Colonial New York*. Baltimore, Md.: Johns Hopkins University Press, 2002.

McCusker, John. *Money and Exchange in Europe and America, 1600–1775*. Chapel Hill: University of North Carolina Press, 1975.

McCusker, John, and Russell Menard. *The Economy of British America, 1607–1789*. Chapel Hill: University of North Carolina Press, 1985.

McCusker, John, and Kenneth Morgan. *The Early Modern Atlantic Economy*. Cambridge, U.K.: Cambridge University Press, 2001.

Morgan, Edmund S. *American Slavery, American Freedom: The Ordeal of Colonial Virginia*. New York: W. W. Norton, 1975.

Morgan, Philip. *Slave Counterpoint: Black Culture in the Eighteenth-Century Chesapeake and Lowcountry*. Chapel Hill: University of North Carolina Press, for the Omohundro Institute of Early American History and Culture, 1998.

Morris, Richard B. *Government and Labor in Early America*. New York: Columbia University Press, 1946.

Newell, Margaret. *From Dependency to Independence: Economic Revolution in Colonial New England*. Ithaca, N.Y.: Cornell University Press, 1998.

Perkins, Edwin J. *American Public Finance and Financial Services, 1700–1815*. Columbus: Ohio State University Press, 1994.

———. *The Economy of Colonial America*. New York: Columbia University Press, 1988.

Price, Jacob. *Capital and Credit in British Overseas Trade: The View from the Chesapeake, 1700–1776*. Cambridge, Mass.: Harvard University Press, 1980.

Salinger, Sharon. *"To Serve Well and Faithfully": Labor and Indentured Servants in Pennsylvania, 1682–1800*. New York: Cambridge University Press, 1987.

Walton, Gary, and James F. Shepherd. *The Economic Rise of Early America*. New York: Cambridge University Press, 1979.

Wood, Peter. *Black Majority: Negroes in Colonial South Carolina from 1670 through the Stono Rebellion*. New York: Alfred A. Knopf, 1974.

18th Century EDUCATION

The 18th century was a time of rapid educational development in America, especially in New England. Great strides were taken in elementary schooling and in levels of reading and writing literacy. Grammar schools and colleges increased in number, while academies and social libraries were founded, the latter marking the opening stages of a "reading revolution." With the advent of the American Revolution, educational opportunities were expanded for many Americans, including women and free blacks. Despite the Revolution's ideals of equality, however, severe disparities in education that were inherited from the colonial period persisted, and, for some groups, especially southern slaves, even worsened.

New England Schooling and Literacy

New Englanders were among the most literate populations in the British Empire, and their commitment to education continued after the American Revolution. Outside of Rhode Island, New England legislatures intensified efforts begun in the previous century to require towns to provide literacy education for inhabitants' children. In Massachusetts, for example, the colonial assembly continually raised fines on towns failing to comply with the school laws. Colonial legislatures also experimented with a variety of tax schemes to raise revenue for local schools, including taxing public lands. In 1700 the Connecticut assembly went so far as to create a public school fund, consisting of revenue raised in each town by a tax on ratable property. Towns had to pay school taxes whether school was kept or not. Should a community fail to keep a school, it would receive no "school money" from the colony, which would then hold the money in reserve for future distribution to county grammar schools.

At the same time, New England communities, beset by rising pressures on local resources, experimented with ways to comply with colony school laws. The single greatest source of socioeconomic strain was rapid population growth, brought on by persistently high fertility rates. From 93,000 people in 1700, New England soared in population to 713,000 in 1780. While some of the excess population moved westward, much of it spilled over into unsettled lands of established communities, placing increasing demands on their limited educational resources. The response to this was the subdivision of towns into precincts or parishes, and the creation of "dame schools" and "moving schools" to accommodate the growing educational needs of the new neighborhoods. Begun during the 1670s in Massachusetts on a limited basis, dame schools were taught by neighborhood women at low cost, and they appealed to communities strapped for money to teach reading. Children graduating from a dame school would often go on to a writing school, an institution that also spread rapidly through New England during the 18th century.

The growth of writing education was made possible by another innovation—the "moving school"—which towns increasingly relied on to fulfill obligations to deliver literacy to rapidly rising populations of children. To offset the high cost of teaching writing, a single master would be expected to hold school in each precinct, moving from one to the other over the course of the year. What communities gained in quantity from moving schools, however, they lost in quality. Critics pointed to the seasonal nature of schooling as inadequate to the educational needs of children. Increasingly, neighborhoods reorganized themselves into school districts, run by school committees empowered to distribute local taxes to schools. So swift was the shift from moving schools to district schools that Connecticut formally legalized the system in 1766, followed by Vermont in 1782 and Massachusetts in 1789.

This combination of central and local control over schooling, undergirded by household reading instruction of children by mothers, was a potent one, leading to a rapid rise of reading and writing literacy throughout New England. Because the innovations in schooling allowed communities to deliver education to all children, literacy rates—as measured by signatures on wills, deeds, and other documents—increased for women as well as for men. After hovering around 70 percent for the period 1670–1710, the rate of male signing literacy rose to 85 percent by 1760 and 90 percent by 1790. From 45 percent in 1710, the rate of female signature literacy increased to over 60 percent during the 1760s. Although a gap between male and female literacy still existed in the rural areas of New England by the end of the 18th century, women in urban areas had erased it, acquiring near universal signing literacy and parity with men.

Because New England towns put most of their educational resources into literacy schooling, little was left over for grammar school education. Although Massachusetts, for example, required all towns larger than 100 residents to establish grammar schools, the law was followed mainly in the breech of it. Even raising fines for noncompliance failed to force towns to found grammar schools—in 1765 only 48 of 140 towns with 100 families or more had them. As public support for grammar schools continued to decline, New Englanders who could afford it turned to private academies to give their children a classical education, especially in the post-Revolutionary period.

Schooling and Literacy in the Mid-Atlantic and the South

Outside of New England, state-supported local schools never took root in America. Along with household instruction in reading, the middle and southern colonies relied mostly on denominational and private schools for literacy education. In the middle colonies, consisting of New York, New Jersey, Pennsylvania, and Delaware, no uniform church-state system controlled education, as was the case in Congregational New England. Although Pennsylvania called for the establishment of state-supported schools at its founding in the 1680s, nothing came of it. Rather, the middle colonies, reflecting conditions of religious toleration and sectarian diversity, placed literacy education in the hands of individual church groups and private entrepreneurs.

Pennsylvania in 1715 formally recognized the right of private and religious bodies to maintain schools and to hold property for that purpose, and Delaware followed suit in 1743. In Philadelphia and New York, the two cities of the region, private schools operated by entrepreneurial schoolmasters expanded most rapidly, bringing literacy education to the children of the families of the artisans, tradesmen, and shopkeepers that were increasingly concentrated there. There were at least 260 private schoolmasters in New York in 1780, and 283 in Philadelphia in 1783. In addition to teaching reading and writing, entrepreneurial teachers delivered highly eclectic curricula to their constituents, including instruction in sewing, fencing, dancing, art, and music. Their primary aim, however, was advancement in reading and writing.

In the rural areas, denominational schools were more successful than entrepreneurial schools, due in part to the evangelical capacity of churches to create communities, with schools, in areas of wide population dispersal. Among the denominations spearheading education in these areas were the Quakers, who reached out to girls as well as to boys, to the poor, and to blacks; and the Presbyterians, who settled most of the borderlands south of New York and constituted majorities in many frontier communities. The Anglicans became a force for basic literacy in the middle colonies after the formation of the London-based Society for the Propagation of the Gospel in 1701. The society waged the most organized literacy campaign in 18th-century America, sending 65 schoolmasters to all the colonies between 1714 and 1763 to instruct the poor, blacks, and Native Americans in basic literacy.

Because of the absence of ecclesiastical monopolies over education in the middle colonies, particularly in New Jersey, Pennsylvania, and Delaware, denominations were free to pursue multiple opportunities in advanced education. The Presbyterians took the lead in developing academies, founding 52 of them between 1723 and 1783, primarily in the middle colonies. The Presbyterians also inaugurated a new age of college building when they founded the College of New Jersey (later Princeton) in 1746. The Anglicans quickly followed suit with King's College (later Columbia) in 1754; the Baptists with the College of Rhode Island (later Brown) in 1764; the Dutch Reformed Church with Queen's College (later Rutgers)

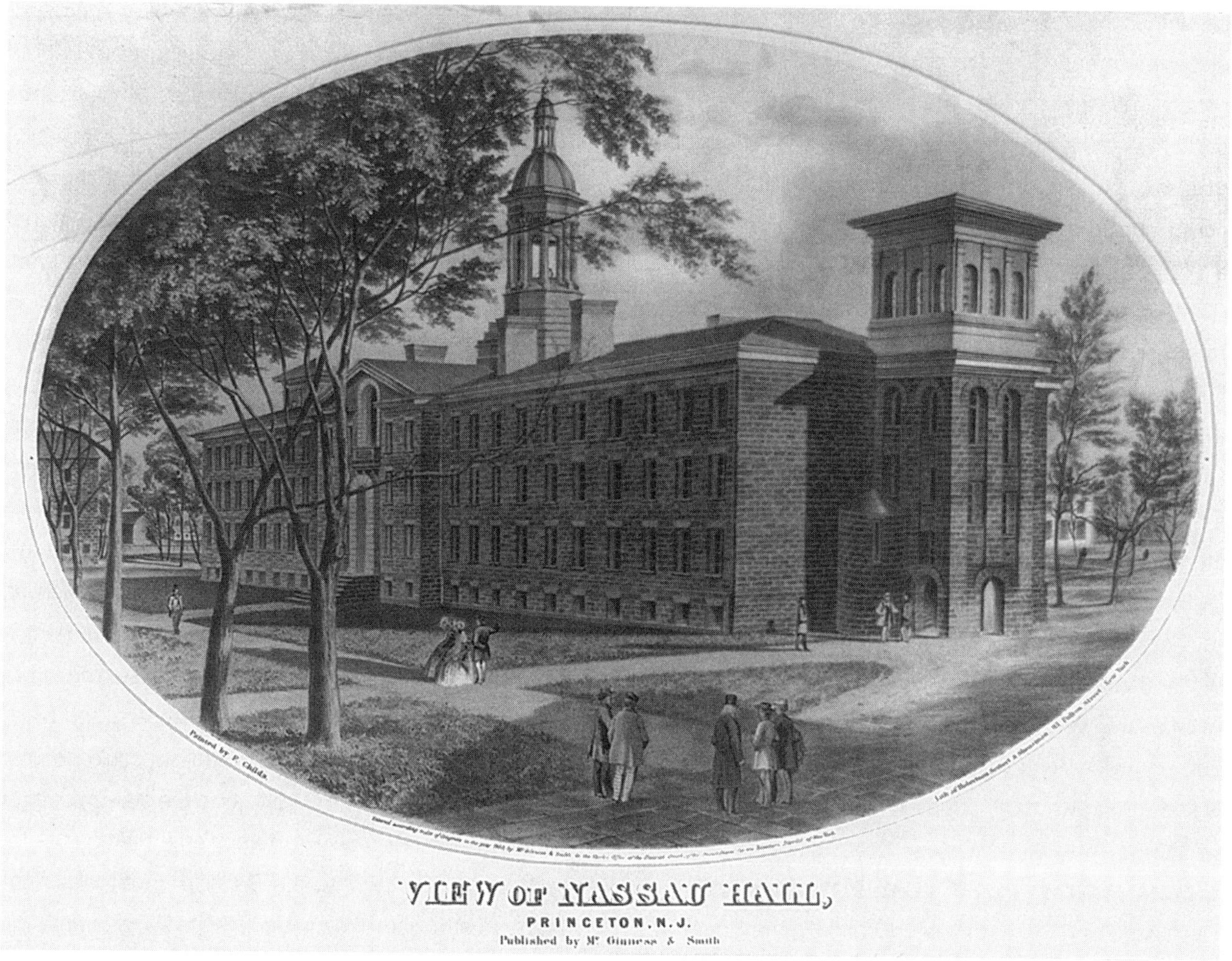

Founded in 1746 as the College of New Jersey, what is now Princeton University was British North America's fourth college. This engraving from around 1860 shows Nassau Hall, which contained the entire college for almost half a century and was the site of meetings of the Continental Congress in the spring and fall of 1783. ***(Library of Congress)***

in 1766; and the Congregationalists with Dartmouth in 1769. The College of Philadelphia (later the University of Pennsylvania), founded in 1755, was the only college established in the age of "college enthusiasm" that lacked denominational affiliation, although it soon fell under Anglican control.

Although they relied as heavily on the ministry for leadership as their predecessors—Harvard (1636), William and Mary (1693), and Yale (1701)—the new colleges were nevertheless guided by a new religious vision, one inspired by the Great Awakening that peaked in the 1740s and 1750s. Activist New Light clerics from the middle colonies, intent on expanding the supply of pro-revival preachers, were especially influential in founding the College of New Jersey and Queens College, but they also played an important role in setting up Rhode Island and Dartmouth colleges. Despite their denominational affiliations and evangelical sympathies, they all opened admission to students from nonaffiliated churches, and all adopted curricula broad enough to train candidates for the learned professions as well as the ministry.

The southern colonies lacked many of the educational forms of their northern counterparts, including state-sponsored public schools and entrepreneurial schools. Although denominational schools spread south from Pennsylvania into Virginia and the Carolinas, these rarely penetrated the Eastern Seaboard, where plantations proliferated. Major planters used private tutors to instruct children in reading and writing, while yeoman farmers often used "old-field" schools set up by individual parents, who hired schoolmasters on a term-to-term basis to do so. With respect to curriculum, these schools were similar to northern schools, although their enrollments were considerably lower.

Because of the haphazard nature of education in the middle and southern colonies of America, literacy rates in both regions tended to be lower than those in New England, although communities could attain surprisingly high levels of male signing, in the range of 70–80 percent, if the conditions were right. Thus in Perquimans County, North Carolina, nearly 80 percent of the men were literate by the end of the colonial period, a rate nearly comparable to that in New England. The conditions in Perquimans, where there were few plantations and a large population of Quakers, were rare, however. When it came to colony and statewide literacy achievement, the school systems of New England were without peer.

Education and the Enslaved

Overshadowing the history of education in the South was slavery. As the slave population in the South rose (increasing from over 32,000 in 1700 to over 509,000 in 1780), so did southern planter opposition to slave literacy, which was seen as a possible incitement to riot. A year after the Stono Rebellion in 1739, in which 44 blacks and 21 whites lost their lives, the South Carolina assembly passed legislation outlawing the teaching of writing to slaves. The reason cited was that instructing slaves in writing would be accompanied by "great inconveniences," including the forging of passes and subversive slave communication. The Georgia legislature followed suit with a similar law in 1755, and in 1770 it proceeded to ban teaching slaves reading.

Despite planter resistance to slave schooling, campaigns to instruct southern slaves in reading and writing existed in the colonial South. The Society for the Propagation of the Gospel sent teachers into the region to create schools for slaves, but they met with limited success due to the weakness of the southern Anglican church. Most notable among the society's efforts to educate slaves were Alexander Garden's day school for young Africans, which opened in Charlestown, South Carolina, in 1743, and Joseph Ottolenghe's mission to the enslaved of Savannah, Georgia, which started up in 1751. Garden's "Negro School" met with some initial success, enrolling at one point over 60 children, who were taught how to read the Bible. But both projects were short-lived; Garden's school closed down shortly after his death in 1756, and Ottolenghe's ceased operations around 1758.

More successful were the educational efforts of the itinerants of the Great Awakening, an intercolonial revival of religion that swept through America from the 1730s into the 1750s. Moving south into Virginia and other southern colonies, northern Presbyterian preachers such as Samuel Davies and John Todd and Baptist evangelists such as Shubal Stearns held classes in reading for slaves participating in religious revivals. The southern Awakening led to the growth of black churches, black preachers, and black instruction in literacy. By 1795 the Baptists could boast a membership of about 17,000 blacks in the states south of Maryland. While not requiring literacy as a prerequisite for preaching or membership, the Baptists nevertheless encouraged instruction in reading within the slave community.

Denominational campaigns to educate slaves and free blacks also existed in the North. While the Anglican-sponsored Society for the Propagation of the Gospel established a mission in New York City in 1704 to catechize slaves and teach them some reading, the Associates of Dr. Thomas Bray, founded in 1724, was the first Anglican organization to actually create schools for northern blacks—in Philadelphia in 1758, New York City in 1760, and Newport, Rhode Island, in 1762. New England Congregationalists under the leadership of Cotton Mather, a Boston minister, set up an evening school to instruct blacks and Indians in reading the scriptures that lasted from January 1718 to the end of 1721. The Quakers, many of whom were committed to slave emancipation, saw their first school for blacks open in 1750, when Anthony Benezet started teaching slave children in his Philadelphia home at night. By 1770 he had raised enough money to build a separate black school and hire a schoolmaster. It is important to note that, of the many initiatives to educate free and enslaved blacks during the 18th century, most were limited to education in reading, the reigning belief being that writing was a badge of freedom.

Books, Libraries, and Readers

A primary consequence of expanding schooling and literacy in America was the growth in demand for schoolbooks and the publication of American imprints. There were no changes in reading preferences among Americans, as religious books, especially the Bible, were predominant throughout the century. Nor were there changes in reading audiences, which either expanded or decreased according to wealth, gender, education, and region. Still, fictional works, such as Samuel Richardson's *Pamela,* grew gradually in popularity.

Another indicator of the expanding demand for books was the social or subscription library, which appeared for the first time in 1731 in Philadelphia. Founded by Benjamin Franklin and his Junto club, the social library spread rapidly through America. Indeed, 51 of them were established in New England alone in the period from 1733 to 1780. In addition to social libraries, circulating libraries arose starting with the 1760s. While social libraries had a limited membership, circulating libraries disseminated books to as many readers as were willing to pay a nominal fee. They therefore appealed to a larger audience, including women. As surviving circulating-library records show, many of the books borrowed were fiction, and they were turned over quite rapidly, with some readers borrowing as many as 21 books a month. Although libraries would not enter a period of extraordinary expansion until after 1790, it is clear that the rudiments of what would become a "reading revolution" were already in place well before that time.

Combined with the spread of literacy, reading, and other forms of print was the rapid growth of newspapers and pamphlets after midcentury. Such changes democratized public discourse and created a new public sphere, one that organized disparate groups of readers from different walks of life around common sets of ideas. When Britain attempted to centralize its control over the colonies after 1763, the response was the spread of common literary resistance and the outbreak of rebellion in 1776.

The American Revolution

The American Revolution gave rise to a national debate over the future of the country, one centered on education and the issue of how to transmit democratic values

One indication that literacy was expanding during the 18th century was the growth of subscription libraries throughout the colonies. The above painting by Charles E. Mills shows Benjamin Franklin opening the first subscription library in Philadelphia in 1731. *(Library of Congress)*

to a new generation of Americans. Although educational reformers emphasized public schooling over parental education, the family remained important as a site for education despite simultaneously experiencing changes that altered the traditional educative roles of the parents.

Significantly, the Revolution engendered ideals of "Republican Motherhood" that greatly expanded the role of mothers in household education. Republics, unlike monarchies, depended for their survival on the education of all citizens in the values of representative government. But the expansion of the market economy after the Revolution forced fathers out of the household, while the decline of household production reduced mothers' domestic labor. The result among the more prosperous mothers of America was a rise in the leisure time they could devote to household instruction of children, not only in literacy, which they had done prior to the Revolution, but also in the new values of the republic. Accompanying the call for Republican Motherhood was a campaign for female education, which reflected a rising regard for women's moral and mental abilities. The campaign proved an enormous success, delivering an advanced academic curriculum to qualified women in all regions of Revolutionary America. At the same time, however, well-educated women were urged to apply their mental energies to the home, particularly to the raising of patriotic children. While the Revolution liberated women's intellect, it also sought to confine it to matters domestic.

The American Revolution also expanded efforts to bring literacy to slaves and free blacks. Even as the denominational campaigns for black literacy continued, the Revolution nudged Americans toward more secular efforts to educate blacks. Many of these accompanied plans to emancipate slaves. Thus, New Jersey mandated the teaching of slaves prior to their emancipation in the state's 1788 law, while New York prepared for abolishing slavery by ordering masters to teach minors in slave families how to read the scriptures. The antislavery societies springing up during and after the Revolution had slave literacy at the top of their agendas. In 1794 the American Convention of Abolition Societies encouraged members to instruct free black and slave children in "common literature." Over the next decade, antislavery activists started black schools that focused on basic literacy in Charlestown; Savannah; Washington, D.C.; Philadelphia; Wilmington, Delaware; Georgetown, Maryland; Alexandria, Richmond, and Norfolk, Virginia; as well as in many northern communities.

The educational gains made by blacks in the post-Revolutionary period looked increasingly threatening to whites, however, and northern and southern communities alike questioned their right to literacy. In some northern cities, blacks were separated from whites in schools, and their schools in turn were singled out for attack by mobs. In the long run, the Revolution failed to eliminate educational discrepancies that had plagued the country since the 17th century. Gender, race, and region would persist in restricting educational opportunities for Americans, in tragic defiance of the egalitarian ideals of the Revolution.

Yet 18th-century educators made an important contribution to subsequent American educational development in the district system of schooling, which satisfied local demand for elementary education well into the 19th century. District schools spread during the era of the new republic, and rates of enrollment rose, for girls as well as boys, reflecting an increasing acceptance of female education. Well before the advent of common-school reform, the early American system of district schools democratized literacy, at least in the North, and helped Americans prepare for a modern, liberal world.

—Gerald F. Moran

Further Reading

Amory, Hugh, and David D. Hall. *A History of the Book in America.* Vol. 1, *The Colonial Book in the Atlantic World*. Cambridge, U.K.: Cambridge University Press, 2000.

Berkin, Carol. *Revolutionary Mothers: Women in the Struggle for America's Independence*. New York: Alfred A. Knopf, 2005.

Cohen, Sheldon S. *A History of Colonial Education, 1607–1776*. New York: John Wiley, 1974.

Cornelius, Janet Duitsman. *"When I Can Read My Title Clear": Literacy, Slavery, and Religion in the Antebellum South*. Columbia: University of South Carolina Press, 1991.

Gross, Robert A., and Mary Kelley. *A History of the Book in America.* Vol. 2, *An Extensive Republic: Print, Culture, and Society in the New Nation, 1790–1840*. Chapel Hill: University of North Carolina Press, 2010.

Kaestle, Carl E. *Pillars of the Republic: Common Schools and American Society, 1780–1860.* New York: Hill & Wang, 1983.

Lockridge, Kenneth A. *Literacy in Colonial New England: An Enquiry into the Social Context of Literacy in the Early Modern West*. New York: W. W. Norton, 1974.

Middlekauff, Robert. *Ancients and Axioms: Secondary Education in Eighteenth-Century New England*. New Haven, Conn.: Yale University Press, 1963.

Monaghan, Jennifer E. *Learning to Read and Write in Colonial America*. Amherst: University of Massachusetts Press, 2005.

Pangle, Lorraine Smith, and Thomas L. Pangle. *The Learning of Liberty: The Educational Ideas of the American Founders*. Lawrence: University Press of Kansas, 1993.

Sobel, Mechal. *The World They Made Together: Black and White Values in Eighteenth-Century Virginia.* Princeton, N.J.: Princeton University Press, 1987.

Warner, Michael. *The Letters of the Republic: Publication and the Public Sphere in Eighteenth-Century America*. Cambridge, Mass.: Harvard University Press, 1990.

18th Century EMPIRES

British, French, Spanish, and Native American empires all competed for trade and territory in 18th-century North America. The sparsely populated Spanish colonies formed the edge of a powerful and populous Central and South American empire. The French colonies strengthened their hold on Indian trade and alliance in the first half of the century. The British colonies grew at an exponential rate, leading to political and economic conditions that eventually overwhelmed the imperial governmental structure. The breakdown of the relationship between Great Britain and its colonies in the American Revolution fractured the imperial world based on monarchical political culture and mercantilism and led to a new republican world based on representative government and free trade.

Colonial Growth

Different settlement patterns, economic activities, and social organization among New Spain, New France, and British America caused wide variations in rates of population growth. French colonists located settlements and forts along the St. Lawrence River, the Great Lakes, and in the interior between the Illinois country and Louisiana along the Mississippi River. Although some settlers farmed, the focus on trapping and the fur trade, as well as a gender imbalance, hindered French colonial population growth in comparison with British America. By the early decades of the 18th century, the British-American colonies had a population approximately 15 times greater than that of New France. The economic foundations of Britain's colonial empire lay primarily in staple agriculture, which consistently demanded both more land and more laborers. By the mid-18th century, the population of New York alone was roughly double that of French Canada and Louisiana. At the Peace of Paris in 1763, New France had a population of approximately 79,000, while British America's population neared 2 million.

The population of the viceroyalty of New Spain, between 2.5 and 3 million in 1750, was greater than that of the British American colonies. However, the vast majority of Spanish colonists lived in the Caribbean, Central America, and Mexico; only a small fraction resided in Spain's upper North American settlements, such as Santa Fe in New Mexico and St. Augustine in Florida. This population disparity resulted primarily from the presence of precious metals, which formed the basis of New Spain's economy, in South America and Mexico. Additionally, while the British colonies experienced an influx of immigrants from all over Europe, including over 100,000 Germans by 1783, Spain prohibited non-Spanish immigration to its American colonies, which limited population growth.

Britain's North American colonies, in sharp contrast, experienced staggering population growth, due to both immigration and natural increase. In 1700 the population was 265,000 (including slaves). By 1770 it had reached 2,283,000. One reason the colonies' population grew so dramatically was the availability of arable land, which enabled young men to obtain freehold property and become independent and thus to marry at a younger age, consequently producing more children in the course of marriage. The availability of land, as well as a relatively tolerant religious environment, drove a massive influx of immigrants into the Middle Atlantic region and later the southern backcountry. Between 1754, when the French and Indian War began, and the outbreak of fighting in the Revolution in 1775, approximately 125,000 immigrants arrived from Great Britain alone.

Population growth in the British Empire drove economic development in exports of agricultural products, as well as in other areas such as shipbuilding, the carrying trade, and the slave trade. British America also increasingly participated in a coastal trade among the colonies and with the West Indies. Additionally, colonial imports of manufactured goods increased dramatically by midcentury. The overall increase in volume of trade and economic activity stretched the limits of imperial government because this growth was not supported by structural improvements. For example, since English laws forbade exportation of sterling coin to the colonies, the colonies increasingly needed a uniform monetary system to replace the inadequate and confusing combination of barter, book credit, Spanish coin, and paper money issued separately from each colony. In the absence of adequate financial reforms, these developments strained the framework of Britain's empire.

Institutional Structure

Colonial government varied widely among the British, French, and Spanish empires, particularly regarding representative government. Each echoed, to some extent, governmental forms at the center of empire. Reflecting their parent countries' absolutism, New France and the Spanish colonies were closely governed by their monarchs. New France, for example, was unified under one government, appointed by the king, and governed without an assembly. The viceroyalty of New Spain was centralized as well, and tightly controlled by a colonial bureaucratic, judicial, and ecclesiastical framework. A viceroy and provincial governors ruled without a representative assembly. The imperial systems also differed in how they funded colonial administration. For example, in New Spain, the Crown's percentage (one-fifth) of church tithes and mining profits paid for colonial government, whereas British America lacked such a system and relied primarily on colonial assemblies to raise funds.

British colonies often achieved semi-autonomous political status, with elective assemblies balancing royal governors, replicating the parliamentary institutions that checked England's constitutional monarchy following the Glorious Revolution. Throughout the 18th century, colonial assemblies vied with royal governors for political power. They clashed primarily over finances, particularly since the assembly voted the governor's salary. The power struggle resulted in a gradual but marked rise in the power of assemblies at the expense of the royal prerogative. Additionally, colonists understood the Glorious Revolution of 1688 somewhat differently from their counterparts in England. Although the settlement following the Glorious Revolution placed political power in the king-in-Parliament, most colonists continued to interpret the king as independent of Parliament. Thus, colonists believed their primary imperial link was to the king, an interpretation that caused conflict later in the century.

The British Crown strove to create more central control and a standard for colonial government during the 18th century. This continued a process begun in the previous century by Charles II, James II, and William and Mary. Charles II focused on revoking corporate and proprietary charters, and succeeded with Massachusetts Bay in 1684. His brother and successor, James II, established the Dominion of New England (1686–89), which consolidated a number of New England and Middle Atlantic colonies under one royal governor, abolished representative assemblies, and revoked land grants throughout the Dominion. The Glorious Revolution, which replaced James II with his Protestant daughter Mary and her husband, William, stadtholder of the Netherlands, ended this short-lived experiment in absolutism.

Nevertheless, the Crown continued its efforts to increase colonial control into the 18th century through administrative consolidation of royal colonies and purchasing proprietary charters. In 1702, New Jersey became a royal colony in this manner. The Crown took control of South Carolina in 1719 and purchased the proprietorships of both North and South Carolina in 1729. Although the Crown issued a proprietary grant for Georgia in 1732, it subsidized the colony's settlement, and the charter provided for a royal takeover in 1752.

Despite consistent efforts at centralization and standardization, British colonial government remained inconsistent, with a mix of royal, proprietary, and corporate colonies. Royal colonies came closest to the English model, with an appointed royal governor, appointed council, and elected assembly meant to imitate the institutions of king, Lords, and Commons. In this model, the council acted as court, advisory council to the governor, and upper legislative house. However, in proprietary colonies (by the mid-18th century, only Pennsylvania and Maryland) the proprietor appointed the governor. In the corporate, or "charter," colonies (Connecticut and Rhode Island), the governor, council, and assembly were all elected. This inconsistent imperial system created serious problems.

Some of the problems with imperial governance began in London. A jumble of overlapping, sometimes conflicting, institutions managed colonial affairs, and this system often did not work well. The secretary of state for the southern department bore the responsibility for colonial policy, while the Privy Council supervised colonial administration, dispatched instructions and commissions to colonial governors, and reviewed colonial legislation. Additionally, the Board of Trade and Plantations managed colonial correspondence, obtained information, created reports and maps of the colonies, and advised on matters of administration. This seemingly comprehensive structure actually caused inefficiency and created a rather byzantine process of communication and legislative review, wherein each colony had to submit legislation to London for approval.

Colonial input into this system was limited and often added to the confusion. Interest groups and colonial agents played an informal yet crucial role in maintaining political channels of communication between colonies and mother country. However, agents and their patrons fell in and out of favor, and interest groups often lacked the influence to shape policy. Currency legislation provides numerous examples of this lack of influence. The practice of allowing individual colonies to issue large amounts of money to fund war expenditures and then demanding that such currency be taken out of circulation at war's end caused a series of devastating booms and busts in the colonial economy. However, well-connected London merchants opposed colonial paper money for their own reasons, and therefore colonial agents and interest groups failed to achieve imperial reform on the troubling currency issue.

Political Culture

In the 18th century, far-flung empires were held together, in large part, through political culture—the ideology, customs, and rituals through which people understood and took part in politics. British political culture centered on patriarchy, monarchy, order, affection, and interest. Patriarchy cast the monarch as protective father and his subjects as loyal children. This created an exchange of both affection and duty between king and subject. Rituals and ceremonies strengthened this imperial relationship, and holidays such as Coronation Day and the monarch's birthday celebrated the British Protestant monarch and ties of empire with parades, bonfires, and feasts. Likewise, Spanish subjects displayed political culture in rituals that emphasized state power and monarchy. For example, when a new viceroy arrived in America, the local authorities received him with elaborate ceremonies. The viceroy then proceeded along a historic route to Mexico City decorated for his journey. In the colonial capital, elaborate court rituals mimicked those of the royal court in Madrid.

For European empires involved in the Americas, religion functioned as a powerful component of political culture for two reasons. First, religious institutions buttressed the authority of political states; and second, colonists defined themselves politically in terms of religion. The French and Spanish defined themselves as spreaders and defenders of the Catholic faith, Christianizing heathen Indians and preventing the spread of Protestant heresy in the Americas. Likewise, British colonists defined themselves politically as freeborn Protestant Britons and viewed the colonies of absolutist Catholic France and Spain as antithetical and threatening to their own security and freedom. These beliefs contributed to and shaped imperial warfare, as all participants believed themselves to be involved in a global battle between good and evil, in which they battled the antichrist. Many Protestants fought to rid North America of papists in order to bring on the second coming of Christ and one thousand years of peace, a belief known as millenarianism.

British colonists also experienced a strong imperial connection through material culture. The consumer revolution of the mid-18th century made available a wide range of manufactured goods that linked colonists and mother country. In addition to goods that colonists valued because they symbolized metropolitan fashion and taste, many goods also represented monarchical political culture. For example, stoneware tankards and jugs bore royal symbols, and tavern signs commonly depicted royal coats of arms; even decorative silverware bore royal images. Thus, colonists experienced a very real imperial connection in their daily lives.

Social Structure

Socially, inequality defined 18th-century empires. Society was organized hierarchically into what was known as the "great chain of being." According to this social construct, everyone had a proper place in a social order delineated by fine distinctions. People in the lower or middling orders showed deference to their superiors, while superiors were required to show condescension in turn, which in British America meant assisting those lower in the social order by treating them to alcohol and food on Election Day or lending money. In New Spain, Spaniards controlled the upper levels of government, while an elite group of creoles controlled politics at the provincial level. In this colonial society, *mestizos* and *castizos*, people of mixed Spanish and Indian descent, occupied a lower social status. The upper levels of society created an oligarchy, wherein leading groups of families ran both society and government.

Eighteenth-century society and politics overlapped in the highly personal political practice of patronage, wherein connections of family and friendship rather than talent often determined political appointments. This practice assured loyalty and thus created a strong base of support known as "interest." The French colonial system was essentially an elaborate system of royal appointments, channeled through patron-client relationships. In the British Empire, Benjamin Franklin made use of patronage and successfully constructed a large political network both in the colonies and in London. For example, Lord Bute arranged for Franklin's son, William, to be appointed royal governor of New Jersey at the age of 22. Moreover, while Franklin resided in London

Benjamin Franklin made great use of the 18th-century practice of patronage, successfully building a large political network both in the colonies and in London. This engraving of an 1859 painting by Robert Whitechurch shows Franklin appearing before the Lords in Council in Whitehall Chapel, London, in 1774. Franklin was serving as a colonial agent in London at the time and made many efforts to resolve the imperial conflict with America. He is at the Council to present the concerns of the American colonists. *(Library of Congress)*

as a colonial agent (1757–62 and 1764–75), his protégés and friends, including the printers William Strahan and H. S. Woodfall, assisted him in his widespread efforts in the newspapers to resolve the imperial conflict. Patronage created problems in Britain's American colonies, however, because colonial administrators in London often monopolized the power to make colonial appointments themselves. This left colonial governors with few opportunities to construct their own base of support.

Trade and Mercantilism

Eighteenth-century imperial systems based their political economies on mercantilism. Under the assumption that wealth was limited, empires aspired to create a favorable balance of trade with other nations by exporting more than they imported, thus retaining a surplus of specie. Under this system, colonies existed to enrich their parent country through trade. Colonies supplied raw goods, including sugar, tobacco, furs, rice, and indigo, and in return the parent country shipped manufactured goods to its colonies. This system relied on regulations, such as navigation laws, restrictions on colonial manufacturing, and bounties, to encourage colonies to produce raw goods the parent country needed. Empires especially sought naval stores—the goods needed to supply a navy—such as hemp, pitch, tar, and timber.

Mercantilism was intended to make empires relatively self-sufficient and to prevent rivals from gaining any advantage, thus maintaining a balance of power in Europe. After centuries of warfare over religion, dynastic control, and territory, people took it for granted that if any single nation-state became too powerful, it would naturally seek to invade and control its neighbors. Thus, empires competed for territory, colonies, and trade not only for their own gain, but also to prevent their imperial rivals from acquiring the tools of domination.

Maritime power proved essential to imperial success in both trade and war. Therefore, the contest over trade, territory, and wealth in North America often focused on competition for domination of waterways, coastlines, and strategic outposts from which to raid enemy shipping or defend trade. In fact, the first permanent English settlement in North America, at Jamestown, was designed in part to check Spanish expansion and raid Spanish shipping. Wars often hinged on naval power and on cooperation between land and sea power, as in the crucial victory at Yorktown in 1781 during the American Revolution, when a combined French and American land force and the French navy surrounded British troops under General Cornwallis on the Yorktown Peninsula. Although all three European empires in North America possessed powerful navies, the British Empire rightfully claimed supremacy throughout the century.

Native Americans

Native Americans, such as the Iroquois Confederacy, formed the linchpin in contests of diplomacy and trade as empires vied for their military and economic allegiance. Beaver pelts and deerskins proved highly lucrative to colonial traders, while Indians desired European manufactures, including clothing, jewelry, cooking implements, liquor, tools, guns, and ammunition. The French and British competed for this valuable trade; the French, however, dominated Native trade and alliances until their defeat in the French and Indian War.

The interaction between Native Americans and the Spanish, French, and British colonists differed substantially. The Spanish Empire dominated Native peoples through conquest and exploitation. Franciscan priests founded missions and focused on converting Indians, often forcibly, while the Spanish government set up the *encomienda* system, which essentially created a forced labor, or tribute, system. Spanish governors granted lands to colonists, who then had the right to demand tribute in the form of labor or other services from the Native peoples who lived on that land. Forced conversion and tribute devastated Native population and culture.

The French colonial system provided Indians with more advantages and closer cultural ties than did the British. The French not only provided a steady trade, but also supplied their Native allies with gunsmiths to repair weapons free of charge, as well as interpreters. Partly due to the gender imbalance in New France, French traders and trappers routinely married Native women and spent their winters in Indian villages, thus strengthening social and cultural ties.

The rivalry between Britain and France to convert Native souls was a serious one, partly because of the centuries-old religious contest between Protestantism and Catholicism. Additionally, although many missionaries genuinely cared for Native peoples' salvation, imperial leaders recognized religion as a useful tool of control. Whoever managed to convert peoples they viewed as heathens had an upper hand in conquering new territories and gaining power, wealth, and trade. Catholic missionaries routinely traveled and lived among Native Americans, a matter of great concern to British Protestants. Jesuits had great success in New France, converting thousands of Indians.

The value not only of their trade, but also of their military alliance gave Native empires a great deal of power in the 18th century. The most famous example was the Iroquois Confederacy, or Six Nations, which consisted of an alliance among the Seneca, Cayuga, Onondaga, Oneida, Mohawk, and Tuscarora Indians. Courted by both the British and French, Native peoples like the Iroquois exploited European balance-of-power politics and played one empire off another in order to maintain their own independence and to protect their lands and communities. The huge sums the British and French spent annually on Indian presents indicated the importance they attached to Indian diplomacy. In 1746 alone, France spent 54,000 livres (a significant sum) on Indian presents. Indians had the ability to tip the scales in favor of one empire or another with their assistance.

Imperial Warfare

Imperial rivalries erupted repeatedly into warfare in North America beginning in the late 17th century and continuing throughout the 18th century. Before 1750 most of these wars began in Europe, due to balance-of-power politics and dynastic succession. Imperial wars naturally spread to the colonies because of the competition over colonial wealth, trade, and territory.

Queen Anne's War (1702–13) provides an example of the pattern of imperial conflict that originated in Europe in the first half of the 18th century. Known in Europe as the War of the Spanish Succession, it was precipitated by a problem of dynastic succession. It created an alliance between France and Spain that threatened to upset the delicate balance of power in Europe because of perceived French gains in wealth, trade, and territory. In response, the English, Dutch, and Austrians formed an alliance that led to war. This imperial war spread to the British and French colonies in America, where competition for resources, trade, and strategically placed colonies shaped military strategy, such as the British-colonial capture of French Acadia. Acadia's harbors and naval stores, as well as its position near the mouth of the St. Lawrence River and valuable fisheries, made it a desirable imperial possession. The Treaty of Utrecht that ended the war exchanged territory and made trade concessions in an effort to restore the balance of power in Europe.

By the mid-18th century, however, the center of imperial warfare shifted from Europe to America when the French and Indian War began in the Ohio Valley in 1754. Three primary conditions in America created the context for this shift. First, the British colonial population was growing rapidly, necessitating territorial expansion and causing conflict with the French in the disputed territory of the Ohio Valley. Second, the rapid growth of trade increased competition between empires over resources, territory, waterways, and Native alliances. Third, the stark contrast between the colonial systems of constitutional, Protestant Britain and absolutist, Catholic France and Spain heightened imperial conflict.

That the French and Indian War—which became known in Europe as the Seven Years' War—began not in Europe but in America is indicative of the growing importance of the American trade and territory to imperial balance-of-power politics. The conflict began when Virginia sent a force commanded by George Washington to challenge France's right to build forts in the Ohio Valley, an area both empires claimed. Formally declared in 1756 between Britain and France, the war spread throughout Europe, and indeed throughout the world, as far away as India and the Philippines. Britain and France, and later Spain and Prussia, fought to establish supremacy on the world stage of trade and territory. This conflict redrew the

Benjamin West's 1771 painting *The Death of General Wolfe* depicts a scene at the British siege of Quebec during the French and Indian War that serves as an allegorical commentary on the state of the British Empire in 1759. The war redrew the imperial map in North America and significantly diminished France's American holdings and Native Americans' diplomatic power. Once united in a common struggle, the Americans, Britons, and their Native allies would soon be violently struggling against each other. *(Library of Congress)*

imperial map in North America, marked the downfall of France's American empire, and significantly diminished Native Americans' diplomatic power.

British victory and the Peace of Paris in 1763 radically changed British, French, Spanish, and Native empires in North America. Great Britain gained Florida from the Spanish and Canada, as well as the American interior to the Mississippi River (with the exception of New Orleans), from France. Just prior to the peace negotiations, France secretly ceded New Orleans and the land west of the Mississippi to its ally, Spain. Thus, the French and Spanish presence and influence in North America was significantly reduced, although not entirely removed. The British Proclamation Line of 1763 also significantly changed the postwar imperial map. This line, which roughly followed the Appalachian Mountain range, was intended to restrict colonists from settling on Indian lands, thereby preventing conflict between the two groups. However, the Proclamation Line created a great deal of resentment in colonial settlers and land speculators who had fought in the French and Indian War primarily to gain access to that land.

Imperial Reform

By midcentury, British colonial and imperial leaders recognized the need for imperial reform in response to colonial growth and development and problems of defense and colonial management. Some reformers recommended using the French model of uniform colonial government with a centralized power structure. This would replace the confusion and inefficiency of the British colonial system that encompassed three different types of colonial government and a decentralized system in which center and periphery shared government and policymaking.

Indian affairs provides an example of the flaws inherent in the existing system. In the British colonies prior to the mid-18th century, each colony managed Indian affairs individually, including legislation and trade regulation. Although intercolonial cooperation in Indian diplomacy occurred regularly, the British colonies' disparate policies caused confusion and resentment among the Indians. Reformers, such as Sir William Johnson, superintendent for Indian affairs in the north, recognized this defect in British-Indian relations and sought to rectify it by placing Indian affairs firmly under imperial control and creating uniform colonial laws for Indian trade and diplomacy. The British government responded in 1764 by writing a "Plan for the Future Management of Indian Affairs." Although never implemented, the plan represented the effort on both sides of the Atlantic to make the empire run more smoothly through reform.

Comprehensive reform plans were not implemented primarily because repeated warfare had strained imperial resources and finances for both the parent country and its colonies. As a result of the French and Indian War, Britain's debt increased from £74,600,000 to £122,603,336. This created an annual interest of over £4 million, roughly half the national budget. Beginning with the Sugar Act in 1764 and the Stamp Act in 1765, Britain attempted to bring its colonies under tighter fiscal control and to develop colonial revenue. This created colonial resistance and raised fundamental questions regarding the constitutional relationship between Britain and its North American colonies.

Although the official government program insisted on parliamentary supremacy, opinion in Britain on colonial policy and the optimal political organization of the empire varied widely and included ideas such as a federal union, divided sovereignty, a written constitution, a formal union, and colonial representation in Parliament. Imperial possibilities that originated from Britain, however, in addition to being hampered by financial concerns, could not keep pace with rapidly developing events in the colonies. Additionally, political opponents in Britain who supported these more flexible imperial constructs, including the Earl of Chatham, the Duke of Richmond, and Dr. Richard Price, found themselves in the minority, unable to topple the secure political bulwark the king and ministry had built up in Parliament through placemen, pensioners, and electoral control of the rotten borough system. Therefore, the ministry continued its plan of coercion rather than conciliation until it proved too late.

The imperial relationship between Britain and its colonies disintegrated for many reasons: Disagreement persisted over whether sovereignty in an empire could be divided between Parliament and colonial assemblies; distance between the imperial center and periphery caused slow communications; imperial institutions and governmental policy failed to keep pace with colonial growth and development; political power struggles and ministerial turnover made it difficult for Britain to manage its colonies; Enlightenment ideology and new ideas regarding free trade challenged the imperial status quo; the Crown implemented only limited reforms; and colonial officials lacked sufficient royal patronage to build interest. Unlike the Spanish and French, the British never fully standardized or centralized their colonial government, and the colonial structure developed very differently in the absence of an aristocracy and eventually undermined imperial authority.

Fractured Empire

Although Britain's Canadian and West Indian colonies remained loyal, the American Revolution (1775–83) split the empire and replaced monarchical government with republican government in North America. Britain's loss of its colonies caused a shift in focus to the West Indies and India and prepared the groundwork for the second British Empire. It also led to a focus on continental politics and power struggles, which culminated in the Napoleonic Wars. The American Revolution also triggered the Age of

Revolution that rocked the French Empire in the Haitian and French revolutions in the last decade of the 18th century and the Spanish Empire in the 19th. North America and the empires that had dominated it changed dramatically throughout the 18th century. By century's end, although empires still played a significant role on the world stage, the old imperial order was no more.

—Heather Schwartz

Further Reading

Alden, John R. *John Stuart and the Southern Colonial Frontier: A Study of Indian Relations, War, Trade, and Land Problems in the Southern Wilderness, 1754–1775*. Ann Arbor: University of Michigan Press, 1944. Reprint, New York: Gordian Press, 1966.

Anderson, Fred. *The Crucible of War: The Seven Years' War and the Fate of Empire in British North America, 1754–1763*. New York: Alfred A. Knopf, 2000.

Bowen, H. V. *Elites, Enterprise, and the Making of the British Overseas Empire, 1688–1775*. New York: St. Martin's Press, 1996.

Bushman, Richard L. *King and People in Provincial Massachusetts*. Chapel Hill: University of North Carolina Press, 1985.

Calloway, Colin G. *The American Revolution in Indian Country: Crisis and Diversity in Native American Communities*. Cambridge, U.K.: Cambridge University Press, 1995.

———. *New Worlds for All: Indians, Europeans, and the Remaking of Early America*. Baltimore, Md.: Johns Hopkins University Press, 1997.

———. *The Scratch of a Pen: 1763 and the Transformation of North America*. New York: Oxford University Press, 2006.

Christie, Ian, and Benjamin W. Labaree. *Empire or Independence, 1760–1776: A British-American Dialogue on the Coming of the American Revolution*. New York: W. W. Norton, 1976.

Elliott, J. H. *Empires of the Atlantic World: Britain and Spain in America, 1492–1830*. New Haven, Conn.: Yale University Press, 2006.

Ferling, John. *Struggle for a Continent: The Wars of Early America*. Arlington Heights, Ill.: Harlan Davidson, 1993.

Fowler, William M. *Empires at War: The French and Indian War and the Struggle for North America, 1754–1763*. New York: Walker & Co., 2005.

Graham, Gerald S. *Empire of the North Atlantic: The Maritime Struggle for North America*. Toronto: University of Toronto Press, 1950.

Greene, Jack P. *The Quest for Power: The Lower Houses of Assembly in the Southern Royal Colonies, 1689–1776*. Chapel Hill: University of North Carolina Press, 1963.

Jacobs, Wilbur R. *Wilderness Politics and Indian Gifts: The Northern Colonial Frontier, 1748–1763*. Lincoln: University of Nebraska Press, 1950.

Kammen, Michael. *Empire and Interest: The American Colonies and the Politics of Mercantilism*. Philadelphia: J. B. Lippincott, 1970.

Labaree, Leonard W. *Royal Government in America: A Study of the British Colonial System before 1783*. New Haven, Conn.: Yale University Press, 1930.

McConville, Brendan. *The King's Three Faces: The Rise and Fall of Royal America, 1688–1776*. Chapel Hill: University of North Carolina Press, 2006.

McCusker, John J., and Russell R. Menard. *The Economy of British America, 1607–1789*. Chapel Hill: University of North Carolina Press, 1985.

Pagden, Anthony. *Lords of All the World: Ideologies of Empire in Spain, Britain, and France, c. 1500–1800*. New Haven, Conn.: Yale University Press, 1998.

Parry, J. H. *Trade and Dominion: The European Overseas Empires in the Eighteenth Century*. New York: Praeger, 1971.

Royot, Daniel. *Divided Loyalties in a Doomed Empire: The French in the West from New France to the Lewis and Clark Expedition*. Newark: University of Delaware Press, 2007.

Shannon, Timothy J. *Indians and Colonists at the Crossroads of Empire: The Albany Congress of 1754*. Ithaca, N.Y.: Cornell University Press, 2000.

Sosin, Jack. *Whitehall and the Wilderness: The Middle West in British Colonial Policy, 1760–1775*. Lincoln: University of Nebraska Press, 1961.

Taylor, Alan. *The Divided Ground: Indians, Settlers, and the Northern Borderland of the American Revolution*. New York: Alfred A. Knopf, 2006.

18th Century ENVIRONMENT

An upheaval in relationships between people and the natural environment took place in 18th-century North America that was as transformative as the era's better-known political revolution. The practical, economic evidence of what some historians have called an "ecological revolution" can be seen in the expansion of commercial agriculture (and with it the expansion of slavery); the movement of hunters and European settlers westward into Appalachia, displacing and destroying thousands of Native communities; and the connection of the vast majority of people in the American colonies to Europe's global network of trade. European immigrants, African Americans, and American Indians working in the service of world markets exploited the natural world on a larger scale than had been the case when only North America's Native inhabitants were farming, hunting, and building towns and villages.

The results of a more intensive exploitation of nature were often harmful to both people and the environment, leading to the expansion of slavery; the felling of vast tracts of forests; the degradation and scattering of American Indian communities; steep declines in populations of beaver, deer, and wolves; and, by century's end, the construction of dams and canals, which diverted water to power mills and transported goods, respectively. At the same time, however, many people prospered as a result of the ecological revolution, which contributed to new wealth, large cities, and ultimately to new ways of thinking about the natural world.

A Climate of Change

The stage on which the ecological and political revolutions of the 1700s took place was eastern North America. During most of the 18th century, land was relatively easy to obtain by moving west or south, cutting down forests, or seizing claim to river valleys where Indian farmers had already cleared the land. But by the end of the American Revolution, the era of easy-to-claim land was over, and the eastern third of the new United States was beginning to look much more crowded—with immigrants from the British Isles, Scandinavia, Germany, and elsewhere—and much more like a part of Europe than the Eden many earlier settlers had sought.

Immigrant farmers in the Americas faced the same challenge that Europeans faced: For most of the 1700s, a cooling period, known as the Little Ice Age, made farming challenging, but by the end of the century this period was giving way to a warming trend and greater unpredictability in climate. Severe storms, killing frosts, and new crop diseases were on the rise, taking a toll on farmers in the colonies. A volcanic eruption in Japan in 1788–89 sent clouds of dust into the atmosphere, lowered global temperatures temporarily, and devastated food supplies. Erratic weather patterns in the late 18th century may have influenced farmers to seek stability through increased trade and reliable cash crops that promised to tide them over during hard times, thus reinforcing the trend toward a market-based economy.

Disappearing Forests

The region of North America into which settlement was expanding in the 18th century is known as the Eastern Woodlands. Here, for centuries before Europeans arrived on the scene, Indian groups used fire to manage their forested landscape. It was used to create open meadows attractive to deer, elk, turkey, and quail; to burn paths for travel; to clear land for farming; to engineer better defensive positions against enemy attacks; and to eliminate mosquitoes, ticks, and other pests. But even with the managed burning carried on throughout the Eastern Woodlands, enormous tracts of trees remained available for colonists to exploit.

Soon the American colonies became an integral part of the European economy—and a vital resource, in particular, for Mother England. Most European settlers in the 18th century came from regions of scarce forests. The English, for example, were already experiencing shortages by the late 16th century, but their expanding navy required timber, as did miners (for mine shorings), barrel makers, and textile factories. At first, the northern colonies answered England's need for timber, with New Hampshire alone providing up to 500 enormous white pines for masts each year. By 1715 the American colonies were essential to the English navy's power, providing half of all Britain's naval stores. Later in the century, as population pressures depleted New England's forests, entrepreneurs looked toward the South, where stands of evergreens provided not just timber, but also pitch and tar for preserving wood and preventing leaks in ship hulls. Of course, some forest products were consumed at home, particularly millions of cords of wood for fuel. In addition, the burning of forests and stumps to clear land for agriculture created potash used in soap, glass, and gunpowder.

Because trees were seen as inexhaustible in colonial America, few good records of deforestation in the era exist, but certainly tens of millions of acres were cleared for farming, fuel, and pasture. By the end of the 18th century, forest clearing along the East Coast had three major ecological consequences: The diversity of animal species declined as animals such as bears and wolves lost valuable habitat; the lack of a tree canopy created hotter, drier soils and made the land more vulnerable to erosion and flooding; and the lack of tree cover affected streams and rivers, which were subject to more sediment and runoff because tree roots were no longer stabilizing the soil.

Farming by Natives and Immigrants

Many American Indian communities practiced similar patterns of agriculture in the Eastern Woodlands. In the spring, small stands of trees were burned, and new areas—usually near rivers or streams—were planted with corn, beans, and squash. Then families left their villages to hunt, fish, and gather berries and fruit, moving back to their farms to harvest crops in the fall. Some of the harvest would be preserved for the colder months, and it would be supplemented by hunting deer and other game in the winter.

A similar cycle of planting and hunting took place on the Great Plains near the Missouri and other rivers where soil was rich. In addition to deer and smaller mammals, Plains Indians hunted the abundant bison, which were still migrating across the grasslands in herds of millions. By the 18th century, Plains Indians had incorporated horses (reintroduced to the continent by the Spanish in the 1500s) into their way of life, which changed their overall relationship with the environment. Horses required constant movement to fresh grass in summer and reliable forage in winter, so some tribes moved from a semi-nomadic to a fully nomadic existence. In addition, social differentiation based on how many horses a group owned became more common. Despite a great deal of diversity in modes of subsistence, all American Indian cultures tried to maximize and diversify their food sources to defend against hunger during the inevitable lean times of drought or severe winters.

In contrast with American Indians, most colonists farming in North America in the 18th century were tied in large and small ways to European markets. In the South, major export crops such as indigo and rice were common. In the North, farmers produced some grains, including maize, or corn, to exchange for European goods. By the mid-1700s, many farms in the English colonies were producing surpluses, which helped feed growing cities and towns up and down the East Coast and allowed for the exporting of grain. Regions soon began to specialize. The area west of Philadelphia, for example, produced wheat and milled flour, some of which was exported to the West Indies, along with wooden staves for barrels, providing money so the farmers and middlemen could pay for new luxury goods from Europe. At the same time, Europeans could obtain sugar from the West Indies while prospering from transporting slaves to work the plantations. Thus, the land and forests of North America became absolutely integral to the global sugar economy.

To Europeans, land in the English colonies seemed almost infinite, so they often failed to follow the sustainable practices of fertilizing and leaving fields fallow that they had used in their homelands. Instead, they simply moved on to new land when they exhausted a particular area. As populations grew and farms were divided among many siblings, maintaining large enough yields of wheat, rye, corn, and oats on smaller plots became difficult. Political tensions arose at midcentury, in part from environmental pressures. In particular, farmers who were struggling to survive on shrinking tracts of land, with soils depleted of nutrients, protested and resisted tax increases of any kind.

During the Revolutionary War, demand for meat to feed soldiers led more farmers to turn to livestock as a market commodity. Many farmers in the North and Appalachia expanded their fields of grasses and clover for livestock, using whatever spaces they could find to create open meadows for grazing. Cattle and sheep provided not only meat but also milk and wool, which could be transformed into valuable products for market. Livestock also produced manure that could be recycled to fertilize fields. In the South and backcountry, hogs were more valuable and common than cattle or sheep because they were so easily adaptable and easy to feed. Usually set free to forage in—and often devastate—the forests and pastures around farmsteads, they thrived on native plants, nuts, and roots, while the southern landscape became dotted with smokehouses to cure the staple meat.

The gradual expansion of livestock among American farmers in the 18th century was one of the most long-lasting changes in human-nature relationships on the continent. Pasturing cattle, sheep, and hogs changed the composition of plant species in northern and southern colonies by favoring those that were less edible by livestock, such as white pine and red cedar, while hardwoods like oak and birch declined. At the same time, livestock disseminated seeds of European weeds in their manure. The use of horses for plowing expanded the amount of land each family could manage, dramatically increasing pressure for expansion into new territories. And finally, one other long-lasting result of the expansion of livestock in the 1700s was a drastic decline in the population of wolves in the eastern United States, as settlers tried to protect the domestic animals that had become so essential to their survival.

Landscapes of Slavery in the South

The institution of slavery profoundly affected the relationships between people and the environment in the South, in part because it made the production of tobacco, indigo, and rice (and later cotton) possible and profitable. Enslaved Africans brought specific practices related to the environment from their homelands, merging these traditions with a variety of European traditions. What emerged in the 18th century was a landscape of plantations, small farms, and scattered towns in Virginia, the Carolinas, Louisiana, Florida, and Georgia, mainly focused on the production of a few commodities for European and American markets.

In the 18th century, tobacco cultivation spread from traditional plantation strongholds in tidewater Maryland and Virginia, where the crop had depleted the soil of nutrients, to newer, smaller farms inland and upriver. After the American Revolution, tobacco cultivation spread to fresh territory in Kentucky and Tennessee. However, rice was the crop that truly dictated new relationships with nature in the 18th-century colonies, primarily in coastal Louisiana, South Carolina, Georgia, and Florida.

In Louisiana, some of the first African slaves to arrive in 1719 introduced rice to the riverbanks and bayous. Rice was an ideal crop for the flood-prone area, and within two years plantations near New Orleans were producing thousands of pounds of it annually. The delicate grain required skilled, intensive labor, and the management of large amounts of land and water. Slaves cleared floodplains of trees and shrubs so that seeds could be sown in bare soil, and they built elaborate dams, gates, dikes, and sluices to control the flow of water into and out of fields. As fields moved farther inland in the late 1700s, more complex systems of dams, levees, and culverts were required. By 1720, partly due to the expansion of rice plantations and their heavy demand for laborers, South Carolina's population included twice as many slaves as whites. By the end of the century, much of the low country had become a human-engineered landscape, rather than a natural one, making it a tribute to the ideals of rational, scientific management of the world that was prominent among the elite. At the same time, historians have found that plantation slaves carved out their own spaces, which were aligned with their needs for less commodity-driven, more personal landscapes.

The other crop that dominated southern agriculture in the 1700s was indigo, which produced a brilliant, valuable blue dye. Again, slaves knew this plant well because it grew wild in many regions of West Africa. Once a few planters in Louisiana began to develop the industry, plantations expanded and took over areas farther inland in Louisiana, Florida, and South Carolina—places too dry for rice. Like rice, indigo was labor-intensive, requiring many hands to cultivate and process it. But it was also a very reliable export commodity, and it made planters rich. However, because old-growth forests were cut down to make way for plantations, the cultivation of indigo simplified and sometimes eroded the landscape. By the end of the 18th century, many indigo planters gave in to competition outside the United States, and cotton and sugarcane became the dominant cash crops in the 1800s.

Backcountry Transformations

With the Proclamation of 1763, the British tried to stop colonists from settling beyond the ridge of the Appalachians,

Expanded Colonial Settlement into Backwoods Regions, End of the 18th Century

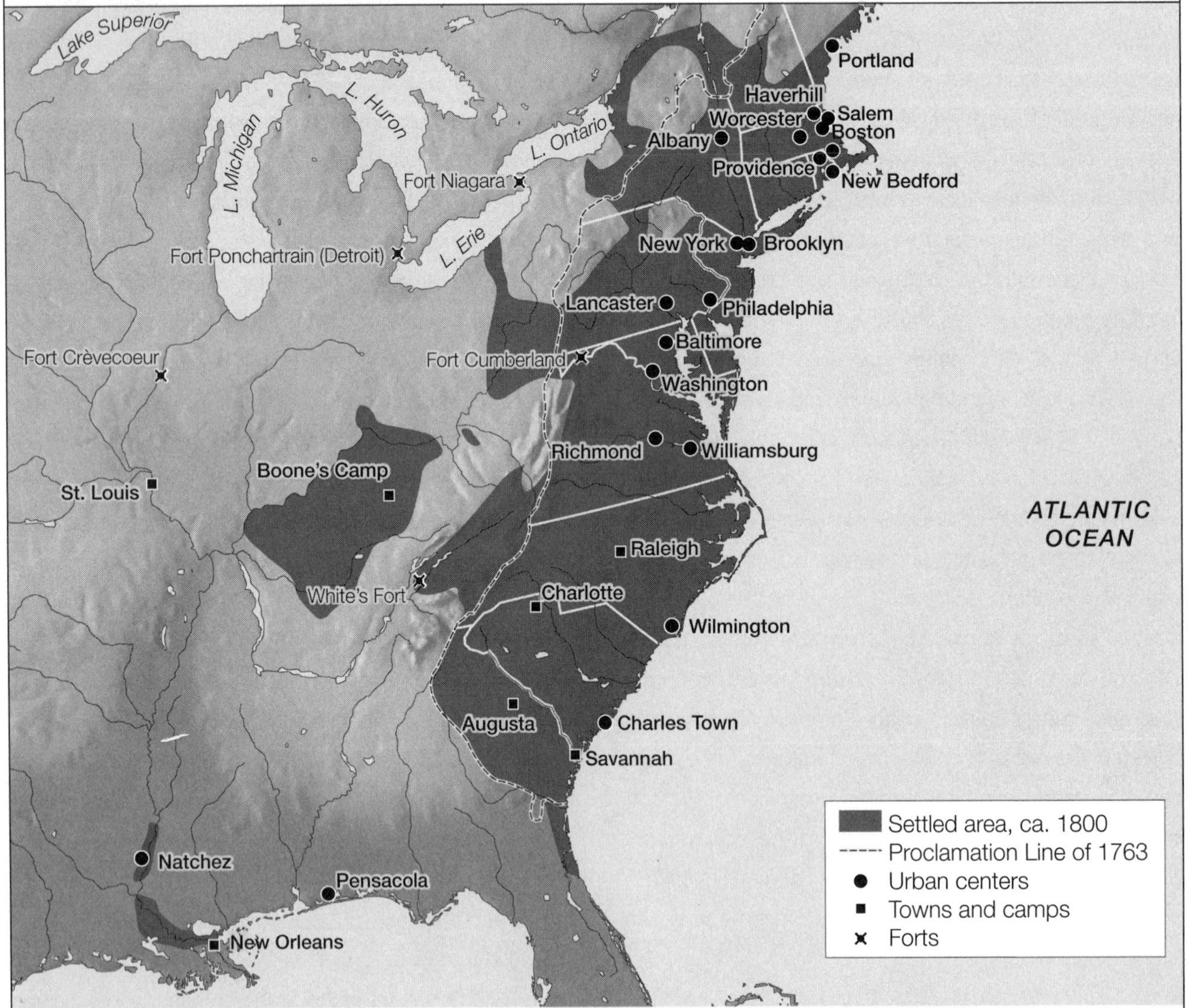

Source: U.S. Geological Survey, *The National Atlas of the United States of America* (Washington, D.C.: U.S. Dept. of the Interior, 1970).

The settling of the backcountry by colonists beyond the boundary established by the Proclamation Line of 1763 continued the environmental transformation of the eastern half of North America, a process that had begun when Europeans first attempted to settle the eastern coast of the continent in the 16th century.

leaving the territory west of the mountains for occupation by Native Americans. This was done with the hope of avoiding conflicts. But speculators and settlers paid no attention. Whites kept moving inland, putting more and more pressure on Native occupants of what would become West Virginia and Tennessee, as well as western Virginia, North Carolina, and South Carolina. Hunters were often the first to establish settlements in the mountains and foothills. They resided there during hunting season and used packhorses to carry out deerskins and other goods. Hunters and traders opened routes to the west and made business contacts with Indians. Settlers gravitated toward these routes, and toward fields and meadows already cleared by Indians.

By 1790 there were thousands of settlers developing the resources of the Tennessee Valley, with thousands more on the Cumberland Plateau and in the eastern foothills of the Blue Ridge Mountains. The Appalachian region as a whole had at least 80,000 inhabitants—primarily English and Scots-Irish immigrants, but also Germans, Africans, Irish, and Scandinavians. Cattle and sheep grazed in open meadows that Indians had maintained by burning for generations. European settlers established small corn, flax, and wheat fields near their homes (often local variations of log cabins), and they planted orchards and native crops of beans, tobacco, pumpkins, and squash. Just as had been the case in New England and the coastal southern colonies, trees were the most essential resource: They were used for firewood, building materials, roof shingles, tool handles, and fencing. Along this new frontier, patterns of deforestation and the influence of livestock on plant life also reoccurred.

Native Americans and traders worked hand in hand in the 1700s to dramatically change the backcountry landscape by removing white-tailed deer, elk, and bison from the region. Deer hides made their way to Europe to become gloves and book binding, while Indian hunters received rifles, axes, and bullets in exchange. At the height of the deerskin trade in the mid-18th century, more than 500,000 deer hides a year were shipped to Europe from the American colonies.

European demand for deerskins and the pelts of raccoons, otters, and beaver led to the overhunting of the creatures, and in the case of the beaver it ultimately caused a population crash toward the end of the 1700s. For centuries, American Indians had hunted beaver without endangering the animals' overall population, in part because Indian population density was relatively low. But as more and more Indian hunters were brought into the global market, they contributed to the beaver's near extinction. Indians demanded European-made goods, including metal tools and cooking vessels, guns and gunpowder, and linens. Europeans demanded beaver pelts for hats and clothing. The exchange was ideal from an economic point of view, as each partner in the transaction had something the other needed. From the point of view of maintaining the animal population, however, the resulting unrestrained hunting was a disaster.

Another Revolution: Ideas about Nature

During the 18th century, most people living in the American colonies and, later, the United States were farmers, hunters, and fishers. They therefore interacted with and understood nature through their bodies, through their daily physical contact with the sky, earth, plants, and animals. European immigrants, free and enslaved Africans, and Native Americans all understood nature in this way. Intellectually, however, they approached the natural world differently, based on their inherited religious and cultural ideas, which evolved and shifted over the course of the century. For example, the Ojibwa and Micmac people begged forgiveness of animals when they killed them for food or clothing, believing in a holistic world in which human and animal souls were intertwined. Many Europeans, on the other hand, held religious beliefs that emphasized a rigid division between man and nature—and between humans and animals—with only humans possessing souls, and with humans enjoying a God-given dominion over the natural world.

As European market capitalism came to dominate more and more of North America over the century—tying Indians, Europeans, and Africans into complex webs of market relationships—new ways of thinking about, controlling, and using land, animals, and plants came to dominate as well. For Europeans, land once viewed as a resource to sustain a family was now expected to generate profits. Europeans who sought to feed markets and viewed animals and trees as commodities to be traded did not have long-term sustainability in mind. The notion of nature as a set of commodities and resources for exploitation and profit continued to dominate American thinking well into the 19th century. Algonquians, Iroquois, Creeks, and other Native groups generally did not view land as personal property, and they did not believe that a single person or group could own it. Instead, they divided territories into zones where certain groups had rights to hunt, fish, or grow crops, without the notion of controlling the land itself. They also tended to hunt and fish with the goal of sustaining animal populations over the long term.

At the same time that ordinary Americans were embracing nature as a commodity, elites in Europe and the new United States were adopting the views of Enlightenment philosophy and science, which trumpeted the power of the human intellect to dissect, understand, and improve upon the natural world. Rejecting traditional notions of nature as a mysterious realm in which natural disasters, crop failures, and disease were attributed to magic or battles between God and the devil, Americans schooled in Enlightenment thought—including leaders such as George Washington, Thomas Jefferson, and Benjamin Franklin—were determined to use scientific methods and new inventions to bring nature into the service of their fellow citizens. This Enlightenment emphasis on progress and the perfectibility of the human condition through human reason and effort provided philosophical support for the economic projects of the late 18th century that increased human control and manipulation of the landscape.

But the germ of a new mode of thinking had emerged by the end of the century, in the form of a revolt against purely scientific and empirical understandings of nature. Certainly, the sense of a dark, frightening, unknown wilderness had disappeared as Americans brought more of the continent under their control. But as the 18th century ended, Romantic philosophers, writers, and artists sought to reinvest wilderness, and nature as a whole, with spiritual meaning. Romantics saw untamed forests, mountains, and waterfalls as places where humans could come in contact with God through his most awe-inspiring creations. So, at the turn of the new century in the United States, a second ecological revolution was about to take place. Industrialization produced a sharp critique of the way humans were exploiting and polluting the environment, and wilderness was elevated to a new sacred status through the popular movement to establish national parks, a quintessentially American ideal.

—Shelley Sperry

Further Reading

Carney, Judith A. *Black Rice: The African Origins of Rice Cultivation in the Americas*. Cambridge, Mass.: Harvard University Press, 2001.

Chaplin, Joyce E. *An Anxious Pursuit: Agricultural Innovation and Modernity in the Lower South, 1730–1815*. Chapel Hill: University of North Carolina Press, 1993.

Cowdrey, Albert E. *This Land, This South: An Environmental History*. Rev. ed. Lexington: University Press of Kentucky, 1996.

Cumbler, John T. *Northeast and Midwest United States: An Environmental History*. Santa Barbara, Calif.: ABC-CLIO, 2005.

Davis, Donald Edward. *Where There Are Mountains: An Environmental History of the Southern Appalachians.* Athens: University of Georgia Press, 2000.

Edelson, S. Max. *Plantation Enterprise in Colonial South Carolina*. Cambridge, Mass.: Harvard University Press, 2006.

Hahn, Steven, and Jonathan Prude, eds. *The Countryside in the Age of Capitalist Transformation: Essays in the Social History of Rural America.* Chapel Hill: University of North Carolina Press, 1985.

Lewis, Michael, ed. *American Wilderness: A New History*. New York: Oxford University Press, 2007.

Merchant, Carolyn. *American Environmental History: An Introduction*. New York: Columbia University Press, 2007.

———. *Ecological Revolutions: Nature, Gender, and Science in New England*. Chapel Hill: University of North Carolina Press, 1989.

Opie, John. *Nature's Nation: An Environmental History of the United States*. Fort Worth, Tex.: Harcourt Brace, 1998.

Rice, James D. *Nature and History in the Potomac Country: From Hunter-Gatherers to the Age of Jefferson.* Baltimore, Md.: Johns Hopkins University Press, 2009.

Silver, Timothy. *A New Face on the Countryside: Indians, Colonists, and Slaves in South Atlantic Forests, 1500–1800.* New York: Cambridge University Press, 1990.

Steinberg, Ted. *Down to Earth: Nature's Role in American History.* 2d ed. New York: Oxford University Press. 2008.

Stilgoe, John. *Common Landscape of America, 1580–1845*. New Haven, Conn.: Yale University Press, 1982.

Sturtevant, William, ed. *Handbook of North American Indians*. 15 vols. Washington, D.C.: Smithsonian Institution, 1978–2008.

Sutter, Paul. S., and Christopher J. Manganiello, eds. *Environmental History and the American South: A Reader.* Athens: University of Georgia Press, 2009.

Thomson, Keith. *A Passion for Nature: Thomas Jefferson and Natural History*. Chapel Hill: University of North Carolina Press, 2009.

Williams, Michael. *Americans and Their Forests: A Historical Geography.* New York: Cambridge University Press, 1989.

18th Century EXPLORATION AND DISCOVERY

Exploration can entail a wide range of activities, from casual meanderings in familiar lands to carefully planned expeditions to little-known places. But one thing that unifies most everything called "exploration" is the quest for scientific knowledge. Whether the search for exotic plant specimens or for precise geographic data, exploration is always about adding to what is known about the wider world. At present, that wider world has come to include the deep sea and outer space, but in the 18th century it was much more circumscribed. For the most part, systematic scientific exploration was limited to regions adjoining the world's major bodies of water. Very few explorers penetrated the inland reaches of the world's continents. The vast inland hinterlands of Africa and North America, for example, remained almost exclusively the province of speculative geographers.

Having said this, it should also be useful to distinguish between two different kinds of exploration, landed and seaborne. Although the two share much, they differ in the fundamental sense that the primary operational platform of the latter is the oceangoing sailing ship. This made them much more costly and, in turn, much more likely to require state sponsorship, since governments were really the only organizations with either the resources or the strategic incentive to undertake such costly, complex projects.

Such elaborate oceanic expeditions, along with the more modest undertakings of lone overland travelers, transformed what was known about North America in the 18th century. It is a story of failure as much as it is one of success, but its consequences are undeniable: a fuller grasp of just what the world was.

Seaborne Exploration before the Seven Years' War

The locus of seaborne exploration in the 18th century was the Pacific. After two centuries of extensive commercial exploitation and imperial conquest, the Atlantic littoral was largely known to Europeans. The Pacific was another matter. But until the 1760s, formal exploratory ventures to the Pacific were rare. Most European activity in the Pacific before the 1760s was directed toward trade and plunder. That is, it was either a function of European interest in the lucrative markets of the Far East, or it was a function of the European efforts to plunder the riches of rival nations. The latter usually amounted to state-sponsored piracy, otherwise known as privateering.

Similarly, insofar as there was any state involvement in British, Spanish, French, or Dutch activity in the Pacific, that involvement was limited and disinterested. That is, European states whose subjects sailed the Pacific had no concerted policy that focused on the Pacific. None of them saw the region as a pressing arena of colonization, and none of them had any broad strategic vision that involved incorporating the Pacific into their imperial holdings. Insofar as they did, that vision was incredibly truncated. Spain, for example, traversed the Pacific with its treasure galleons for nearly 250 years and claimed territories such as California, Peru, and the Philippines, but this was not a function of some larger imperial plan to incorporate the vast Pacific basin into the Spanish Empire. In a sense, the treasure galleons—those huge, sailing vaults that annually carried silver from Acapulco to the Philippines—were anomalous, born primarily of the perceived dangers of moving Peruvian silver through the Atlantic.

Seaborne Exploration after 1760

Beginning in the early 1760s, this fragmented, incoherent approach to the Pacific gave way to something of an imperial contest, as European powers sought to lay claim to the globe's remaining uncolonized oceanic littoral. That contest would continue at least until the outbreak of the

French Revolution, which momentarily distracted Europe from far-flung empire-building, and it would generate, arguably, the most substantial, sophisticated, and coherent body of geographic and scientific data to date.

This race for Pacific dominion, and the attendant surge in state-sponsored exploratory voyages, is best understood as an outgrowth of the Seven Years' War (1756–63). Though the formal peace, signed in 1763, briefly ended the open antagonism of the 18th century's two great imperial rivals, France and Great Britain, it did not end more covert antagonism. Indeed, in some ways it only heightened that antagonism.

France

Before the Seven Years' War, the French controlled much of North America (Canada and Louisiana); after the war they retained no possessions at all on the mainland continent east of the Mississippi. There were a number of problems with this. First, it meant that France's ability to supply its islands in the West Indies—most importantly Martinique and Guadeloupe—were sharply curtailed. To feed their sugar-harvesting slaves, French planters would now have to purchase food from the British or the Spanish, thereby enriching potential imperial rivals. To some French policy-makers and enlightened "philosophes," the Pacific and the fabled great "Southern Continent" (the vast landmass cartographers generally believed to occupy the southern reaches of the Pacific, including the still unexplored landmasses associated with New Zealand and Australia) seemed like a potential alternative.

Second, the French had come to depend very heavily on Spanish silver, obtained through trade in Chile, Peru, and Mexico. In the early decades of the 18th century, French ships carried something near 100 million pesos worth of silver back to France. After the war, French ships ferrying silver back to France could find no safe harbor in New Orleans or the Canadian Maritime provinces while Anglo-American ships had access to the vast Atlantic seaboard of North America. Suddenly the Pacific seemed like the last best option for incorporating Spanish silver into the French economy.

Third, having lost its mainland possessions in America, France now found itself with only a very few overseas colonies. Not only were colonies a source of valuable commodities and important trade, they were also the principle bargaining chip in what had become a global quest for dominance. Every colony constituted a potential source of wealth, a potential base of military operations, and a potential strategic advantage in the race for favorable trade in Asia and America.

Thus, the mystery of the "Southern Continent" and much of the rest of the Pacific contributed to the urgent sense that any true imperial power needed to begin claiming the Pacific's vast coastal territories, lest a rival do so first. In particular, it was entirely possible that whoever claimed those lands would discover something akin to what Spain had discovered in the 16th century: a seemingly limitless fountain of precious metals. It was also possible that the winner of that race would discover lands of incalculable strategic value. In addition to offering safe harbor for ships making the arduous Pacific crossing, such lands might provide a large supply of vital strategic commodities, such as tall hardwood trees that could be used for ship masts.

All of these concerns inspired the French to organize the first of a series of expeditions in 1763, just as the Peace of Paris was bringing the Seven Years' War to its formal conclusion. Commanded by Louis-Antoine de Bougainville, a distinguished soldier who had fought in the Seven Years' War, the voyage sought to reassert the French Empire, first by laying claim to the Falkland Islands. The plan was to gain control of those islands, just east of Tierra del Fuego, and in turn gain control of the southeastern gateway to the Pacific. The French intended to follow this first strategic step with more claims in the Pacific itself.

Britain

Though it won the Seven Years' War, and though its imperial status was essentially unchallenged, Britain suddenly found itself with a series of very difficult problems as well. Like all empires, this one was incredibly costly to maintain. Without infusions of valuable trade goods and "specie" to compensate for the administrative costs entailed by its newly expanded dominions, Britain's new supremacy would be—and indeed was, as the American Revolution demonstrated—short-lived. Similarly, if a newly dedicated France succeeded in its own imperial designs in the Pacific, the results for Britain could be catastrophic. The British Empire was a fragile thing indeed, and Britain's rival states were well aware of this.

An indication of just how important the British government had begun to take Pacific exploration is suggested by the fact that the Admiralty, the government agency charged with governing the vast British Navy (by far the largest and wealthiest branch of the British government), was given control of Pacific exploration. While the Admiralty had some role in earlier voyages of reconnaissance, never before had its exploratory mandate been as comprehensive or as rigorous. Hence, in 1764, Britain's first naval expedition to the Pacific in many decades took to the seas. Commanded by Commodore John Byron, the voyage took a year and began by probing French claims in the Falkland Islands. Byron was then supposed to sail around Cape Horn and head north, along the American coast in search of the treasured Northwest Passage, the putative northern waterway linking the Atlantic and Pacific oceans. After a treacherous passage around the Cape, however, Byron's men began falling to scurvy, and his ships, the *Dolphin* and the *Tamar*, began running low on supplies. Rather than risk his crew's life by traveling into the little-known northern Pacific, he followed prevailing westerly winds toward the Solomon Islands, never touching the west coast of the Americas. He returned to England in May 1766 with little to show for his efforts, and his expedition generated very little novel scientific data.

But in an indication of how important and how urgent the Admiralty had come to view Pacific reconnaissance, it almost immediately returned the *Dolphin* to sea, this time under the command of Captain Samuel Wallis. The purpose of this voyage, which began in August 1766, was spelled out in the secret instructions issued by the Admiralty to Wallis. He was to sail around Cape Horn and then tack west to the Great Southern Continent. The voyage would be a bold strike for the British Empire in the South Pacific.

Again, though, much like Byron before him, rather than further risk the lives of his scurvy-suffering, malnourished crew by sailing west into the unknown, Wallis ignored the Admiralty's orders and sailed for the Solomon Islands. Along the way he discovered the "Society Islands," of which Tahiti was the best known. In May 1768, Wallis returned to England with his leaky, broken ship, and a crew that had barely survived its years at sea.

Of course, the French were not idly observing Britain's Pacific thrust. Shortly after Wallis left port, another French expedition led by Bougainville took to the seas. After fighting the British in Canada as aide-de-camp to the famous Montcalm, the ill-fated commander of French forces there during the Seven Years' War, Bougainville was now fighting them in the Pacific. Having left Europe shortly after Wallace, he followed the *Dolphin* in the same miserable passage around Cape Horn, arriving in Tahiti a year after Wallis. His one great achievement was to have lost a mere seven men to shipboard sickness.

What is striking about these early exploratory voyages is their collective failure. None of them discovered the sought after Southern Continent or the equally important Northwest Passage; indeed, aside from Tahiti and a few other Polynesian islands, they did not discover much of anything. One of the primary reasons for this was sickness: For all of these captains, a voyage into the Pacific meant terrible bouts of scurvy and malnutrition, bouts so bad that for periods of time their ships almost had to sail themselves.

The Cook Voyages

The story of Captain James Cook's three Pacific expeditions is very different. Thanks to a rigorously enforced nutritional regimen, strict rules for shipboard cleanliness, and Cook's own navigational mastery, these voyages generated more scientific data than all the previous Pacific expeditions combined, and they probably generated more raw geographical and scientific data than any such expeditions in history. The first of Cook's voyages, begun in August 1768, charted the eastern coast of Australia and established that New Zealand was a distinct, unattached landmass. The second, which lasted from 1772 to 1775, conclusively disproved the existence of any great southern continent. And the third, perhaps the most ambitious of the three, and the one that culminated in Cook's death at Kealakekua

Bay on the island of Hawaii, yielded navigational charts for the Northwest Coast of North America from Vancouver Sound to Alaska and the Aleutian Islands. Indeed, Cook charted the Northwest Coast so carefully and skillfully that the British Navy continued using his charts well into the 20th century. But what is perhaps most remarkable of all among Cook's many achievements was the fact that not a single sailor aboard his ships during any of his voyages died from scurvy, malnutrition, or any of the other scourges that had been so common a part of long-distance seafaring. Indeed, although Cook had not recognized that scurvy could be controlled through the consumption of Vitamin C–bearing citrus fruits, he did recognize that cleanliness and a constant diet of fresh food—as opposed to the sailor's normal diet of salt meats, hardtack, beer, and grog—would preserve shipboard health and, in turn, allow the ever-longer periods at sea needed for exploration in the distant reaches of the Pacific.

In terms of their relevance to North American history, Cook's voyages are best understood in the context of a nascent trade between China and Anglo-America. Cook's final voyage, in particular, established the lucrative potential of the Northwest Coast fur trade. Supple sea-otter skins, obtained by Cook's crew at Nootka Sound on Vancouver Island, fetched handsome sums in Canton. News of the potential profitability of this trade spread upon

The Routes of Captain James Cook's Three Voyages, 1768 to 1780

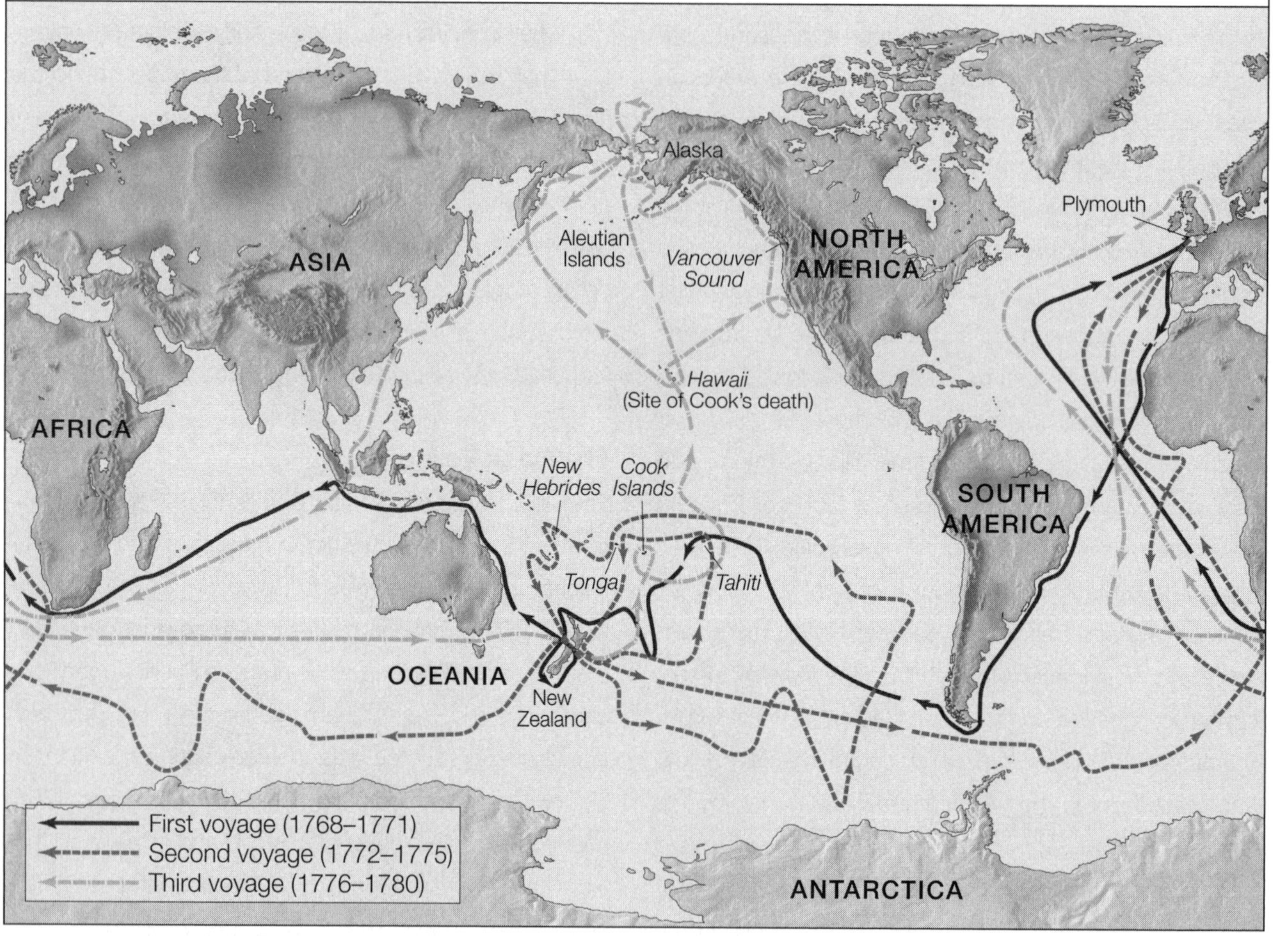

This map shows the three voyages undertaken by Captain James Cook, which are thought to have generated more raw geographical and scientific data than any such expeditions in history. One of the most significant of Cook's discoveries was the profit potential of the Northwest Coast fur trade.

the voyagers' return to Britain in 1780, and by 1785 a small number of British ship owners had begun sending vessels to Nootka. Meanwhile, merchants in the newly established United States were themselves looking for ways to capitalize on this new China trade. No longer bound by British trade restrictions, but facing a hazardous Atlantic trade, American merchants began looking to the Pacific and China for lucrative business opportunities. One of them, Robert Morris, who was a former smuggler and the principle financier for the Continental Congress, enlisted a former member of Cook's final voyage, the Connecticut-born John Ledyard, as supercargo for an expedition to the Northwest Coast. Financing for the voyage never came together, however, and Morris's partners elected to leave the Northwest Coast to the British. The situation would change after the 1787–90 voyage of the Boston ship *Columbia*, which established the Northwest Coast as a viable arena for New England maritime trade.

Overland Exploration

Overland exploration of 18th-century North America was largely the work of individuals and their patrons. The British government had little interest in the vast interior of North America, even after the conclusion of the Seven Years' War, when much of that interior came under British control. In the immediate aftermath of the American Revolution, the confederation of American states, which eventually became the United States, may have had substantial interest in the continental hinterland, but it lacked the means and the political capital to translate that interest into any kind of large-scale exploratory project. To be sure, there were dozens of colonials, and later Americans, who generated abundant scientific data about the American backcountry, but these tended to be lone travelers, subsidized by private patrons or nongovernmental scientific societies. Perhaps the best known of these were a Quaker father and his son, John and William Bartram.

With the patronage of Peter Collinson—a prominent London merchant, fellow Quaker, and member of London's Royal Society, who had been introduced to Bartram by Benjamin Franklin—John Bartram (1699–1777) traversed the colonial countryside, primarily east of the Appalachian range, in search of botanical specimens. Many of these specimens ended up in the collections of prominent European botanists, including the British king, George III, and the great Swedish taxonomist Carl Linnaeus. But John's son William (1739–1823) was the more notable explorer.

Encouraged by another prominent London Quaker and Royal Society member, Dr. John Fothergill, William undertook an ambitious expedition to the American Southeast between 1773 and 1777, making his way through the Carolinas, Georgia, northern Florida, and west as far as Baton Rouge. Traveling alone on horseback or in the company of local Native American guides, Bartram assembled a rich catalog of flora, fauna, and ethnographic observation. In 1791 he published an account of his travels that proved immensely popular, both in the United States and Europe. The book appealed to a growing Romantic sense that nature must be looked upon less as a transparent, rational set of mechanical actions than as a mysterious, often ineffable arena of strange and contradictory impulses.

Jefferson

Important and influential though Bartram's travels were, they had nowhere near the broad geopolitical and scientific impact of the state-sponsored seaborne voyages, particularly those of Cook. And it would not be until the Lewis and Clark Expedition of 1804–06 that an overland expedition would achieve anywhere near the impact of these British oceanic voyages. What is important to recognize, though, is that the concerns that lay behind the Lewis and Clark Expedition were present many years before it actually occurred. And while the expedition is best known for the heroism of its leaders and the abundant scientific data they collected, its origins—much like that of the 18th-century Pacific voyages—lay as much in politics as in science. Almost simultaneously with the conclusion of the American War for Independence, Thomas Jefferson—the principle architect and patron of Meriwether Lewis and William Clark's expedition—began expressing concern about the unknown American West. The main problem was that the existence of a Northwest Passage remained an open question. Jefferson feared that if such a passage were discovered by the British, they would possess a foothold for renewed imperial activity in North America. As early as 1783, Jefferson thus suggested that the Revolutionary War soldier and notorious Indian killer (and older brother of William Clark) George Rogers Clark lead a preemptive expedition to the Northwest Coast.

Nothing came of this, but Jefferson's concerns did not abate. Indeed, while serving as American minister to France, Jefferson developed a new scheme to explore and lay claim to the Far West. This one involved John Ledyard, the Connecticut-born member of Cook's final voyage. After failing to finance a fur trade expedition to the Northwest Coast, Ledyard (1751–89) found himself residing in Paris and associating with Jefferson and his expatriate American circle. His financial prospects in a freefall, Ledyard seized on Jefferson's suggestion that he traverse the North American continent from west to east. Such a journey, Jefferson hoped, would confirm once and for all the existence of a river passage from the headwaters of the Missouri west to the Pacific Ocean. It would also, Ledyard hoped, make this impoverished aspiring gentleman from Connecticut an international celebrity.

The easterly route was dictated by Jefferson's belief that it would take best advantage of the American river system. This view was informed by the colonial traveler Jonathan Carver (1710–80), whose 1778 *Travels in the Interior of North America*, and its accompanying map, seemed to indicate a single continental watershed, lying somewhere near the west-flowing headwaters of the Columbia River and the east-flowing headwaters of the Missouri. If Ledyard could make his way upstream to the single range designated by Carver as the "Shining Mountains," he would be able to quickly travel down the much-longer Missouri to the relative safety of the Mississippi Valley.

In the spring of 1787, bearing letters of introduction from Jefferson and the Marquis de Lafayette, Ledyard set out, alone and on foot. His plan was to travel across Russia and Siberia to the Kamchatka Peninsula, and from there, travel aboard a Russian fur-trading vessel to North America. It was as bold a plan as it was foolish, and the only thing surprising about it is that it did not end in Ledyard's death. After several months of diplomatic wrangling and arduous travel along Russian post roads, Ledyard reached the fur-trading entrepot of Yakutsk, some 4,000 miles east of Moscow. Prevented by winter weather from continuing his journey, a lingering Ledyard elicited the suspicion of fur merchants in the larger city of Irkutsk. Thanks to Cook, these merchants had suddenly found themselves competing for North Pacific furs for which they had, not a decade earlier, been the sole buyers. Empress Catherine II soon intervened, and Ledyard was expelled from Russia via Poland and Prussia.

Conclusion

It was the Scottish fur trader Alexander Mackenzie (1764–1820), traveling with a small party of fur trappers and Native guides, who finally traversed the North American continent in 1793. But even this successful overland journey was indicative of the fundamental fact of exploration in 18th-century North America: It was largely an oceanic undertaking. Unable to secure financing for a transcontinental voyage from the British government, Mackenzie turned to Montreal's Northwest Company, a fur-trading enterprise. But the company's interests, not surprisingly, were almost entirely commercial. An efficient route to Canada's West Coast, its directors believed, would afford a lucrative outlet for English manufactured goods, and an equally lucrative trade in Northwest Coast furs. No such route presented itself, and Mackenzie's voyage has thus also become something of a footnote to the better-known Lewis and Clark expedition. But even that expedition, with the support of the federal government and the direct patronage of the American president, had little immediate impact. It did nothing to alter British imperial ambitions, and very little to further America's, and its scientific findings took nearly a decade to appear in print.

—Edward G. Gray

Further Reading

Bartram, William. *Travels and Other Writings.* Edited by Thomas P. Slaughter. New York: Library of America, 1996.

Beaglehole, J. C. *The Exploration of the Pacific.* 3d ed. Stanford, Calif.: Stanford University Press, 1966.

———. *The Life of Captain James Cook.* Stanford, Calif.: Stanford University Press, 1974.

Carver, Jonathan. *Jonathan Carver's Travels Through America, 1766–1768: An Eighteenth-Century Explorer's Account of Uncharted America.* Edited by Norman Gelb. New York: John Wiley & Sons, 1993.

Cook, James. *The Journals of Captain James Cook.* Edited by J. C. Beaglehole. Cambridge, U.K.: Published for the Hakluyt Society by Cambridge University Press, 1955–1974.

Gibson, James R. *Otter Skins, Boston Ships, and China Goods: The Maritime Fur Trade of the Northwest Coast, 1785–1841.* Seattle: University of Washington Press, 1992.

Goetzman, William H. *New Lands, New Men: America and the Second Great Age of Discovery.* New York: Viking, 1986.

Gray, Edward G. *The Making of John Ledyard: Empire and Ambition in the Life of an Early American Traveler.* New Haven, Conn.: Yale University Press, 2007.

Howse, Derek, ed. *Background to Discovery: Pacific Exploration from Dampier to Cook.* Berkeley: University of California Press, 1990.

Jackson, Donald Dean. *Thomas Jefferson and the Stony Mountains: Exploring the West from Monticello.* Urbana: University of Illinois Press, 1981.

Ledyard, John. *The Last Voyage of Captain Cook: The Collected Writings of John Ledyard.* Edited by James Zug. Washington, D.C.: National Geographic Society, 2005.

Mackenzie, Alexander. *The Journals and Letters of Sir Alexander Mackenzie.* Edited by W. Kaye Lamb. Cambridge, U.K.: Published for the Hakluyt Society by Cambridge University Press, 1970.

Mapp, Paul. "Silver, Science, and Routes to the West: The Pacific Ocean and Eighteenth-Century French Imperial Policy." *Common-place* 5, no. 2 (January, 2005). Available online. URL: www.common-place.org/vol-05/no-02/mapp/index.shtml. Accessed March 8, 2010.

Slaughter, Thomas P. *The Natures of John and William Bartram.* New York: Alfred A. Knopf, 1996.

Taylor, Alan. "Jefferson's Pacific: The Science of Distant Empire, 1768–1811." In *Across the Continent: Jefferson, Lewis and Clark, and the Making of America*, edited by Douglas Seefeldt, Jeffrey L. Hartman, and Peter S. Onuf. Charlottesville, 2005.

Williams, Glyn. *Voyages of Delusion: The Quest for the Northwest Passage.* New Haven, Conn.: Yale University Press, 2003.

18th Century FAMILY AND CHILDHOOD

In contrast to the early decades of European settlement in America, where the divine right of authority placed king over subject, husband over wife, and parents over children, the ideas of the Enlightenment, including its questioning of divine right, effected a change in the relationships in American families. Location, religion, ethnicity, and a variety of other factors created diversity in the experiences of families and children during the 1700s, yet some general changes can be observed over the course of the century. Although many women faced pregnancy every two years, increasing their chances of dying from complications, as the 1700s progressed and mortality rates improved, more people created kinship networks, thus increasing community and family ties in many parts of the colonies. Paternal control of the family relaxed, reflecting the larger, changing political climate of the nation and the availability of new land. In American families, governing by consent assumed increasing importance, eventually creating a means by which families became not only autonomous from the community and church but that also became an essential training ground for young American citizens.

Colonial Parenting

Early in the 1700s, colonial fathers often dictated, on the basis of parental privilege, their children's education, career, and selection of a spouse. In New England, religion and control shaped family dynamics. Families did not operate independently of their community, and the community enforced both religious and social regulations. Disobedience in children was viewed as a disobedience to God, reinforcing a culture of strict paternal authority. Curbing the willfulness of small children was believed to be the key to raising children who would follow religious and social regulations. Many of the items associated with childhood during this time, such as swaddling clothes, standing stools that kept toddlers standing in one place, and leading strings intended to keep children physically constrained, also indicate a need or desire to control children's behavior. In this environment fathers and mothers demanded respect from children, and little tolerance existed for play or frivolity. By the 1700s, nonetheless, older children exhibited some increased control of their own behavior, as illustrated by the increasing rate of young women who were pregnant at the time of their marriage. But fathers could use inheritance as a control mechanism, ensuring that children remained beholden to parents until their deaths.

Not all colonists managed their homes and families according to stringent religious principles. Without the pressures of mandatory submission to authority directing their parenting, the middle colonists, especially the Quakers in Pennsylvania, were among the first to introduce permissive, more openly affectionate parenting. This type of parent-child relationship focused on childhood as a particularly important time of life, not necessarily for disciplinary reasons, but as a period for children to explore and express themselves. Unlike New England parents, who were discouraged from showing too much affection, Quakers, in particular, were not frowned upon in their communities for providing loving attention to their children.

Similarly, southern colonial families did not focus on discipline as a hallmark of child rearing. They did face, however, the worst mortality rates of any colonists. This loss of life created many combined families with stepchildren, half-children, and guardianships for orphans. Southern families in particular used a network of adults to help provide educational opportunities for their children and guardians in the event of an emergency. These networks did not necessarily include biological relatives, instead establishing fictive kin for children whose family life was disrupted.

Native American Families

Unlike their colonial neighbors, Native American children experienced permissive childhoods. Native American parents rarely physically disciplined their children and did not expect them to undertake difficult physical labor until they came through rites of passage. Each group possessed its own way of ushering children into the adult world of the tribe, including vision quests, ceremonial hunts, and menstruation huts for girls. Warfare between colonists and Native Americans and between tribes sometimes resulted in the adoption of captives to replace the deceased. Children in particular could be fully integrated into the tribe and given new parents, siblings, and an extended family. These cross-cultural adoptions caused suffering in colonial families, particularly when their kidnapped children did not wish to return to their biological families after life in a tribe.

Changing Ideas about American Families

As the century progressed, parents viewed children less as property and more as individual personalities capable of contributing more than simply labor to the household. Several factors contributed to this change, weakening the power that older generations held over their children and giving young people greater autonomy. The ideas of the Enlightenment shaped changing attitudes of family and childhood. Childhood ceased to be a period to hurry through and became a time for parents to guide children in developing their unique talents. The religious revival called the First Great Awakening (ca. 1730–55) gave young people the option to convert to faiths different from that of their parents, thereby loosening parenting control. Finally, as the American Revolution approached, colonists who believed they were treated like children by the English monarchy rethought their understanding of childhood.

Conflict also changed family dynamics. Many families suffered through the two major conflicts of the century, the French and Indian War (1754–63) and the American Revolution (1775–83), as well as other smaller conflicts between colonists and Native Americans. These trials encouraged the independent nature of Americans and also can be linked to the beginnings of change for patriarchal authority and the concept of childhood. Conflicts throughout the century resulted in westward expansion. This availability of new land, coupled with soil exhaustion from tobacco and the reduced availability of good land for farming in New England, meant that young people often moved away from their parents to start new lives.

As the historian Steven Mintz pointed out, indications other than geographic separation support the idea of changing family dynamics and increasing childhood independence. For example, during the second half of the century, naming practices of children began to change. Instead of giving children the names of dead siblings or other relatives, parents began adding middle names, a possible indication that parents respected the individuality of each child. In addition, material items designed specifically for children grew in popularity. Books and toys became an increasingly important part of education and play. Young people also stopped bowing to their parents and asking them for their blessing each morning. Devices formerly used to constrain the movement of children lost their popularity.

Although the 18th century marks an important transition in how Americans defined childhood and managed their families, many children still had to shoulder adult responsibilities at an early age. Some children worked alongside their parents on farms, while others lived with neighbors to learn farming or housekeeping. Apprenticing children to tradesmen still remained a vital form of hands-on training for adult jobs. This meant that some children faced separation from their immediate families.

The labor of children remained important for most families, but the departure or death of a parent created additional pressures on children as workers. In particular, the American Revolution placed hardships on many American families. Both Loyalists and Patriots experienced shortages of supplies, the absence of family members, and in some cases the deaths of husbands, sons, and brothers. This traumatic time meant that children took on more important work roles in their families, and some even enlisted, notwithstanding that the minimum age for the army was technically 16. At the end of the conflict, childhood took on increased importance in the new nation. In order to create a well-informed citizenry capable of self-governance, children needed to be brought up with respect for the principles of the Revolution. Women—earning the sobriquet "republican mothers"—were charged with this responsibility. In contrast to the beginning of the century, when men provided most of the instruction to children, and boys were the primary learners, in the new republic all children needed to have a basic education, and thus women held new responsibility in shaping the character of young Americans. This change brought not only new public schooling opportunities for the next century, but also more private girls' academies for education.

As the roles of parents changed, so did the roles of spouses. During the 1600s the choosing of one's spouse could be determined by a young person's parents. By the 1700s the goal of picking a loving and respectful partner based on mutual affection and consent increased in importance. The formalities of a marriage depended on location. In areas that lacked resident clergy, marriages could be celebrated without a formal ceremony. In New England the church controlled the rules surrounding marriage, including making a public a declaration of intent to marry, known as *banns*, so that objections could be raised. Regulations about marriage and divorce ultimately rested with the states in the new U.S. government, although in 1783 Congress dictated rules about divorce for the Northwest Territory in the Northwest Ordinance. In most places the laws of coverture—the idea that men controlled the property of women and represented them in government—dictated rules about marriage and inheritance for women. When states created laws regarding marriage, they limited the rights of women based on this precedent. These laws removed from the church the power to regulate marriage and gave it to the government.

Slave Families

Although the structure of family life changed for European descendants during the century, the life of slave families and children changed little, except for their increasing numbers. Slaves could not legally marry, further weakening their ability to create an immediate family structure, although informal

This lithograph from 1867 titled *Virginia One Hundred Years Ago* depicts an 18th-century Virginia plantation family visiting their slave quarters and being greeted by a family of slaves. An ever-present threat to the stability of a slave family was its possible division through the sale of a family member, the death of an owner, or the giving of a family member as a gift in a marriage settlement. *(Library of Congress)*

binding ceremonies did take place. Allowing slaves to marry would have extended a civil right available only to citizens. Slave children were expected to begin doing some work by 5 or 6 years of age. By 12 most children worked in the fields, and mortality rates remained higher than for white children during the entire century. Despite the hardships associated with life as a slave, many tried to attain some semblance of family life. Even though slave couples could not legally marry, many did live together as husband and wife, even if only a few days a month. The greatest obstacle to the slave family was its possible division through sale. As a result of the hazards of slave life, many slaves expanded their immediate family to include nonrelated people referred to as brother, sister, aunt, or uncle. This establishment of fictive kin proved important in the event that biological family members were separated by sale or death. Although the number of slave families separated by sale did not increase drastically until the 1800s, the possibility of family members being divided after the death of an owner or because they were given as gifts in a marriage settlement was threatening to family stability. The small number of free African Americans in the North managed to create immediate families and community ties within the bounds of Anglo society.

Diversity and Change

The diversity of peoples and experiences in 18th-century America created a variety of familial patterns. However, the ideology of the Revolution created an overall environment that fostered change. Education of both sexes took on increasing importance; consent and self-determination altered the relationships between children and parents; marriage focused on consent, and gradually this consent increased the property rights of women. The increasing number of slaves imported into America meant that more families faced the difficulties brought about by forced servitude. Native American families also felt the strain of American expansion as they were pushed into new territory and faced the loss of loved ones from armed conflict. While their children struggled to adjust to this new world, white American children reaped the benefits—receiving more education, experiencing fewer restraints, and gaining increasingly more time to enjoy being children. These changes, although not uniform, established trends that continued into the next century.

—Megan E. Birk

Further Reading

Calvert, Karin. *Children in the House: The Material Culture of Early Childhood, 1600–1900*. Boston: Northeastern University Press, 1992.

Cott, Nancy. *Public Vows: A History of Marriage and the Nation*. Cambridge, Mass.: Harvard University Press, 2000.

Demos, John. *A Little Commonwealth: Family Life in Plymouth Colony*. New York: Oxford University Press, 2000.

———. *The Unredeemed Captive: A Family Story from Early America*. New York: Vintage, 1995.

Frost, William J. *The Quaker Family in Colonial America: A Portrait of the Society of Friends*. New York: St. Martin's Press, 1973.

Gordon Reed, Annette. *The Hemingses of Monticello: An American Family*. New York: W. W. Norton, 2008.

Grassby, Richard. *Kinship and Capitalism: Marriage, Family, and Business in the English-Speaking World, 1580–1740*. New York: Cambridge University Press, 2001.

Gutman, Herbert. *The Black Family in Slavery and Freedom, 1750–1925*. New York: Random House, 1976.

Marten, James, ed. *Children in Colonial America*. New York: New York University Press, 2007.

Mintz, Steven. *Huck's Raft: A History of American Childhood*. Cambridge, Mass.: Belknap Press of Harvard University Press, 2004.

Morgan, Edmund S. *The Puritan Family: Religion and Domestic Relations in Seventeenth-Century New England*. New York: Harper & Row, 1966.

Smith, Daniel Blake. *Inside the Great House: Planter Family Life in Eighteenth-Century Chesapeake Society*. Ithaca, N.Y.: Cornell University Press, 1980.

18th Century FOOD

When white Americans came of age after the American Revolution, they had to perform a cultural balancing act. On the one hand they had to develop an identity that separated the new republic from Europe. The process of establishing a national persona was multifaceted and ongoing, but in general it demanded that Americans embrace the most conspicuous differences between their nascent society and the established customs of the motherland—they had, in essence, to celebrate the comparative "wildness" of the American environment. On the other hand, while young Americans eagerly sought to highlight the rough-hewn values of the frontier, they could not go so far as to identify with the wilderness "savages"—the Indians—whom they had worked so diligently to dispossess and banish. The cultural challenge of juggling European refinement and American primitiveness touched the lives of every white American. The threat of going native, balanced against the threat of falling into overcivilized luxury, consistently tempered early Americans' effort to establish their national character. It is in the context of this tension that early Americans created what we might call American cuisine.

Indeed, by the time of the American Revolution, the colonies' diverse culinary landscape had evolved into an "American" mode of eating. Distinctly regional culinary habits—habits whose differences resulted in part from racial and ethnic contributions, as well as radically different living conditions—had gently coalesced by the end of the 18th century. Increasing coastal commerce and the development of a "consumer revolution" that knew no bounds helped standardize material life, especially as it played out in the kitchen. These factors eventually helped early Americans develop their distinctive way of eating, based on the frontier "virtues" of simplicity, self-sufficiency, pragmatism, and a studied lack of pretension. By the early 1800s American cookbooks were playing increasingly important roles in American kitchens and, more important, offering middle-class women accessible recipes written, as a popular example put it, "in the American mode."

Within that American mode, a survey of the diverse diets that developed throughout the 18th century reveals regional habits reflective of distinct environmental, cultural, and agricultural backgrounds.

One Extreme: New England

New Englanders worked diligently to replicate the culinary habits of England, which were based primarily on meat (preferably beef or lamb), garden vegetables, and bread, as well as porridges, meat pies, and soups. The region's development of mixed agriculture, its lack of staple crops, and a population of middle-class settlers were all factors contributing to the broad effort to eat like proper English families. Typical households settled on modest-size farms, grew vegetable gardens and orchards, kept livestock for beef and dairy, seeded their fields with English clover grass, and cultivated as much English grain—wheat, rye, and oats—as precious labor allowed. Mixed farming demanded little foreign labor—certainly few slaves—and by the 18th century necessitated only sporadic interaction, if any, with Indians, a factor that kept New Englanders relatively insulated from alien food traditions. With their comparatively open access to the metropolis and high literacy rates, New Englanders were also more likely than other colonists to import and rely on directives found in English cookbooks and farming manuals. Their successful approximation of English ways—in matters culinary as well as others—stands as one of the region's most notable accomplishments. It was an accomplishment, moreover, that made their diet—despite a heavy reliance on Indian corn—as familiar as it could have been in a strange new world.

Another Extreme: The Lower South

Whereas New Englanders pursued as close a replica as possible of English food habits, the Lower South pioneered a nearly complete abandonment of traditional English eating customs. An intense dedication to extensive rice cultivation, a climate and environment with little resemblance to that of the homeland, a heavy reliance on slave labor, and routine interaction with Native American cultures led to a way of eating that sophisticated Europeans characterized as something close to barbaric. In essence, the demands of a staple-based plantation economy were not supportive of cultivating traditional culinary habits—too much land, labor, and culture in general was invested in rice. Carolinians, in particular, seemed to have had no trouble with their culinary diversions. And it was in the Deep South, in general, where colonists were more likely to tolerate and even celebrate meals deriving from indigenous customs.

Several examples convey this cultural predilection. "We were entertained," the English surveyor of Carolina John Lawson wrote, "with a fat boiled goose, venison, raccoon, and ground nuts." On another occasion, Lawson consumed a stew made by "Congree Indians" that consisted of "3 teal [a kind of duck] and a possum," politely pronouncing the dish "a curious ragoo." Despite the "curious" nature of the local cuisine, however, Lawson, as well as plantation-owning Carolinians, willingly adopted many of its less-refined characteristics, noting that settlers were "never wanting of a good appetite" so long as they relied on "the adjacent woods" and rivers "well-stored with fish." It is hard to imagine a proper New Englander entertaining such an adaptable attitude, one that spoke to the region's lack of traditional animal domestication and steady rotation of food crops.

The region's strong adherence to slavery further distinguished southern eating habits from the motherland and New England. With Africans and African Americans constituting a majority of the population (in some places reaching 90 percent), and with masters granting slaves land to grow their own crops (it was cheaper than importing food), African-based culinary traditions inevitably rose from the bottom up. Slave diets were quite different from that of whites initially, but as slaves developed their own food systems, whites were more likely to partake in the bounty, mixing imported food with what slaves produced on the ground (literally). Writing about "Guinea Corn," for example, the naturalist Mark Catesby noted how it was "propagated, and that chiefly by the negroes, who make a bread of it, and boil it in the manner of firmity." Once again, in terms of food, it would have been hard to find attitudes and practices more radically different from those prevailing in New England.

Between the Extremes

Other regions of the landscape that would become the United States fell between the extremes of New England and the Lower South, developing a range of culinary identities that were at once unique and reflective of other regions. The middle colonies—Pennsylvania in particular—gravitated in many ways toward the New England model of food production. It developed a cuisine commensurate with an economy based on large-scale wheat and dairy farming, an ethnically diverse population, a many-tiered labor force that included slaves and servants, and a vibrant urban-rural system of exchange. These factors, combined with the region's Quaker-inspired ethos of frugality and flexibility, inspired a diet that was measured but diverse, reliant on beef, cheese, and bread, but readily open to pork, scrapple, or corn mush.

The Chesapeake Bay region—Virginia especially—hewed closer to the Carolina model, but did not replicate it. Settlers there fashioned a cuisine that reflected the region's emphasis on tobacco, servants, and, after 1700 especially, slaves. The situation was not unlike in South Carolina, where rice determined the overall structure of the colony and, in so doing, left whites to explore an amalgam of food traditions, by which they blended the traditional with the unfamiliar. The difference, though, is that the smaller slave population, and the fact that slaves generally did not have their own gardens, led to the Virginians favoring tradition over adaptation. Wine, sherry, fresh beef, and occasional supplies of vegetables and fruit allowed at least the wealthier English colonists to approximate some aspects of traditional English cuisine. Most other residents of this region, however, remained comparatively dependent on what the wilderness offered (in food or animal forage), what Native Americans traded, or what the masters had left over, thus reflecting the habits of their cohorts down south. Large quantities of salted pork, cornmeal, and wild game were the norm for many Virginians and Marylanders.

Culinary Convergence

While these local modes of eating persisted, a more cohesive way of eating began to emerge in the years just preceding the Revolution. Two main factors contributed to this convergence: the increase in intercoastal trade and the rising availability of British goods. Trade up and down the East Coast developed on the back of the rum and molasses trade that flourished between the mainland and Barbados after 1720. By the 1750s, colonists, especially those who lived along the coast, were regularly enjoying access to food from other regions. Okra, for example, made its way from South Carolina to Rhode Island. Virginian ham sold in South Carolina. New England cod went to the middle colonies. Pennsylvania sent pork and butter throughout the colonies. By the 1770s, regional ingredients had become, as a result of the increasingly systematic nature of intercolonial trade, much less localized. An intercolonial food exchange was under way, and a more uniform way of eating was one result. Regional differences slowly become less pronounced and, to an extent, more reflective of the mother country.

The dispersal of what had once been strictly local ingredients was due in part to the growing uniformity of the colonial cooking experience. Utensils, recipes, and kitchen space throughout British America began to look increasingly alike. The reasons had to do with supply, demand, and cultural imperatives. "It is really possible," wrote a German visitor to the colonies in the 1750s, "to obtain all the things one can get in Europe in Pennsylvania." This observer was noting a commercial trend that historians have since called a "consumer revolution." He was speaking of Philadelphia, but he could just as easily have been referring to other stopping points on the East Coast, including New York, Charleston, Boston, Newport, or Baltimore. With rising colonial incomes and declining prices of English durable goods, white Americans after 1730 significantly enhanced their collective living standard to include, among other luxuries, expanded kitchens stocked with primitive potbelly/six-plate stoves, English cooking tools, tables and chairs, and English cookbooks. These accoutrements supported a material transformation that allowed English colonists to approximate British metropolitan life with some level of accuracy. As Ben Franklin put it in the late 1760s, colonists "had not only a respect, but an affection, for Great Britain, for its laws, its customs, and manners." Buying from the motherland was crucial to this broader identity, one that cut across regional deviations. This connection applied especially well to food and cooking. Ironically, on the eve of Revolution, colonists were enjoying access to more ingredients, as well as the English utensils and cooking

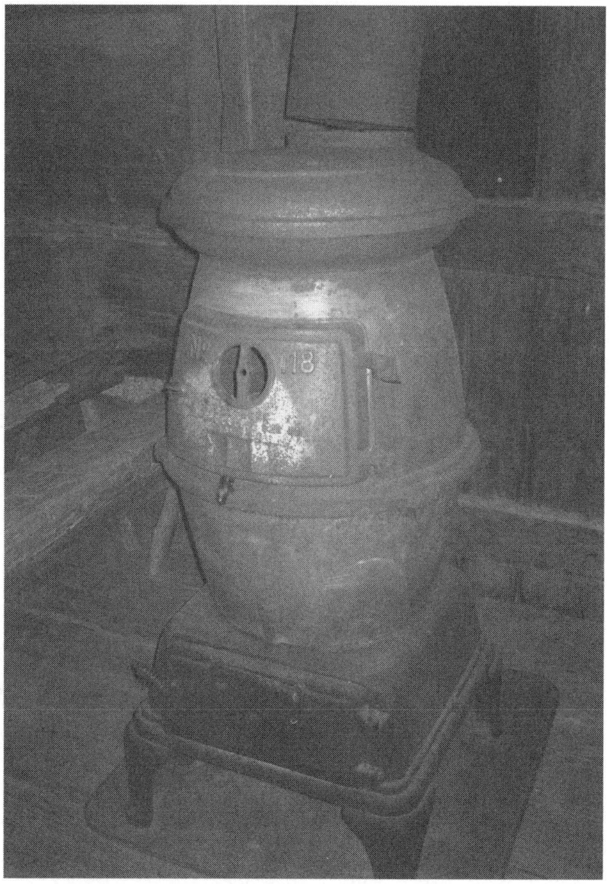

Toward the middle of the century, white Americans' living standards rose significantly thanks to rising colonial incomes and declining prices of English durable goods. The expansion of available kitchen accoutrements during the so-called consumer revolution allowed English colonists to mimic the trappings of British metropolitan life with relative ease. There were potbelly stoves similar to the one pictured above in a select handful of households by the 1730s. ***(Ewlyahoocom)***

manuals, that enabled them to anglicize the relatively rough-hewn cuisine, of which many were often ashamed.

For all the colonists' success in replicating English eating habits during the consumer revolution, the Revolutionary War put an abrupt halt to the transition from provinciality to metropolitan sophistication. Just when British America was beginning to feel integrated into the cultural patterns of the empire, politics intervened. The empire's unwelcome infringements—taxes, for example—turned Americans into reluctant but committed revolutionaries. Independence, in turn, inspired political changes that rapidly redefined America—despite its 750,000 slaves—as the pinnacle of genuine, rather than feigned, liberty. This development posed a profound cultural problem that had tremendous implications for the young American identity. The United States had a general idea what its new political system would look like. It had no idea, however, what its new cultural values would be. In critical ways, colonists turned to food to seek answers.

An Early American Cuisine

Expressing cultural identity through food allowed Americans to seek a balance between refinement and wilderness. Promoting his play *The Father* in 1789, William Dunlap advertised the production as "a frugal plain repast," in contrast to the "high seasoned food" offered by European playwrights. The comparison was apt. In America, thoughts about proper food began with virtuous qualities such as frugality, roughness, flexibility, and a radical openness to experimentation. American cuisine, as a reflection of the American people, was touted as pragmatic, self-sufficient, adaptable, and completely lacking in artifice.

Whether any of this was actually the case is beside the point. The mere fact that Americans were actively promoting their food as a distinct contrast to fussy and overrefined European cuisine highlights a defining aspect of an emerging national identity. Whereas many colonists, especially those in the North, had spent much of the colonial era trying to minimize the ruggedness of American life, early Americans now began to celebrate it, although in a much more measured fashion than before. Few white Americans (including many southerners) were willing to champion the extreme culinary examples provided by the rural South. Nevertheless, early Americans, consciously or not, promoted dietary habits embracing the tolerance and flexibility that enabled southerners to accept Native American and African influences on their diet and, in turn, transform English inherited practices into American culinary creations. At the same time, they eschewed the refinement New Englanders had long sought, without completely rejecting their habits. Again, the goal was to strike a balance.

The new American diet was more a way of thinking about food than it was a transition to a specific list of foods or defining dishes. Evidence of early Americans achieving a balance between tradition and contemporary conditions—that is, embracing an adaptive attitude toward food—appears frequently enough to offer a sense of this change. Patrick Henry condemned Thomas Jefferson's taste for fine French food, warning him never to "abjure his native victuals." A British foreign minister invited to dine with James Madison in 1777 remarked that the meal "was more like a harvest home supper than the entertainment of the Secretary of State." Jefferson, who occasionally brewed beer from corn, explained to a friend that "I have no recept [recipe] for brewing and I doubt if the operations of malting and brewing could be successfully performed from a receipt." In other words, conditions and ingredients varied. One had to adapt.

These examples reveal Americans walking a fine line between European refinement and provincial ruggedness. Without consciously doing so, Americans were drawing on two deeply engrained elements of their diverse culinary heritage as they expanded westward, confronted new "wild" territories, and worked to subdue the wilderness. The rough nature of the colonial frontier, which English Americans once associated with the indigenous population, became a national characteristic that early Americans could now, with the British model dissipating, embrace with measured enthusiasm. Likewise, the refinement of the idealized English (and European) diet was now a quality that young Americans could overtly condemn—rather than praise, as they once had—without completely dismissing its welcome trappings. Through the virtues that American food embraced—frugality, simplicity, pragmatism, unpretentiousness—the United States could grow into an upstanding nation while avoiding the enervating habit of oversophistication into which the British had fallen. It could announce, as Thomas Jefferson did, "how unripe we yet are," all the while knowing that ripeness, like an overly refined cuisine, was something to avoid. Most importantly, they could strike this balance by growing, cooking, and eating food.

—James E. McWilliams

Further Reading

Baron, Stanley. *Brewed in America: A History of Beer and Ale in the United States.* Little, Brown, 1962.

Breen, T. H. *Tobacco Culture: The Mentality of the Great Tidewater Planters on the Eve of the Revolution.* Princeton, N.J.: Princeton University Press, 1985.

Clark, Peter. *The English Alehouse: A Social History, 1200–1830.* New York: Longman, 1983.

Conroy, David. *In Public Houses: Drink and the Revolution of Authority in Colonial Massachusetts.* Chapel Hill: University of North Carolina Press, 1995.

Cronon, William. *Changes in the Land: Indians, Colonists, and the Ecology of New England.* New York: Hill & Wang, 1983.

Fischer, David Hackett. *Albion's Seed: Four British Folkways in America.* New York: Oxford University Press, 1989.

Greene, Jack P. *Pursuits of Happiness.* Chapel Hill: University of North Carolina Press, 1988.

Hess, Karen. *The Carolina Rice Kitchen: The African Connection.* Columbia: University of South Carolina Press, 1992.

Jones, Evan. *American Food: The Gastronomic Story.* New York: Dutton, 1981.

Littlefield, Daniel C. *Rice and Slaves: Ethnicity and the Slave Trade in Colonial South Carolina.* Champaign: University of Illinois Press, 1991.

McMahon, Sarah F. "A Comfortable Subsistence: The Changing Composition of Diet in Rural New England." *William and Mary Quarterly*, 3d series, 42 (January 1985): 26–65.

McWilliams, James E. *A Revolution in Eating: How the Quest for Food Shaped America.* New York: Columbia University Press, 2005.

Merrell, James H. *Into the American Woods: Negotiations on the Pennsylvania Frontier.* New York: W. W. Norton, 1999.

Morgan, Philip D. *Slave Counterpoint: Black Culture in the Eighteenth-Century Chesapeake and Lowcountry.* Chapel Hill: University of North Carolina Press, 1998.

Thompson, Peter. *Rum Punch and Revolution: Taverngoing and Public Life in Eighteenth-Century Philadelphia.* Philadelphia: University of Pennsylvania Press, 1999.

Ulrich, Laurel Thatcher. *The Age of Homespun: Objects and Stories in the Creation of an American Myth.* New York: Oxford University Press, 2001.

18th Century FOREIGN AFFAIRS

From 1700 to 1763, the American colonies followed the rest of the British Empire in maintaining a hostile relationship with the French, Spanish, and most Native American nations. This hostility grew out of European imperial rivalries.

By the 1740s, all three empires (British, French, and Spanish) claimed large, overlapping frontier zones from the Caribbean to Canada, further encouraging conflict. British victory in the Seven Years' War (1756–63) appeared to seal North America's fate, but the problems of imperial governance led instead to the American Revolution and another round of European war. The realities of the imperial crisis caused the rebellious colonists to seek French, Spanish, Dutch, and even Native alliances, albeit under duress. This continued haphazardly until the outbreak of the French Revolution, which split the American polity and ultimately led America into a hostile relationship and the Quasi-War with France at the end of the century.

Securing the Frontier: 1700–1739

At the beginning of the 18th century, colonial Americans would find themselves in a situation that would become all too familiar, enmeshed in a war generated by dynastic and imperial rivalries in Europe. As colonies, they had no autonomous foreign policy and no control over international relations. The primary thrust of colonial governments' diplomacy, such as it was, was to attempt to parlay with the various Native tribes and nations on their borders, in order to thwart the considerable French influence over them. During Queen Anne's War (1702–13), Indian raiding was a top security concern for New Englanders, whose forces were deployed attacking French maritime Canada. Colonial governments repeatedly, and usually unsuccessfully, tried to lure the Native populations away from alliances with the French, whose interest in fur trading and tendency to intermarry with Native people gave them strong alliances with the Indian nations.

The expansion of the population farther inland in the 1720s and 1730s provided the context for continued diplomacy between the colonial governments and Native Americans. For example, New York joined with the Iroquois League in 1727 in building a post at Oswego on Lake Ontario. In some cases, colonial governors provided elaborate entertainments for visiting Native "princes." In 1753, for instance, a Cherokee delegation visiting Williamsburg, Virginia, on a diplomatic mission was treated with a performance of Shakespeare's *Othello* as well as mock sword fighting and fireworks. From around 1710 onward, Native leaders would also sometimes visit London and be received by dignitaries, including, in some cases, the sitting monarchs.

This expansion also brought the settlers of the three major European empires into geographic proximity with one another, often on land whose ownership was unclear. This proximity became, in more than one instance, the source of diplomatic tensions in Europe. Such tensions heightened interest in diplomacy with Amerindian nations, but it also foreshadowed renewed warfare among the European powers that would entangle the Native populations as well.

War, Diplomacy, and Empire: 1739–1775

In 1739, 26 years of nominal peace between Britain, France, and Spain gave way to a quarter-century of imperial rivalry, including the War of Jenkins' Ear (1739–48), King George's War (1744–48), and the French and Indian War (1754–63). These wars reflected conflicts over control of trade in Spanish America, the struggle for dominance in India, and the three-power rivalry for control of the interior of North America.

The reality of imperial warfare led the colonists and the London government to renew their efforts to reach diplomatic accords with the Native American nations. This became an especially important goal in the period before and during the Seven Years' War. For example, London approved of the Albany Congress of 1754, where colonial politicians parlayed with Iroquois leaders in an effort to restore the Covenant Chain, the alliance between the Iroquois and British North Americans.

While generally concerned with defending the colonies, British officials sometimes ignored colonial interests. British Americans generally resented the return of the French fortress of Louisbourg in Canada that had been approved of by British diplomats in the Treaty of Aix-la-Chapelle in 1748. The 1763 Treaty of Paris, which enabled the drawing of the Proclamation Line of 1763, effectively barring British Americans from settling the lands west of the Allegheny Mountains won from the French, is another example of the same phenomenon. Ultimately, British diplomats served the interests of the British government, and of the empire as a whole, while colonial needs were often subordinate in the equation.

Hampered by debts from the midcentury wars, and following the example of their European competitors, the British leadership under King George III hoped to centralize the colonial administration in the mid-1760s. In conjunction with renewed enforcement of the Navigation Acts passed a century earlier, the Sugar Act (1764), Stamp Act (1765), and Townshend Acts (1767) all sought greater revenue from the colonies in order to retire the British national debt and pay for the regular troops stationed in British America, while also extending greater control over the colonies. Colonists opposing British taxes and regulations provoked violent confrontations in the Boston Massacre (1770) and *Gaspee* Affair (1772). Protests over the Tea Act of 1773, culminating in the Boston Tea Party, convinced the British that the colonies were increasingly ungovernable. In response, Parliament passed the Coercive Acts (or "Intolerable" Acts) of 1774, designed to punish the rebellious colonies, which began the political spiral into the war of the American Revolution.

From British Colonies to the United States: 1775–1800

Under the weight of British political pressure, thousands of colonists joined a rebellion against the mother country in 1775–76. The Revolutionary War (1775–83) fundamentally changed the relationship with Great Britain and created a new diplomatic reality for the emergent American nation, which was now allied with its former enemies, the French and Spanish, against its mother country.

As early as 1775, American agents were searching for European assistance. Once the rebellion began, Americans quickly sought to establish relations with other countries. The writing of the Declaration of Independence was driven in part by the need to formally establish the imperial separation, in order to parlay formally with European powers. Early in 1776, the French and Spanish governments refused open support for the rebel colonies, but through Pierre de Beaumarchais and the American envoy Silas Deane, they arranged for the secret transfer of arms, munitions, and other military stores to American forces. By December 1776, Arthur Lee and Benjamin Franklin had joined Deane in Paris, and they used threats of reconciliation with Great Britain to goad France into open alliance. The French monarch, Louis XVI, signed a treaty with the new nation in 1777, shortly after the American victory at the Battle of Saratoga, and a French declaration of war followed in 1778. Spain joined the war in 1779, and in 1780 the British, fearing Dutch intervention, declared war on the Netherlands.

By 1783, Americans had achieved their independence on the ground, and the Treaty of Paris confirmed their gains. Both they and the French retained a sentimental attachment to the alliance of 1778, and American diplomats in Europe and North Africa worked quickly to build good relations with other powers. Franklin represented American interests in Sweden in 1782–83, Prussia offered early recognition, and trade relations were soon opened with the German free cities of Hamburg and Bremen. By 1785, friendly relations with Morocco eased American entry into the Mediterranean, setting the stage for American opposition to the Barbary corsairs around the turn of the 19th century.

Despite these turns in its favor, the young United States remained insecure between two large colonial empires, with Britain to the north and Spain to the south and west. Anglo-American relations remained tense, as ambiguous provisions in the Treaty of Paris gave room for mutual suspicion. Americans continued to confiscate

Once the rebellion against Britain began, American agents sought to secure European assistance in their struggle. Benjamin Franklin was one such agent, and he helped goad France into open support of the Revolutionary cause. In the above print, Franklin bows as he greets the French king Louis XVI at Versailles on March 20, 1778. ***(Library of Congress)***

Loyalist property and collect on Loyalist debts, while press gangs at sea still forced Americans to serve in the Royal Navy. In addition, British forces retained control of forts in the Great Lakes region that were supposed to have been ceded to the infant republic. To the south, a resurgent Spanish Empire eyed further gains in Georgia, Alabama, Mississippi, and Tennessee. And as long as Americans remained lightly settled in the trans-Appalachian West, both colonial empires saw the opportunity to support Native American opposition to the new republic.

The first major threat to American independence came neither from Britain nor from Spain, however, but from France. In its early phases, from 1789 to 1792, the French Revolution was welcomed by most Americans, along with the possibility of alliance with a sister republic. In 1793, Citizen Edmond Genêt, the new French envoy to the United States, exploited this popularity with a tour across the Atlantic seaboard, starting in Charleston, South Carolina. President George Washington had issued a neutrality proclamation on April 22, 1793, hoping to stay out of Europe's War of the First Coalition. Genêt recruited individual Americans for privateering against British vessels, however, and for a colonial war against Spain. Genêt's activities provoked a constitutional crisis and protests from President Washington, but when a new French government recalled Genêt early in 1794, Alexander Hamilton extended one of the young republic's first offers of asylum.

The end of the Genêt Affair opened new opportunities for the United States, which Hamilton and Washington quickly seized. They instructed John Jay, their envoy in London, to ask the British for better compliance with the 1783 Treaty of Paris. Despite his weak negotiating position, Jay benefited from Britain's ongoing war against France. By the end of 1794, the Jay Treaty confirmed substantial British concessions in North America and the Atlantic. Though American public opinion was split, if not enflamed, by the treaty, in Europe it led to further American success. By 1795, Charles Pinckney, the American envoy to Spain, reported a treaty of his own, with Spain surrendering its ambitions in the trans-Appalachian Southwest.

These diplomatic victories in Europe had important ramifications for the American frontier. Informally backed by the British, Indians in the Northwest Territory had defeated American expeditions led by Arthur St. Clair and Josiah Harmar in 1791–92. By 1794, negotiations with Great Britain encouraged that nation to withdraw its support of the Native tribes, allowing Anthony Wayne to achieve greater success in the Northwest, and the treaties of 1794–95 formally ended European support for Native Americans in the West. Tennessee joined the Union in 1796, and Americans in general surged across the Appalachians.

In the wake of American reconciliation with both Britain and Spain, ties with France grew worse. With a young Napoleon Bonaparte leading its armies into Italy, France again invoked the alliance of 1778. Beginning in 1797, however, President John Adams sought to continue

Washington's policy of neutrality—a stance that led to the undeclared Quasi-War with France from 1798 to 1800. Although Adams maintained the United States' official neutrality, the investment of his political capital cost him the election of 1800, and Thomas Jefferson's administration reversed the brief progress of Anglo-American relations.

In sum, the United States emerged during the 18th century as a continental empire largely secure against attacks by Native Americans but still vulnerable to the throes of European imperial politics. Early in the century, Britain's North American colonies faced down the Indian threat and secured a larger territorial frontier. By 1763, the colonies' expansion brought much stronger intervention by Great Britain in North American affairs and a decisive defeat to Britain's imperial competitors in the region. Subsequent British mismanagement helped provoke the American Revolution, however, leaving a weak but independent United States. Through a policy of neutrality and dexterous diplomacy, the young republic survived amid competing European empires and set the stage for further expansion.

—Brendan McConville

Further Reading

Anderson, Fred. *Crucible of War: The Seven Years' War and the Fate of Empire in British North America, 1754–1766.* New York: Alfred A. Knopf, 2000.

———. *The War That Made America: A Short History of the French and Indian War.* New York: Viking, 2005.

Banks, Kenneth. *Chasing Empire across the Sea: Communications and the State in the French Atlantic, 1713–1763.* Montreal: McGill–Queens University Press, 2002.

Bemis, Samuel Flagg. *Diplomacy of the American Revolution.* New York: Appleton-Century, 1935. Reprint, Bloomington: Indiana University Press, 1957.

Casto, William. *Foreign Affairs and the Constitution in the Age of Fighting Sail.* Columbia: University of South Carolina Press, 2006.

Dull, Jonathan R. *Diplomatic History of the American Revolution.* New Haven, Conn.: Yale University Press, 1985.

Estes, Todd. *The Jay Treaty Debate, Public Opinion, and the Evolution of Early American Political Culture.* Amherst: University of Massachusetts Press, 2006.

Franklin, Benjamin. *The Autobiography and Other Writings.* London: Penguin Classics, 1986.

Frazier, Patrick. *The Mohicans of Stockbridge.* Lincoln: University of Nebraska Press, 1992.

Hamilton, Alexander, James Madison, and John Jay. *The Essential Federalist and Anti-Federalist Papers.* New York, Classic Books America, 2009.

Hinderaker, Eric. *Elusive Empires: Constructing Colonialism in the Ohio Valley, 1673–1800.* Cambridge, U.K.: Cambridge University Press, 1997.

Mauduit, Israel. *Considerations on the Present German War.* London: John Wilkie, 1760.

Preston, David. *The Texture of Contact: European and Indian Settler Communities on the Frontier of Iroquoia, 1667–1783.* Lincoln: University of Nebraska Press, 2009.

Shy, John. *A People Numerous and Armed: Reflections on the Military Struggle for American Independence.* Rev. ed. Ann Arbor: University of Michigan Press, 1990.

Silver, Peter. *Our Savage Neighbors: How Indian War Transformed Early America.* New York: W. W. Norton, 2009.

Simms, Brendan. *Three Victories and a Defeat: The Rise and Fall of the First British Empire.* London: Basic Books, 2008.

Stagg, J. C. A. *Borderlines in Borderlands: James Madison and the Spanish-American Frontier, 1776–1821.* New Haven, Conn.: Yale University Press, 2009.

Taylor, Alan. *American Colonies: The Settling of North America.* New York: Viking, 2001.

Ward, Matthew. *Breaking the Backcountry: The Seven Years' War in Virginia and Pennsylvania, 1754–1765.* Pittsburgh, Pa.: University of Pittsburgh Press, 2004.

White, Richard. *The Middle Ground: Indians, Empires, and Republics in the Great Lakes Region, 1650–1815.* Cambridge, U.K.: Cambridge University Press, 1991.

18th Century GENDER AND GENDER ROLES

Gender, an interlocking set of ideas about what did and what should make men and women different from one another, as well as what characteristics defined masculinity and femininity, was a critical component of 18th-century thought. In 18th-century America, gender was important to how people lived day to day: their family life, their work, and their religion. It was important to how their society was shaped politically, socially, and economically. Gender not only reflected beliefs about masculine and feminine qualities and behavior, but also a hierarchy of values attached to those ideas that ranked male over female. Gender, like other cultural values and ideals, was *prescriptive* but not always *predictive* of human behavior.

Eighteenth-century people used gendered language to express ideas about particular men and women and their behavior, particularly sexuality. They also used gendered language to describe arenas of human interaction including war and politics. In the 18th century the French and Indian War, the American Revolution, and efforts to create a new American government, for example, were all discussed and interpreted in light of new ideas and concerns about gender. While novels of the period exhibited new forms of marriage, contrasting arranged marriages with marriages of love, a parallel description emerged during the American Revolution of "tyrannical" arranged marriages and "despotic" monarchical government. Through their words and their actions, men and women helped give shape and substance to gender as a system of ideas and practices.

Ideas about gender had strong, traditional European components but were not necessarily fixed. As these ideas encountered new circumstances and new challenges in colonial and early national America—challenges such as slavery, race, and war—people contested them. Some scholars have noted a connection between 18th-century ideas about gender and ideas about race or status. In the British North American colonies, English ideas about manhood, for example, came to express ideas about *white* masculinity and measured all men against that standard. The value placed on men's independence came to stand not just for political or economic independence, but also to distinguish free, white men from enslaved black men. Likewise, both positive and negative cultural values associated with femininity took on racial overtones.

English Household and Gender Ideals in America

Eighteenth-century English ideas about gender were especially influential in 18th-century America. These ideas derived from long cultural traditions and Protestant religious teachings and centered on the roles of men and women in the patriarchal, or male-controlled, household. An adult man was expected to be the head of his household and responsible for all his dependents, including his wife, their children, and any servants. Men were expected to be the major providers for their family. By law, men controlled their family's wealth and directed its labor. Male heads of household were the primary political actors in a community.

An adult married woman was her husband's helpmate, but she was subordinate to him, by law and custom. Women were expected to be submissive, modest, and good housekeepers. Women often worked to help support their families, but what income they produced was the property of their husbands, and they could have no formal role in politics. Women were supposed be virtuous and especially careful of their sexual character; a young woman's chastity was essential to her reputation. While men were expected to be rational and moderate, society expected women to be more emotional.

Both men and women were expected to display the virtues of good Christians, but each according to his or her role. Protestant religious teachings emphasized the importance of the household and elevated the role of the male household head. Household heads were to lead religious instruction in the home, modeling good Christian behavior, reading from the central text, the Bible, and ensuring the proper behavior of their dependents. Just as male householders composed the collective political body of a community, they were the key to the authority of a religious community.

These rigid roles informed how 18th-century people organized the daily acts of family and work, in addition to how they evaluated behavior as appropriately masculine or feminine. Men and women were expected to marry; stereotypes about effeminate bachelors and unattractive spinsters confirmed these expectations. Women were responsible for the care of children, while men were responsible for the appropriate religious (and other) education of their sons and daughters. Boys and girls were trained to fulfill their respective household positions and carry out the accompanying social, economic, and political duties. By many measures, more women acted religiously than did men, by joining churches and by filling the pews each day of worship. But their role in the conventional Protestant churches that dominated British America was, like their role in households, subordinate.

Labor was divided along gendered lines. Ideally men and women were expected to fulfill distinct but complementary work roles, although in practical terms women did as much physically arduous labor as men, and often the same types of work. For example, on farms fieldwork was a male job, but it often required all available hands. Women were primarily responsible for household labor involving children, food, and clothing, as well as some specific garden and dairying, while men were responsible for extra-household labor. On a farm that meant field and livestock work, while in more urban areas it might mean artisanal or professional work. Under particular circumstances these spheres of work might overlap; a shopkeeper's wife, for example, might be expected to spend time working with goods or customers, and a master shoemaker or cooper's wife would help feed and house any apprentices or servants that helped with her husband's work. Widows, particularly in cities, might take over areas of their late husband's business. But these were exceptional situations, and acceptable because they were exceptional.

Other Cultural Influences

English household models of gender were mostly, but not entirely, shared by other European cultures. Among the Dutch, for example, women enjoyed a more powerful position in the household and within property law. When the English took over the Dutch colony of New York and English law superseded Dutch law in the late 17th and early 18th centuries, those comparative advantages disappeared.

Some religious groups altered aspects of English household-based gender ideals. Quakers, for example, who were prominent in the Mid-Atlantic region, particularly Pennsylvania, upended some standard English ideas about gender. Quakers believed in the equality of souls (male and female, black and white), which many Protestants emphasized but few translated into social practice. The Quaker faithful embraced women in their ministry and in the governance of their church. These ideas and practices were so contrary to English cultural traditions that Quakers themselves felt the tension keenly. Prominent and wealthy Quakers wrote about difficulty in observing both English practices of gender hierarchy and Quaker equalitarianism.

Gender and Racial Ideas

English and other European ideas about gender and household continued to shape how colonials evaluated and understood the Native American communities they encountered. Among the first European observations about Native Americans were remarks on the different ways in which Indians organized labor and family life. In most Indian communities, agriculture was the women's province, and in many such communities village centers were female space because men were so often absent—exactly the reverse of European models. Europeans viewed these differences as markers of the inferiority of Indian culture and tried to enforce practices among Indians that would better conform to European standards.

Europeans also interpreted African men and women in light of their own standards of gender and sexuality. Roughly similar to Native American groups, Africans seem to have had complementary male and female patterns of work responsibility, and women played an important role in agricultural societies. Europeans interpreted these patterns as perverse—an inversion of appropriate gender roles. Even as Europeans went about organizing the enslavement of African women and men and expropriating their labor, they explained the distinctions between black people and white people in gendered and sexualized terms that they felt could justify this violence. For example, the historian Jennifer Morgan points out that Felix Spoeri, writing in 1661, remarked that the African women he observed in Barbados were capable of breast-feeding their children even as they worked in the fields: "When slave mothers go to work, they tie the young children across their backs. While they work they frequently give their children the breast, across the armpits, and let them suckle." Putting African women to work in the fields—work that generally was not associated with women in European culture—already suggested that African women were to be seen as distinct from European women. To suggest that African women could do "men's work" and nurse their children at the same time similarly suggested there was something about their physical and emotional capacity that was different from white women. Thus "women's work" could be preserved for white women—and the categories of gender further refined along racial lines.

Gender, Law, and Economy

Rigid ideas about men's and women's distinct nature and responsibilities could lead to other forms of coercion. Europe's long history of witchcraft accusations and panics traded in part on ideas about gender, particularly in denigrating older women perceived to be inappropriately powerful. In America, men seen as insufficiently masculine and women seen as insufficiently feminine were mocked, gossiped about, or worse. A good reputation, and one that conformed to these gendered ideals, was crucial for men in getting and retaining credit, for example. Young women's marriageability was largely dependent on their good reputation. One measure of the importance of a good reputation, measured according to standards of gender, is the large number of slander suits that appeared regularly in colonial courts in which gender and sexuality were at issue.

Other aspects of law and the court system were influenced by concepts of men's and women's character and behavior. In New England, strongly Puritan forms of legal proceedings in the 17th century had held men and women to roughly the same standards of sexual behavior. By the 18th century, under the influence of more strictly English-style law, courts were prosecuting women for sexual misbehavior (especially when they bore children out of wedlock) but not men. "Fornication" cases, which generally constituted the largest number of criminal cases in county courts, became a way for the community to discipline the sexual conduct of young, unmarried women, while they cast young men's sexual behavior as more acceptable. As the historian Cornelia Hughes Dayton pointed out, this 18th-century double standard pressed particularly hard on women from poorer backgrounds, whose families did not have the resources to protect them either from a court appearance or from the reputation of sexual looseness, which more often was attached to them than to young women from wealthier families.

The expanding, more commercial economy of the 18th century was probably responsible for these changes in the court culture. Earlier courts, under Puritan influence, had been deeply invested in having both men and women repent what they saw as sinful behavior, while later courts were more interested in protecting men's creditable commercial reputations; thus fornication became largely seen as a female crime. Also, as the 18th century progressed, women constituted a smaller proportion of litigants involved in debt suits, because women were less likely to be involved in the geographically extensive network of credit relations that was becoming more important than the local, more intimate creditor-debtor relations in which they had played a larger role. Many women kept small shops in busy port cities, retailing cloth and foodstuffs, for instance, which required engaging in local, face-to-face credit exchanges. Few women, however, were wholesalers or merchants arranging coastal or transatlantic shipments, involving more-impersonal long-distance credit that relied on masculine evaluations of "creditworthiness."

In a commercial economy, men worried a lot about how they cultivated and portrayed their reputation. Money was at stake. Merchants carefully crafted their communications to highlight qualities associated with masculinity. Business success relied on this masculine reputation, and, as one merchant noted explicitly, business failures could leave one "unmanned." Manly honor, reliability, and mastery were the stuff of success. In regularly using this sort of language, merchants helped perpetuate the notion that gender and the expanding credit economy—which they were also crucial in facilitating—were linked. Men's good credit, they were saying, was the key to this new economy. And by saying so, they helped make it so.

Gender and Wartime

The language of masculinity was mobilized in other important contexts throughout the 18th century, including very prominently in times of war. The two most significant conflicts of the century, the Seven Years' War (called, in the colonies, the French and Indian War) and the American Revolution, both drew on ideas about gender to explain the deteriorating relationships among the opposing parties and the violence that ensued. The Seven Years' War was the last and greatest in a series of wars that engulfed the colonies in North America in the territorial competition among European empires. The French and the British competed for Indian allies in this as in earlier wars. Especially hard hit was Pennsylvania, the western areas of which lay between British and French claims and included important river access to the French colonies in both Canada and Louisiana. In Pennsylvania, political groups disagreed about the causes and necessity of war, as well as who should pay for the colony's defense, even as violence between colonists and Indians in the backcountry increased. Those disagreements were not only expressed in gendered terms, but also reflected different ideas about how masculinity should be expressed in wartime.

Masculine qualities associated with war, such as aggression or bravery, were by no means the only appeals to masculinity. The historian Nicole Eustace points out that during a debate about raising taxes for military expenses, for example, the Speaker of the Pennsylvania Assembly, the Quaker Isaac Norris, cast aspersions on the unwillingness of the colony's proprietor Thomas Penn to pay more taxes himself. "How odious it must be," Norris asserted, "to a sensible manly People, to find *him* who ought to be their Father and Protector, taking Advantage of Publick Calamity and Distress, and their Tenderness for their bleeding Country, to force down their Throats, Laws of Imposition, abhorrent to common Justice and common Reason!" Norris's characterization of the men of the colony ("a sensible manly People") and his derision of the proprietor ("him who ought to be . . . Father and Protector") both turned on an understanding of masculine responsibilities. He invoked the political and moral responsibility of colonial householders to hold their leaders to account in the service of protecting their families and communities. And he invoked the proprietor's failure to uphold his patriarchal responsibility for the people of Pennsylvania.

Another example comes from the aftermath of the war, when a group of backcountry men known as the Paxton Boys murdered peaceful Indians in retaliation for their perceived assistance to other Indians who were attacking colonial settlements during what was called Pontiac's Rebellion. The Paxton Boys seemed to flaunt an image of frontier masculinity, justifying their violence with the claim that they only killed enemies of the colony. Reactions from other Pennsylvanians involved images of both gender and status. Benjamin Franklin called the Paxtons "savage white Christians" in rebuke, clearly implying it was they, not the Indians, who were the savages. Franklin's terminology played on elite Philadelphians' and others' notions of backcountry settlers as less civilized men than themselves. Ideas about how warfare reflected and produced the best and the worst in men and women were important throughout this and other conflicts.

Both before and during the American Revolution, the politics of gender became entwined in the contests over independence. Patriot women were encouraged to show appropriately feminine support for their cause, often through their production, consumption, or nonconsumption of household goods. Key British imports targeted for boycott, including cloth and tea, already were associated with women. For decades writers had drawn attention to the ways that tea parties, somewhat like the famous salons of Europe, could become forums in which women might exercise covert social and maybe even political power. These writers cast aspersions on the ways that, by bringing together groups of people in a private setting for conversation, elite women's tea parties created a feminine forum that was unsupervised by men, and in fact when men entered that space they were supervised by women. In an episode that left only a few traces in the historical record, women in Edenton, North Carolina, seemed to fulfill all these cultural anxieties. In 1774 more than 50 women organized a tea party at which they determined to boycott tea and crafted a statement of their intent, in hopes of encouraging others to follow their example. Early the next year a print claiming to depict "A Society of Patriotic Ladies, at Edenton in North Carolina" was printed in a London magazine. The image showed some of the women with sharply masculine faces and seated at a table under which a dog was lifting its leg on a cask of tea and licking the face of a neglected child. Tea, then, was not only a British product whose taxation the colonists resented, but a product that could be used in an activity that was potentially subversive of gender roles.

The infamous print titled "A Society of Patriotic Ladies, at Edenton in North Carolina" appeared in a London magazine in 1775 and satirized the organized boycott of English tea by a group of more than 50 Edenton women. The masculine-faced boycotters are depicted not only as being unfeminine in their political activities but also as neglectful mothers, as the lone child under the table suggests. ***(Library of Congress)***

Women's production and wearing of homespun yarn and cloth became associated with Revolutionary-era patriotism. Spinning and weaving were important parts of women's household labor, particularly in New England (in contrast to England and Europe, where weaving was male work). As important as it was for a family economy, homespun could rarely provide enough cloth to meet all a family's needs, and the volume of cloth imported from Britain increased over the first three-quarters of the 18th century. But during the Revolutionary era, cloth, like tea, was an economically and symbolically important target of the boycott. Homespun cloth was associated with independence, and women's spinning was promoted as an act of patriotic virtue. Community spinning bees, often organized by ministers as charity work, sprang up to supply needier families with similarly patriotic garb—though in some accounts these spinning bees were themselves political acts of patriotism.

Women's clothing and fashion accessories were also interpreted in gendered political terms. The most fashionable items had always been those that reflected the metropolitan tastes of Europe's capitals, London and Paris. During the Revolutionary era, however, fashion was seen as a form of feminine indulgence and was linked to the excesses of European aristocracy, which was caricatured as feminine and weak. Particular dress details, such as certain laces or sleeve styles, were seen as reflecting either patriotic or Tory political sympathies and values. Simplicity was displayed as a sign of both feminine and masculine American political virtue. In John Singleton Copley's famous 1768 portrait of the wealthy silversmith and prominent Bostonian Paul Revere, for example, Revere wore expensive linen and sported gold buttons, but his hair is simple and unpowdered. The very fashionable high hairstyles, which for women involved adding bulk and rolls to their hair,

John Singleton Copley's famous portrait of Paul Revere from 1768 shows the Bostonian dressed in expensive linen and sporting gold buttons, but, significantly, his hair is simply styled and unpowdered. American colonists derided the fashionable high hairstyles worn by European men and women as emblematic of the feminine indulgence, excess, and weakness of the European aristocracy. *(Artchive)*

were popular in Europe for both men and women and provoked particular disdain, though many elite women kept wearing them. Mocking depictions of European men in high hair emphasized the femininity and inadequacy of their culture and their politics.

Writers who invoked the relationship between masculinity and the Revolution could be blunt. As during the French and Indian War, people emphasized different aspects of manhood to explain political and military identities. Thomas Paine, author of the inspirational pamphlet of the Revolution, *Common Sense*, wrote that his work was about the "manly principles of independence" and that any man who was loyal to the king was "an apostate from the order of manhood." Songs and toasts rang through the male gatherings at taverns, celebrating male martial bravery and fortitude. A song by the Bostonian William Billings, for example, praised the American soldiers as they faced the more experienced British troops: "The Foe comes on with haughty Stride; / Our troops advance with martial noise, / Their Vet'rans flee before our Youth, / And Gen'rals yield to beardless Boys." In Billings's depiction, the Americans' youth, innocence, vigor, and virtue are contrasted with the age and corruption of England. This was a common way to compare the two societies, their people, and their political values.

Changing Attitudes about Gender, Politics, and Household Roles

Because ideas about gender were grounded in household-based conventions, and because those ideas often underpinned how people understood political and economic as well as social and familial relationships, when attitudes about marriage and children began to shift in the late 18th century it had far-reaching effects. Ideal notions of how men and women should behave and how they should relate to one another seemed to change. These changes included new ideas about husbands, wives, and the marriage relationship, and fathers, mothers, and parenting. In popular culture, strict patriarchy and the power of men's household position gave way to an emphasis on affection and mutuality within families. Print culture, especially the increasingly popular novels, emphasized the importance of "sensibility," a sensitive quality of feeling, in marriage and other family relationships. Traditional European ideas about marriage had supposed that men and women would marry with the consent of their parents, and that a marriage was less a meeting of hearts and souls than a practical arrangement—albeit one that could lead to love—that heavily considered the financial and social status of the two partners. By the end of the 18th century, however, more people embraced the notion that marriage should be based on love and free choice rather than dictated by parents and based on financial interest.

Young men and women were encouraged by the example of the heroes and heroines in the books they read to expect that they would create a marriage of rewarding partnership with their beloved. They were also cautioned to avoid some of the dangers that those fictional characters encountered. Two of the most widely read novels of the 18th century were Samuel Richardson's *Pamela* and *Clarissa*. In both novels the heroine is an innocent, virtuous young woman who prizes love over money. Both Pamela and Clarissa are tempted by men who initially want only to seduce them. Both women face difficulties with their families because of their romantic choices. The lessons of these novels were clear: Women should protect their virtue and reputation, and men should do likewise. Their families should support their romantic choices.

These idealized notions of marital choice, companionate marriage, and supportive parenting were reflected in political language and imagery. England was often depicted as a tyrannical parent in an era that began to value a very different mode for parents, especially fathers. George Washington was lionized not only as the hero of the American Revolution, but as the father of the young country. He was not the stern and power-mad father of old, but the benevolent, more moderately authoritative father that the new era celebrated. There was an ideal maternal figure to accompany this fatherly image. A "republican mother" was glorified as the kind of woman who would cultivate moderation and an ethic of service in both her sons and her husband. And of course she would raise her daughters to do the same. She still had no direct role in politics or governance.

As the young country emerged from revolution to republic, gender was no less important to how people lived or to how they thought. But over the 18th century, dominant notions of gender had shifted. Though these adaptations did not change the essentially hierarchical nature of gender and gender relations, they may have made for more adaptable gender roles.

—Karin Wulf

Further Reading

Brown, Kathleen. *Good Wives, Nasty Wenches, and Anxious Patriarchs: Gender, Race, and Power in Colonial Virginia.* Chapel Hill: University of North Carolina Press, 1996.

Dayton, Cornelia Hughes. *Women before the Bar: Gender, Law, and Society in Connecticut, 1639–1789.* Chapel Hill: University of North Carolina Press, 1995.

Ditz, Toby L. "Shipwrecked; or, Masculinity Imperiled: Mercantile Representations of Failure and the Gendered Self in Eighteenth-Century Philadelphia." *Journal of American History* 81:1 (June 1994): 51–80.

Eustace, Nicole. *Passion Is the Gale: Emotion, Power, and the Coming of the American Revolution.* Chapel Hill: University of North Carolina Press, 2008.

Fliegelman, Jay. *Prodigals and Pilgrims: The American Revolution against Patriarchal Authority.* Cambridge, U.K.: Cambridge University Press, 1986.

Foster, Thomas. *Sex and the Eighteenth-Century Man: Massachusetts and the History of Sexuality in America.* Boston: Beacon Press, 2007.

Godbeer, Richard. *The Overflowing of Friendship: Love between Men and the Creation of the American Republic.* Baltimore, Md.: Johns Hopkins University Press, 2009.

Haulman, Kate. "Fashion and the Culture Wars of Revolutionary Philadelphia." *William and Mary Quarterly*, 3d series, vol. 62, no. 4 (October 2005): 625–662.

Hemphill, Dallett. *Bowing to Necessities: A History of Manners in America, 1620–1860*. New York: Oxford University Press, 1999.

Heyrman, Christine Leigh. "Religion, Women, and the Family in Early America." Divining America, TeacherServe. National Humanities Center. URL: http://nationalhumanitiescenter.org/tserve/eighteen/ekeyinfo/erelwom.htm.

Jabour, Anya. *Marriage in the Early Republic: Elizabeth and William Wirt and the Companionate Ideal*. Baltimore, Md.: Johns Hopkins University Press, 1998.

Juster, Susan. *Disorderly Women: Sexual Politics and Evangelicalism in Revolutionary New England*. Ithaca, N.Y.: Cornell University Press, 1994.

Kann, Mark. *A Republic of Men: The American Founders, Gendered Language, and Patriarchal Politics.* New York: New York University Press, 1998.

Klepp, Susan E., and Karin Wulf, eds. *The Diary of Hannah Callender Sansom: Sense and Sensibility in the Age of the American Revolution.* Ithaca, N.Y.: Cornell University Press, 2010.

Knott, Sarah. *Sensibility and the American Revolution.* Chapel Hill: University of North Carolina Press, 2008.

Lindman, Janet. *Bodies of Belief: Baptist Community in Early America.* Philadelphia: University of Pennsylvania Press, 2008.

Morgan, Jennifer L. *Laboring Women: Reproduction and Gender in New World Slavery.* Philadelphia: University of Pennsylvania Press, 2004.

Ulrich, Laurel Thatcher. "Wheels, Looms, and the Gender Division of Labor in Eighteenth-Century New England." *William and Mary Quarterly*, 3d series, vol. 55, no. 1 (January 1998): 3–38.

18th Century GOVERNMENT

At the beginning of the 18th century, the British colonists on the Eastern Seaboard were governed by ramshackle institutions crudely modeled on those of England under the auspices of a variety of types of charters derived from the English monarchy. By the century's end, the American people were governed under a single national constitution and had remarkably uniform governing institutions, with their rights guarded by state as well as federal constitutions.

This transformation came in two stages. In the 18th century's first six decades, colonial governments were remade on the model provided by London's institutions. Colonial courts became dominated by English procedure, the English jury system became the norm, and colonial assemblies began to act as Parliament did. The American Revolution ended this overt Anglicization of institutions, as institutions and governing practices were republicanized after 1776.

Colonial Government

At the beginning of the 18th century, all governments in British America derived their legitimacy from three types of charters or grants given directly or indirectly by the Crown of England between 1607 and the opening of the 18th century. There were royal charters that established colonies directly under Crown control; charters to settler companies that allowed them some leeway in creating governing structures; and proprietorships, under which individual owners, or groups of owners, operating under a royal grant, had broad leeway in shaping their colony's government. Initially, New England was dominated by charter-company governments, while in the Mid-Atlantic south to Maryland proprietorships predominated, with New York being an exception. In the south, all the colonies were founded as private ventures, only to be formally royalized shortly after their establishment.

Throughout the latter half of the 17th century, English monarchs had sought tighter controls over their distant North American colonies. In the 1680s, King James II went as far as to abolish all governing institutions and legal boundaries in the region between Pennsylvania and Maine, forming the whole into one supercolony called the Dominion of New England, with its capital at Boston. Local institutions were done away with, and a variety of charters and proprietorships revoked.

The overthrow of James II during the Glorious Revolution of 1688–89 brought an end to the Dominion of New England, but after 1700 a general tendency to royalize colonial governments by revoking charters and proprietorships developed and began to change British America. Massachusetts, New Jersey, Maryland, and eventually North Carolina, South Carolina, and Georgia all saw governing powers once in private hands surrendered to the British Crown. The institutions of government and law began to be remodeled along the lines of metropolitan London's. To a large degree, the government of towns and villages remained as they had been at the end of the 17th century, but at the county and colonywide level, governing institutions were, across the 18th century's first six decades, made over along British lines.

Early in the 18th century, the governing and legal institutions based on these various colonial charters were a primitive jumble created from local precedent in England and adaptation in America. Local government was the most important to the vast majority of farmers and their families. Towns and villages in northern New Jersey, New York east of the Hudson, and the New England colonies northward were dominated by town meetings or councils; to the south, the primary local governing institutions tended to be countywide ones. The town councilors were almost always leading men with substantial property who would also play a role in governing the local church and other institutions. The town meetings distributed unassigned property, and assigned subcommittees to fix roads, control hogs, assess property for taxation, and distribute relief to the town poor. Local justices of the peace, usually considerable property holders in the community but often lacking any formal legal education, held monthly courts that settled small civil and criminal matters. In other words, the town meetings and local justices provided the basic government services necessary for life in the early modern world.

The county courts, the colonies' primary legal body and the place where most British American subjects came into contact with the broader empire, had a haphazard quality. There was a seriously lack of trained lawyers and judges in the American colonies in the 18th century's first decades. In fact, in many areas, there was open hostility to lawyers and professional politicians, and court procedures reflected this. The lack of trained lawyers inhibited the standardization of legal practices and allowed for incredible leeway in understanding of legal statutes as well as the ideas of legality or illegality. Trial by jury was becoming more common but was not yet a settled practice in all areas, and again, many jurymen had little or no understanding of the finer points of the law, expected of jury members in the 18th century.

The most important institutions for an individual colony were its legislature and executive offices. These made most of the decisions that affected the population as a whole, and they were supposed to link the body of the people to the empire by joining the people's representatives with those sent by London authorities. The franchise was limited in most areas to male property holders (freeholders) over the age of 21, so the political community eligible to participate in politics or serve in government was small in proportion to the total population. Nonetheless, annual elections in the New England colonies, and periodic ones elsewhere, allowed the freeholders some say in the government. Legislatures in most area were bicameral (Pennsylvania being the exception, having a unicameral government established early in the 18th century), with the upper houses appointed by the imperial officials or by proprietors living in London and the lower houses elected by the freeholders. Only in Connecticut and Rhode Island were the upper houses elected directly, although Massachusetts retained the right to indirectly elect its upper house from the body of the lower house.

The legislatures had considerable power. They established taxes, could order roads or bridges built in some circumstances, played a role in appropriating money for the militia and the defense of the colonies, and controlled the issuing of paper money, backed by various schemes to assure the money's value. Their control over the money supply was far from complete, though, as London authorities established tight restrictions in this regard, allowing the colonies to print money during wartime and then ordering its removal from circulation when the wars ended. Both houses worked with (and sometimes against) governors appointed by the London authorities (or by proprietors living in London, as was the case with Pennsylvania and Maryland). Only Connecticut and Rhode Island—still operating in the 18th century under the charter-company governments formed in the 1630s—were allowed to elect their own governors, a task they confronted yearly. Governors acted as the living links between London and the colonies, and again had significant powers. In the colonies to the south of New England, they could call assembly elections, call out the militia, and in some areas act as members of the colonial supreme or extraordinary courts. They had a say in the distribution of some unappropriated lands. They could veto, set aside, or alter money bills, though like the legislatures, the governors' actions in this regard were bounded by instructions and regulations from London.

The governor often fell into conflict with their assemblies over money and power issues. The assemblies, who were supposed to pay the governors regularly, sometimes withheld salary from these officials for months and even years to punish them for obeying their instructions from London too carefully. Lewis Morris, for example, the royal governor of New Jersey between 1738 and his death in 1746, had not been paid for years at the time of his death, and the colony's assembly even put off his struggling widow years later when she tried to collect the pay in arrears!

The haphazard character of governing institutions began to change in the 1720s and 1730s as the colonies became better integrated into the first British Empire. The broader cultural tendency to emulate the styles of Great Britain manifested itself strongly in government and law. Two groups played a central role in this transformation: the first generation or cadre of professionally trained lawyers, some of whom received their education at the Inns of Courts in

London; and the imperial bureaucrats sent from London as governors and other officials, who were markedly better prepared and educated as the century progressed.

The transformation of the bench and bar was perhaps the more pronounced of these changes, as it had a very direct impact on British Americans in all colonies. The establishment of primitive law schools in the offices of leading attorneys in the Mid-Atlantic and the South beginning in the 1720s and 1730s, and New England in the 1750s and 1760s, combined with the willingness of some colonial gentlemen to send their sons and other younger relatives to London for a formal legal education, changed dramatically the functioning of the courts and the law. Gone, or at least less common, were the unlearned judges and even justices of the peace. In their place came magistrates familiar directly or indirectly with the courts of London, well-read in the law, increasingly wearing robes and periwigs in emulation of the English courts, with a detailed knowledge of English court procedures, legal precedent, and jury procedure. The courts became more standardized in their functioning, the appeal process was clarified, and trial by jury became normalized in all appropriate cases.

Royal governors such as Thomas Pownall (above), the governor of Massachusetts, were able to manage their colonies' legislatures in a way that was acceptable to the London authorities. Pownall served as royal governor from August 1757 to June 1760, at which point he returned to England. *(Library of Congress)*

Also becoming rarer were individuals pleading on their own account. The use of trained lawyers to represent conflicting parties became commonplace. Often this development provoked protests, especially during the periodic debt crises caused by instabilities in the colonial paper money supplies, but it nonetheless continued to expand as the century progressed. Trained judges and lawyers became the norm rather than the exception by the 1760s.

The appointment of better-trained imperial bureaucrats worked the same kind of transformation on other government institutions. Royal governors like Robert Hunter and Jonathan Belcher in the first half of the 18th century and later Thomas Pownall, William Franklin, and James Wright, among others, were able administrators who understood how to manage the legislatures within their respective colonies in a manner acceptable to the London authorities. Most of them stayed in office for years on end, gradually making the governorships effective executive offices along decidedly British lines.

Revolutionary Government

Governing became increasingly difficult as the unrest over taxation in British America after 1764 expanded into a general crisis within the empire. Mobs prevented royal officials from collecting taxes or enforcing trade regulations. These same officials suffered attacks on their homes and property and ultimately their persons. In 1773 and 1774, in the Boston Tea Party's wake, the upheaval intensified and imperial institutions began to collapse. Even the royal courts ground to a halt as jurymen began challenging the authority of royal judges and denying the empire generally. In their place came a loose network of revolutionary committees and congresses, basing their authority on the will of the people only. These extralegal bodies gradually assumed the power of taxation in most locales, established rude courts to deal with political enemies as well as common criminals, gained control of the militia, and assumed the other functions of government, even down to the mundane local tasks handled by town meetings.

Such a haphazard arrangement could not last, and in 1776 and 1777 new, republican constitutions based on popular sovereignty were created in most states. Pennsylvania, Georgia, and the nascent state of Vermont did away with upper houses in their governing structures, while the other states retained a bicameral structure. Everywhere, the fear of arbitrary power being concentrated in the hands of one person led American constitution writers to diminish the power of governors. Writing new constitutions for a new society was often fraught with difficulty, but these challenges paled besides the governmental problems caused by open warfare on American soil. Congress was forced out of Philadelphia twice, once for nearly a year as the British occupied the city in 1777. In a number of states, the members of the new governments were forced to flee the British. In the case of Georgia and South Carolina later in the war, the governments completely collapsed in the face of British invasion. County courts of sessions in some areas did not meet for years, and there were districts in many states where the new governments simply could not exert control as fighting broke out among Americans of different loyalties. Both the states and the Congress tried to fund the seemingly endless war by repeated emissions of paper money, but this spread misery beyond the zone of fighting by sparking hyperinflation that in turn led to the loss of confidence in the new governments.

The effective end of fighting in 1781 brought the opportunity to stabilize the new regimes, and in many areas government again began to function, if not normally, at least consistently. The courts restarted, town meetings returned to their normal tasks, elections for assemblymen and governors were now held yearly in almost all the states, and new political ceremonies that celebrated the figures and events of the struggle for independence became the norm. Popular sovereignty was accepted as the legitimate source of government everywhere, and it seemed the society might settle down to enjoy the fruits of its remarkable victory over the world's greatest superpower.

Articles of Confederation

Serious underlying problems of government and constitutional order remained, though, even as the Treaty of Paris formally ending the war was signed in 1783. The Articles of Confederation government, which had been ratified in 1781, remained in place, but its authority was weak. It did not have the power to raise troops, tax internally, or embody a formal federal judiciary. The Congress did not have control of the money supply, and states continued to issue and withdraw money from circulation, causing serious economic problems and a breakdown in debtor-creditor relations. Congress also needed to pay and demobilize the army, units of which had not been paid for years. No formal plan yet existed for the establishment of new states in the vast lands beyond the Appalachian Mountains won in the war, and in some areas—Maine, western North Carolina, what became Vermont, and the northern Connecticut River valley—groups of settlers and speculators were trying to establish new states based on their own authority as part of "the people." There was broad dissatisfaction with the state constitutions, and the continual calls for new state conventions to draw up new constitutions led to an increased sense of disorder.

The issues of the unappropriated lands, the money supply, and discontent with the state governments were addressed by the Articles of Confederation government, but only the first problem, that of governing western lands, was adequately resolved by that government. The confederation government got the individual states to relinquish their claims to the trans-Appalachian interior, and passed a series of ordinances, culminating in the three Northwest Ordinances of 1784–87, that outlined a method to establish new governments in the interior. But the central government's inability to stabilize or even assert control over the money supply, and the resulting breakdowns in debtor-creditor relations and interstate commerce, created problems both within states and between them. Debtors claimed the courts were controlled by creditors and their lawyers. Many, incited by financial issues, called for constitutional changes on the state level that would fundamentally alter government's role in people's lives.

The Articles of Confederation did not give the federal government the power to raise troops, tax internally, or form a federal judiciary. The problems of the money supply and contracts, and more generally of order, led elements in each state to call for a new centralized, federal government. The new U.S. Constitution (above) drafted in 1787 greatly enhanced the federal government's power, allowed for the creation of a federal judiciary, and established in theory federal supremacy over state law. *(National Archives)*

The functioning of governments faltered and then broke down in several states, under the strains caused by these problems. These convulsions were most notable in Massachusetts, leading to Shays's Rebellion, a period of widespread, violent unrest in the central and western portion of the state in 1786 and 1787.

The problems of the money supply and contracts, and more generally of order, led elements in each state to call for a new centralized, federal government. In 1787, delegates to a constitutional convention gathered in Philadelphia to shape a new government based on a new constitution.

Though bitterly debated, this new constitution was adopted in 1788 by the majority of the states. It greatly enhanced the central government's power over taxation, the military, and interstate commerce, allowed for the creation of a complex federal judiciary, complete with a supreme court, and established in theory federal supremacy over state law. The chief executive, now called the president, was given strong powers, and the Senate acted as a check on the House of Representatives. And the federal model was soon emulated by states that had experimented with unicameral governments. By 1791, state and federal institutions were remarkably uniform in their structure, with two-house legislatures, strong governors, and nominally independent judiciaries.

The 1790s were dominated by efforts to make the new federal government work in practice and to mesh its workings with those of the states. These efforts were fraught with difficulty. The collection of internal taxes led to violent resistance, culminating in the Whiskey Rebellion in Pennsylvania in 1794. State governments jealously guarded their prerogative against federal intrusion. Legal procedures and institutional power were immature and unfixed in their character, and this included the federal Supreme Court, whose constitutional power was still unclear. The development of the first party system led to intense fighting over control of institutions on all levels of government, and at times it seemed as though the two parties were teetering toward civil war. The Federalists wanted a strong government with extensive powers of taxation and an ample military, while the Jeffersonian Democratic-Republicans demanded a small central government and power vested in the states. The contested election of 1800 led to Jefferson assuming the presidency, and gradually the system of government became more normalized in people's lives.

—Brendan McConville

Further Reading

Bailyn, Bernard. *The Ordeal of Thomas Hutchinson*. Cambridge, Mass.: Harvard University Press, 1976.

Beeman, Richard R. *Plain, Honest Men: The Making of the American Constitution*. New York, Random House, 2010.

———. *The Varieties of Political Experience in Eighteenth-Century America*. Philadelphia: University of Pennsylvania Press, 2006.

Bonomi, Patricia U. *A Factious People: Politics and Society in Colonial New York*. New York: Columbia University Press, 1973.

Breen, T. H. *American Insurgents, American Patriots: The Revolution of the People*. New York: Hill & Wang, 2010.

Elkins, Stanley, and Eric McKitrick. *The Age of Federalism: The Early American Republic, 1788–1800*. New York: Oxford University Press, 1995.

Holton, Woody. *Forced Founders: Indians, Debtors, Slaves, and the Making of the American Revolution in Virginia.* Chapel Hill: University of North Carolina Press, for the Omohundro Institute of Early American History and Culture, 1999.

Mann, Bruce. *Republic of Debtors: Bankruptcy in the Age of American Independence*. Cambridge, Mass.: Harvard University Press, 2003.

McConville, Brendan. *The King's Three Faces: The Rise and Fall of Royal America, 1688–1776*. Chapel Hill: University of North Carolina Press, for the Omohundro Institute of Early American History and Culture, 2006.

Nicholson, Colin. *The "Infamas Govener": Francis Bernard and the Origins of the American Revolution*. Boston: Northeastern University Press, 2000.

Wood, Gordon S. *Creation of the American Republic, 1776–1787*. Chapel Hill: University of North Carolina Press, for the Omohundro Institute of Early American History and Culture, 1998.

18th Century HEALTH AND MEDICINE

Medicine was in a state of transition in 18th-century America. While many premodern practices and theories were still widespread, the 18th century saw the beginnings of recognizably modern medical practice. Experimental science and clinical observation began to replace the received wisdom of the ancient world, the first American medical schools were established, and male physicians began to replace midwives in obstetrics. At the same time, physicians and other medical practitioners confronted new challenges in the form of devastating epidemics.

Theories of Health and Disease

The understanding of the causes of illness in the 18th century was still rooted in the humoral theory of disease, a system first developed by the ancient Roman physician Galen. In this theory, the body is composed of four "humors": blood, phlegm, black bile, and yellow bile. Each humor was associated with a degree of moisture and a temperature: phlegm, for instance, was cold and wet, while yellow bile was warm and dry. Each individual had a dominant humor in his or her body, which gave rise to personality differences. Some of the words we still use to describe personality, such as "phlegmatic," derive from this ancient belief.

Disease resulted when one humor overwhelmed the others. Each individual was prone to diseases that stemmed from their naturally dominant humor. A person dominated by the "hot" humors, for instance, would be prone to fevers. A person's age and sex also contributed to humoral balance. Men were "hotter" and "dryer" than women; older people were "colder" and "dryer" than young people. However, given the right circumstances, any person could develop any disease. Too much of a certain food, an upsetting experience, or exposure to bad weather could all upset the humoral balance and cause disease.

Eighteenth-century Americans recognized spiritual as well as physical causes of disease. God could send illness as a "correction" for sin, and many pious individuals spent time at prayer when they fell sick. Some deeply religious parents took this thinking a step further and interpreted their children's illnesses as punishment for their own sins. Prayer, fasting, and consultation with a minister were as much a part of curing illness as a visit from a physician.

Most physical treatments were aimed at restoring humoral balance, through rebalancing the body's temperature and moisture, or through purging excessive, putrefying humors. A practitioner would first determine the nature of the disease—was it a hot, dry disease with a fever, or a cold, moist disease, such as a cold? He or she would then prescribe medicines as a counterbalance. For instance, a "cold" disease would be treated with "hot" medicines such as ginger tea, served as hot as the patient could bear. Many 18th-century treatments also involved driving "excessive" humors from the body. While any humor could be in excess, blood and bile were the usual culprits. Bile could be driven out with emetics and laxatives, and excessive blood would be removed through bleeding and leeches. To remain in good health, a person needed to avoid excessive eating and drinking, dress appropriately for the weather, and avoid emotional extremes.

However, a new theory of disease was emerging in the medical schools of Europe. Elite colonial physicians who studied there brought this new theory, called the "solidist" theory, back home with them. Solidist theory holds that health and disease depend on the state of blood vessels and nerves. When these tissues are healthy, bodily fluids such as blood and "nerve fluid" move freely throughout the body. When tissues are either overstimulated or debilitated, the flow is blocked and the person becomes ill. In this view, diseases caused by overstimulation require "depletive" treatments, while diseases caused by debility require strengthening medicines.

In practice, many of these treatments looked much the same as those recommended by humoral theory. Overstimulation required bleeding and purging, much as imbalanced humors did. Only when a disease was classified as "debility" did the treatments vary: In those cases, physicians prescribed rich, strengthening foods and "stimulants" such as alcohol and opium. Most practitioners adopted an eclectic view of medicine, incorporating both theories of disease into their practices.

Types of Medical Practitioners

As was the case in the previous century, most medical care was provided by practitioners with little formal education. Most laypeople, especially women, had extensive knowledge of herbal medicines and other folk remedies. If a person became sick, the first healer they turned to was likely to be a family member or neighbor.

Other kinds of informal practitioners included bonesetters and other itinerant practitioners who specialized in one procedure, such as tooth-drawing or the removal of bladder stones. Many of these traveling "doctors" also sold medicines and tonics of their own invention, the ingredients of which they kept secret but which frequently included a large amount of alcohol. Itinerant doctors and surgeons traveled set routes from town to town. When they arrived, they advertised their presence in the local newspaper or by printed broadside. While some claimed to have formal credentials, most simply let their reputations or extravagant advertisements speak for them.

Midwives were on the boundary between informally trained practitioners, such as traveling bonesetters, and credentialed practitioners, such as physicians and surgeons. Midwives delivered most of the babies in the 18th century. In addition, midwives took care of many "female complaints," including infertility. Some also offered more general services to their communities, such as basic first aid, herbal medicines, and nursing care. Midwives usually began their practices with an informal apprenticeship with another woman, gradually gaining enough experience to practice on their own. Since it was impractical for a woman with young children to practice midwifery, most midwives began their careers in middle age. Midwives were assisted in their work by their patients' female relatives and neighbors, who traditionally gathered to support mothers in childbirth.

The medical profession itself had three different levels: surgeons, apprentice-trained physicians, and physicians with a university degree. Surgeons were formally trained but had a lower status than physicians. Their lower rank stemmed from the premodern tradition that a "gentleman" did not work with his hands. Since surgery was a manual skill, it was a lesser profession than medicine, which depended on knowledge and education. Many surgeons learned their trade in the military, and then continued to practice once their service was ended. Surgeons set bones, removed cancerous tumors, and performed amputations. As the century progressed, the old distinction between physicians and surgeons disappeared, and surgery rose in status alongside the rest of the medical profession.

Most who called themselves physicians or doctors did not have a university degree. The usual career path for a doctor was to learn his skill through an apprenticeship. Most of these apprentice-trained doctors were respected members of their communities and made a good living, but they did not yet have the high status that physicians would achieve in the 19th and 20th centuries.

The 18th century also saw the emergence of a new kind of physician: an ambitious young man from a good family with a degree from an elite university who saw himself not just as a healer but as a scientist. These men usually studied in London or Edinburgh, where they learned anatomy through dissection of cadavers, observed surgical procedures in hospitals, assisted researchers with medical experiments, and attended lectures on the latest developments in medical science. Edinburgh students then wrote a thesis based on clinical observation or original experiments. Dr. Benjamin Rush, noted for both his contributions to American medicine and his leadership during the Revolution, was an excellent example of this new breed of physician.

Dr. Benjamin Rush exemplified the new breed of physician that emerged in the 18th century. He studied in Edinburgh, and after receiving his medical degree he worked in London hospitals and later wrote the first American chemistry textbook, titled *Syllabus of a Course of Lectures on Chemistry. (Library of Congress)*

Americans who obtained their degrees through this system usually returned to establish practices in large cities, where they catered to the elite families who could afford their services. However, their influence on the profession was out of proportion to their small numbers. The European-trained physicians were the founders of the first American medical schools, and they helped transform American physicians from craftsmen to professionals.

Eighteenth-Century Changes in Medicine

The 18th century saw important changes in several areas of medical practice. European-trained surgeons developed new techniques for common operations, male physicians began delivering babies, and some doctors began advocating for inoculation to prevent smallpox.

Surgery in the 18th century was severely limited by two things: lack of anesthesia, and lack of sterile technique. The lack of anesthesia meant that operations had to be performed as quickly as possible to limit the patient's pain. The lack of a germ theory and antisepsis meant that almost all surgical wounds became infected. As a result, surgery was considered a treatment of last resort, and very few operations entered the chest or the abdomen. Surgeons dealt with trauma cases and lesions of the skin, eyes, or extremities. Within these limitations, however, the new science of the 18th century allowed some innovations in surgery. European-trained American surgeons developed new methods of treating bladder stones, removing cancerous tumors, and tying off arterial aneurysms.

The 18th century also saw important changes in childbirth and obstetrics. American doctors trained in Edinburgh and London popularized the use of obstetrical forceps—a tool that helped doctors deliver infants who were stuck in the birth canal. Physicians could offer both the forceps to assist with difficult births and laudanum (an opium derivative) to soothe pain. As a result, some affluent women in American cities began to look to male physicians instead of midwives to provide safety and comfort in childbirth. This change remained controversial. Midwives rallied to defend their profession, arguing that their methods were gentler and protected a woman's modesty. The claims of greater safety made by physicians were undermined by the damage done by men using forceps without proper training or experience. Throughout the 18th and 19th centuries, physicians and midwives practiced in parallel, and for many women a midwife remained the only available option. However, the 18th century marked the beginning of physician-assisted birth in America.

Another important change in 18th-century medicine was the introduction of smallpox inoculation. Inoculation is not the same as vaccination, although the two techniques are similar. While vaccination uses a related virus to induce an immune response, inoculation injects a full-strength smallpox virus under the skin of the patient. For reasons that are still not clear, this method usually results in a mild, survivable case of smallpox, which nevertheless gives the patient full immunity.

Inoculation had been used in Africa and Asia for centuries, reaching Europe around 1700. In America, the method was first proposed by Onesimus, an African slave in the household of the Reverend Cotton Mather of Boston. In 1721, the Boston physician Zabdiel Boylston collaborated with Mather to try inoculation in America. When a smallpox epidemic broke out in the city, Boylston injected smallpox scabs under the skin of his six-year-old son and two of his slaves. All three survived the procedure, and none developed smallpox again.

Mather and Boylston's successful experiment was greeted with strong opposition. Many feared (with reason) that inoculated patients would spread smallpox to healthy populations; others questioned the ethics of deliberately inducing disease in healthy persons. Eventually, the city of Boston banned the practice, and other towns and cities followed suit. Within 30 years, however, the tide of public opinion had turned. By the time of the Revolution, inoculation was accepted enough that Benjamin Franklin, John and Abigail Adams, and other leaders had themselves or their children inoculated. Smallpox inoculation represented a crucial first step in the prevention of a terrible disease.

Epidemics and Infectious Disease

Despite progress in such areas as inoculation, epidemic disease was a major killer during the 18th century. The thriving port cities were often the first victims, as ships from around the world brought deadly germs to America. In addition, the growing population of the cities combined with lack of proper sanitation to create epidemics of waterborne disease.

Smallpox continued to erupt in America throughout the century and remained widely feared. Unlike in Europe, where smallpox had a permanent foothold, smallpox in America would disappear for a time before recurring. When epidemics broke out, the virus would encounter a population with no immune members, resulting in a high death toll. The typical pattern was for a ship carrying an infected passenger to dock in a city. As the disease spread, frightened inhabitants fled to the countryside, bringing the disease with them. Thus, an outbreak that began in Boston could spread as far as Canada. Outbreaks in New York City followed the fur trade along the Hudson River and spread far into the interior of the continent. Outbreaks occurred in New England about every 10 years; in New York and Pennsylvania, with their important ports of New York City and Philadelphia, they occurred about every 5 years. The South suffered the least, perhaps because there was only one major port city, Charleston, South Carolina.

Some of the most significant outbreaks occurred during wartime. Both the Seven Years' War (1756–63) and the Revolutionary War (1775–83) were accompanied by outbreaks of smallpox. The disease followed the armies and thrived on the malnutrition, social disruption, and crowded conditions created by war. During the Revolutionary War, George Washington initiated an inoculation campaign to keep his troops healthy. Even with such measures in place, many more soldiers (and civilians) died of smallpox than in battle.

Yellow fever was another disease that attacked port cities. Yellow fever is a mosquito-borne, tropical virus. It attacks the digestive tract and the liver, giving rise to the jaundice (yellowing of the skin and eyes) for which it is named. It probably originated in Africa and came to the Americas on trading ships. The first epidemic broke out in Boston in 1693, but the disease appeared more often in Philadelphia and Charleston, where the hot, humid summers allowed the vector mosquitoes to survive. In 1699, one outbreak in Charleston killed half of the members of the colonial assembly.

Unlike smallpox, yellow fever did not spread far beyond its point of origin, and it always disappeared when the weather became cold enough to kill mosquitoes. Since yellow fever was perceived as a disease of cities in the summer, many wealthy urbanites began purchasing country houses where they could spend their summers without fear of infection.

Philadelphia suffered a devastating epidemic in 1793. A shipload of French refugees from the revolution in Haiti arrived in Philadelphia that July, and the epidemic began shortly thereafter. Since Philadelphia was then the nation's capital, the work of the federal government shut down after President Washington and Congress fled the city. By the time the epidemic ended in November, somewhere between 3,000 and 5,000 of the city's 55,000 inhabitants had died.

Even when there were no epidemics of yellow fever or smallpox, 18th-century cities were unhealthy places. The sanitary practices of the time could not guarantee a clean water supply, and outbreaks of "flux" or "bloody flux" (typhoid and dysentery) were common. In cities, two or three families often shared one privy or pit toilet. While the usual practice was to fill in and re-dig privy pits every few years, the growing population meant that privy vaults filled quickly. In areas with a high water table, the contents could easily seep into wells and contaminate drinking water. In addition, some cities had ordinances requiring that garbage, street sweepings, and animal manure be disposed of in the river, creating another potential source for water contamination. In the countryside, population densities were lower, but leaky privies and the common habit of relieving oneself on the ground meant that rural areas were not immune either.

Intestinal diseases were particularly deadly to children. Parents feared the "summer flux," which carried off many infants and toddlers. Unlike yellow fever and smallpox, which appeared dramatically and then disappeared, the flux was a constant threat in most areas.

The Beginnings of Modern Public Health, Medical Education, and Hospitals

The crises created by epidemics led to some of the first public health measures in American cities. Smallpox outbreaks led to a number of quarantine laws, some of which were rooted in ancient practices. For example, ships with sick passengers were required to wait 20 days before unloading. Some cities went further, placing all members of infected households under house arrest or requiring them to hang colored cloth on their doors. New England cities and Charleston, South Carolina, founded publicly funded quarantine hospitals, which were built on islands or other isolated sites to protect the city from contagion.

After the 1793 yellow fever outbreak in Philadelphia, the city founded a permanent public health committee. The committee established a public hospital to care for victims of the epidemic, sent workers to sweep and scrub the homes of the sick, and created street cleaning crews to sprinkle water on the roads to control dust and remove garbage and other filth from the city streets. In early 1794 these services were made a permanent part of city government. Soon thereafter, the public health committee authorized the building of the first city water treatment plant.

Hospitals were another innovation of the 18th century. While previous centuries had cared for the sick poor in almshouses and poorhouses, the 18th century saw the first institutions staffed by physicians and dedicated exclusively to the care of the sick. The first was the Pennsylvania Hospital in Philadelphia, founded in 1751 by Benjamin Franklin and Dr. Thomas Bond; the second, New York Hospital, was proposed in 1769 by Dr. Samuel Bard and opened in 1791. In both cases, the hospital provided both medical services and training and research material for physicians.

Finally, the 18th century saw the beginnings of modern medical education. The hospitals in New York and Philadelphia attracted many of the young men who had trained abroad. These same physicians saw the need for an Edinburgh-style medical school in America. In Philadelphia, John Morgan and a group of prominent physicians founded a medical school as part of the College of Philadelphia (later the University of Pennsylvania) in 1765. The curriculum was based on that of the University of Edinburgh, stressing direct clinical observation as a supplement to academic lectures and reading. King's College (later Columbia University) opened its own medical school along similar lines in 1767, and it became the first American school to award the MD degree.

All of these events foreshadowed the development of a scientifically based, professionalized practice of medicine and public health that would dominate the 19th and 20th centuries. While the 18th century remained part of the premodern medical world in many ways, important changes were already under way.

—*Rebecca J. Tannenbaum*

Further Reading

Bell, Whitfield. *The Colonial Physician and Other Essays.* New York: Science History Publications, 1975.

Benes, Peter, ed. *Medicine and Healing: Proceedings of the Dublin Seminar for New England Folklife*. Boston: Boston University Press, 1992.

Brown, Kathleen M. *Foul Bodies: Cleanliness in Early America*. New Haven, Conn.: Yale University Press, 2009.

Cash, Philip, Eric H. Christianson, and J. Worth Estes, eds. *Medicine in Colonial Massachusetts, 1620–1820*. Boston: Colonial Society of Massachusetts, 1980.

Duffy, John. *Epidemics in Colonial America*. Baton Rouge: Louisiana State University Press, 1953.

Earle, A. Scott. *Surgery in America: From the Colonial Era to the Twentieth Century*. 2d ed. New York: Praeger Publishers, 1983.

Estes, J. Worth, and Billy G. Smith, eds. *A Melancholy Scene of Devastation: The Public Response to the 1793 Philadelphia Yellow Fever Epidemic*. Canton, Mass.: Science History Publications, 1997.

Fenn, Elizabeth A. *Pox Americana: The Great Smallpox Epidemic of 1775–82*. New York: Hill & Wang, 2001.

Leavitt, Judith Walzer. *Brought to Bed: Childbearing in America, 1750 to 1950*. New York: Oxford University Press, 1986.

Powell, John Harvey. *Bring Out Your Dead: The Great Plague of Yellow Fever in Philadelphia in 1793*. 1949. Reprint, New York: Arno Press, 1970.

Reiss, Oscar. *Medicine in Colonial America*. Lanham, Md.: University Press of America, 2000.

Tannenbaum, Rebecca J. *The Healer's Calling: Women and Medicine in Early New England*. Ithaca, N.Y.: Cornell University Press, 2002.

Ulrich, Laurel Thatcher. *A Midwife's Tale: The Life of Martha Ballard, Based on Her Diary, 1785–1812*. New York: Alfred A. Knopf, 1990.

18th Century HOLIDAYS AND FESTIVALS

The world of the 18th century was profoundly different from our own time, and the holidays people remembered and the way they celebrated them were quite different from our customs. And as it was also a time of change, the holidays celebrated were radically transformed between 1700 and 1800.

That century saw three profound shifts in the character and nature of public holidays. The first of these was the acceptance of the idea of annual holidays, especially in the area north of Maryland. The second change was the movement of formal celebration to newly settled areas of the frontiers throughout the century. And the final shift was the wholesale replacement of the public holidays of the British Empire, which had been introduced at the beginning of the century, by a radically new set of holidays designed to establish a specific American identity. All these holidays, both imperial and those specifically American, played a central role in 18th-century society and politics.

Imperial Holiday

At the opening of the 18th century, few formalized public holidays existed in British America. In the northern and middle colonies, the presence of large numbers of Calvinist and Quaker settlers inhibited public celebration. Calvin had warned against annual holidays and rites, which he saw as a sign of ungodliness and an invitation to sin. Christmas and Easter were frowned upon, and political holidays were likewise disdained. Quakers saw such celebrations as disruptive to orderly society. In the southern colonies, the lack of urban centers in what had already become a dispersed, plantation-based society kept public celebrations isolated to the few substantial towns, such as Charles Town and Williamsburg.

Political convulsions within the first British Empire began the process of change that would see annual public holidays established throughout British America. The overthrow of the Catholic king James II in the Glorious Revolution (1688–89) by his Protestant son-in-law and daughter, William and Mary, led to decades of intermittent warfare with Bourbon France. The colonists, eager to show their allegiance to an empire at war and under increased pressure to accept more centralized authority in order to coordinate imperial defense, began to adopt imperial holidays recommended to them by the London authorities.

The first such holiday widely accepted was November 5, known alternatively as Pope's Day, Guy Fawkes Day, or Powder Plot Day. The holiday celebrated the foiling of a Catholic plot against King James I and the English Parliament in 1605. Introduced in the 1690s, the holiday was initially marked by sermons in Protestant churches followed by bonfires and toasting. By the end of the 18th century's first decade, though, it would involve, at least in New England port towns, rowdy processions of artisans, sailors, apprentices, slaves, and even some gentlemen. These crowds would push large carts carrying effigies of the Catholic pope, monks, and the devil, and would parade through towns until dusk, when the effigies would be destroyed. By the 1730s, Boston crowds of thousands held rival processions, followed by bloody battles on Boston Common between the North End crowd and the South End crowd for possession of the other neighborhood's pope effigy—contests almost always won by the North End.

The introduction of other holidays tied to the British royal family and the empire soon followed Pope's Day's establishment in the American colonies. The monarch's birthday, the queen's birthday, the Prince of Wales's birthday, the monarch's coronation day, and other days associated with the Hanoverian dynasty's reign in Britain became annual holidays remembered in every colony. The government's purpose in establishing them (or encouraging their establishment) was to tie the colonies to the empire and to inculcate a British identity, and a specifically Protestant-British historical worldview, in the population.

Pope's Day, also known as Guy Fawkes Day or Powder Plot Day, was the first holiday to be celebrated widely by 18th-century Americans. Guy Fawkes, pictured above being arrested, was a British soldier who participated in the failed Catholic plot to assassinate the Protestant King James by blowing up the palace at Westminster during the state opening of Parliament, while James I and his chief ministers were meeting inside. The holiday was celebrated with bonfires, processions, effigies of Fawkes, and toasting. ***(Jupiter Images)***

Initially, these royalist celebrations were quite limited in their character. There would be sermons at the local Protestant churches, a review of the local militia, and perhaps a bonfire and a treat of ale for the local population. But, like Pope's Day, they became over time far more elaborate, all-day affairs that involved thousands of people in the major port towns as either participants or spectators or both. Governors, councils, assemblymen, other officials, and militia units would gather in the morning hours. Flags would be raised, there would be a cannonade, followed by a review and parading of the militia, with the civilian officials and leading men of the community following in their own procession. There would then be banqueting for the leading gentlemen and their families, in which toasting the empire and the monarch would play a central role. The government or leading men would supply alcohol and roasted oxen or other cattle for the general population. In the evening, fireworks would be set off, and the homes of the leading men would be illuminated with candles.

In the 1720s and 1730s, formal holidays celebrating the empire's national subgroups, particularly the English, Welsh, Scottish, and Irish peoples, came to be established in the American colonies as migrants from all areas of the British Isles poured into the provinces on the Atlantic's western shore. St. George's Day, St. David's Day, St. Andrew's Day, and St. Patrick's Day all became days of celebration marked by sermons, feasting, toasting, cannonades, processions, flag raisings, and illuminations. These holidays were sanctioned by the government and became part of the empire's formal political calendar. As difficult as it may now be to believe, St. Patrick's Day celebrated Protestant monarchy and Ireland's inclusion in the British Empire. Only in the 19th century would it become the Catholic and Irish nationalist holiday known.

These holiday celebrations were spectacles that drew thousands in the major towns. They also were among the few opportunities in a given year for women and children to demonstrate their political sentiments. Groups of gentlewomen sang patriotic songs, extolling the virtues of the British Empire and monarchy. Children sometimes were given a role in the rites; this was especially true of Pope's Day, which sometimes featured children marching with the effigies, and even used children inside the effigies of the pope and the monks to move the heads as the procession careened down the streets of British America's ports each November 5.

Reports of these holiday celebrations spread by word of mouth, but as newspapers and almanacs became more common in the 18th century, the impact of the holidays became greater, as print accounts spread wherever people read and discussed the news. As the holidays were often major events, the accounts were quite detailed and spread word far and wide of the manner of performance of these ceremonies.

While the royal and national holidays were commemorated in one form or another in every colony, there were regional and local holidays as well. In New England, days of thanksgiving in late autumn had been decreed by the various colonial assemblies or governors, though Thanksgiving would not become a national holiday until the American Civil War. The graduation days of Harvard and Yale, and later the College of Rhode Island (now Brown University) and Dartmouth, were holidays in their respective colonies, as was election day, when freeholders chose their representatives (and in Rhode Island and Connecticut their governors as well).

One of the unique aspects of the election day holidays in New England was the custom of what was called "Negro Election" or "Negro Coronation." The major New England towns had significant African American slave populations before the Revolution, as well as free people of color, and these populations would hold their own elections, and their own celebrations, at the same time as the white population. Those in Massachusetts and New Hampshire towns would elect "kings," while those in the charter colonies of Connecticut and Rhode Island would elect "governors" to rule over them for the coming year. Feasting and dancing would follow, sometimes paid for by the African American populations, and sometimes by white masters. White masters often recognized these elections and would sometime work through the African American "king" or "governor" to regulate behaviors in slave communities.

In the Mid-Atlantic colonies, the Dutch-speaking populations, a remnant of the 17th-century Dutch New Netherland colony, kept a number of holidays associated with the Dutch Reformed Church and Dutch culture generally. The most important of these were holidays associated with Christmas (St. Nicholas's Day), New Year's Day, marked by the firing of guns into the air during visits to friends and relatives, and especially Easter, or Paas, as the Dutch New Yorkers called it, along with a number of days related to it. Perhaps the best known of the other Easter-related holidays was Pinkster, or Pentecost, the seventh Sunday after the marking of Christ's resurrection. These holidays fused religious remembrance with folk customs rooted in the beliefs and practices common in the Netherlands in the 17th century and were kept in parts of New York and New Jersey.

As with Negro Election in New England, Pinkster had an African American component. Afro-Dutch slaves, of which there were a significant number in the Mid-Atlantic colonies, would elect a king or ruler for their festival, which would include feasting and music. Major African American Pinkster celebrations took place at Albany and in New York City. These celebrations seem to have fused aspects of African religion with the Reformed Christianity of the Dutch. The African Americans at Albany engaged in something called the "Toto Dance," which may have had some African origins, although they also by the end of the century conducted great processions, led by their elected king, in imitation of the processions conducted by the white majority.

The prevalence of the Church of England in the Mid-Atlantic colonies and the South encouraged the keeping of the church's holidays in those regions. These included Christmas and Easter, which were largely ignored in New England. These holidays were kept in much the same fashion as they are today, with decoration, feasting, and the exchange of gifts and visiting, especially on Christmas.

These annual holidays were not the only celebrations, of course. Weddings, frolics, house raisings, and more formally the entrance of an imperial governor into his new colony would lead to enthusiastic celebrations, sometimes planned, sometimes not. The weddings and the frolics were often raucous and wild affairs that would continue all night. The coronation of a new monarch would likewise lead to widespread celebrations across the colonies, although these were of a more formal nature.

By the 1730s, these holidays and festivals were well-established parts of life in the towns and villages near salt water across British America. The massive movement of population to the southern and western frontiers established populations too far away to participate in such festivities. Nevertheless, the importance of holidays to 18th-century populations created a demand for them on the frontier.

Holidays and Festivals on the Frontier

The movement of European and African populations to the frontiers of British America brought holidays and festivals to those areas, supplanting the ritual cycles maintained by a number of Native American groups. The same holidays that had been established in the longer-settled areas of the coast were remembered in the interior, but the difference in settlement patterns and population density again transformed them.

In 1700, European and African populations almost all lived within 50 miles of salt water, the exceptions being the Dutch-dominated settlements upriver along the Hudson and English settlements in the Connecticut River Valley in Massachusetts. The ocean was highway and food source; it provided ties to Europe and the Caribbean, as well as ample supplies of fish protein. High birth rates and an acceleration in European and African immigration—the latter coerced, of course, by slave traders—led to a massive pattern of movement that redistributed population. Although all the colonies felt this process, it was most evident in the Mid-Atlantic region and southern interior, which saw massive population influxes.

Both imperial authorities and the immigrants themselves felt the need to retain some holidays and demonstrate their loyalty to the British Empire and the Hanoverian kings (George I, George II, George III), who ruled, it sometimes seems, by means of celebration. As early as 1716 the resident garrison of the "house . . . the most outward settlement on this side of Virginia" is recorded as firing their guns and engaging in ceremonies of celebration when the colony's governor came on an inspection tour. In the 1740s William Stephens, an official in the newly settled colony of Georgia, initiated the celebration of a number of imperial holidays in what was really just a collection of crude settlements, the southernmost in mainland British America. In the early 1740s the 56 male freeholders of Savannah were treated to flag raisings, cannonades, and toasting on St. George's Day, St. Andrew's Day, King George II's birthday, and Pope's Day. By 1743 and 1744 the population was demanding extensive celebrations, a demand Stephens gave in to, even though the colony was going broke.

For certain, these frontier celebrations were different from those in the large cities. The communities were too new, dispersed, and ill planned for the authorities to conduct celebrations as they did in Boston, New York, or Charles Town. Stephens noted another problem: The settlers at Savannah in large part were not English, or even necessarily from the British Isles. There were German-speaking Swiss, Germans, French, Scots-Irish, Scottish, and Dutch settlers, as well as a few Englishmen. Those of these non-English ethnic groups no doubt also somehow remembered their own cultural and religious holidays, but records of their doing this are few at best.

The holidays and festivals established after 1700 were a powerful force tying the colonists to Britain, but even these would not survive the imperial upheaval that began in 1764 when the London government attempted to extend its tax structure into the American provinces. In the revolution that followed, holidays and festivals would be remade in a decidedly American fashion, the results of which we still live with today.

Holidays Made American

The outbreak of what is now known as the Stamp Act crisis (1765–66) initially did nothing to dampen participation in the imperial holidays, which celebrated the king and the royal family; the colonists saw their disputes as between them and Parliament, not the monarchy. In fact, many in the colonies believed that the monarch, the young George III, would support their stance of no taxation without representation. So the imperial holidays continued to be celebrated, often enthusiastically, right up to 1774.

By that time, though, a change had begun in the cycle of celebrations. New days associated with the resistance to what was seen as tyrannical British power were added to the calendar of yearly holidays, most notably the anniversary of the Boston Massacre of 1770 and the anniversary of the repeal of the Stamp Act in 1766. These celebrations were highly politicized and included speeches and sermons denouncing arbitrary power and British taxation of America. Some even included mock funeral rites for "Liberty" or "The Rights of Englishmen."

The closure of the port of Boston in 1774 because of the dumping of tea in the harbor, and the outbreak of heavy fighting in New England the following year led to the final abandoning of the imperial holidays in most parts of America. The anniversaries of the first meeting of the Continental Congress (May 10, 1775) and of the fighting at Lexington and Concord became days of remembrance, as did the anniversary of the battle of Bunker Hill and the British evacuation of Boston on March 17, 1776 (also St. Patrick's Day, of course). As the war progressed, other battles and war-related events were remembered annually, including the Christmas battle of Trenton, the American victory at Saratoga, and eventually the British evacuation of New York City in November 1783 after almost eight years of occupation. Some of these holidays survived into the 19th and 20th centuries; the Boston Marathon is run on Patriot's Day (the third Monday in April), which commemorates the Lexington and Concord battles.

However, two of the new holidays, the Fourth of July or Independence Day, which began to be celebrated in 1777 and continues on unbroken until today, and George Washington's Birthday, which was first celebrated during the war and is now combined with that of Abraham Lincoln to form the February holiday of Presidents Day, became central parts of American culture and important parts of American political history. In both cases, the practices used in the imperial past to mark monarchical anniversaries were now adapted to celebrate independence and republican government. Flag raisings, cannonades, toasting, parading, and sermons were all used to mark the day of independence and its central military hero, Washington. As early as July 4, 1777, a Rhode Islander in Newport would report that he heard a "continued firing of cannon . . . up the river [Narragansett Bay] . . . in honor of the Declaration of Independence," and he would report hearing the same each year thereafter.

The holidays, held and remembered even in the darkest days of the war in areas free of British control, were more than mere festivals. They were part of a concerted effort to create a new American, republican identity and citizen, and to create a new historical and social time line that celebrated what had always been "American" and "republican" about British America. They were, in essence, part of the national founding and the national foundation.

As with the royal holidays, these new, patriotic annual festivals were soon marked in the period's print culture. *The New Pennsylvania Almanac*, published in 1786 in Philadelphia, listed on its calendar the battles at Trenton (1776) and Princeton (1777), as well as February 6 [1778], labeled "French Alliance"; March 17, "St Patrick" and "Boston evacuated"; May 10, "Congress Met, 75"; May 12, "Charleston surrend. 80"; June 1, "Boston Port shut, 74"; July 4, "Independence 76"; August 27 [1776], "Battle of Long Island"; and "September 8, Battle Eutaw, 81 [in South Carolina]." This particular almanac also listed the religious holidays remembered by the Episcopal Church of America, and other days of religious note to Christians.

While the new holidays were enthusiastically celebrated at the war's end in 1783, the divisions in American society soon made the politically charged holidays of

After the Declaration of Independence, in 1777, two new holidays began to be celebrated: the Fourth of July, or Independence Day, and George Washington's Birthday, which was first celebrated during the Revolutionary War. Both holidays were celebrated using practices formerly used to mark imperial holidays, such as flag raisings and parades. The above engraving from 1794 shows George Washington—"The protector of his country, and the supporter of the rights of mankind"—encircled by the Seal of the United States and 13 state seals. ***(Library of Congress)***

July Fourth and Washington's Birthday battlegrounds for opposing views about the meaning of the American Revolution and the shape of the government. The nationalists (later adopting the name of Federalists) wanted a stronger central government. These were the men who supported the Constitutional Convention of 1787 and created the document Americans now live by. They feared that the language of the Declaration of Independence would encourage radicalism and runaway democracy and thus sought to control the celebration of the Fourth of July. Instead they used Washington's Birthday to celebrate their own vision of America and the American Revolution; Washington was a Federalist (though revered by all political parties) and an advocate of strong government. Their opponents, first the Anti-Federalists of 1787–88 who opposed the Constitution, and later the Jeffersonian Republicans of the 1790s, celebrated the Declaration (written by their leader, of course) and used the celebrations of the Fourth of July and Washington's Birthday to call for a more egalitarian, radical understanding of the Revolution and a more popular form of republican government. By 1800 the parties were often holding rival holiday celebrations, and violence between the contending parties on those days was not unknown.

Holidays and festivals played a central if changing role in 18th-century America. In an era before radio, TV, and the Internet, the celebrations brought people together, communicated and expressed shared values, and played a central role in politics. The forces that established and changed the celebrations in the 18th century—the needs of the far-flung British Empire to hold its subjects together, the massive movement of population to the frontiers, and the American Revolution itself—did not alter the basic fact that people needed and wanted to celebrate their political and religious beliefs in public, together. In so doing, they helped us better understand the changes of the 18th century.

—Brendan McConville

Further Reading

Cressy, David. *Bonfires and Bells: National Memory and the Protestant Calendar in Elizabethan and Stuart England.* Berkeley: University of California Press, 1989.

McConville, Brendan. *The King's Three Faces: The Rise and Fall of Royal America, 1688–1776.* Chapel Hill: University of North Carolina Press, for the Omohundro Institute of Early American History and Culture, 2006.

Newman, Simon. *Parades and the Politics of the Street: Festive Culture in the Early American Republic.* Philadelphia: University of Pennsylvania Press, 1997.

Travers, Len. *Celebrating the Fourth: Independence Day and the Rites of Nationalism in the Early Republic.* Amherst: University of Massachusetts Press, 1997.

Waldstreicher, David. *In the Midst of Perpetual Fetes: The Making of American Nationalism, 1776–1820.* Chapel Hill: University of North Carolina Press, for the Omohundro Institute of Early American History and Culture, 1997.

18th Century HOUSE AND HOME

The thousands of houses erected in Britain's mainland colonies during the 18th century embodied thousands of individual decisions made by builders and homeowners. Despite the great diversity that these decisions produced, it is still possible to discern patterns in housing and furnishings that provide insights into changing building practices, standards of living, cultural diversity, geographic mobility, and social status. For some, the quality of housing improved significantly during this century, with advances in terms of comfort, privacy, and refinement. Yet, for most colonists, the character and quality of their housing changed very little, even though they often consumed growing quantities of imported goods in their homes. If anything, the 18th century witnessed a growing disparity in housing stock as wealthy planters, merchants, and professionals built large and fashionable brick, timber-frame, or, more rarely, stone Georgian-style mansions, while the majority made do with cabins and houses built of logs or clapboards and that lacked plaster walls, wood floors, or glass windows.

Housing in New England

Overall, continuity rather than change characterized 18th-century New England architecture. Carpenters continued to hew, join, and raise post-and-beam box frames, primarily using oak or pine. Gable roofs remained the norm, though the pitch of these roofs lessened over the course of the century. Oak, pine, or cedar shingles covered roofs, and oak or pine clapboards covered most exterior walls, which as a rule remained unpainted. A single chimney usually stood at or near the center of two-room houses or on the gable end of those with only one ground-floor room. Well into the second quarter of the century, interior finishes continued to focus on decorating the exposed building frame. The only widespread change was the gradual replacement of leaded casement windows, which swung out to open, with sash windows, which moved up and down.

While most New England houses shared these traditional features, the region's 18th-century housing stock exhibited variations in size and plan that reflected economic and social stratification. The vast majority of the dwellings that dotted the countryside were still single-story, one- to three-room farmhouses that stood in isolation. Some of these were single-room cottages measuring only 10 by 14 feet. Most common were probably one-story, two-room, hall-and-parlor houses of 600 to 800 square feet, with a central chimney and a small entry, into which the front door opened. Some were slightly larger houses of 800 to 900 square feet with three rooms (hall, parlor, and kitchen), a massive off-center chimney, and a corner staircase to the garret above. Windows would have been at a premium in all of these houses, and paint was uncommon on either interior or exterior surfaces. Privacy also would have been at a premium, since the homes in New England had, on average, seven occupants.

The two-story 18th-century New England houses that today outnumber their more humble contemporaries have survived in disproportionate numbers. Only in urban areas and wealthier farming regions such as northeastern Massachusetts and the Connecticut River Valley did two-story houses of 1,200 to 1,400 square feet constitute a majority of the housing stock on the eve of the American Revolution. As a rule these two-story houses used traditional plans, with dedicated rooms, and employed architectural ornament. After mid-century their interior finish made greater use of plaster, paint, and raised paneling. Until late in the century, some residents continued to build houses with jetties, or overhangs, between the first and second floor. Most common were hall-and-parlor houses with two rooms on each floor, flanking a center chimney. The classic New England saltbox house, with its integral lean-to and sweeping rear roof, was built in most areas of the region. Saltboxes usually had three to five rooms below and three bedchambers above. Even in these larger houses, room use usually remained multipurpose, for parlors still contained the best bed, and various other functions continued to take place in rooms throughout the house. Cooking was increasingly limited to kitchens, however.

Housing in the Mid-Atlantic Region

Greater variety and more evidence of change were found in the houses built during the 18th century in the colonies stretching from New York to Delaware. This variety and innovation resulted from the particular history and ethnic diversity of the Mid-Atlantic, most of which had been part of the Dutch colony of New Netherland until it was conquered by the English in 1664. Today, only a few 17th-century dwellings with obvious Netherlandic architectural features still stand in this region, and with one or two possible exceptions, these surviving houses post-date the 1664 English takeover of the colony. Yet recognizably Dutch dwellings of two or three stories, built in brick with stepped gables, remained a prominent part of New York's 18th-century cityscape, though by midcentury, if not earlier, new buildings that were recognizably English in appearance became more common. Along the Hudson River, on Long Island, and in northeastern New Jersey, better-off descendants of the Dutch colony's settlers built story-and-a-half houses with two to four rooms. While some of these dwellings retained features of Netherlandic origin, such as anchor-bent framing, exposed joists, and perhaps porches, they also incorporated more obvious architectural innovations, such as gambrel roofs, symmetrical facades, sash windows, and central passages, which were not rooted in 17th-century building traditions of the Netherlands. In northern New Jersey and neighboring New York, houses built of stone survive in disproportionate numbers, but they were originally a small minority in a landscape where most residents lived in wooden versions or even more modest, one-room timber-frame or log houses of 400 to 500 square feet.

In the settlements along the Delaware River, immigrants from England and Wales in the late 1600s and early 1700s drew upon traditional British plans and building practices as well as more recent developments in urban building. From its earliest years Philadelphia's architecture employed features found in contemporary English cities, such as brick construction, sash windows, pentices or pent eaves (a narrow roof that projected from a wall between the first and second story), central or side passages, angled corner fireplaces, and gable-end walls lacking windows. Merchants built imposing brick houses, while upwardly mobile tradesmen and craftsmen spent considerable amounts of money on multiroom brick homes that approached modern middle-class standards in their finish. The majority lived in two-story brick or wooden houses as tenants, and the smaller the dwelling the greater the crowding.

Settlers in rural areas of the Delaware Valley initially erected wooden dwellings based on traditional British plans. Over time, some colonists incorporated some urban features as well as more traditional ones into two-story houses built of wood, brick, or stone in the Pennsylvania countryside and in southwestern New Jersey. But these houses, covering 900 to 1,600 square feet, rarely constituted more than a third of the housing stock even in this prosperous region, and they were outnumbered by single-story, one- or two-room, timber-frame or log dwellings of 400 to 600 square feet. Here and in the backcountry farther south, German immigrants erected stone and log houses that embodied elements of their own building traditions, though by the later 1700s and early 1800s their homes, like those built by the descendants of the settlers of New Netherland, incorporated elements of newer English building practices.

Housing in the South

During this century, established building traditions in Virginia and Maryland also exhibited more signs of change than were seen in 18th-century New England architecture. Over the course of the century, a growing number of planters and city dwellers, such as successful merchants, tradesman, and shopkeepers, built two- to four-room, story-and-a-half houses with masonry foundations, well-built frame or brick walls, and plastered interiors. They contained anywhere from 500 to 1,200 square feet. Weatherboards, which were long, thick, sawn boards that overlapped, replaced narrow, riven clapboards as the preferred covering for exterior walls, and shingles replaced clapboards for covering roofs. Some exteriors were painted, and brick chimneys replaced wooden chimneys. As a result, many more 18th-century houses—most of them dating from after the American Revolution—survive, in comparison to their less permanent 17th-century predecessors. Still, within these houses, old assumptions about where to work, sleep, eat, and cook—ideally in a kitchen located in a separate building—remained in place.

Many poorer residents in the South—white freeholders as well as enslaved blacks—lived in smaller, less substantial structures that lacked wood floors, plaster walls, and glass windows. Like many 17th-century dwellings in the region, these structures had a spindly frame covered by riven clapboards, while some had wooden chimneys lined with clay. Interiors were dark, dirty, and crowded. Except on the largest plantations, there was very little housing built exclusively for slaves, who lived in outbuildings and in nooks and crannies of the main house. One 18th-century dwelling intended for slaves does survive in Mecklenburg County, Virginia, though it was modified and expanded in the 19th century. Originally, it measured only 12 by 16 feet; it had a single narrow door and small windows with sliding shutters, but no glass. At the end of the century, the 1798 federal direct tax—the so-called window tax—rated over half the houses in Virginia and Maryland as substandard and therefore exempt from taxation.

As the 18th century progressed, a growing number of these small houses and cabins inhabited by poor whites and some blacks—slave and free—were built of round or squared-off logs. In parts of Virginia and Maryland, one-quarter to three-quarters of the population lived in such log dwellings. In the Carolinas and Georgia, almost three-quarters of the houses were small, wooden dwellings of log or clapboard that were exempt from taxation; in Kentucky and Tennessee in 1798, 80 to 90 percent were so insubstantial or in such poor condition that they were tax exempt. Virtually all of these homes lying beyond the Allegheny Mountains were log houses and cabins.

Log Construction

The spread of log construction throughout the mainland British colonies was the most dramatic architectural development during the 18th century. This development is noteworthy because 17th-century English colonists had brought with them no knowledge of log construction. Swedes and Finns erected the first log buildings along the Delaware River in the 1630s and 1640s. Subsequently, German settlers brought their own traditions of log construction to the Delaware Valley. Once introduced, the techniques of log building spread to other ethnic groups and to distant regions. Scots-Irish immigrants, who settled in or passed through the Delaware Valley region, adopted log construction and carried it into the back-country of Virginia and the Carolinas, as did immigrants from Germany. On the frontiers of New England, colonists were erecting log huts and cabins by the mid-1700s, if not earlier. During the third quarter of the century, Native Americans also began to build and live in log cabins. By 1800, log dwellings had become the most common form of housing in the new United States, though very few of these log homes survive today.

Log construction offered colonists an inexpensive form of housing that could be built from readily available materials without the assistance of a carpenter and with few tools. Indeed, the only necessary tool was an ax. Some were intended to be no more than temporary structures suited to families setting up farms, and these were eventually replaced or abandoned. Others were lived in for years, or for decades in some instances. The simplest, and probably the most common, one-room log cabins often lacked foundations and glazed windows, and they had dirt floors and wooden chimneys. More substantial log houses had two stories, stone foundations and chimneys, and a glazed window or two, and they might even be plastered on the inside or covered with weatherboards on the exterior. On average, single-story log houses contained 400 to 600 square feet, and like other contemporary dwellings they housed, on average, seven people.

Domestic Architecture in the Georgian Style

Standing in striking contrast to these log structures and the one-room, timber-frame houses that together housed the vast majority of the population were the larger, more architecturally ambitious homes built by wealthy colonists in coastal cities and the countryside. In the first two decades of the 18th century, merchants and government officials in Boston and Portsmouth, wealthy tobacco planters in Virginia, and the rich rice planters in South Carolina began

Designed and built in 1716–18 by John Drew, a ship-joiner and architect, the MacPheadris-Warner House in Portsmouth, New Hampshire, offers an example of the Georgian style of architecture that was popular among wealthy colonists in coastal cities and the countryside, especially in the first two decades of the 18th century. Above is a photo of the house from 1902. *(Library of Congress)*

to build brick houses in a new style known today as Georgian. They drew selectively upon English design ideas that were rooted in a Renaissance architectural vocabulary, melded them with existing building practices, and adapted them to local social conditions and resources to create distinctive expressions in a recognizably Georgian style. Notable early examples were Boston's 1690–91 Foster-Hutchinson House, the 1712 Clark-Frankland House, and the 1712–13 Andrew Faneuil House, all of which are no longer standing. Existing structures in this style include the 1716–19 MacPheadris-Warner House in Portsmouth, New Hampshire, and the 1706–22 Governor's Palace in Williamsburg, which has been reconstructed.

Several features distinguished these houses from 17th-century houses and most other 18th-century dwellings. They had symmetrical facades; large sash windows; square, four-room plans, bisected by a central passageway; and classically inspired architectural details on the exterior. At the same time, they rejected as no longer fashionable such features as overhangs, pent eaves, and, ideally, pitched roofs. The interiors contained high-ceilinged, wainscoted, and plastered rooms in which wooden surfaces might be painted yellow ocher, verdigris, or Prussian blue, or they might be grained to suggest more exotic materials such as cedar or marble. These interiors were seen as being more refined, more polite, and thus better suited to entertaining. Having passageways and, as a rule, eight to ten rooms, such houses provided their occupants with a degree of a privacy absent in the vast majority of 18th-century homes. Later in the century, some Georgian-style houses had projecting pavilions and Palladian windows on their facades, along with neoclassical interior detailing.

Beginning around midcentury, elements of this style and its central-hallway plan were incorporated into more modest Georgian houses constructed in the countryside by members of the rural gentry and clergy. Even though they were usually built of wood, these rural mansion houses—with their two chimneys, elaborate doorways, and other architectural embellishments, such as corner quoins and boxed cornices—stood out amid the single-story or two-story center-chimney houses. As a rule, they contained between 2,800 and 3,200 square feet. The impact of these houses was often heightened by the use of either a large gambrel roof with its double pitch or a hip roof in which four roof planes tapered to the ridgeline. Exteriors of these mansion houses were usually painted in "stone colors"—shades of gray and tan—with the trim picked out in white, suggesting a solidity of masonry that was belied by their wooden clapboarding.

Housing and the Spread of Consumer Goods

To distinguish themselves from their less wealthy neighbors, and to impress royal officials and English merchants with their stature and "Englishness," the occupants of these mansion houses began to cultivate a lifestyle that was qualitatively different from that of their neighbors. The performance of genteel social rituals depended on new types of imported goods, such as tea and ceramics, as well as locally produced furniture, such as sets of chairs and specialized tables for tea drinking, dining, and card playing. For their owners, these houses, with their new goods and furnishings, were not only markers of wealth and assertions of status, they were also critical props necessary for the proper display of genteel social knowledge. Such houses provided the ideal stage for cultural expressions designed to affirm ties that bound together members of the colonial elite while distancing them from other members of society.

At the same time, the goods that supported such rituals were inherently fragile, usually new, and commercially available to others. Analyses of estate inventories and storekeepers' account books, along with archaeological excavations, have revealed that not just the elite but also growing numbers of middling colonists and residents of the new nation were acquiring some of these newly available consumer goods. Like the residents of Georgian mansions, colonists of the middling sort—farmers and craftsmen—began to consume tea, coffee, and chocolate, and they began to buy imported English textiles, looking glasses, candlesticks, knives and forks, and pewter and ceramic goods. More modest homes also contained more beds, more chairs, and more tables than had been present in the dwellings of 17th-century colonists.

Once luxuries, such goods and furnishings became necessities—or what contemporaries called "conveniences." More was involved than improving basic standards of living or standards of sanitation, for these consumers were more likely to buy a punch bowl than a chamber pot. For their consumers and owners, these new goods served primarily as props of a more refined and respectable lifestyle. In addition, these props and markers could be acquired for money, were not dependent upon birth, were widely recognizable, and were readily portable.

For increasing numbers of Americans, consumer goods may have been affordable, but improved housing was not. As a result, the population's growing purchases of imported beverages and domestic furnishings helped drive late-18th-century investment in architecture as a means of maintaining status in settled regions of the country. While the increase in consumers' ability and desire to obtain goods could serve to blur social distinctions and differences in wealth, expenditures on large and costly houses reinforced them. In newly settled areas where expenditures of labor and money went into clearing land, obtaining livestock, and planting crops, relatively little time and few resources were spent on either consumer goods or housing. By the end of the 18th century, the contrasts in housing between coastal regions and the western interior, between cities and the countryside, and between rich and poor were stark.

—Kevin Sweeney

Further Reading

Bushman, Richard L. *The Refinement of America: Persons, Houses, Cities*. New York: Alfred A. Knopf, 1992.

Carr, Lois Green, and Lorena S. Walsh, "The Standard of Living in the Colonial Chesapeake." *William and Mary Quarterly*, 3d ser., 45, no. 1 (January 1988): 135–159.

Carson, Cary, Ronald Hoffman, and Peter J. Albert, eds. *Of Consuming Interests: The Style of Life in the Eighteenth Century.* Charlottesville: University Press of Virginia, 1994.

Chappell, Edward A. "Housing the Nation: The Transformation of Living Standards in Early America." In *Of Consuming Interests: The Style of Life in the Eighteenth Century*, edited by Cary Carson, Ronald Hoffman, and Peter J. Albert, 167–232. Charlottesville: University Press of Virginia, 1994.

Clemens, Paul G. E. "The Consumer Culture of the Middle Atlantic, 1760–1820." *William and Mary Quarterly*, 3d ser., 62, no. 4 (October 2005): 577–624.

Crowley, John E. *The Invention of Comfort: Sensibilities and Design in Early Modern Britain and Early America.* Baltimore, Md.: Johns Hopkins University Press, 2001.

Garvin, James L. *A Building History of Northern New England.* Hanover, N.H.: University Press of New England, 2001.

Gowans, Alan. "The Mansions of Alloways Creek." In *Common Places: Readings in American Vernacular Architecture,* edited by Dell Upton and John Michael Vlach, 367–393. Athens: University of Georgia Press, 1986.

Graham, Willie. "Preindustrial Framing in the Chesapeake." In *Constructing Image, Identity, and Place: Perspectives in Vernacular Architecture,* no. 9, edited by Alison K. Hoagland and Kenneth A. Breisch, 179–196. Knoxville: University of Tennessee Press, 2003.

Herman, Bernard. *Town House: Architecture and Material Life in the Early American City 1780–1830.* Chapel Hill: University of North Carolina Press, for the Omohundro Institute of Early American History and Culture, 2005.

Lanier, Gabrielle M. *The Delaware Valley in the Early Republic: Architecture, Landscape, and Regional Identity.* Baltimore, Md.: Johns Hopkins University Press, 2004.

Lounsbury, Carl. "The Dynamics of Architectural Design in Eighteenth-Century Charleston and the Lowcountry." In *Exploring Everyday Landscapes: Perspectives in Vernacular Architecture,* no. 7, edited by Annmarie Adams and Sally McMurry, 58–72. Knoxville: University of Tennessee Press, 1997.

Main, Gloria L. "The Standard of Living in Southern New England, 1640–1773." *William and Mary Quarterly*, 3d ser., 45, no. 1 (January 1988): 124–134.

Michel, Jack. "'In a Manner and Fashion Suitable to Their Degree': A Preliminary Investigation of the Material Culture of Early Rural Pennsylvania." In *Working Papers from the Regional Economic History Research Center*, 5, no. 1, edited by Glenn Porter and William H. Mulligan, Jr., 1–83. Greenville, Wilmington, Delaware: Eleutherian Mills-Hagley Foundation, 1981.

Ryan, Thomas R. "Cultural Accommodations in Late-Eighteenth-Century Architecture of Marbletown, New York." In *Shaping Communities: Perspectives in Vernacular Architecture,* no. 7, edited by Carter L. Hudgins and Elizabeth Collins Cromley, 137–149. Knoxville: University of Tennessee Press, 1997.

Shammas, Carole. "The Housing Stock of the Early United States: Refinement Meets Migration." *William and Mary Quarterly*, 3d ser., 64, no. 3 (July 2007): 549–590.

Steinitz, Michael. "Rethinking Geographical Approaches to the Common House: The Evidence from Eighteenth-Century Massachusetts," in *Perspectives in Vernacular Architecture*, no. 3, edited by Thomas Carter and Bernard L. Herman, 16–26. Columbia: University of Missouri Press, 1989.

Sweeney, Kevin M. "Mansion People: Kinship, Class and Architecture in Western Massachusetts in the

Mid-Eighteenth Century." *Winterthur Portfolio* 19, no. 4 (Winter 1984): 231–255.

Wacker, Peter O. "Relations between Cultural Origins, Relative Wealth, and the Size, Form and Materials on Construction of Rural Dwellings in New Jersey during the Eighteenth Century." In *Géographie historique du village et de la maison rurale: actes du colloque,* edited by Charles Higounet, 201–230. Paris: Centre National de la Recherche Scientifique, 1979.

Wells, Camille. "The Eighteenth-Century Landscape of Virginia's Northern Neck." *Northern Neck of Virginia Historical Magazine* 37, no. 1 (1987): 4217–4255.

———. "The Planter's Prospect: Houses, Outbuildings, and Rural Landscapes in Eighteenth-Century Virginia." *Winterthur Portfolio* 28, no. 1 (Spring 1993): 1–31.

Zink, Clifford W. "Dutch Framed Houses in New York and New Jersey." *Winterthur Portfolio* 22, no. 4 (Winter 1987): 265–294.

18th Century IMMIGRATION

Over the course of the 18th century, well over 700,000 immigrants from Africa and Europe arrived in British North America. The English remained a major group, but they came to be outnumbered by Africans as well as immigrants from Germany, Ireland, Scotland, and France. Whether these newcomers came voluntarily or involuntarily, they radically transformed the ethnic, cultural, and religious composition of the existing population. The increase in ethnic diversity was especially notable in the middle colonies. In Pennsylvania—a particularly popular destination for European immigrants due to its religious freedom and availability of land—the proportion of the English declined to only around 35 percent of the white population by the time the first United States census was taken in 1790.

The Course of Immigration during the 18th Century

Immigration to British North America was relatively low in the first three decades of the 18th century. Of the 55,000 newcomers during this period, an estimated 30,000 originated in Africa, and 25,000 arrived from northern and western Europe. Beginning around 1730, immigration from Europe increased steadily, and roughly 36,000 Europeans arrived in the 1730s. During the same period, 40,000 Africans were brought to North America to meet the demand for labor in the southern colonies. Between 1740 and 1770, immigration increased to an average of 130,000 per decade, with half coming from Africa. The imperial crisis and the American Revolution caused a drop in immigration, which increased only slowly after independence, with an estimated 100,000 Europeans arriving in the United States in the last two decades of the century.

While religious and political factors drove emigration from Europe, the majority left for economic reasons, including overpopulation, resulting agrarian crises, and rises in land rents. During the 18th century, British North America gained a reputation as the "best poor man's country," as an asylum of liberty, and as a land of opportunity. Immigrants were attracted to British North America by the abundant land, natural resources, and freedom from governmental interference in private affairs. Moreover, ship captains and merchants actively recruited emigrants in their efforts to make a profit in the lucrative and largely unregulated immigrant trade. The majority of European immigrants did not have the resources necessary to pay for their passage across the Atlantic. Instead, they chose to enter into agreements with a vessel's owner or captain that provided them with transatlantic passage in return for several years of servitude in America. At the end of the term, the servant was usually entitled to "freedom dues," which could include clothing, tools, or even land. By the time of the Revolution, an estimated 250,000 Europeans had come to North America as servants. During the 18th century, German and Irish immigrants replaced the English as major sources of bound labor, and most of them settled in the Mid-Atlantic region.

English

During the 18th century, England ceased to be the main source of immigrants in North America, in part because England had become increasingly concerned about the emigration of its domestic population. As a result, the English government began to pass laws that were designed to prevent the departure of its subjects, especially skilled laborers. At the same time it more actively promoted the settlement of foreigners in North America.

Significant numbers of English immigrants continued to arrive in North America throughout the 18th century, however. The total between 1700 and 1775 numbered around 80,000, with peaks during breaks in European warfare in the 1720s, 1750s, and 1770s. As many as 50,000 of these newcomers were convicts, the majority of whom ended up as indentured servants on tobacco plantations in the Chesapeake region. Immigration from England rose in the early 1770s, with an estimated 6,000 newcomers arriving between 1773 and 1775 alone. More than half of them were indentured servants, and the majority settled in Virginia and Maryland. While Americans of English descent retained their dominance in parts of New England, mostly because of legislation that discouraged non-English newcomers from settling there, their proportion declined overall, especially in the middle colonies. A study of surnames recorded in the 1790 census revealed that the percentage of people from England made up around 60 percent of the white population and 49 percent of the entire population of British North America in 1776.

The Revolution sharply reduced English immigration. For roughly two decades after independence, English laws continued to discourage emigration, especially of skilled artisans and manufacturers. Late in the century, however, a number of radicals emigrated, including the clergyman, scientist, and outspoken supporter of the American and French revolutions Joseph Priestley, who moved to Pennsylvania after his home in England was destroyed during the Birmingham Riots of 1791.

Africans

African slaves were the largest non-English group to arrive in British North America during the 18th century. As many as 400,000 men, women, and children were forcibly transported from Africa to British North America in order to meet the growing demand for agricultural labor. Most of them came from West Central Africa, the Bight of Benin, the Bight of Biafra, and the Gold Coast. Slavery existed in every North American colony. Most slaves lived and worked on plantations in the South, but there were also substantial slave populations in the North. There was a free black population that was concentrated in northern cities, but the number of free blacks declined in the decades leading up to the Revolution, as legal restrictions made it increasingly difficult for owners to free their slaves. On the eve of the American Revolution, roughly one out of five Americans was either an African immigrant or the descendant of one, and the vast majority of them were enslaved.

The Revolutionary War and the republican ideology that stressed liberty and equality had a dramatic effect on the institution of slavery in the North. As the result of legal action, including "freedom suits" brought by slaves, all of the northern states soon legislated for the abolition of slavery. By the end of the century, there were significant free black communities in the North and also in the Upper South.

Germans

The German-speaking people who arrived in North America in the 18th century included populations from a number of places, including the Palatine, Austria, Switzerland, and Alsace. Although a few Germans came to North America in the 17th century, large-scale German immigration did not commence until after the turn of the century. In 1709, politics and economic hardships, caused primarily by overpopulation, scarcity of land, and warfare, compelled 13,000 Palatines to journey to London, lured by rumors that Queen Anne would provide them with free passage to and land in America. The British government eventually sent 600 of these individuals to North Carolina, and another 3,000 were sent to New York, in exchange for several years of labor in its naval stores factories along the lower Hudson River. By 1712, the project was abandoned, and while some Germans remained on the Hudson, others moved to New York's frontier and into Pennsylvania. News of the success of some of these settlers contributed to a growing migration. In 1717, three ships arrived from Germany. Between 1727 and 1740, an average of 6 vessels carrying German-speaking people landed in North America every year; this number increased to 10 ships annually until the outbreak of the Seven Years' War in 1756 temporarily halted the trade. Over 100,000 Germans settled in North America during the 18th century, including about 5,000 mercenary soldiers who fought for the British during the American Revolution.

The German migration was generally a family migration. Most of the immigrants were farmers, and the vast majority belonged to the Lutheran and Reformed churches. An estimated two-thirds of the German immigrants came to America as indentured servants or "redemptioners." Whereas indentured servants were contractually bound to the ship's captain, who could sell them in America, redemptioners signed contracts to pay their fare in America in any way they chose after their arrival, including with funds provided by friends and family or by signing indentures. Most ended up in the Mid-Atlantic region, and many servants experienced upward mobility after the conclusion of their terms.

Some German immigrants eventually moved south, from Pennsylvania into Virginia's Shenandoah Valley and into Georgia, along the most important route of migration in colonial North America, the Great Wagon Road. Many more Germans settled in southeastern Pennsylvania, where they exhibited a strong tendency to preserve their customs and manners. These Pennsylvania Germans, commonly referred to as the Pennsylvania Dutch, are considered a separate ethnic group, with distinct forms of folk art, music, and language.

Irish and Scots-Irish

Reliable statistics about Irish immigration during the colonial period are not available. It is clear, however, that the Irish constituted one of the largest non-English immigrant groups during the 17th and 18th centuries. Population studies suggest that over 250,000 Irish—and perhaps as many as 400,000—came to America between 1700 and 1775. Only around one-fifth to one-fourth of them were Catholic, and another fifth were Anglican. The majority of Irish Catholics were single males who came as indentured servants, but the group also included members of the dispossessed Irish gentry. Overall, despite persistent economic struggles and religious discrimination, Irish Catholics were inhibited from emigrating by traditions that stigmatized emigration as involuntary exile.

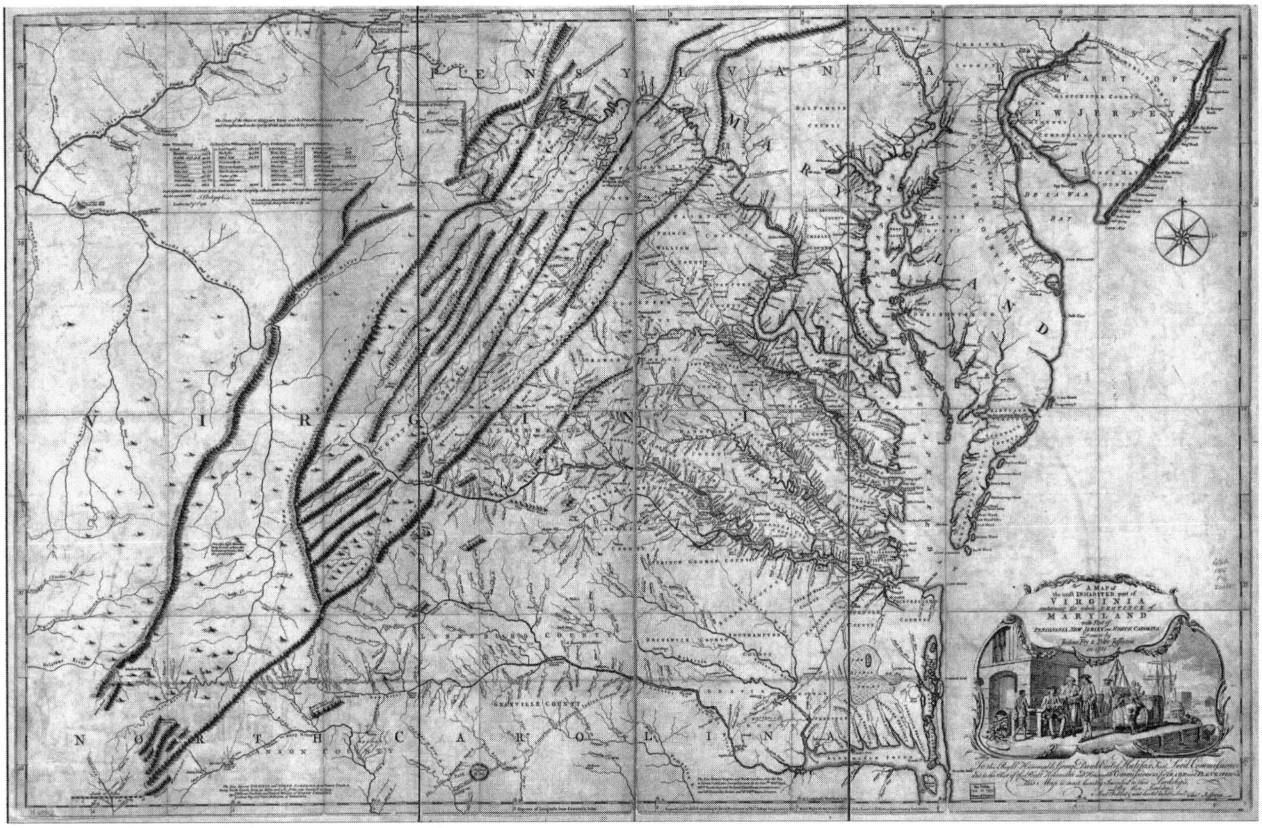

The so-called Great Wagon Road, used by many Germans and Scots-Irish families to travel south into the backcountry, was the most important route of migration in colonial North America. The above map was drawn by Joshua Fry and Peter Jefferson in 1751 and features "the most inhabited part of Virginia containing the whole province of Maryland with part of Pensilvania, New Jersey and North Carolina." It was based on firsthand surveys and contained the first accurate representation of the Allegheny Mountains. *(Library of Congress)*

The largest group of emigrants from Ireland were Scots-Irish, an American term used to describe Presbyterians from Scotland who had settled in the Ulster region of Northern Ireland in the 17th century. Over 100,000 of them went to North America in the 18th century. These people emigrated for a combination of economic, religious, and political reasons. They labored in Ireland under an economic system that severely restricted opportunities to trade freely, and, like all Irish tenants, they were forced to pay high rents to English landlords. Moreover, they were viewed with suspicion by the largely Catholic Irish population, while at the same time suffering discrimination due to their status as non-Anglicans. The termination of land leases in 1717 and 1718 triggered the first significant waves of emigration. Over the following decades, a steady stream of Scots-Irish made their way to America, with particularly large numbers arriving in the years 1725 to 1729, 1740 and 1741, and especially 1771 to 1775, when an agrarian crisis and the collapse of the linen trade caused 40,000 Scots-Irish to emigrate. An average of 5,000 arrived every year in the 1780s and 1790s, with almost all of them paying their way. Among them was a small group of perhaps 100 to 200 political refugees who came in the wake of the failed Irish Rebellion of 1798.

While some of the early Scots-Irish immigrants settled in New England, the local population soon viewed them with suspicion, in part because of their particular brand of Calvinism, but also because many of the newcomers were poor. The majority of Scots-Irish settled in the far more welcoming middle colonies, where Philadelphia, and New Castle and Wilmington in Delaware, became major ports of entry. By midcentury, Pennsylvania's Cumberland County was dominated by Scots-Irish. Over the next two decades, some of them moved south, establishing a string of frontier communities along the Great Wagon Road, in Pennsylvania, Virginia, and Georgia.

Scots

While Scots had been settling in North America since the beginning of European colonization, their numbers increased steadily after the Act of Union of 1707 opened trade between Scotland and the colonies. However, the first significant numbers of Scots who arrived in North America during the 18th century did not go there voluntarily. Over 1,400 Jacobites defeated in the rebellions of 1715 and 1745, along with hundreds of criminals and religious dissenters, were shipped to the colonies in the first four decades of the 18th century. Beginning in the 1730s, voluntary immigration increased, and around 30,000 Scots arrived in America in the years up to 1760. Emigration from Scotland did not reach significant numbers until the 1750s, when large numbers of Scottish soldiers went to America to fight in the French and Indian War. The decision of many of them to stay in America and persuade friends and neighbors to follow their lead triggered a flood of emigration. An estimated 25,000 Scots reached America's shores between the end of hostilities with France in 1761 and the outbreak of the Revolutionary War in 1775.

Emigrants from Scotland came from two distinct regions, the Lowlands and the Highlands. Highlanders generally came with their families. Large numbers of them arrived in the 1760s in response to persistent poverty that was aggravated by a series of crop failures, the raising of rents, and the "Highland Clearances" that followed the Jacobite Rebellion of 1745. They tended to settle in close-knit communities, primarily in New York's Hudson Valley and the Cape Fear region of South Carolina. The emigration of Lowlanders peaked in the 1770s. Primarily lured by the availability of cheap land, most of them came as indentured servants without their families.

The vast majority of Scots were Presbyterian. A relatively high proportion of the merchants and factors (brokers) in port cities were Scottish. Many were active in politics, and even though some supported the Revolutionary cause, most of them remained loyal to the British Crown. After Britain lost possession of its colonies, many left for Canada or returned to Scotland. Nevertheless, according to census records, there were around 260,000 people of Scottish stock in the United States in 1790, or more than 6 percent of the population.

French

During the colonial period, French immigration came from several distinct sources. In the 18th century, small

During the French and Indian War, thousands of Acadians were forcibly removed from Nova Scotia by the British beginning in 1755, an expulsion known as the Grand Dérangement. Many of these French immigrants were dispersed throughout the 13 colonies. The above painting by Thomas Davies from 1758, titled *A View of the Plundering and Burning of the City of Grimross*, depicts the St. John River Campaign, during which British soldiers torched the village and forced the families to flee. *(National Gallery of Canada)*

groups of French Huguenots continued to arrive directly from France or by way of the Netherlands, where they had sought refuge from religious persecution. Most were artisans, skilled farmers, or merchants. They settled throughout the 13 colonies, with concentrations in New York, Pennsylvania, Virginia, and North Carolina. Partly because they were few in number, and also because many had spent a generation or more outside of France before their arrival in North America, they tended to marry into non-Huguenots communities. By the middle of the century, they had largely disappeared as a distinct ethnic group.

A very different group of French emigrants arrived from Canada. In 1755, the British forcibly removed between 6,000 and 8,000 Acadians from Nova Scotia because of suspected disloyalty. Many were dispersed throughout the 13 colonies, where they were generally unwelcome because of their Roman Catholicism. Many of them did not survive the displacement, known as the Grand Dérangement. However, some of them eventually established small communities in various parts of the North Atlantic region. In the 1760s, between 2,000 and 3,000 Acadians, called Cajuns, settled in Louisiana, then a Spanish colony with a strong French presence.

A third kind of French immigrant arrived during and after the French Revolution. At least 10,000 French refugees settled in the United States in the late 1780s and 1790s. The majority, including several thousand people of mixed descent, came from the French colonies in the Caribbean. Among this group were "free people of color," many of them wealthy planters, who fled Saint Domingue during the slave rebellion in the early 1790s. The majority of the French refugees settled in urban centers along the eastern seaboard, especially Philadelphia.

Other Immigrant Groups

Other ethnic groups with a numerically small but notable presence in the 13 colonies included Jews, Welsh, Swedes, and Dutch. The first significant groups of Jews that arrived in the 18th century included primarily Ashkenazim from central and eastern Europe who escaped war and persecution, and Sephardim from Portugal who left their homeland due to the Inquisition. After establishing communities in England and Holland, some of them eventually settled in Rhode Island, New York, Pennsylvania, South Carolina, and Georgia. In 1740, Parliament enacted a law for the American colonies that offered naturalization to Jews, a right that brought considerable privileges, including relief from trade restrictions and the right to own property. The majority of Jewish immigrants during the colonial period pursued careers in commerce, and most settled in cities along the Atlantic coast. By 1776 there were between 2,000 and 3,000 Jews in the colonies.

Significant immigration of people of Welsh, Swedish, and Dutch origin did not commence until after 1800; however, all of them were well represented in the colonies. There were a few Welsh communities in southeastern Pennsylvania, Delaware, and the Carolinas. A few hundred Swedes immigrated to America in the 18th century to join the Swedes that had arrived earlier. Similarly, a few Dutch settled in the colonies in the 18th century. Small Dutch communities of Quakers and Mennonites remained in Pennsylvania, but regions that had formerly been dominated by the Dutch, most notably New York, gradually lost their Dutch character over the course of the century.

By the end of the colonial period, ethnic diversity had increased significantly. New England remained the most ethnically homogenous region, with an overwhelmingly white and English population, in part because it was the least welcoming for non-English immigrants. Nevertheless, there were some Africans, Scots-Irish, Scots, Huguenots, and Jews in New England. The middle colonies were the most ethnically diverse, with large German and Scots-Irish concentrations, as well as many Scots, French, Swedes, Dutch, and Africans. Only about half of the region's population was of English origin. Most of the people in the southern colonies were of English background, but there were significant minorities of Germans, Scots-Irish, and Scots. What set this region apart from the other colonies was the large African population. Throughout the colonies, the English tended to be overrepresented in the tidewater region, while the backcountry was much more ethnically mixed.

Immigration and the American Revolution

At the end of the Seven Years' War, England began to tighten its previously relaxed immigration policies as part of an effort to reorganize the British Empire. In addition, the government wanted to curb English emigration, which surged to unprecedented levels in the late 1760s and early 1770s. It vetoed colonial laws designed to promote immigration, including a statute by Georgia that promised free transportation to Protestant emigrants from Britain, and a North Carolina act that offered land grants to Highlanders from the Isle of Skye. Customs officials in England and Scotland were ordered to keep detailed records about the numbers and motives of emigrants, and in 1773 the colonies were prohibited from passing their own naturalization laws.

Of course, the outbreak of the Revolutionary War that resulted in the founding of the new nation changed all that. The single most important immediate effect on American immigration policies was the transformation of British subjects into aliens. The English now faced the same kind of scrutiny as newcomers from other European nations. More generally, wartime experiences with Loyalists, as well as long-held suspicions that subjects of despotic governments could not easily become liberty-loving citizens, raised doubts about the character of foreigners and their contributions to the new republic.

In the 1790s, the U.S. Congress passed three successive Naturalization Acts that reflected a growing tension between the idea of the nation as a haven for the oppressed and the realities of partisan divisions and deep-seated prejudices. The Naturalization Act of 1790 offered naturalization to any "free white person" who had resided in the country for at least two years, proven his "good character," and taken an oath to "support the constitution of the United States." Within a few years, the influx of foreigners fleeing from the crises triggered by the French Revolution raised fears of newcomers meddling in politics, especially since a high proportion of the new arrivals were political refugees with radical views. In 1795 a new Naturalization Act was passed, increasing the length of residency to five years. The third law, passed in 1798, was clearly a political measure by the Federalists designed to increase national security when war with France seemed inevitable, and also to deprive their political opponents, the Jeffersonian Republicans, of a major source of their support. The new law, passed as one of several measures collectively known as the Alien and Sedition Acts, required 14 years of residency before an applicant could be admitted. Enemy aliens were barred from naturalization while their native country was at war with the United States.

Within two years of the election of Thomas Jefferson to the presidency of the United States in 1800, the Alien and Sedition Acts were repealed, and the residency requirements for naturalization returned to five years. The restriction to "free white persons" remained unchanged, however, and nonwhite foreign-born persons continued to be barred from becoming American citizens. Overall, Americans preferred European immigrants who were propertied, hardworking, Protestant, and republican. Yet self-interest and the principle of offering refuge to the European victims of despotic governments ensured that the new nation opened its doors and granted access to citizenship to virtually any European who desired to take part in the republican experiment.

—Friederike Baer

Further Reading

Barkan, Elliott R., ed. *A Nation of Peoples: A Sourcebook on America's Multicultural Heritage.* Westport, Conn.: Greenwood Press, 1999.

Baseler, Marilyn C. *"Asylum for Mankind": America, 1607–1800.* Ithaca, N.Y.: Cornell University Press, 1998.

Berlin, Ira. *Many Thousands Gone: The First Two Centuries of Slavery in North America.* Cambridge, Mass.: Belknap Press of Harvard University Press, 1998.

Butler, Jon. *The Huguenots in America: A Refugee People in New World Society.* Cambridge, Mass.: Harvard University Press, 1983.

Daniels, Roger. *Coming to America: A History of Immigration and Ethnicity in American Life*. 2d ed. New York: Perennial, 2002.

Dinnerstein, Leonard, and David M. Reimers. *Ethnic Americans: A History of Immigration.* 5th ed. New York: Columbia University Press, 2009.

Dobson, David. *Scottish Emigration to Colonial America, 1607–1785*. Athens: University of Georgia Press, 1994.

Faber, Eli. *The Jewish People in America.* Vol. 1, *A Time for Planting: The First Migration, 1654–1820.* Baltimore, Md.: Johns Hopkins University Press, 1992.

Fogleman, Aaron. *Hopeful Journeys: German Immigration, Settlement, and Political Culture in Colonial America, 1717–1775.* Philadelphia: University of Pennsylvania Press, 1996.

Griffen, Patrick. *The People with No Name: Ireland's Ulster Scots, America's Scots Irish, and the Creation of a British Atlantic World, 1689–1764.* Princeton, N.J.: Princeton University Press, 2001.

Leyburn, James G. *The Scotch-Irish: A Social History.* Chapel Hill: University of North Carolina Press, 1962.

Miller, Kerby A. *Emigrants and Exiles: Ireland and the Irish Exodus to North America.* New York: Oxford University Press, 1985.

Nolt, Stephen M. *Foreigners in Their Own Land: Pennsylvania Germans in the Early Republic.* University Park: Pennsylvania State University Press, 2002.

Otterness, Philip. *Becoming German: The 1709 Palatine Migration to New York*. Ithaca, N.Y.: Cornell University Press, 2004.

Thernstrom, Stephan, ed. *Harvard Encyclopedia of American Ethnic Groups*. Cambridge, Mass.: Harvard University Press, 1980.

Wokeck, Marianne. *Trade in Strangers: The Beginnings of Mass Migration to North America.* University Park: Pennsylvania State University Press, 1999.

18th Century LABOR AND LIVELIHOOD

In the American colonies, labor shaped people's lives. The labor they performed, and the relationships outlined by that labor, may be broken into broad categories, which often overlapped and changed over the course of the 18th century. First, people who lived in the emerging urban areas worked at jobs different from those of the majority of North Americans, who were involved in agriculture. Second, labor in urban and rural areas was different for men and women, but the type of work each sex performed depended on whether those men and women were bound, enslaved, or free. Third, while the huge majority of people worked with their hands, a minority worked as managers, lawyers, and businessmen. Finally, enslaved and free laborers lived and worked differently, and the differences grew more pronounced over time.

Many labor relationships changed over the course of the 18th century. New ways of thinking about productive relationships combined with political disputes to reshape labor practices. More specifically, as the colonial economy matured in North America, some colonists felt constrained by their relationship to Britain. They sought to break free from British political rule so they could pursue other economic activities. As much as political upheaval drove change, workers, employers, and owners sought to modify their relationships for economic reasons. But not everyone shared the same goals. Workers wanted greater stability and steadier income, while owners and employers sought to reduce their costs and risk and to maximize their revenue and profits. The push for these changes came from many directions, and people who desired one brand of change often confronted people who sought another. Some succeeded in accomplishing the change they sought, while others failed.

When groups of people negotiated changes in their working relationships, they did so from vastly different positions. Employers, landlords, and owners possessed far more economic and political power than did workers, tenants, and enslaved people. Not surprisingly, they exerted greater control over the political and legal mechanisms that determined labor and labor relations. In most cases, these interactions produced more standardized economic relationships that favored owners and employers, who enforced their desires through the political and social institutions they dominated. In any case, both sides worked hard to keep whatever advantage they acquired, because these interactions were a zero-sum game: Whatever workers gained, employers and owners lost.

Urban Laborers: Free and Enslaved

In general, people living in cities worked at jobs different from those of people living in the countryside. In cities such as New York, Philadelphia, and Charleston, South Carolina, white and black, free and enslaved men, women, and children worked as much as they could, or were forced to work, to survive. While some free urban residents worked as skilled craftsmen or businessmen and earned handsome incomes, the majority worked at semiskilled and unskilled jobs and struggled to provide enough food for their families. Enslaved people worked in many of the same kinds of jobs, but they reaped none of the profits from their labor and they faced additional hardships because of their status.

Sailors usually made up the largest group of workers in 18th-century cities. Often called "Jack Tars" because of how they waterproofed their pants, sailors faced hard and dangerous work for little pay. Even under the best of circumstances, working on a ship was drudgery. Sailors hauled, loaded, and off-loaded cargo, kept the ship clean, fixed the rigging, and repaired sails. They ate poorly and slept belowdecks in dark and wet quarters. All the while, ships pitched and rolled in heavy winds and harsh seas, and a misstep could cause a debilitating injury or death.

Pay was affected both by the time of year and external forces. Sailors living in colder climates usually worked 9 to 10 months per year. Frozen waterways and rough seas inhibited shipping in winter months. On the other hand, sailors earned more during wars such as the Seven Years' War (1756–63). Overall, however, captains and mates made more than other mariners onboard ship, and sailors remained some of the poorest free workers in the community.

Fishermen, on the other hand, can be divided into at least two groups. Some fishermen lived and worked much like sailors. They spent long periods at sea, working at the same tasks as other sailors. But they spent much of their time handlining or hauling in nets of fish, which they preserved and stored belowdecks. Others, such as New England farmers, fished because the region's poor soil inhibited crop yield. As a result, these farmers looked to the sea and nearby rivers and lakes to supplement household production.

Sailors and fishermen spent large chunks of time away from home. Some fishermen went out and returned the same day, but most sailors ventured to open sea and spent days, weeks, or even months away from home. When not at sea, sailors often worked at jobs associated with shipping. They made and repaired ropes and sails, loaded and unloaded ships, or moved cargo from one place to another. Laborers received low wages for this kind of work, and they often lived on the edge of poverty. Most urban laborers also faced extended periods of unemployment every year. When facing dire circumstances, families often resorted to begging or appealed for public relief. When a family could not earn enough to survive and could not acquire enough public relief to remain in their dwellings, they sometimes ended up in a local almshouse. Others lived on the streets, scavenging for food until they could find work.

Long absences put pressure on families to provide for themselves until the sailor or fisherman might return home with his wages in hand. The families of farmers who also fished did the work those men usually performed to make up for the lost labor. Wives and children of sailors, however, worked at menial, unskilled jobs to add to the household's income. Women often took in laundry or sewing to earn extra money. Wives of sailors also took in borders to offset living costs. Children worked at whatever job might earn them money. They collected rags or garbage, carried light loads, worked for craftsmen such as blacksmiths or carpenters who had no apprentices, or, in some cases, simply wandered the streets begging for money or food. When women and children could find work, they earned roughly half what a man earned, or less.

Women in cities enjoyed greater job opportunities than their rural counterparts. Married women tended to operate stores, taverns, or public houses, or they made and repaired clothes while their husbands were at sea. Others became midwives. They continued tending their businesses if they became widows. Some women, however, resorted to prostitution to survive or to provide for their children. Few of these jobs or businesses paid well, and women, especially widows, remained some of the poorest residents of North American cities.

Lower-class workers sometimes competed with enslaved Africans for work. That competition intensified as the urban slave population increased over the 18th century. Nearly one in five white households in New York City contained a slave, and slightly more than half of Charleston's population was enslaved. Owners forced their slaves to perform unskilled and semiskilled work around the house. They also taught slaves to perform skilled labor—some slaves worked as carpenters or smithies, for example. Owners also rented out skilled slaves to earn extra revenue. Slaves who labored as craftsmen achieved a measure of freedom few other slaves enjoyed, and some even earned money for themselves. Employers could rent slaves for far less than they paid white laborers, and white laborers grew to resent slaves. By the end of the century, urban white workers found themselves working at only the most dangerous kinds of jobs because slave owners refused to let their valuable "property" risk work-related injury.

In northern cities, whites performed most of the skilled labor. Craftsmen such as tailors and cordwainers, for example, earned more than sailors and unskilled or semiskilled workers; those who employed journeymen and apprentices or who owned slaves fared better.

Nevertheless, even wealthier craftsmen and businessmen faced moments when they had to cut workers, sell slaves if they owned them, or in some way turn property into cash to survive economic downturns.

A few craftsmen, such as silver- or goldsmiths, as well as a few merchants and shippers, thrived and grew rich. In Boston, for example, the noted Revolutionary leader John Hancock inherited a shipping empire and became one of the richest men in North America. While war, bad weather, and periodic lulls in the economy certainly affected his income, Hancock's wealth enabled him to weather these economic storms more comfortably than his poorer neighbors.

Wars such as the Seven Years' War and the Revolutionary War challenged the livelihoods of urban workers. War increased the demand for commodities such as cured meat, salt, and gunpowder, which helped some workers, but it also meant fewer jobs on land and at sea when governments restricted trade. But a few merchants capitalized on war. Rather than abide by laws prohibiting trade with the enemy, some merchants smuggled goods across enemy lines. Smuggling was a common practice during peacetime as well, and many North American merchants simply continued their activities during war, even though that meant trading with enemies. During the Seven Years' War, for example, British customs officials investigated the economic activities of many New York City merchants who were trading with Britain's enemies. Some of these same men later traded with Britain while their countrymen were waging a war for independence against the Crown. For them, wealth trumped political allegiances.

Over the course of the 18th century, shop owners moved away from a system of craftsmen, journeymen, and apprentices toward manufacturing and wage labor. The change began in cities such as Philadelphia and New York before 1776, but the trend accelerated after the war. In the crafts system of the early 18th century, craftsmen employed apprentices and journeymen to produce goods. Apprentices usually worked with a craftsman for four to seven years, during which time the craftsman taught the apprentice all the steps required to turn raw materials into a finished product. Once an apprentice demonstrated proficiency, the craftsman allowed the apprentice to become a journeyman, marking the occasion by giving the apprentice his own set of tools. Many journeymen continued to work with the craftsman while they acquired the capital necessary to establish themselves in their own shops. Late in the 18th century, however, some craftsmen began replacing their apprentices and journeymen with unskilled or semiskilled laborers. Rather than teach laborers every step in the production process, they taught each laborer one step in the process. It took craftsmen far less time to teach workers one step of the process, and they could easily replace workers who performed poorly. Craftsmen also paid these less-skilled workers less than they would have spent on training apprentices. The shift made laborers more easily replaceable and drove down wages. Many employers cut wages further by hiring women and children, who earned far less than men for the same job.

The shift to manufacturing drove a wedge between employers and wage laborers that extended beyond the workplace. In the crafts system, craftsmen, their families, journeymen, and apprentices often lived and worked under one roof. Thus, craftsmen provided more than simply job training; they created a community. Craftsmen served as the head of their households, teaching journeymen and apprentices how to behave and how to act as good citizens in their communities. But the shift to wage laborers undermined those relationships. As craftsmen shifted toward hiring wage laborers, they also refused to let their laborers live with them, and they began to move away from the people who worked at their shops. As a result, the shift toward manufacturing also physically divided urban communities economically, socially, and culturally.

Urban slaves also faced changing working and living conditions in the late 18th century. In the post-Revolutionary period, and especially during and after the Haitian Revolution of the 1790s, whites in the new United States grew increasingly worried about widespread slave revolt. The slave uprising in Haiti epitomized whites' fears in the South of armed slaves bent on killing their owners. To prevent similar slave uprisings on the mainland, whites tightened their control over urban slaves. After enacting harsher penalties for disobedience, escape, or insurrection, whites exerted greater control over the movements of enslaved people. In

Charleston after the American Revolution, whites required slaves to wear badges indicating to whom they belonged. Blacks without badges had to prove their status, or they faced dire consequences.

Rural Laborers

Farmers dominated the North American countryside in the 18th century. Most farmed similarly sized lots, diversified their agricultural production to ensure some measure of success, sold goods at market, and relied on family labor to perform the backbreaking work needed for successful agricultural production and to produce what the household needed to survive. Farmers cut down trees, burned out the stumps, cleared stones, drained wet land, leveled the terrain, turned the soil, fenced in paddocks, built houses and barns, planted and harvested crops, and cared for livestock. These farmers all relied on essentially the same tools to grow food for their households, and their production practices changed very little over the course of the 18th century.

Farmers increased production by increasing the number of hands in the fields. For most farmers, wives and children represented additional hands, and because subsistence stood in the balance, everyone worked wherever needed. In general, however, men, women, and children tended to follow regular labor patterns. Men and older male children often worked in the fields with draft animals clearing and plowing land, tending crops, and reaping the harvest. They also sheared sheep and slaughtered animals for meat. Women and female children often cared for vegetable gardens near the house and tended the cows and chickens. They also cooked the food consumed on the farm, spun cloth, and made clothes. Again, despite these divisions, men and women worked wherever necessary, and it is more accurate to think of a household's production than of what a man or a woman might produce on a farm.

Most farm families lived perilously close to the edge of subsistence. Any small misfortune could lead to a failed crop and hunger or, worse, starvation. A broken tool, too much or too little rain at the wrong time, blight or some other kind of crop disease, an infestation of pests, diseased livestock, or injury to the farmer easily threw agricultural production into jeopardy.

What farmers grew varied by region. Along the coast of New England, where the soil was rocky and sandy, farmers grew wheat and other hardy crops. Where the soil was better, farmers tended to grow grain such as wheat and corn. In the Middle Atlantic, farmers grew wheat and other grains, but they also sold lumber for additional income, and many farmers grew fruit trees. Most of these farmers produced a great variety of vegetables, kept cattle and dairy cows, some pigs and chickens, and traded their surplus goods with their neighbors for things they needed.

Where farmers in the North relied on family members to increase production, farmers in the southern region bought slaves. But they rarely used that new labor to produce subsistence crops. Instead, southern farmers used slaves to grow cash crops. In Virginia, small farmers relied on family labor and grain production for survival, but if they acquired a slave, they usually put that slave to work growing tobacco to sell at market. Farther south, in South Carolina, farmers who could afford to purchase a slave often put the slave to work growing indigo and rice.

In the later 18th century, some farmers who lived near cities took advantage of their proximity to growing urban populations. Around New York, Boston, and Philadelphia, for example, farmers shifted away from grain production to raise livestock. They sold meat and dairy goods to urban residents and to ships. Meat and dairy production also changed how these farmers traded at local markets. Most farmers traded agricultural goods for what they needed, but dairy and meat farmers sold their products for cash and used the money to buy what they needed.

Not all these farmers owned the land they occupied. Tenants made up approximately one-fourth to one-third the total number of farmers in North America, and, in some parts of North America, most farmers rented land. In New York's Hudson Valley, for example, most of the arable land was owned by a few families who rented that land to tenants. Tenants were usually required to pay rent with wheat, a valuable trade commodity that landlords turned into flour and then shipped throughout the Atlantic world. In Virginia's Northern Neck and Maryland, regions also characterized

Male farmers in the North put their wives and children to work in the fields in order to increase production. In southern colonies like Virginia and South Carolina, farmers could boost production and profits by buying slaves to grow cash crops like tobacco. In the above engraving slaves work on an 18th-century tobacco plantation. *(Jupiter Images)*

by landlordism, tenants usually paid rent with tobacco. And in sections of Kentucky, upward of 80 percent of farmers rented land and paid rent with wheat and corn.

Where tenants lived much like farmers who owned similarly sized lots, being a landlord proved to be lucrative. Over the course of the 18th century, the Livingstons of New York, for example, turned the goods their tenants paid in rent into commodities they shipped throughout the Atlantic market. They became one of the wealthiest families in North America, rivaled only by Virginians such as the Carters, who owned hundreds of slaves and employed hundreds of tenants to produce tobacco. Similarly, the Fairfaxes of Virginia rented land to thousands of tenants in the Northern Neck and took in hundreds, if not thousands, of pounds of tobacco in rent every year. Both families sold the tobacco and accrued fortunes. Indeed, landlordism was so lucrative that even George Washington tried his hand at it, though he was never as successful as his neighbors.

If great estates dominated regions such as New York's Hudson Valley and Virginia's Northern Neck, plantations worked by enslaved Africans characterized much of the rest of rural Virginia, Maryland, and the Carolinas. The plantation system emerged slowly in the 17th century but exploded in the 18th, as planters increasingly relied on enslaved Africans for labor. In the Chesapeake, planters forced thousands of enslaved people to turn hundreds of thousands of acres into tobacco fields. To the south, planters in South Carolina relied on slaves to produce indigo, a valuable dye, and rice.

Slaves in the 18th century worked under two distinct systems. In the Chesapeake, slaves generally labored a certain number of hours per day, usually between 9 and

12 hours, depending on available daylight and weather. They often worked six to seven days per week, and their work routines were governed by overseers and planters. On some plantations in South Carolina, on the other hand, slaves were responsible for performing certain tasks, like planting the rice crop or draining the fields. Once the task was completed, their time was more or less their own. The task system developed not out of a desire to grant slaves more freedom but because planters wanted to protect their investment in human property against the crushing heat and malaria of the area.

Whether working under time or task constraints, rural slave labor was made possible and profitable through violence. Overseers and owners quickly learned that while many slaves worked hard on their own, others resented their enslavement and refused to work as hard as planters desired. To make slaves work in brutal conditions at hard labor for long periods of time, owners and overseers regularly whipped, beat, or starved slaves. Some planters held whipping orgies during which they picked slaves at random and whipped them. Additionally, they threatened slaves with the sale of their loved ones if they failed to work hard enough. Both tactics, beatings and threats, also worked to deter slaves from escaping or rebelling against their owners. Slaves who escaped and were captured, or who participated in rebellions, were treated harshly. Captured runaways were often whipped, scarred, beaten, or mutilated. Insurgents often faced brutal execution. Female slaves also faced rape at the hands of their owners.

Independence from Britain failed to inspire a widespread manumission of enslaved Africans. While slavery diminished in the North after the Revolution, slavery became more entrenched in southern states. Some owners manumitted their slaves, but most slave owners were more like Thomas Jefferson, who freed only a handful of the nearly 600 slaves he owned over the course of his life. Slave owners who considered manumitting their slaves quickly changed their minds when news of the bloody slave revolt in Haiti reached the United States. They worried that free and enslaved blacks might imitate Haitian rebels and slaughter white planters.

Over the course of the 18th century, the number of slaves in the Chesapeake declined. But the decline grew more out of changing agricultural practices than a desire to bestow independence on slaves. Planters in the Chesapeake moved away from tobacco production, which was labor intensive, toward grain production, which required less labor. They made the shift because decades of intensive tobacco farming had depleted the soil's nutrients and led to decreasing yields. By the middle of the 18th century, tobacco farming was becoming less profitable. Wheat prices, on the other hand, rose consistently over the course of the 18th century, and while planters might not get as rich growing wheat as they might growing tobacco, they preferred the steady income of wheat production over the fluctuating value of tobacco crops. Planters who switched to grain required fewer workers in the field, and those slaves worked less often. So, as planters such as George Washington began moving from tobacco to wheat, they realized they needed fewer slaves. Some planters manumitted excess slaves, but others sold them to traders who transported that human cargo south and then west.

Conclusion

While tenant and yeoman farmers throughout North America labored in 1800 much as they had in 1700, other inhabitants experienced far more dramatic changes in how they labored. By 1800, the biggest change in labor practices had emerged in cities, where craftsmen increasingly hired wage laborers to reduce labor costs. In the process, however, these employers began a trend that profoundly reshaped the urban landscape. The shift may have opened doors to greater wealth and political power for some, but the vast majority of Americans faced declining wages and prospects. By the end of the century, most laborers earned less money and lived closer to the edge of poverty and despair. Slavery dissipated and then largely disappeared in northern states, but the institution became increasingly entrenched in the South. Planters changed their perspectives on slavery as well. Before the American Revolution, many slave owners thought of slavery as a necessary evil, but by 1800 more and more planters considered slavery the cornerstone of their society. These two broad categories of labor, free and enslaved, emerged slowly in the 18th century. By the end of the century, however, they increasingly defined more than work and work relationships in the new United States, as they came to characterize the country's people and the difficult choices they still had to make.

—Thomas Humphrey

Further Reading

Berlin, Ira, and Ronald Hoffman, eds. *Slavery and Freedom in the Age of the American Revolution*. Charlottesville: University Press of Virginia, 1983.

Bliss, Willard F. "The Rise of Tenancy in Virginia." *Virginia Magazine of History and Biography* 108, no. 4 (1950): 427–441.

Egerton, Douglas R. *Death or Liberty: African Americans and Revolutionary America*. New York: Oxford University Press, 2009.

Henretta, James A. "Families and Farms: *Mentalité* in Pre-Industrial America." *William and Mary Quarterly* 35, no. 1 (1978): 3–32.

Humphrey, Thomas J. *Land and Liberty: Hudson Valley Riots in the Age of Revolution*. DeKalb: Northern Illinois University Press, 2004.

Innes, Stephen, ed. *Work and Labor in Early America*. Chapel Hill: University of North Carolina Press, 1988.

Kierner, Cynthia A. *Traders and Gentlefolk: The Livingstons of New York, 1675–1790*. Ithaca, N.Y.: Cornell University Press, 1992.

Kim, Sung Bok. *Landlord and Tenant in Colonial New York: Manorial Society, 1644–1775*. Chapel Hill: University of North Carolina Press, 1978.

Kulikoff, Allan. *The Agrarian Origins of American Capitalism*. Charlottesville: University Press of Virginia, 1992.

———. *From British Peasants to Colonial American Farmers*. Chapel Hill: University of North Carolina Press, 2000.

———. "The Progress of Inequality in Revolutionary Boston." *William and Mary Quarterly* 28, no. 3 (July 1971): 375–412.

Lockley, Timothy James. *Lines in the Sand: Race and Class in Lowcountry Georgia, 1750–1860*. Athens: University of Georgia Press, 2001.

McConville, Brendan. *These Daring Disturbers of the Public Peace: The Struggle for Property and Power in Early New Jersey*. Ithaca, N.Y.: Cornell University Press, 1999.

McCurry, Stephanie. *Masters of Small Worlds: Yeoman Households, Gender Relations, and the Political Culture of the Antebellum South Carolina Low Country*. New York: Oxford University Press, 1995.

McCusker, John J., and Russell R. Menard. *The Economy of British America, 1607–1789*. Chapel Hill: University of North Carolina Press, 1991.

Morgan, Philip D. *Slave Counterpoint: Black Culture in the Eighteenth-Century Chesapeake and Lowcountry*. Chapel Hill: University of North Carolina Press, 1998.

Pruitt, Bettye Hobbs. "Self-Sufficiency and the Agricultural Economy of Eighteenth-Century Massachusetts." *William and Mary Quarterly* 41, no. 3 (1984): 333–364.

Rothenberg, Winifred Barr. *From Market-Places to a Market Economy: The Transformation of Rural Massachusetts, 1750–1850*. Chicago: University of Chicago Press, 1992.

Schocket, Andrew M. *Founding Corporate Power in Early National Philadelphia*. DeKalb: Northern Illinois University Press, 2007.

Smith, Billy G. *The "Lower Sort"; Philadelphia's Laboring People, 1750–1800*. Ithaca, N.Y.: Cornell University Press, 1990.

———. "The Material Lives of Laboring Philadelphians, 1750 to 1800." *William and Mary Quarterly* 38, no. 2 (1981): 163–202.

Sundue, Sharon Braslaw. *Industrious in Their Stations: Young People at Work in Urban America, 1720–1810*. Charlottesville: University of Virginia Press, 2009.

Vickers, Daniel. *Farmers and Fishermen: Two Centuries of Work in Essex County, Massachusetts, 1630–1850*. Chapel Hill: University of North Carolina Press, 1994.

Wermuth, Thomas S. *Rip Van Winkle's Neighbors: The Transformation of Rural Society in the Hudson River Valley, 1720–1850*. Albany: State University of New York Press, 2001.

Wood, Peter H. *Black Majority: Negroes in Colonial South Carolina from 1670 through the Stono Rebellion*. New York: Alfred A. Knopf, 1974.

18th Century LAW

During the 18th century, American law was transformed in fundamental ways. First, the judicial system shifted from one in which colonial courts were subject to English supervision through appeals to the English Privy Council, to one in which two court systems, state and federal, operated simultaneously over the same territory. Second, substantive law, increasingly English throughout the 18th century, became more distinctively American after independence. Third, American lawyers obtained more authoritative sources to locate the law, such as printed law reports. Finally, American legal education began to change, away from an apprenticeship system to one in which lawyers were trained exclusively in university law schools.

The Judicial System

In 1700 each American colony had its own distinctive set of courts, although they shared certain features. Most colonies had a network of trial courts that heard criminal and civil cases, as well as some form of high court, sometimes called a supreme court, that could hear appeals from cases in the trial courts. Some of the judges of the supreme courts and the trial courts had legal training, but many did not. Like England, all colonies also commissioned justices of the peace in each county. The justices of the peace were generally prominent and wealthy men, although they were usually not lawyers. They tried various petty offenses and also superintended roads and performed other county administrative duties. The colonial courts were subject to English supervision through appeals to the English Privy Council, which was effectively the true supreme court for all the American colonies, even though few American litigants could afford to pursue a costly and time-consuming appeal overseas. Colonial American courts were often busy places in the 18th century. Litigation rates, for example, increased dramatically between 1700 and 1730, particularly with respect to commercial and debt cases. Most civil lawsuits, however, did not go to trial but were settled privately between the parties.

American independence brought significant changes to the judicial system, and most states drafted new constitutions specifying the structure of the state judiciary. Appeals to the English Privy Council ended. Most states, however, retained their local trial courts and a high court that could hear appeals from the trial courts. This appellate structure marked a significant departure from English legal practice. In England, appeals were relatively uncommon, and the highest "court" was the House of Lords, one of the houses of Parliament. Under the English system, therefore, the judicial power was not fully independent of legislative power. By separating judicial and legislative functions, the new American state constitutions sought to ensure a relatively independent role for the judiciary. Although appeals played a prominent role in the legal systems of many countries in continental Europe, American appellate courts would eventually develop a significant body of appellate law, which would prove to be one of the most distinctive American contributions to common-law legal practice.

American independence also led to the creation of a parallel system of federal courts. After independence in 1776, the Continental Congress drafted the Articles of Confederation, which served as America's first constitution. The Articles, ratified in 1781, did not provide for a comprehensive federal court system. Instead, the Articles provided for only one federal court, the Federal Appellate Prize Court, which heard appeals from state courts in cases arising under admiralty and maritime jurisdiction—that is, cases involving shipping and the high seas. Because ocean shipping was a large component of the 18th-century American economy, admiralty and maritime cases often involved large sums of money and tended to attract America's best lawyers.

Many Americans, however, such as Alexander Hamilton and James Madison, sought a stronger federal government and a more powerful system of federal courts. Their disappointment with the Articles of Confederation led to the ratification of a new United States

Constitution, which Americans still live under today. Article III of the new constitution established the judicial branch of the federal government, stating: "The judicial Power of the United States, shall be vested in one supreme Court, and in such inferior Courts as the Congress may from time to time ordain and establish." This language represented a compromise made at the Constitutional Convention in 1787 between delegates who favored creating only a supreme court and those who favored both a supreme court and lower federal courts as well. Under this compromise, Congress could create lower federal courts, but it was not obligated to do so. The Constitution required federal judges to be nominated by the president and confirmed by majority vote of the U.S. Senate. Federal judges would serve, as did English judges, during "good behavior"—that is, for life, in almost all cases. They could be removed from office only by impeachment, which required a majority vote of the U.S. House of Representatives and a two-thirds vote of the Senate. By guaranteeing life tenure and making it difficult to remove federal judges, the framers sought to ensure judicial independence from ordinary politics. Article III also guaranteed jury trial in criminal cases in federal court, and the Seventh Amendment, ratified in 1791, guaranteed jury trial in most civil cases as well.

The federal judiciary was formally organized when the first Congress convened under the new constitution. In the Judiciary Act of 1789, Congress provided for a United States Supreme Court composed of six justices (the Constitution had not specified the number of justices) and for a system of lower federal courts. It also provided that the Supreme Court could review decisions of both the lower federal courts and the state supreme courts. John Jay, the first chief justice of the United States, took office in 1789 and served until 1795, when he was replaced briefly by John Rutledge, and then by Oliver Ellsworth, who served until 1800.

Federal courts have authority over the same geographic territory as state courts, but their power to hear cases, which lawyers call "jurisdiction," differs. State courts are courts of general jurisdiction, meaning they can hear almost any type of legal dispute that a litigant might bring. Federal courts, by contrast, are courts of limited jurisdiction; they can hear only those cases specifically identified in Article III of the Constitution. Two broad categories of jurisdiction provide for most cases brought in federal courts: federal question jurisdiction, which are cases that arise under federal law; and diversity jurisdiction, which are cases in which the parties to the dispute are from different states or countries. These limits on federal jurisdiction mean that most types of cases, such as divorces, child custody disputes, property, contracts, and personal injury cases, and disputes over the interpretation of a will, are heard almost entirely in state courts. Disputes over the proper scope of federal jurisdiction frequently occur, however, because this system of two sets of courts operating over the same territory sometimes creates conflicts of authority.

Substantive Law

There are two significant European legal systems, the civil law system and the common-law system, both of which have their origins in the years between 1100 and 1300. The civil law system was used in most of the nations of continental Europe, as well as in Scotland. This system was ultimately rooted in Roman law, as recorded in the 6th-century *Corpus Juris Civilis* of the Emperor Justinian. Civil law systems relied heavily on university-trained lawyers and judges and did not employ juries as fact-finders. North American colonies established by the French and Spanish, such as Louisiana and the southwestern United States, employed civil law systems. Louisiana state law is still based on this system.

The common-law system, by contrast, was unique to England. The common law was far less rooted in Roman law, its practitioners did not study in universities, and it relied primarily on juries of laymen for most fact-finding functions. When the first English settlers came to America in the 17th century, they had to decide how much English law to retain. Some colonies, especially in New England, experimented freely, abandoning juries and citing the Old Testament as a significant source of legal authority, especially in criminal matters. In other colonies, English common law fully prevailed.

This legal diversity narrowed significantly in the years prior to American independence. In a process that historians have referred to as the "Anglicization" of American law, colonial legal systems in the English colonies increasingly resembled their English counterparts, and English common-law doctrines and institutions came to dominate American life. Legal practice became professionalized, as practicing lawyers displaced laymen as judges and counsel. This newly professionalized bench and bar (as judges and lawyers came to be called) frowned on earlier deviations from the substance and practice of English law.

Independence led lawyers and legislators to reform their inherited English law, so as to conform better to American circumstances. While confirming English common law as the basis of the legal order—a decision known as the "reception of the common law"—statutes and common-law legal doctrines differed more and more from their English predecessors, a change that historians have referred to as the "Americanization" of American law. State courts and legislatures made significant changes, for example, to English rules on property ownership and inheritance. In most parts of England, if a landowner died without a will, his eldest son would inherit all his property. This rule, known as primogeniture, was replaced in America with the rule that property would be divided equally among all the landowner's children, daughters as well as sons. Courts and legislatures also modified some of the harsher aspects of English criminal law, reducing the number of crimes punishable by death and gradually abolishing imprisonment for debt.

American law deviated sharply from English law in the matter of slavery. The colonies had long recognized the legality of slavery, even though this status was ambiguous under English common law. English law became increasingly hostile to slavery, while American jurisdictions developed proslavery legal rules. Statutes and practice made it difficult for masters to free slaves and for slaves to marry, own real property, enter into contracts, and testify in court. Slave status typically descended through the mother, meaning that many children fathered by white men with female slaves would themselves remain in slavery, including the children that Thomas Jefferson fathered with his slave Sally Hemings. After independence, however, northern states began providing for the gradual emancipation of slaves, although in some states this process took half a century to complete. The emancipation movement was a consequence of the spirit of liberty raised by the American Revolution itself. Antislavery advocates argued that slavery was inconsistent with the "self-evident truth" announced in the Declaration of Independence "that all men are created equal." In southern states, despite the hopes of some 18th-century leaders that slavery was on a path to ultimate extinction, the emancipation movement never succeeded. The invention of the cotton gin in the early 19th century made slavery increasingly economically viable and helped to entrench slavery even more deeply in southern law and custom.

Legal Literature

In a common-law legal system, tradition and custom are significant sources of law. Part of this tradition includes prior decisions by courts, which lawyers refer to as "precedent." But lawyers need a way to identify this precedent, a way to "find" the law. At the beginning of the 18th century, American lawyers could rely on several sources. First, they might rely on published reports of individual cases. But there were many problems with this. No American courts published their own decisions until after the Revolution, so American lawyers could only consult English cases. The books printing these English decisions were difficult to obtain, frequently very expensive, and were often written not in English, but in a form of French known as "law French." French had been the language of court after the Norman invasion of England in 1066, and the practice of using French in the English law courts had persisted for many subsequent generations.

Eighteenth-century American lawyers instead turned eagerly to English legal treatises, which digested and summarized the body of English case law. The four volumes of Sir Edward Coke's *Institutes*, written in the first half of the 17th century, provided American lawyers with a learned, although frequently obscure, analysis of English common law. Most 18th-century American lawyers spent some time working through Coke's dense volumes, especially his *First Institute*, which focused entirely on land law. American lawyers also consulted English justice-of-the-peace manuals, which instructed the lay justices of the peace on the subtleties of English common law and procedure.

Between 1765 and 1769 Sir William Blackstone published his famous *Commentaries on the Laws of England*, an elegant four-volume summary of the English common law. American lawyers devoured these volumes, often in pirated American editions. Indeed, more volumes of Blackstone appear to have been sold in America than in England. For many aspiring American lawyers, until well into the 19th century, Blackstone became the basis of their legal education and their main source for knowledge of English common law. Abraham Lincoln, for example, carried Blackstone's volumes when riding from courthouse to courthouse in rural Illinois in the 1840s and 1850s. As late as 1860, when he was running for president, Lincoln advised a young man that the path to becoming a lawyer started with reading Blackstone.

Sir William Blackstone published *Commentaries on the Laws of England*, a four-volume summary of English common law, between 1765 and 1769. These volumes would become the basis for the legal education of American lawyers well into the 19th century. *(Library of Congress)*

After independence, Americans began publishing decisions of American courts for the first time. In 1789 the first volume of Ephraim Kirby's *Connecticut Reports* was published, and other reporters soon followed in other states. Alexander Dallas began publishing decisions of the Pennsylvania Supreme Court in 1790 and decisions of the U.S. Supreme Court in 1798. With the advent of published decisions, American lawyers now had authoritative texts for American precedents, allowing lawyers to develop increasingly informed arguments based on these decisions. With the advent of printed law reports, American law became more accessible and more professional.

The Legal Profession

The path to a legal career was quite different in the 18th century from what it is now. American lawyers in almost all states must now earn a college degree and graduate from a three-year law school before taking the bar exam and becoming lawyers. Before American independence, however, there were no law schools at all in the United States. Instead, aspiring lawyers could choose one of two paths. The first was to travel to England and attend what was known as an "Inn of Court," a professional guild that admitted lawyers to the English bar. There were four English Inns: Lincoln's Inn, Gray's Inn, Middle Temple, and Inner Temple. "Barristers," as they were called, were the only attorneys who were permitted to argue in court. Americans who could afford such an education trained alongside more senior English lawyers by observing English common-law courts in action and by assisting with drafting legal documents. Middle Temple was especially popular with Americans, attracting approximately 150 American students over the course of the 18th century. Five members of Middle Temple signed the Declaration of Independence, and seven signed the United States Constitution.

The second path was to serve for a few years as an apprentice to a more experienced lawyer in America. John Adams, for example, became a lawyer this way as a young man in Massachusetts. Apprenticeships varied widely in quality, however; although some apprentices learned a significant amount, others did little more than shuffle papers. Adams himself was appalled to discover, at the end of his clerkship, that he still had no idea how to file a motion in court. Nonetheless, by 1800, the apprenticeship was by far the most common means of becoming an American lawyer.

In 1784 America's first law school, Litchfield Law School, opened in Litchfield, Connecticut. Despite its location in a one-room building in a remote Connecticut town, the school attracted students from all across the country. Litchfield's two proprietors, Tapping Reeve and James Gould, operated the school as a private, for-profit law school. The curriculum was based heavily on Blackstone's *Commentaries* and covered a wide variety of common-law subjects. The school functioned until 1833, and its graduates eventually included 3 U.S. Supreme Court justices, 56 state supreme court justices, 28 U.S. senators, 101 congressmen, 14 state governors, and 6 U.S. Cabinet members. Other for-profit law schools like Litchfield opened throughout the country in the late 18th and early 19th centuries, and for many years they were more prominent than university-based legal education. But, beginning in the 1820s, many of these schools either closed or were acquired by colleges and universities.

University legal education began in America in 1789, when a lawyer named George Wythe was appointed "Professor of Law and Police" at the College of William and Mary in Williamsburg, Virginia. Wythe was the first American appointed to a faculty position in the field of law. Indeed, Wythe was only the second person in the common-law world to teach common law at a college or university, the first being William Blackstone a few decades earlier at Oxford. Wythe's students included John Marshall, the future chief justice of the United States. His courses included the relatively new subject of constitutional law. Wythe was succeeded at William and Mary by St. George Tucker, a significant scholar who produced an American edition of Blackstone's *Commentaries*. But these attempts at introducing legal education at the college level were not widely followed, and when they were, they were often of low quality. Not until the 19th century would significant university legal education really flourish in America.

These four broad changes in American law over the course of the 18th century proved enduring and remain hallmarks of American legal practice. From relatively modest beginnings, the American legal system would grow in size and in sophistication. Increasing numbers of Americans would turn to the legal system and to lawyers on issues ranging from property to business disputes to far-reaching questions about basic constitutional rights.

—Carlton F. W. Larson

Further Reading

Amar, Akhil Reed. *America's Constitution: A Biography*. New York: Random House, 2005.

Bilder, Mary Sarah. *The Transatlantic Constitution: Colonial Legal Culture and the Empire*. Cambridge, Mass.: Harvard University Press, 2004.

Dargo, George. *Law in the New Republic: Private Law and the Public Estate.* New York: Alfred A. Knopf, 1983.

Dayton, Cornelia Hughes. *Women before the Bar: Gender, Law, and Society in Connecticut, 1639–1789*. Chapel Hill: University of North Carolina Press, 1995.

Friedman, Lawrence M. *A History of American Law*. 3d ed. New York: Simon & Schuster, 2005.

Gerber, Scott Douglas, ed. *Seriatim: The Supreme Court before John Marshall*. New York: New York University Press, 1998.

Grossberg, Michael, and Christopher Tomlins, eds. *The Cambridge History of Law in America: Early America (1580–1815)*. Cambridge, U.K.: Cambridge University Press, 2008.

Hoffer, Peter Charles. *Law and People in Colonial America*. Baltimore, Md.: Johns Hopkins University Press, 1998.

Horwitz, Morton. *The Transformation of American Law, 1780–1860*. Cambridge, Mass.: Harvard University Press, 1977.

Hulsebosch, Daniel J. *Constituting Empire: New York and the Transformation of Constitutionalism in the Atlantic World*. Chapel Hill: University of North Carolina Press, 2005.

Larson, Carlton F. W. "The Declaration of Independence: A 225th Anniversary Re-Interpretation." *Washington Law Review* 76 (July 2001): 701–791.

———. "The Revolutionary American Jury: A Case Study of the 1778–1779 Philadelphia Treason Trials." *SMU Law Review* 61 (fall 2008): 1441–1524.

Mann, Bruce H. *Neighbors and Strangers: Law and Community in Early Connecticut*. Chapel Hill: University of North Carolina Press, 1987.

———. *Republic of Debtors: Bankruptcy in the Age of American Independence*. Cambridge, Mass.: Harvard University Press, 2002.

Marcus, Maeva, ed. *The Documentary History of the Supreme Court of the United States, 1789–1800*. 8 vols. Edited by New York: Columbia University Press, 1985–.

Murrin, John M. "The Legal Transformation: The Bench and Bar of Eighteenth-Century Massachusetts." In *Colonial America: Essays in Politics and Social Development*, edited by Stanley N. Katz. Boston: Little, Brown, 1971.

Nelson, William E. *Americanization of the Common Law: The Impact of Legal Change on Massachusetts Society, 1760–1830*. Cambridge, Mass.: Harvard University Press, 1975.

Rakove, Jack N. *Original Meanings: Politics and Ideas in the Making of the Constitution*. New York: Alfred A. Knopf, 1996.

Reid, John Philip. *Constitutional History of the American Revolution*. 4 vols. Madison: University of Wisconsin Press, 1986–1993.

Tomlins, Christopher, and Bruce H. Mann. *The Many Legalities of Early America*. Chapel Hill: University of North Carolina Press, 2001.

18th Century LEISURE AND RECREATION

The 18th century witnessed a significant transformation in leisure and recreation as commercial leisure enterprises multiplied, especially in towns and cities. This expansion occurred despite constant criticism and legislative action against such activities, a crusade first led by religious authorities and later by Revolutionary leaders. These critics and opponents decried the indulgent risk-taking, social mingling, and vain displays of status characteristic of the growing variety of leisure events. Yet the elements they disliked only became more prominent over time, and by the end of the century, many of the new republic's prominent leaders invested in leisure enterprises and used these competitive and relatively democratic events to rally political support.

In the 18th century, *leisure* or *recreation* were not antonyms for *work*, as they would later become. Rather, *recreation* referred exclusively to physical exercises such as hiking, walking, and calisthenics. *Leisure* carried class connotations and referred to the free time of a gentleman, which he was supposed to use to cultivate his mind and manners. Games, sports, and theater only slowly came under the rubric of *leisure* in the late 18th and early 19th centuries, as a more robust commercial leisure industry emerged and offered a democratic experience that was increasingly at odds with the widening inequalities of daily life in the early republic. Still, well into the 19th century, work, recreation, and leisure remained indivisible in many circumstances. The best example of this continuity is the enduring presence of the rural *frolic* or *working party*, which brought neighbors together to complete barns, harvests, and textile projects within a festive atmosphere of physical competition and libation. So, in the context of the 18th century, *leisure* activities cannot be divorced from everyday life or work.

Growth and Development

Even though domestic and rural leisure activities were more common and witnessed less change during the 18th century, the rise of organized public commercial leisure activities triggered the era's moral debates. These activities resulted from two periods of intense economic expansion in the middle and then the final decades of the century. Each era provided wealthy elites with the means to finance a larger array of leisure activities and allowed growing urban populations to attend them.

The emergence of organized public commercial leisure can be traced through three major types of venues: taverns, racetracks, and theaters. Taverns, the traditional bastion of public leisure in England and in 17th-century America, multiplied almost exponentially between 1720 and 1760. By the end of that period, every major American city boasted at least one tavern for every hundred or so residents. Virtually every rural crossroads, too, was marked by a "public house" offering a mix of liquor, food, political discussion, business negotiation, and a range of table games, from cards and dice to backgammon and billiards.

In the 17th century, horse races had often been held along the roads in front of taverns, and they were just as likely to be sparked by spontaneous tavern debate as they were to be planned in advance. But the mid-18th century saw the rise of Thoroughbred racing, which required a rare and expensive breed imported from England and known for its endurance. So, in addition to the century-old short dashes, which produced the American quarter horse (named for its quarter-mile races), 18th-century Americans also attended Thoroughbred races run around permanent, mile-long oval racetracks. Mimicking English practice, urbane Thoroughbred owners and their peers formed jockey clubs and scheduled weeklong "race meetings," which attracted spectators from hundreds of miles away. Like taverns, race meetings invited congregants to do business, discuss politics, and broaden their social networks amid an atmosphere of convivial competition.

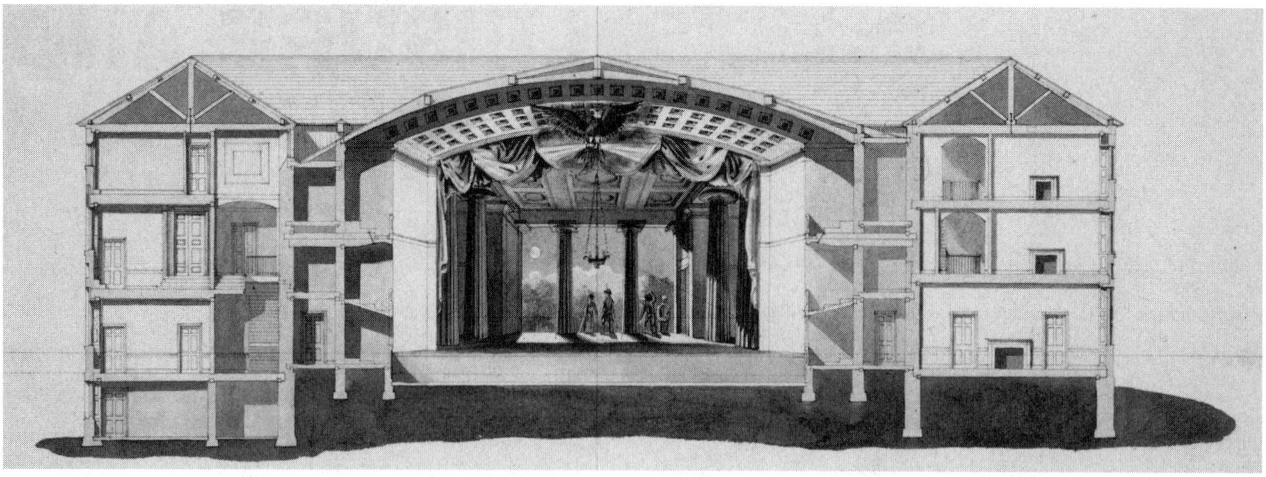

Theater experienced notable growth in popularity during the 17th century, and by the last quarter of the 18th century, a half-dozen cities featured permanent, purpose-built theaters. Above is a drawing from around 1797 showing the interior of a theater housed inside a building in Richmond, Virginia, that also included a hotel and assembly rooms. ***(Library of Congress)***

Theater experienced the most notable growth of all organized leisure activities. Evidence suggests only a few examples of staged drama in America before 1700. By 1770, however, a half-dozen cities featured permanent, purpose-built theaters, and another two dozen towns had hosted at least one professional touring company. By the end of the century, New York, Philadelphia, Boston, and Charleston all boasted two theaters. Throughout the century, theater companies frequently scheduled their tours to arrive in cities during legislative or court sessions, or during race meetings, again evincing the relationship between leisure activities and the "everyday" world of business and politics.

Opposition and Persistence

The expanded presence of taverns, racetracks, and theaters elicited an outcry from religious moralists. Puritans, Quakers, Separate Baptists, Methodists, and even some strict Anglican ministers criticized the gambling, luxury, and social mixing promoted by these events. Allegedly, such activities distracted people from the work and productivity by which their lives were valued or judged, and many moralists saw them as a threat to one's salvation. Such activities supposedly wasted money as well as time, causing the poor to fall deeper into debt and the rich to squander their resources. Finally, the heat of inebriation, competition, and performance frequently inspired challenges and masquerading across class lines. Either by encouraging unfounded elitism through the display of exclusive and worldly luxuries such as Thoroughbreds and box seats, or by reducing the distance between proper elites and their inferiors, leisure activities undermined a social order and hierarchy that many religious leaders considered to be divinely inspired.

The moralists' critiques dated back at least to the 17th century, but the surge of leisure venues and activities invigorated their opposition in the 18th century. Zealots submitted petitions and lobbied colonial legislative assemblies, all in an effort to pass more-restrictive bans against leisure activities associated with gambling, luxury, and social mixing. Most northern colonies already outlawed these activities. Even in the South, where theater and horse racing were legal, laws invited gamblers who had lost more than £10 to sue winners and recover their lost wages. But antileisure laws were not enforced with any regularity anywhere on the continent. The "gambler's code" brought social disgrace on any man who reclaimed his losses through the courts and so discouraged bringing suit. New Englanders banned theater but flocked to taverns for "recitations" of dramatic literature. The King's Privy Council consistently repealed Pennsylvania's strict laws against leisure activities. Indeed, the religionists' persistent requests for stricter enforcement indicate the ineffectiveness of existing regulations.

Yet legal proscriptions did effectively halt the growth of organized leisure for 15 years, during the Revolutionary era between 1774 and 1789. During this period, secular Patriot leaders—including such notable men as John Hancock and Thomas Jefferson—joined the religious moralists. Following a recommendation issued by the Continental Congress in 1774, every colony (and, later, state) explicitly outlawed theater, horse racing, cockfighting, and other activities affiliated with gambling and organized public entertainment. These laws were part of a broader effort to cleanse the country of an allegedly corrupt British culture unsuitable for the sober projects of revolution and creating a republic. Eighteenth-century political theory held that republics required a politically engaged citizenry, lest the people's inattention allow elected leaders to destroy the republic by passing laws that increased their power at the people's expense. In such a fragile political state, the growth of leisure activities seemed to present a significant threat of distraction. Gambling proved difficult to police, but the proclamations did curtail theater, racing, and other large-scale organized public leisure events. The old antileisure refrain, when linked to a secular political agenda, could still prove effective.

Yet the Patriots did not oppose leisure only on moral grounds. The breadth of society that gathered at public leisure activities and venues produced a tension between social distinction and social leveling. On one hand, leisure events gathered diverse members of the community and thus provided an opportunity to display differences in appearance and manners that helped distinguish elites from inferiors. On the other hand, the atmosphere of accessibility, inebriation, competition, and performance inspired inferiors to challenge the presumption of their supposed betters. Bar fights frequently expressed class antagonism. As the Revolutionary rhetoric of equality and liberty spread,

During the Revolutionary era, legal restrictions halted the growth of organized leisure enterprises. Patriot leaders such as John Hancock (left) and Thomas Jefferson (right), both of whom sat in the Continental Congress, joined the religious moralists in opposing activities such as theatergoing and horse racing, which were deemed part of a corrupt British culture and were a waste of time, money, and productivity. ***(Library of Congress)***

elites came under assault for their exclusive seating sections at theaters and racetracks. However, savvy elites—particularly wealthy men interested in political office—had long rallied broad support at taverns by avoiding hauteur and by mingling as equals with poorer and less powerful men. No wonder the Revolutionaries banned leisure activities that emphasized exclusion and competition, such as gambling, racing, and theater, but did not outlaw taverns. The 1774 bans instigated by the Continental Congress were intended not just to cleanse the country morally, but to reduce internal social conflict and unite all Americans against the British foe.

The "republican" rationale for opposing organized public leisure retained its power through the end of the century. As late as 1798, Massachusetts, Pennsylvania, Virginia, and North Carolina all passed fresh legislation against gambling, even promising to "seize and burn" tavern billiard tables. Yet other activities—most notably horse racing and theater—earned legalization because their advocates linked them to productivity and profit. Post-Revolutionary America was torn between the austere moral strictures required to uphold the republic and the rampant opportunity for investment in the absence of colonial economic regulations. Especially as the country emerged from the wartime recession in the 1790s, wealthy Americans again looked to fund leisure activities. But in order to make them suitable for the republic, patrons linked them to investment and productivity. For example, itinerant theater managers owned theaters in the colonial period, while investors owned them in the early republic. This difference helped anchor the theater in the local economy. As a result, every state had legalized theater by 1792. Similarly, racing returned when it was cited as a method for determining superior bloodlines in a booming horse-breeding industry. A new for-profit mentality guided investors in leisure. Before the war, wealthy men funded large-scale leisure activities largely to demonstrate their beneficence. After the war, investors demanded dividends or rising stock values, because the new country's economic ethos required aspiring elites to prove their status through profit and productivity, not just magnanimity.

Profit Motives and Political Power

The return of racing and theater, and the eagerness of investors, sparked another explosion in the number of leisure venues at the end of the century. The market was soon crammed, and profit-seeking investors had to pander to the populace to survive cutthroat competition. Ticket prices held steady despite inflation, so class-specific seating zones became muddled as businessmen attracted a bigger pool of patrons by giving them the opportunity to sit anywhere and assert any status they chose. Although urban taverns became more stratified and less inclusive as price regulations were lifted in accord with post-Revolutionary notions of entrepreneurial freedom, rural taverns and illicit urban gambling halls could not afford to target such a narrow clientele. Overall, the postwar emphasis on maximizing profit from leisure ventures heightened the accessibility of leisure venues and further diminished their ability to distinguish patrons along class lines.

This democratic milieu, saturated with alcohol and competition, made public leisure activities into bastions supporting the power of white men. To be sure, women ran taverns and acted onstage and, accompanied by men, attended the theater and horse races. But a woman who engaged in the raucous world of leisure risked her standing as a lady, while a white man could challenge an alleged superior, escort a reputable woman, or misogynistically harass disreputable women without risking his claims to being a gentleman. Black men worked in taverns and jockeyed racehorses, yet as spectators they faced segregation or even exclusion. These gender and racial restrictions made leisure events into settings that affirmed white men's place atop American society.

Leisure events also reinforced white male power because they were tied to electoral politics. Of course, taverns had long been sites for campaigning. By the 1790s, however, newly legalized theaters mounted partisan productions that criticized leading politicians such as Alexander Hamilton and Thomas Jefferson, while racehorses donned names such as "Anti-Democrat" and "Republican President." The whole nascent commercial leisure industry was thoroughly politicized, which dovetailed neatly with its unmistakably white masculine overtone, since virtually all voters were white men.

Leisure activities were ideal settings for political leaders to recruit supporters. They enabled politicians to engage citizens in a democratic atmosphere, even though both political parties in the early republic were controlled by wealthy elites. Small wonder, then, that many political leaders invested in leisure enterprises. The development of organized public commercial leisure entrenched elites' political power even as it fostered a democratic experience in line with the promise of the Revolution.

—Kenneth Cohen

Further Reading

Cohen, Kenneth. "Well Calculated for the Farmer: Thoroughbreds in the Early National Chesapeake, 1790–1850." *Virginia Magazine of History and Biography* 115, no. 3 (October 2007): 370–411.

Conroy, David W. *In Public Houses: Drink and the Revolution of Authority in Colonial Massachusetts*. Chapel Hill: University of North Carolina Press, 1995.

Faragher, John Mack. *Sugar Creek: Life on the Illinois Prairie.* New Haven, Conn.: Yale University Press, 1986.

Jable, J. Thomas. "Pennsylvania's Early Blue Laws: A Quaker Experiment in the Suppression of Sport and Amusements, 1682–1740." *Journal of Sport History* 1 (Spring 1974): 107–122.

Johnson, Odai. *Absence and Memory in Colonial American Theatre: Fiorelli's Plaster*. New York: Palgrave Macmillan, 2006.

Morgan, Edmund S. *Inventing the People: The Rise of Popular Sovereignty in England and America.* New York: W. W. Norton, 1988. (See especially chapter 8.)

Nathans, Heather. *Early American Theatre from the Revolution to Thomas Jefferson: Into the Hands of the People*. New York: Cambridge University Press, 2003.

Nylander, Jane C. *Our Own Snug Fireside: Images of the New England Home, 1760–1860*. New Haven, Conn.: Yale University Press, 1994.

Salinger, Sharon. *Taverns and Drinking in Early America*. Baltimore, Md.: Johns Hopkins University Press, 2002.

Struna, Nancy L. *People of Prowess: Sport, Leisure, and Labor in Early Anglo-America.* Urbana: University of Illinois Press, 1996.

Thompson, Peter. *Rum Punch and Revolution: Taverngoing and Public Life in Eighteenth-Century Philadelphia*. Philadelphia: University of Pennsylvania Press, 1999.

Withington, Ann. *Toward a More Perfect Union: Virtue and the Formation of American Republics*. New York: Oxford University Press, 1991.

18th Century LITERATURE

Readers of the 18th century witnessed one of the most significant developments in the history of American letters: the transition from religious to secular literature. Like their predecessors in the 17th century, some Congregationalists and Quakers produced sermons, theological treatises, and spiritual autobiographies. By 1740, however, other writers—often following the lead of their countrymen on the other side of the Atlantic—were producing satires, political essays, nature writing, and various forms of autobiography. This turn toward a secular literature, together with the sense of kinship with England's great literary tradition, moved America closer to the big stage of world literature. The colonies and the new republic, in fact, produced two authors, Jonathan Edwards and Benjamin Franklin, of international significance, along with a host of notable writers of autobiography, belles lettres, and political and natural philosophy.

The Religious Legacy: Puritan and Quaker Writings

Much of the significant literature to emerge from America in the preceding century had been written by Puritans, religious dissenters who had quarreled or broken completely with the Church of England. This literature—John Winthrop's sermon "A Model of Christian Charity," Mary Rowlandson's captivity narrative, and the poetry of Anne Bradstreet and Michael Wigglesworth, for instance—reflected the authors' religious concerns with salvation and God's role in human affairs. By the early decades of the 18th century, the Puritans—or Congregationalists, as they were sometimes called in the 18th century—no longer wielded the political and cultural influence they once had, but religious themes continued to pervade American literature. In the 1730s and 1740s, a revivalist movement led by the celebrated preacher George Whitefield swept across the colonies. The Great Awakening, as this movement came to be known, generated new religious excitement and did more to put spiritual matters in the minds of Americans.

When the century began, the major literary figure in New England was Cotton Mather, who carried forward the religious legacy of the 17th century. His magnum opus, *Magnalia Christi Americana* (1702), is, in fact, in the words of its subtitle, an "ecclesiastical history of New-England; from its first planning, in the year 1620, unto the year of Our Lord 1698." Jonathan Edwards, born in 1703, 40 years after Mather, carried on the tradition begun by the Puritans. Edwards, a major figure in the era of the Great Awakening, recounted his private emotional religious experience in his *Personal Narrative*, in which he described the "sort of inward, sweet delight" he experienced in reading a verse from the Bible, his ecstatic contemplation of thunderstorms and other natural phenomena, and his longing for more "holiness." More than an author of one of the best-known spiritual journals of the age, Edwards was perhaps America's greatest religious philosopher, the author of several theological treatises, including *A Careful and Strict Inquiry into the Modern Prevailing Notions of That Freedom of the Will* (1754) and *The Great Christian Doctrine of Original Sin Defended* (1758). Despite his achievements in spiritual autobiography and theology, Edwards is commonly known today almost exclusively for his most famous sermon, "Sinners in the Hands of an Angry God" (1741), in which he called on the unconverted members of his congregation to come to God. In portraying God's complete control over sinful humans, Edwards employed what would become one of the most famous similes in all of American literature, one comparing the sinner to "a spider or some loathsome insect" held over a fire. One of America's greatest religious writers, Edwards nevertheless was not immune to the growing influence of science and reason in Western culture. He wrote a scientific paper on the flying spider and, as some scholars have noted, tried to reconcile science and religion in his work.

Just as Mather and Edwards wrote in the Puritan tradition, Elizabeth Ashbridge and John Woolman gave voice to another distinctive religious subculture, that of the Society

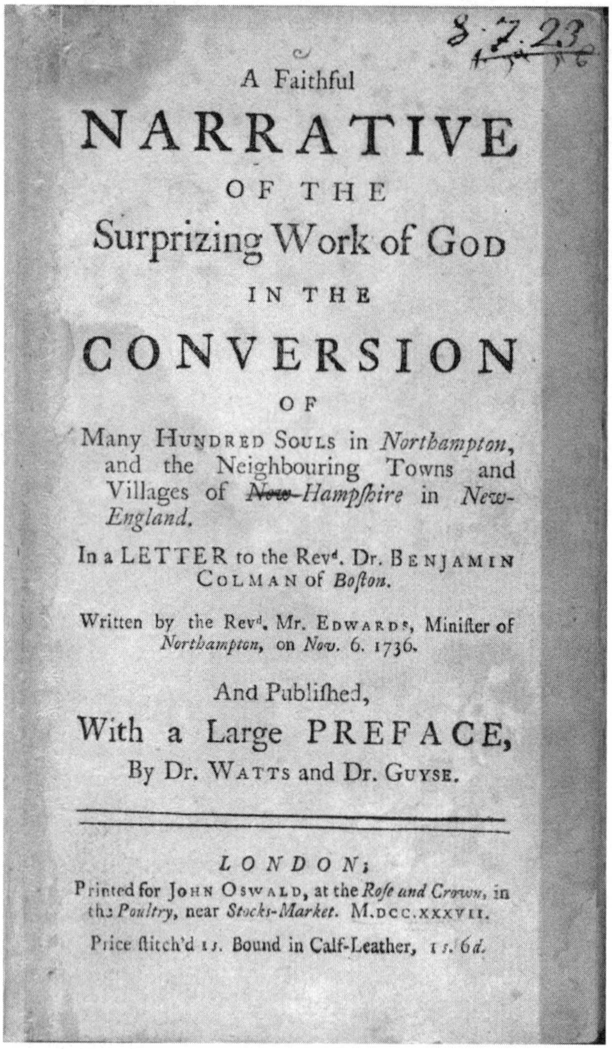

A Faithful

NARRATIVE

OF THE

Surprizing Work of GOD

IN THE

CONVERSION

OF

Many HUNDRED SOULS in *Northampton*, and the Neighbouring Towns and Villages of ~~New~~-*Hampſhire* in *New-England*.

In a LETTER to the Rev^d^. Dr. BENJAMIN COLMAN of *Boſton*.

Written by the Rev^d^. Mr. EDWARDS, Miniſter of *Northampton*, on *Nov*. 6. 1736.

And Publiſhed,

With a Large PREFACE,

By Dr. WATTS and Dr. GUYSE.

LONDON;

Printed for JOHN OSWALD, at the *Roſe and Crown*, in the *Poultry*, near *Stocks-Market*. M.DCC.XXXVII.

Price ſtitch'd 1*s*. Bound in Calf-Leather, 1*s*. 6*d*.

Jonathan Edwards was the greatest American religious philosopher of his time and was notable not only for his theological treatises but also for his synthesis of Puritan intellectual and religious tradition with Enlightenment natural and moral philosophy. Pictured is the frontispiece to Edwards's 1737 treatise on the process of religious conversion, *A Faithful Narrative of the Surprizing Work of God in the Conversion of Many Hundred Souls in North Hampton*. *(Beinecke Rare Book and Manuscript Library, Yale University)*

of Friends, or Quakers, as they are known. Centered in Pennsylvania, a colony that was founded by their own William Penn, the Quakers emphasized an intimate personal relationship with the divine and were known for their repudiation of violence and, eventually, slavery. In *Some Account of the Fore Part of the Life of Elizabeth Ashbridge* (1755), Ashbridge recounts her conversion to the faith, which she once had rejected, as well as the challenges of practicing it in the face of her husband's resistance. Another Quaker work, *The Journal of John Woolman* (1774), is a classic in the genre of spiritual autobiography. Like Edwards in his *Personal Narrative*, Woolman reflects on his own sinfulness, as well as God's powerful, positive presence in his life. In a particularly memorable passage, he describes his boyhood remorse after he threw a rock at a robin and killed it, leaving its brood without a mother. He goes on to reflect on the religious significance of the incident, noting that humans carry a divinely inspired commitment "to exercise goodness toward every living creature." Although he writes explicitly of the "inward life," Woolman, more than Edwards, also treats the challenges the conscience encounters in the midst of a society—particularly one that sanctions slavery—noting that "it is the duty of everyone to be firm in that which they certainly know is right for them."

The Enlightenment

Woolman lived until 1772, and like him, other writers continued to reflect on their faith in writing, but change was clearly on the way. Indeed, by the middle of the 18th century, virtually all of the most noteworthy colonial American literature was secular. In this regard, Benjamin Franklin and his contemporaries were influenced by—and were themselves helping to shape—a major cultural shift in the Western world. In the wake of the scientific revolution that had begun with Copernicus, Galileo, and Francis Bacon in the 16th and 17th centuries, Europe's leading intellectuals—among them England's Isaac Newton and John Locke—were demonstrating and celebrating the power of humans to understand and control the natural and social worlds. The Enlightenment, as the name of this era suggests, was a time for illuminating the workings of nature and human relations. Newton and others did not abandon religion, but they concentrated on what they could know and do here on Earth.

The spirit of the Enlightenment pervades much of the literature emerging from the American colonies in the second half of the century, particularly the works of the era's leading author, who also happened to be its leading scientist. Benjamin Franklin was born in Boston, the city of Mather, and read the famous clergyman's book *Bonifacius, or Essays to Do Good* (1710), which Franklin said might have provided him with an influential "Turn of Thinking." In the 1720s, however, Franklin left Boston and took up residence in the Quaker city of Philadelphia, where he would make his fortune and his reputation as the leading secular writer of the age. The Enlightenment principles of observation, reason, and control are to be found virtually everywhere in Franklin's large and diverse oeuvre. His masterpiece, the unfinished *Autobiography*, tells the story of a man who learned from his observations and experiences, turned his knowledge to good use, and took control of his life, ultimately becoming the original for the rags-to-riches icon that has been a centerpiece of American culture. In one of the most famous passages of this work, Franklin describes his "bold and arduous Project of arriving at moral Perfection"—a plan for using reason to control even morality. Elsewhere, he tells of his strategies for honing his writing abilities, managing his image, and capitalizing on the strengths of others in a group called the Junto—all signs of a man who firmly believed in his own ability to understand and control his environment and delighted in teaching his lessons about self-determination to others. The same theme runs through the aphorisms he included in the annual editions of his *Poor Richard's Almanack* (1732–1757), a best-selling book supposedly compiled by a character named Poor Richard. These aphorisms later provided the substance for Franklin's most famous sketch, "The Way to Wealth," also known as "Father Abraham's Speech." Republished countless times, the sketch helped solidify Franklin's legacy by immortalizing many of his sayings, including "God helps them that help themselves" and "Early to Bed, and early to rise, makes a Man healthy, wealthy and wise." As a leading printer of the era, Franklin was an active participant in the production of emerging literary forms, including not only the almanac, but also the newspaper and the pamphlet. His *Pennsylvania Gazette* and his monographs on education and currency were among the pamphlets that filled the literary marketplace in the 18th century.

The Rise of Belles Lettres

In this new age, in which secular literature enjoyed new prominence, a variety of different genres dominated the literary scene in colonial America. Though sermons and other theological writings were still available, most Americans were probably more likely to be reading the more literary—and often light and entertaining—form of writing known as belles lettres, particularly since this literature was readily available in a new vehicle, the newspaper. After the launch of the nation's first regular paper, the *Boston News-Letter*, in 1704, newspapers provided readers with the news of the day, along with poetry and essays. Other literature was simply shared in manuscript form. Furthermore, a fledgling publishing industry, managed by the likes of Franklin and Matthew Carey, gave Americans access to British books, as well as some works by American authors.

In much of the American literature of this era, readers will see an obvious debt to leading British writers. Indeed, in his autobiography, Franklin recounted his habit of rewriting passages he had found in the *Spectator*, the famous British periodical of the early 18th century, as a means of developing his prose style. Satirical essays and variations on epic poetry were the fashion of the day in the British Isles, and the work of Joseph Addison and Richard Steele, Alexander Pope, Richard Brinsley Sheridan, and their contemporaries clearly left a mark on Franklin and his fellow Americans. Here was a literature known not, as the work of the later Romanticists would be, for its passion or symbolism, but for its humor, its clever turns of phrase, and its urbanity—in a word, for its wit.

Wit was a key ingredient in some of the most important American genres of the era. Like Addison and Steele, writers such as Joseph Dennie, author of the well-known "Farrago" and "Lay Preacher" series, wrote witty essays and published them in newspapers. Some essays, such as ones Franklin wrote under the pen name of Silence Dogood while he was still a teenager, were not only witty, but also satirical, poking fun at people and institutions. Franklin also incorporated satire into hoaxes, such as "A Witch Trial at Mount Holly" and "An Edict by the King of Prussia," in which he took aim at British oppression of the colonies and other targets. Other writers incorporated humor and satire into their autobiographical narratives. *History of the Dividing Line* is William Byrd's satirical account of a surveying expedition in the vicinity of the boundary between his home state of Virginia and North Carolina. A well-to-do planter accustomed to the high culture of London, where he spent part of his life, Byrd employs an urbane style in poking fun at the rural inhabitants he encounters on the trip, characterizing them as lazy, cheap, crude, unkempt, and immoral. Noting that some inhabitants obtain moss in trees by simply cutting the trees down, Byrd wryly observes, "The trouble wou'd be too great to Climb the Tree in order to gather this Provender, but the Shortest way (which in this Country is always counted the best) is to fell it." Although it was not published until the 19th century, *History of the Dividing Line* was available to some of Byrd's contemporaries in manuscript form.

Humorous poetry was common, as well, as evidenced by the productions of a group of writers who came to be known as the Connecticut Wits, or Hartford Wits. John Trumbull satirized education in *The Progress of Dulness* (1772–73). His friend and Yale classmate Joel Barlow adapted one of the era's favorite genres, the epic, for comic purposes. His poem *The Hasty-Pudding* (1793) belongs to a genre known as the mock epic. By employing the lofty language of the epic and applying it to a mundane subject—namely a common meal—Barlow produced a humorous poem in the vein of Pope's famous *The Rape of the Lock*. Another mock epic, *The Anarchiad* (1786–87), was the joint effort of Trumbull, Barlow, Lemuel Hopkins, and David Humphreys. According to a specious introductory note, this poem was found among ruins in North America. In reality, it was a political satire that attacked the conversion to a paper currency and argued that the nation was devolving into anarchy.

Contemporary with such humorous poetry was an abundance of serious poetry, much of it colored by the wave of nationalism that washed over the country in the second half of the century, as Americans mounted a successful revolution against a world power and founded a new nation. Barlow's epic poem *The Vision of Columbus* (1787), for instance, celebrates the promise of the New World, and Timothy Dwight's *Greenfield Hill* (1794) romanticizes life in the Connecticut village where the author was a minister. Nationalistic poetry also issued from the pen of Philip Freneau, the "poet of the Revolution," who attacked Britain and celebrated the American cause in poems such as "To the Memory of the Brave Americans" (1781) and "The British Prison-Ship" (1781). Freneau also wrote notable nature poems, including "The Wild Honey Suckle" (1786) and "On a Honey Bee" (1797). In some respects, Phillis Wheatley resembled contemporaries such as Barlow and Freneau. In tributes to political and religious figures such as the Earl of Dartmouth, George Washington, and George Whitefield, she celebrated freedom, virtue, and religious service in highly formal, stylized heroic couplets—pairs of rhyming lines of iambic pentameter—a favorite form of British poets such as Pope and John Dryden. In one notable respect, however, Wheatley was in a class by herself. Brought to the colonies as a slave, she was freed in 1773 while she was still a young woman. The publication of her *Poems on Various Subjects, Religious and Moral*, in London that same year made her the first black American to publish a book of poetry. Wheatley occasionally reflected on slavery and her race in poems such as "On Being Brought from Africa to America" (1768), which proclaims that "mercy" exposed her to Christianity and argues that Africans can find a place in heaven.

Another slave, Olaudah Equiano, reflected on his experience in prose, producing the first notable example of what came to be a distinctive American genre, the slave narrative. In *The Interesting Narrative of the Life of Olaudah Equiano, or Gustavas Vassa, the African, Written by Himself* (1789), Equiano recounts his captivity in Africa, the horrors of the Middle Passage, his service to an appreciative Quaker master, a terrible beating he received at the hands of white attackers, the commerce he used to store up the funds to purchase his freedom, and his ultimate manumission, as well as the horrors inflicted on other slaves. The result is a scathing condemnation of slavery, which corrupts the white oppressors even while it debases and often destroys the black victims. Equiano, like Frederick Douglass and Harriet Jacobs after him, also tells a personal story, one in which an individual takes control of his fate and, through both industry and reason, overcomes obstacles to improve his condition in life. In this respect, his narrative is a kind of counterpart of Franklin's autobiography, each giving voice to the principle of self-determination.

Long rejected or even prohibited as an immoral or anti-republican art form, particularly by Puritans and Quakers, drama nevertheless took hold in the 18th century, at least in some parts of the country. Most of the plays, staged in cities such as Philadelphia and Williamsburg, came from England and France, but a few American playwrights produced native drama. The first was Thomas Godfrey, whose *The Prince of Parthia* (published in 1765 and performed in 1767) was the first play written by an American to be staged in America. Other notable dramatists included Hugh Henry Brackenridge, William Dunlap, and Mercy Otis Warren. One of the most significant plays of the era was Royall Tyler's *The Contrast* (1787), a comedy of manners featuring a colonial army colonel named Manly and the prototype for the Yankee rustic in a character named Jonathan. In both content and execution, *The Contrast* resembles other 18th-century American drama, which sometimes represented American political aspirations while following the style of British plays.

Thomas Jefferson's Declaration of Independence crystallized the political principles undergirding the Revolution and stands as one of the most stirring documents in the history of American letters. The above painting from 1897 shows Jefferson reading a rough draft of the Declaration to Benjamin Franklin. *(Library of Congress)*

Political and Scientific Writings

Whatever inspiration they provided for the drama, as well as the poetry of Freneau and Wheatley, the events surrounding the American Revolution produced a more lasting literary legacy in the form of eloquent and influential political writings.

Although he was born in England, Thomas Paine became a passionate devotee to the cause of American independence, as well as one of the most important literary forces behind the Revolution. His pamphlet *Common Sense* (1776), in which he rejects the arguments for reconciliation with Great Britain and calls for "a final separation," and a pamphlet series called *The American Crisis* (1776–83), which he wrote while he was a member of the Continental Army, resonated with American patriots, including George Washington's soldiers, who heard Paine's words read aloud before they crossed the Delaware and won a great victory at Trenton. The opening of *The American Crisis* contains some of the most famous words ever penned on American soil: "These are the times that try men's souls. The summer soldier and the sunshine patriot will, in this crisis, shrink from the service of their country; but he that stands it *now*, deserves the love and thanks of man and woman."

If Paine's powerful prose helped drive the American Revolution, Thomas Jefferson's Declaration of Independence crystallized political principles, ultimately inspiring countless Americans over more than two centuries. A model of the elegant prose that characterized writing of the era, Jefferson's brief document recounts the crimes committed by the British

Crown on the American colonies while making a memorable case for the rights of human beings. "We hold these truths to be self-evident," the document famously proclaims, "that all men are created equal, that they are endowed by their Creator with certain unalienable Rights, that among these are Life, Liberty and the pursuit of Happiness."

Less well known, J. Hector St. John de Crèvecoeur's *Letters from an American Farmer* (1782) is another inspiring work of the era. Echoing John Smith's *A Description of New England* and anticipating Franklin's "Information to Those Who Would Remove to America," Crèvecoeur's work is an explicit, often ecstatic, celebration of America as a land of opportunity, a realm where individuals can escape the economic and religious oppression of Europe and where arable land, "rational laws," freedom, and tolerance allow farmers and seamen to achieve independence and prosperity. In the letter entitled "What Is an American," the most famous portion of the work, the author asserts that the American is "a new man" and proclaims, "From involuntary idleness, servile dependence, penury, and useless labour, he has passed to toils of a very different nature, rewarded by ample subsistence. This is an American."

After Paine, Jefferson, Franklin, and their fellow patriots achieved independence, another group of political thinkers outlined their ideas for the new government in a series of essays, first published in newspapers and later collected in book form as *The Federalist*. The essays appeared under the pen name Publius, but the actual authors were three of America's greatest statesmen: Alexander Hamilton, John Jay, and James Madison. Grounded in both the lessons of history and an understanding of human motivation, *The Federalist* presents precisely the kind of reasoned arguments one would expect of Enlightenment intellectuals.

Some of the same leading political writers were at the forefront of another form of secular writing that was on the rise in America: scientific writing. Franklin reported his findings in the field of electricity in writings that were collected and published as *Experiments and Observations on Electricity Made at Philadelphia in America* (1751). Some three decades later, Jefferson completed his *Notes on the State of Virginia* (1784), a compendium of geographical, geological, agricultural, zoological, and political information about his home state. Perhaps the greatest American science writer of the age was William Bartram, who traveled across the South and, in *Travels through North and South Carolina, Georgia, East and West Florida* (1791), described alligators, fish, flowers, and other animals and plants he encountered.

The sermons and other religious writings of the 17th century gave way in the 18th century to a new brand of literature. Whether they explored society or the self, politics or nature, the era's essays, poems, plays, autobiographies, and works of natural and political philosophy exhibit a new interest in the things of this world.

—*Mark Canada*

Further Reading

Bercovitch, Sacvan, ed. *The Cambridge History of American Literature*. Vol. 1. Cambridge, U.K.: Cambridge University Press, 1994.

Byrd, William. *History of the Dividing Line*. In *William Byrd's Histories of the Dividing Line Betwixt Virginia and North Carolina*. Edited by William K. Boyd. Gloucester, Mass.: Peter Smith, 1984.

Crèvecoeur, J. Hector St. John de. *Letters from an American Farmer*. In *Letters from an American Farmer and Sketches of Eighteenth-Century America: More Letters from an American Farmer*. New York: New American Library of World Literature, 1963.

Edwards, Jonathan. *Personal Narrative*. In *Edwards: Representative Selections*. New York: Hill & Wang, 1935.

Elliott, Emory, ed. *American Colonial Writers, 1606–1734*. Detroit: Gale, 1984.

———, ed. *American Colonial Writers, 1735–1781*. Detroit: Gale, 1984.

———, ed. *American Writers of the Early Republic*. Detroit: Gale, 1985.

Franklin, Benjamin. *Writings*. New York: Literary Classics of the United States, 1987.

Jackson, Blyden. *A History of Afro-American Literature*. Vol. 1, *The Long Beginning, 1746–1895*. Baton Rouge: Louisiana State University Press, 1989.

Jefferson, Thomas. "The Declaration of Independence." In *The Papers of Thomas Jefferson*, vol. 1. Edited by Julian P. Boyd. Princeton, N.J.: Princeton University Press, 1950.

Lawson-Pebbles, Robert. *Landscape and Written Expression in Revolutionary America: The World Turned Upside Down*. Cambridge, U.K.: Cambridge University Press, 1988.

Levernier, James, and Douglas R. Wilmes, eds. *American Writers before 1800: A Biographical and Critical Dictionary*. 3 vols. Westport, Conn.: Greenwood Press, 1983.

Ostriker, Alicia Suskin. *Stealing the Language: The Emergence of Women's Poetry in America*. Boston: Beacon Press, 1986.

Paine, Thomas. *The American Crisis*. In *The Complete Writings of Thomas Paine*, vol. 2. Edited by Philip S. Foner. New York: Citadel Press, 1945.

Shields, David. *Civil Tongues and Polite Letters in British America*. Chapel Hill: University of North Carolina Press, 1997.

Slotkin, Richard. *Regeneration through Violence: The Mythology of the American Frontier, 1600–1860*. Middletown, Conn.: Wesleyan University Press, 1973.

Warner, Michael. *Letters of the Republic*. Cambridge, Mass.: Harvard University Press, 1990.

Woolman, John. *The Journal and Major Essays of John Woolman*. Edited by Phillips P. Moulton. New York: Oxford University Press, 1971.

18th Century NATIVE AMERICANS

If 17th-century America was dramatically shaped by Indian power and priorities, the 18th century saw both a magnification and a reversal of that trend. On the Great Plains, where Indians had access to colonial goods without having to deal with colonial settlers, equestrians such as the Sioux and the Comanches were the reigning forces. By contrast, on the East Coast, where European settlement was concentrated, Indians had weakened considerably by the early 18th century, suffering from the hammer blows of disease, warfare, and land loss. Indians remained formidable in places such as Maine, the Appalachian foothills, the Ohio River Valley, and the Great Lakes region, but by the end of the century the Native groups in these regions were also in retreat, confronted by a veritable swarm of white settlers. Across the continent, in coastal California, Indians were spared the ordeal of confronting a mass of colonists, but Spanish missionary efforts unleashed diseases that decimated the indigenous population. Thus, while the mounted bison hunters were rising to power in the center of the continent, their counterparts on the Atlantic and Pacific coasts were in a near freefall.

From the very beginning of their contact with Europeans, Indians had savored European goods and welcomed European traders, which provided the wedge for colonial settlement. European metal tools, such as knives, hatchets, kettles, fishhooks, and sewing needles, were far more efficient than the Indians' stone, bone, and wood equivalents. Firearms, metal-tipped arrows and spears, and iron axes made Indian warriors more formidable than ever before. Fashion-minded Indians also relished the Europeans' brightly colored wool mantles, cloth shirts, pigments, glass beads, and jewelry. Indian leaders who managed to open trade alliances with Europeans and then control the flow of goods to Indian country could consolidate and expand their followings. Likewise, Indian groups who became middlemen between coastal Europeans and interior tribes could enhance their prestige and power. Factors such as these explain why Indians permitted Europeans to enter their territories during the early 17th century.

Plains Indians

Plains Indians came the closest to turning colonialism to their advantage during the 18th century, the Comanches foremost among them. The Comanches ventured onto the southwestern Plains from the Rocky Mountains during the late 17th and early 18th centuries, newly mounted on horseback, allied with the powerful Ute tribe, and primed for expansion. The Comanches' horses originated with the Spanish, who had begun to colonize New Mexico in the late 16th century, but reached them through Indian horse traders like the Utes and Shoshones; it was the Indian-to-Indian trade in horses that mostly accounts for the spread of the animal in Indian country. The Comanches quickly saw the advantages horses afforded: They enabled hunters to cover far more ground, take far more game, and transport far more kill than they ever could on foot; they gave Indian warriors decisive advantages of height and speed; and they permitted the community to move more people and goods over vaster distances than ever before. Seizing the opportunity, the Comanches began warring with the heretofore dominant Apaches for grassland, water, and trade markets. Though the Apaches boasted their own mounted warriors, the fact that they retained horticultural settlements, rather than becoming mounted nomads, left them vulnerable to guerrilla strikes by the more mobile Comanches. The results were decisive: By the mid- to late 18th century, the Comanches were ascendant on the southern Plains, scattering the Apaches to the edges.

From their base in the upper Arkansas River basin, the Comanches broadened their strength through wide-reaching, overlapping trade networks and military conquests stretching from New Mexico to the Mississippi

River. Indians and Spaniards across the southern Plains fell victim to Comanche raids for horses, mules, food stores, manufactured goods, and, not least of all, human captives, most of whom the Comanches enslaved. None of the Comanches' victims, including the Spanish, had the power to suppress these attacks; at the same time, none of them had the willpower to resist the Comanche trade that encouraged these attacks in the first place. Thus, the Comanches sometimes plundered the very communities with whom they traded. They became some of the main suppliers of horses to Indians to their north, of French goods to the Spanish and Pueblo Indians, and of slaves to the Spanish. They even stole horses from the Spanish in Texas to trade to the Spanish in New Mexico, who had little choice but to welcome the trade or else suffer Comanche reprisals.

Comanche territory was bordered on three sides by European colonies—Spanish New Mexico to the west, Spanish Texas and Mexico to the south, and French Louisiana to the east—but those colonies, weakly populated and undersupplied as they were, posed little threat to the Comanches. Indeed, Spanish officials, particularly in Texas, groused that the Comanches allowed their colonies to survive as targets for future raids, and they were certainly right. Colonialism was not an imposition on the Comanches but an opportunity—it was mounts from colonial sources and access to colonial markets that allowed the Comanches to thrive.

Later in the 18th century, the Sioux also used the horse and European trade to become ascendant on the northern Plains. At the beginning of the century, the Sioux resided on the prairies of Minnesota, from which they hunted beaver to exchange for French guns, initially through the brokerage of the Crees and Assiniboines and eventually through French traders themselves. They routinely ventured onto the Plains to hunt, but they did so on foot and with great wariness of well-armed, populous farming tribes on the Missouri River, such as the Arikaras, Mandans, and Hidatsas who jealously guarded the nearby bison herds. Yet by the end of the 18th century the balance of power had shifted, leaving the Sioux poised to explode onto the Plains.

Having depleted the beaver population in Minnesota and adopted the horse, the Sioux were eager to take advantage of an expanding market for bison robes and hides among French and Spanish traders on the Missouri. That opportunity arose when repeated epidemics of smallpox among the Missouri River tribes, between 1780 and 1810, wiped out 90 percent and more of their populations, thereby removing them as a western barrier. Over the next two generations, the Sioux shattered what remained of the tribes and established their dominance westward to the Yellowstone River. When the United States attempted to subdue Plains Indians and seize their lands in the mid- to late 19th century, the Sioux put up a mighty resistance, relenting only when the diminishing bison herds left them starving. The cases of groups like the Sioux and Comanche should disabuse us from charting postcontact Indian history as an uncomplicated downward slope. When Indians had access to European goods through more than one trade partner, and when they managed to keep European settlement at a distance, they were sometimes able to turn colonialism to great advantage.

East Coast Indians

East Coast Indians had initially engaged colonists with the same purpose, but by the start of the 18th century their strategies had largely unraveled. Virginia had decimated the Powhatans of the James and York rivers in a series of wars during the first half of the 17th century, and then displaced or further subjugated most of the surviving groups east of the fall line in Bacon's Rebellion of 1675–76. New England had an equally bloody history of Indian-colonial relations, with the Pequot War of 1636–38 and King Philip's War of 1675–76 breaking Indian power along the region's southeastern coast and leading to the death and enslavement of thousands. Seeking to escape a similar fate, the Piscataways and Nanticokes in Maryland and the Lenapes (or Delawares) in New Jersey retreated into Pennsylvania in the face of often forceful colonial expansion into their homelands.

Events in Carolina demonstrated their foresight. In 1711, the lower Tuscaroras and some of their coastal Algonquian allies, led by Chief Hancock, struck European settlements to protest their expansion on Indian lands and enslavement of Indian peoples. Though the Tuscaroras killed hundreds of settlers and threw North Carolina into a panic in the early months of the conflict, ultimately they were overmatched by the vast coalition that aligned against them. The South Carolina militia, backed by hundreds of Indian allies, such as the Yamasees and Catawbas, came to North Carolina's aid and, over the course of the next year, killed and enslaved hundreds of Tuscaroras. They also persuaded the upper Tuscaroras, who had remained at peace, to turn on their southern counterparts in order to save their own necks. The pressure was too much for the warring Tuscaroras to bear. Most of them escaped northward to take sanctuary with the Iroquois of what is now upstate New York, while others signed a treaty conceding land and authority to North Carolina in exchange for a small reservation.

It speaks volumes about the desperation of Indians in the path of colonial expansion that just a few years later a coalition of tribes, led by the Yamasees, rose up against South Carolina, even after witnessing this carnage. The Indians' tensions with South Carolina had been rising for years despite a longstanding alliance based on a trade of deerskins and Indian slaves for European goods. By the 1710s, Indians like the Yamasees had overharvested their resources. They made up the difference by purchasing on credit, and as they grew further in debt to unsavory traders, they grew fearful that they would be the next victims of enslavement. This danger, combined with grievances over the colony's expansion and Charlestown's bungling diplomacy, led the Yamasees, Ochese Creeks, and other area groups to war against the English in early 1715, to devastating effect. South Carolina would lose some 7 percent of its population during these strikes. When the Cherokees and Catawbas joined the uprising, the colony's future seemed very much in doubt. Yet as the Yamasee War dragged on, Indians began to yearn for a restoration of the trade, and the coalition began to crack. In 1716, South Carolina persuaded the Cherokees to switch sides, thereby forcing the colony's enemies to guard multiple fronts. At this point, the war turned in the English's favor. Though isolated Indian attacks on the colony continued for years, the colony managed to kill, enslave, or scatter its opponents, with most of the survivors fleeing either to Spanish Florida or the emerging Creek Confederacy on the Chattahoochee and Tallapoosa rivers. Indians would never again threaten the very survival of English settlement on the East Coast.

Indigenous wars stoked by imperial conflicts between Spain and England proved equally devastating to the Indians of Florida. During the 16th and 17th centuries, the Spanish militantly forced their missions on thousands of Guales, Timucuans, Apalachees, and Apalachicolas until their influence stretched between St. Augustine to the south and today's Georgia–South Carolina border to the north, and across the Florida panhandle on an east-west axis. The Florida Indians periodically revolted against Spanish demands for labor, tribute, and religious change, and they absorbed epidemics that nearly wiped out their populations, yet on the sliding scale of colonization they were doing relatively well by the late 17th century. They coped with few Spanish settlers and remained largely in control of their daily lives and lands. Ultimately, though, their greatest threat lay outside the colony.

During the late 17th and early 18th centuries, Florida missions suffered multiple slave raids by the Westos, Savannahs, Yamasees, and Creeks, who were encouraged and sometimes led by South Carolinians claiming to be acting in the name of England against Spain. By the time the smoke cleared, 29 missions had either been destroyed or abandoned and the raiders had taken thousands of mission Indians captive (up to 30,000 by one count), to the point that slavers began ranging as far south as the Florida Keys to find targets. Carolina put many of the slaves to work on its expanding rice plantations, but many more were exported to the West Indies and other mainland colonies, making the colony a net exporter of slaves before 1715, despite its own population of African slaves. The Indian slave trade in the Southeast did not die out until the Yamasee War dramatically illustrated the dangers of this enterprise, particularly in contrast to the growing efficiency of the trade in Africans. Ironically, a number of the Yamasee survivors of this war fled south to Florida to take up lands they themselves had depopulated through slave raiding.

Some Indians managed to survive in coastal areas after these wars, but only by accommodating colonial demands for power, land, and labor. Groups such as the Wampanoags, Narragansetts, Pequots, and Mohegans in New England, the Pamunkeys, Chickahominies, and Rappahannocks in Virginia, and the eponymously named "Settlement Indians" in South Carolina moved to reservations with land guaranteed to them by colonial authorities, only to lose that land in increments, usually to answer for debts to colonial merchants. Many of these same groups paid an annual tribute to colonial governors, and they always contributed warriors to the English colonies' wars against France and other Indian nations. Southern Indians also made themselves equally valuable as slave catchers, while many New England Indians expressed their goodwill by hosting missionaries. Perhaps the Indians' greatest appeal to their colonial neighbors was as cheap labor. Working for colonists was essentially the only way most coastal Indians could make ends meet, and thus Indians could be found throughout colonial society as sailors, whalemen, longshoremen, farmworkers, and housemaids, usually in a state of de facto or court-ordered indentured servitude. This workforce included not only men and women but often children, thus robbing Indian communities of substantial numbers of their young and the opportunity to raise them with the people's language and other traditions. It was a steep price to pay for continuing to live on the people's ancestral lands.

Backcountry Indians

In the western reaches of the English colonies, known to Europeans as the "backcountry" or "frontier," Indians retained and often wielded their power. The Wabenakis of Maine and the various Iroquoian and Algonquian residents of the Catholic missions in the St. Lawrence River Valley used hit-and-run tactics to keep northern New England and upper New York on a nearly permanent war footing throughout the 18th century. Though historians often portray these Indians as French auxiliaries, since their attacks on the English often took place in the context of imperial wars, the Indians fought for their own purposes. For instance, the French missions contained large numbers of Indians who had been forced out of New England by the English during King Philip's War. These Indians saw their attacks on the colonists' settlements in the upper Connecticut River Valley as revenge. Likewise, Maine Wabenakis fought to protect their access to critical watersheds and hunting grounds threatened by English expansion. They welcomed French support for their raids, but cared little about the cause of the French king. They remained independent and powerful.

The Iroquois League (comprising the Mohawks, Oneidas, Onondagas, Cayugas, Senecas, and, after 1721, Tuscaroras) entered the 18th century reeling from a century of warfare with their indigenous neighbors and New France, but with their formidable reputation intact. They adopted a multipronged strategy to avoid the dismal fate of their eastern neighbors. For one, they pledged neutrality in all wars between France and Britain, and though certain Iroquois factions, both Francophile and Anglophile, violated this promise at various times, by and large the Iroquois League stayed true. Another critical strategy was to take Indians displaced by colonial expansion and intertribal wars and relocate them in the Susquehanna River Valley on Iroquois country's vulnerable southern flank. By the mid-18th century, Shawnees, Delawares, Mahicans (Mohicans), Nanticokes, Piscataways, and Tutelos had moved to the area, thereby buttressing the Iroquois against white encroachment and attacks from the League's Catawba enemies. Yet even as the Iroquois declared themselves the protectors of these tribes, they sometimes sold off land from which those tribes had moved, as well as land onto which they had relocated, in order to meet British demands, rather than give up parts of Iroquoia proper. Well into the 1760s, this strategy succeeded at maintaining Iroquois lands and preventing embroilment in European conflicts, thereby allowing the league to rebuild its population after decades of loss to disease and war.

The Creeks adopted a similar colonial policy during the early 18th century. The Creeks were already a composite of mostly Muskogean-speaking groups when they began sheltering Indian refugees from the Yamasee War. Then, with the war having demonstrated the folly of relying on just one trade partner, the Creeks developed their own system of balancing European alliances. For instance, they permitted the French to station a garrison at Fort Toulouse in 1716, and the Spanish to build Fort San Marcos on Apalachee Bay in 1718, even as they welcomed mule trains by English traders into their villages. Europeans could see the logic at work here. As one of them commented about the Creek chief, Brims, "No one has ever been able to make him take sides with one of the three European nations who know him, he alleging that he wishes to see every one, to be neutral, and not to espouse any of the quarrels which the French, English, and Spaniards have with one another." As a result, each colonial power "made great presents to [Brims] to regain his friendship . . . which makes him very rich."

The play-off system broke down after the French defeat in the Seven Years' War (1756–63), thereby setting the stage for 60 years of warfare in the Ohio River Valley, Great Lakes region, and interior Southeast. Indians in these zones—including the Shawnees, Delawares, and Miamis in Ohio; the Wyandots, Ojibwas, Ottawas, and Potawatomis in the Great Lakes; and the Creeks in the Southeast—faced a growing Anglo-American population of more than a million people who had little compunction about seizing Indian territory, particularly in the absence of the French threat. With a sense of crisis pervading Indian country, a series of prophets arose who preached that Indians, as a race of people, suffered because the Great Spirit or Master of Life was angry with them. If Indians wanted to regain the Great Spirit's favor, these prophets thundered, they had to swear off alcohol, restore their ritual lives, halt their land sales to whites, and begin weaning themselves from white traders. In 1763 this religious call for Indian unity—particularly from Neolin, the "Delaware Prophet"—inspired a coalition of Ohio River Valley and Great Lakes tribes to rise up against British troops stationed in the woodland posts the empire had acquired from France. After sacking eight British forts and forcing the abandonment of two others, the Indians put down their arms only when the British promised to behave like the French once did, such as by providing the Indians with presents and cheap trade goods, instead of acting like haughty conquerors.

The Revolution and Early Republic

Yet the peace did not last. Indians and frontier settlers swapped attacks throughout the 1760s and early 1770s, culminating in an outright war beginning in 1774 pitting the Shawnees and Delawares against Virginia, in and around modern-day West Virginia. This conflict segued with the American Revolution, a war in which the Indians fought to preserve their own independence, and in which they might be said to have lost more than the British. Most Indians sided with the British, including four of the six Iroquois nations, nearly all of the Ohio and Great Lakes tribes, and, for a time, the Cherokees. They saw that the British were far better equipped than the Americans to maintain the supply of Indian trade goods. These Indians also hoped to persuade the Crown to protect Indian territory, which it promised to do. Instead, Indians allied with the British suffered mightily at American hands. American scorched-earth tactics devastated Cherokee and Iroquois country, sending most of the Iroquois to a permanent refuge in the Grand River Valley of British Canada. Deaths from battlefield casualties, camp diseases, and starvation halved the Iroquois population and sent Cherokee numbers plummeting from 16,000 to 10,000 people.

Indian allies of the United States suffered equally. The tiny Wampanoag village of Mashpee on Cape Cod, numbering no more than 300 people before the war, lost 70 people in 1778 alone, due largely to a camp disease brought home by the one remaining warrior who had survived out of a regiment of 25 men. Likewise, the Stockbridge Mohicans of western Massachusetts sacrificed dozens of men in the service of the Continental army, yet their service and Christian faith won them no favor from their white neighbors, who took advantage of the absence of Mohican fighting men to drive the Indians off of most of their remaining lands. It was an experience shared in varying degrees by most coastal Indians who had sided with the republic.

Seeing how the United States treated its friends, Indians in the interior continued to resist even after the British had surrendered. During the 1790s, the Ohio tribes led by the Shawnee chief Blue Jacket and the Miami Little

The Battle of Fallen Timbers proved a decisive victory for the United States over a Northwest Indian confederation, a victory that came after two decades of border warfare and that secured white settlement of former Indian territory including most of Ohio and part of Indiana. Above is an etching from 1934 by Paul Trester Cahill depicting General Anthony Wayne leading his troops against Indians on the Maumee River in 1794. *(Library of Congress)*

Turtle rebuffed two American armies before going down to defeat at the Battle of Fallen Timbers (1794) and signing the Treaty of Greenville, which ceded most of what is now Ohio and part of Indiana to the United States. Still, the Indians were determined to resist. Just as the region's tribes had united under the prophetic visions of Neolin in the 1760s, so too in the 1810s did they rally around a similar vision by the Shawnee Tenskwatawa, known as the Prophet, to form a resistance movement under his brother Tecumseh. Anticipating trouble, the United States launched a preemptive strike against the militants' settlement at Tippecanoe in 1811. Not surprisingly, given this assault, the Lakes tribes and the Creeks sided with the British during the War of 1812, only to suffer an even greater loss than in the Revolution. The Treaty of Ghent, which ended the war, robbed the Indians of their last European ally who could possibly counterbalance American might. The conclusion of the War of 1812, in this sense, was the end of the Indians' wars for independence east of the Mississippi.

California

Unlike the eastern tribes, Indians in California did not have to cope with the settler colonialism and a rising nation-state, but Spanish missionary work on the Pacific coast reaped an equally devastating toll. California was one of the most densely populated and diverse regions of Native North America during the mid-18th century, with some 300,000 people speaking roughly 90 languages and divided into dozens of different political and ethnic groups—including the Hupas, Yuroks, and Wiyots of the Northwest, the Modocs of the northern interior, the Pomos of the central coast, and the Chumash and Gabrielinos of the southern coast. Spanish evangelization of these people began in 1769 with the founding of San Diego, and by 1804 there were 19 missions up and down the coast, including San Francisco and Santa Barbara. Tens of thousands of Indians entered the missions in search of food, mostly because the massive herds of livestock that accompanied the Spanish disrupted the Indians' hunter-gatherer economies. Yet the missions only contributed to the Indians' decline because they were breeding grounds for disease. Mission Indians suffered a range of ailments, including diphtheria, dysentery, measles, influenza, tuberculosis, pneumonia, and especially an endemic combination of gonorrhea and syphilis. Thus, there were only 21,000 Indians in the missions in 1821, even though over 70,000 had been baptized up to that point. The decimation of California's mission Indians by epidemic disease is the most significant legacy of Spanish evangelization in the area.

The devastation suffered by Indians on the East and West coasts during the 18th century could not have been more alien to the experiences of Indian groups like the Comanches and Sioux, for whom colonialism was a source of strength. Little did they know that the founding of the United States held implications as grave for them as for their eastern counterparts. Indians could thrive in colonial contexts if they had more than one imperial power with which to deal, and as long as they kept white settlement at a distance, but that opportunity declined steadily after the American Revolution. The consolidated might of the republic, which numbered in the millions of people, could not be matched by tribes whose collective strength was in the low hundreds of thousands, and who were divided along numerous lines.

By the end of the War of 1812, neither Britain nor Spain was willing to risk war with the United States over Indian affairs, thus giving the country a near stranglehold on the Indians' supply of goods. As such, though a confederation of tribes in the Ohio River Valley and Great Lakes region put up a mighty resistance during the 1790s, and though the Sioux shot down more than their share of blue-coated cavalry during the campaign to force them onto reservations during the 1860s and 1870s, the nation's power could not be denied for long. The ascendency of the United States ended the double-edged character of colonialism for Indian people; thereafter, but only thereafter, colonialism and subjugation became one and the same.

—David Silverman

Further Reading

Anderson, Gary Clayton. *The Indian Southwest, 1580–1830: Ethnogenesis and Reinvention*. Norman: University of Oklahoma Press, 1999.

———. *Kinsmen of Another Kind: Dakota-White Relations in the Upper Mississippi Valley, 1650–1862*. Lincoln: University of Nebraska Press, 1984.

Baker, Emerson W., and John G. Reid. "Amerindian Power in the Early Modern Northeast: A Reappraisal." *William and Mary Quarterly*, 3d ser., 61, no. 1 (2004): 77–106.

Blackhawk, Ned. *Violence over the Land: Indians and Empires in the Early American West.* Cambridge, Mass.: Harvard University Press, 2006.

Brooks, James. *Captives and Cousins: Slavery, Kinship, and Community in the Southwest Borderlands*. Chapel Hill: University of North Carolina Press for the Omohundro Institute of Early American History and Culture, 2002.

Calloway, Colin G. *The American Revolution in Indian Country: Crisis and Diversity in Native American Communities*. Cambridge, U.K.: Cambridge University Press, 1995.

———. *One Vast Winter Count: The Native American West before Lewis and Clark.* Lincoln: University of Nebraska Press, 2003.

Dowd, Gregory Evans. *A Spirited Resistance: The North American Indian Struggle for Unity, 1745–1815.* Baltimore, Md.: Johns Hopkins University Press, 1992.

DuVal, Kathleen. *The Native Ground: Indians and Colonists in the Heart of the Continent*. Philadelphia: University of Pennsylvania Press, 2006.

Gallay, Alan. *The Indian Slave Trade: The Rise of the English Empire in the American South, 1670–1717.* New Haven, Conn.: Yale University Press, 2002.

Greer, Allan. *Mohawk Saint: Catherine Tekakwitha and the Jesuits*. New York: Oxford University Press, 2005.

Hackel, Steven W. *Children of Coyote, Missionaries of St. Francis: Indian-Spanish Relations in Colonial California,*

1769–1850. Chapel Hill: University of North Carolina Press for the Omohundro Institute of Early American History and Culture, 2005.

Haefeli, Evan, and Kevin Sweeney. *Captors and Captives: The 1704 French and Indian Raid on Deerfield*. Amherst: University of Massachusetts Press, 2003.

Hahn, Steven C. *The Invention of the Creek Nation, 1670–1763.* Lincoln: University of Nebraska Press, 2004.

Hämäläinen, Pekka. *The Comanche Empire*. New Haven, Conn.: Yale University Press, 2008.

Merrell, James H. *Into the American Woods: Negotiators on the Pennsylvania Frontier*. New York: W. W. Norton, 1999.

Milanich, Jerald T. *Laboring in the Fields of the Lord: Spanish Missions and Southeastern Indians*. Washington, D.C.: Smithsonian Institution Press, 1999.

Oatis, Steven J. *A Colonial Complex: South Carolina's Frontiers in the Era of the Yamasee War, 1680–1730*. Lincoln: University of Nebraska Press, 2004.

Ramsey, William L. *The Yamasee War: A Study of Culture, Economy, and Conflict in the Colonial South*. Lincoln: University of Nebraska Press, 2008.

Richter, Daniel K. *Facing East from Indian Country: A Native History of Early America*. Cambridge, Mass.: Harvard University Press, 2001.

Silverman, David J. *Faith and Boundaries: Colonists, Christianity, and Community among the Wampanoag Indians of Martha's Vineyard, 1600–1871*. Cambridge, U.K.: Cambridge University Press, 2005.

Taylor, Alan. *The Divided Ground: Indians, Settlers, and the Northern Borderland of the American Revolution*. New York: Alfred A. Knopf, 2006.

White, Richard. *The Middle Ground: Indians, Empires, and Republics in the Great Lakes Region, 1650–1815.* Cambridge, U.K.: Cambridge University Press, 1991.

———. "The Winning of the West: The Expansion of the Western Sioux in the Eighteenth and Nineteenth Centuries." *Journal of American History* 65, no. 2 (1978): 319–343.

18th Century POLITICS

Political changes within the British Empire's American provinces in the 18th century created a new political reality in the Western world. At the century's beginning, rival families, as well as ethnic and religious groups, vied for authority over local institutions that were often immature, poorly formed replicas of English institutions. Popular participation in politics was common on the local level, but the further up the institutional order one progressed, the more important the patronage of powerful men in provincial capitals and in London became. Advancement to the many government positions that were appointed rather than elected depended on the help of social superiors.

This traditional system of politics eventually fell into crisis. Imperial warfare against France, Spain, and Native Americans, the spread of evangelical religion, population growth, and the Revolutionary crisis fundamentally changed British American politics as the people became more important and interest played a more obvious role in political society. The Revolution amplified these trends, created new institutions, and entirely transformed the language of politics. By century's end the first party system had emerged as a political reality on all levels of society in the new United States. Two political organizations competed, peacefully, for the support of the people in order to gain control of government institutions, and in 1800 the governing group peacefully handed over power to an organized opposition, marking a political revolution. All power derived from the people, and politicians invented new ways to appeal for popular support to gain authority.

Patriarchy and the Course of Provincial Politics

In 1700 the European colonies in the Western Hemisphere were peripheral parts of vast empires in which, under normal conditions, a select few made political decisions. Patriarchy—the rule of the father or fathers—was the political and social norm, and kings and queens were the extended state's central political symbols, "as essential to the political order as the sun is to the order of the solar system," as one colonist put it. "The People," meaning property holders, participated in politics in British America, but largely only to give their consent. Their influence was limited to the election of local officials and the members of the colonial assemblies' lower houses.

British Americans entered the new century hungry to embrace just such a hierarchical order. Between 1660 and 1700, the colonies had been racked by violent disorders and rebellions linked to problems in the British Isles that led to the overthrow of King James II by his daughter Mary and son-in-law William of Orange in the Glorious Revolution of 1688–89. After 1700, violence-weary populations began to embrace an imperially based political system that gave them 40 years of internal peace, during which time disputes were largely settled peacefully and politically.

The rule of the fathers—often literally—became the norm that ensured this peace. The local leaders in British American towns, and even in the smallest villages, were almost always the wealthiest and best-educated men in their towns, counties, or provinces (women did not yet participate in formal politics). They acted as church deacons and sat as the judges and jurymen in the courts. There were few Horatio Alger stories in colonial politics before the Revolution—someone of humble birth who became powerful politically, such as Benjamin Franklin, was the exception created by extraordinary ability, not the rule. The social order, economic system, and political system that emerged after 1700 were interlocked. The same wealthy and wellborn people stood atop each pyramid.

In British America, most of the mainland colonies—and most of the island colonies as well—had institutional governing structures crudely modeled on those of England after the Glorious Revolution, and this tendency became even more pronounced right up until the outbreak of fighting in 1775. In all the colonies, freeholders elected the lower houses of colonial assemblies, as well as some town and county positions, while either the imperial government or proprietors living in the British Isles appointed most governors and upper houses. Only Connecticut, Rhode Island, and Pennsylvania significantly deviated from this model; in the case of the former two, their royal charters allowed them to elect yearly the governors and upper houses, as well as their assemblies. In the case of the latter colony, Pennsylvania's proprietary constitution was unicameral, lacking an upper house.

This institutional reality created two different paths to power in most of British America. One could appeal for popular support from those below in order to gain election to office, or one could solicit patronage from those higher up in the social and political order to win appointment to the many minor appointed posts, the upper house, or, for the truly prominent, a governorship or lieutenant governorship.

Though bounded by general 18th-century norms, each path demanded very different behavior. The man who wanted to be elected to his town council or colonial assembly needed the support of the yeoman landholders who made up the base of the electorate in the colonies, and this was especially vital if he faced opposition from an opponent of similar stature. To get support, the candidate needed name recognition and enough money and resources to court voters. Treating the populace with alcohol and food at elections or militia training days was one method used to secure the allegiance of farmers and artisans. A gentleman leader might also assist social inferiors in need, lend them money, or offer them work in order to keep them employed and assure their support at the time of elections. Before the Revolution, for example, John Hancock, heir to Boston's greatest merchant fortune and a future Founder, gave temporary employment to the shoemaker George Robert Twelve Hewes and thousands of others in the town in order to gain their political support. Such leading individuals would also participate in the processions and toasting common on official royal holidays, such as the king's birthday, that became part of the political calendar in the 18th century, and they would again provide treats for the local population during the festivities.

Such actions paid off on election days. In New England, these were held annually for all elected offices, while in the colonies to the south, only local offices were necessarily elected annually. After receiving a calling, the male population went to the polling place, usually a county courthouse, where they would see the candidate or candidates and then be polled, usually by voice vote. Afterward, the treating began in earnest as winners celebrated with their backers. And winners had good reason to be generous. Once in elected office, men tended to stay there for decades, and to accumulate other offices as well, such as judgeships.

"Treating" was important to securing popular backing, but a gentlemen intent on rising in the empire needed the political help of his social superiors in order to gain the appointed offices at the apex of the governing structures in counties and provinces, and indeed the empire itself. Patronage made the 18th-century political world go around, and it was as true in the colonies as it was in the mother country. As Virginia's lieutenant governor Francis Fauquier noted at midcentury, a man's main qualifications for high office were "birth, his property, his Friends and his own merit." Who you knew, and how they viewed you, were as important or more important than actual qualifications.

Colonial politics were rife with examples of men whose careers were made by the help of a powerful patron. Examples include Lord Cornbury, the early 18th-century New York governor purported by some to be a cross-dresser, who was a cousin of Queen Anne, who appointed him to his post; Benjamin Franklin, who was assisted by several powerful men, including the Philadelphia lawyer Andrew Hamilton; the New Englander Jonathan Belcher, whose personal relationships with members of the Hanoverian dynasty led him to the governorship of Massachusetts Bay, a post he held for 10 years, and then to the governorship of New Jersey, where he served another decade before dying in office; and William Franklin, the natural (born out of wedlock) son of Benjamin Franklin, whose father introduced him to the powerful Lord Bute during a visit to England in the early 1760s. Bute made his new friend, then about age 31, royal governor of New Jersey, a post Franklin would hold until the Revolution displaced him. The list goes on and on. It was therefore not what you knew, it was who (or whom), and friendship and loyalty to one's patrons were far more useful than actual bureaucratic experience in gaining political preferment.

By modern standards, these governments were tiny, with only a few offices, and there were more men eager for these positions than there were places to be filled. Holding office was seen as a sign of high social status, and the leading men of various factions—which in every village, town, and colony were almost always based on kin relationships, ethnicity, or religious affiliation—struggled to gain these posts to assert their own status and assist their friends and families. These factions were not modern parties, and the rivalries were often described in relation to families: the Livingstons versus the Delanceys in New York; the Ogdens versus the Cranes in New Jersey; or, in terms of religious groups, the Quakers versus the Presbyterians in Pennsylvania.

This often blood-based system of political faction and patronage, coupled with a system of appealing for popular support using wealth and status as the major political tools, was a resilient one, linked as it was to a patriotic, patriarchical language that described the 18th-century empire as the greatest political unit in the world, governed by a benevolent father (or at times mother) figure on the throne. And it might have become stronger still had not the imperial wars against the French, Spanish, and the Native Americans created continual need for more money; and had not evangelical preachers arrived to advocate for a personal relationship with God that would, on the spiritual level, sidestep existing social and political institutions and practices; and had not the population of the colonies continued to double every 20 years or so, encouraging conflicts over land ownership in colony after colony.

Preachers, Paper Money, Property, and Politics

Problems that began to emerge in the 1730s led to the formation of a new system of political factions based on the advocacy for or against paper money, evangelical preachers, and land ownership policies that favored small farmers. Ties of blood and ethnic or religious affinity remained vitally important, but new political questions and new mediums of economic exchange began to transform political alignments.

Initially, the names given to these factions referred to their views of evangelical religion. The New Lights, or New Sides, who favored the itinerant evangelicals who had appeared in the 1730s with a powerful message of a personal relationship with God and a strong disregard for the established clergy, were opposed by the Old Lights, or Old Sides, who opposed what they saw as the emotional excess and theological error of evangelical preachers like George Whitefield or Gilbert Tennent and supported the established ministers.

Soon, though, in many places, these labels came to have far broader meanings as other political questions began to be debated, particularly economic issues related to the money supply. A series of imperial wars that pitted the British Empire against France and Spain had led to the creation of a paper money supply in most colonies to help fund the war effort, for there was a chronic shortage of gold and silver in the American colonies. Although paper money allowed for tremendous economic growth, not all parties within the society welcomed this innovation. In many places, New Lights favored the creation of this new money supply to expand economic growth and trade networks, and New Light factions were soon advocating liberal policies concerning the purchase of land from Native Americans and the inclusion of previously obscure men in government. The Old Side or Old Light parties in places like Connecticut, Massachusetts, and New Jersey opposed these innovations and advocated a more traditional economy, polity, and spiritual order, with an interlocked and intermarried leadership group heading all three realms of human activity.

The system of appealing for popular political support remained much as it had been in the century's early decades, but the electoral process became more confrontational in places where issues of religion, paper money, or property ownership came into play. Contested elections did not become the norm, but they did occur again and again during periods of open conflict over these issues, forcing candidates to appeal to the specific interests of their supporters.

These factions struggled for control of different counties and colonies for 20 years or more before the

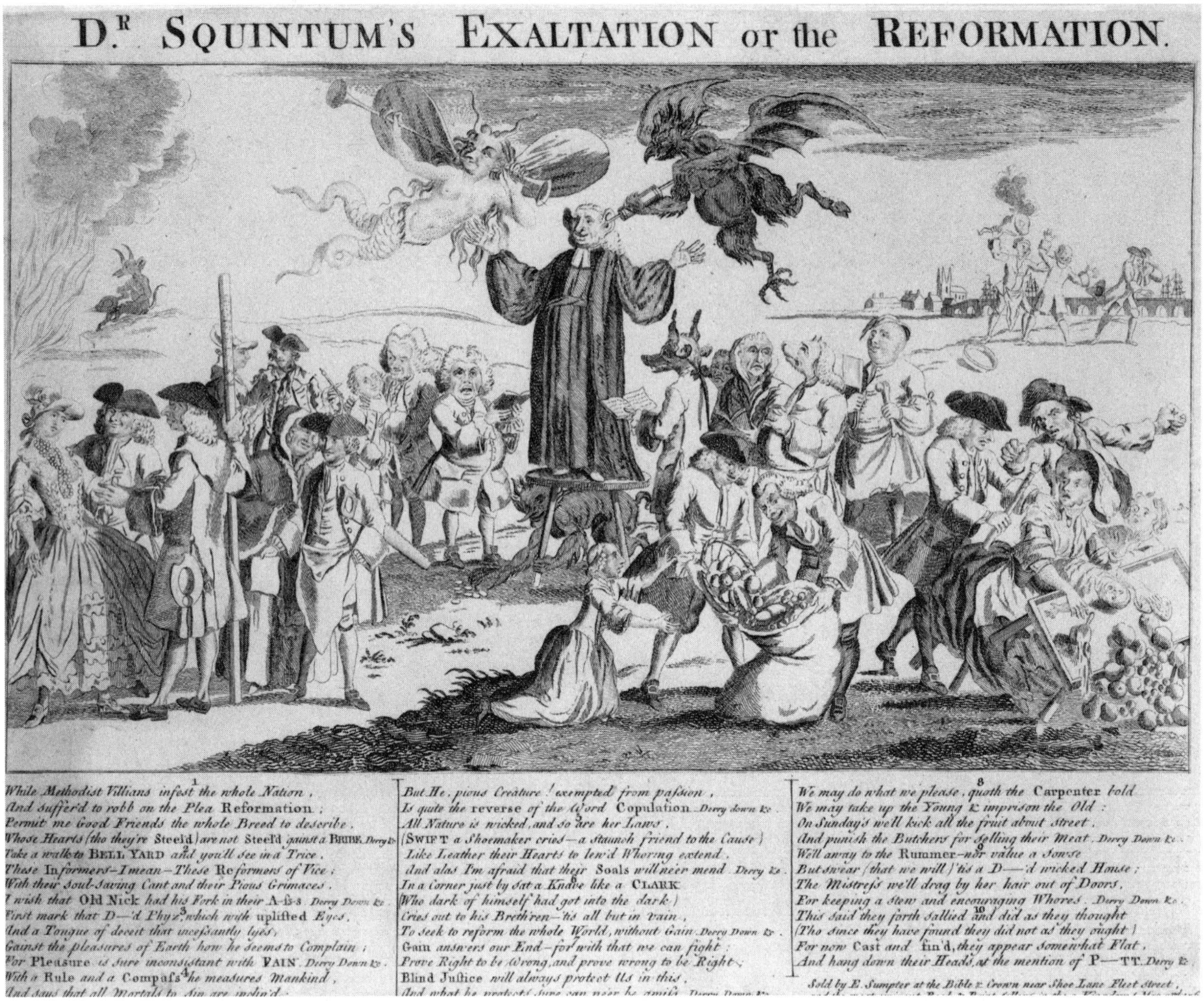

In the 1730s political factions emerged based on blood and ethnic or religious affinity, and the factions' names initially referred to their opposing views of evangelical religion. The "New Lights" disliked the established clergy and supported itinerant evangelicals like George Whitefield, who preached about a personal relationship with God. The "Old Lights" opposed these same evangelical preachers because of their strongly emotional style and their veering away from traditional theology. The above satire of Whitefield suggests that he is using his ministry to enrich himself (note the devil raking in money below the podium) and that he and his supporters, such as those propositioning a prostitute on the left, are morally suspect. *(Library of Congress)*

outbreak of the imperial crisis, which again transformed politics, forever altering their character in North America, and indeed throughout the Western Hemisphere and northwestern Europe, in what is now called the "Atlantic world." The American Revolution marked the beginning of what has alternatively been called the Age of Democratic Revolutions, the Age of Republican Revolution, or simply the Age of Revolutions. All would be accurate, in a sense. The American Revolution profoundly influenced politics in the French Empire, the kingdom of Poland, Ireland, and eventually the Spanish Empire in Latin America, while creating intellectual and political disorder in other societies.

Revolution

The imperial crisis began as an aftershock to the sprawling Seven Years' War (1756–63) and saw France stripped of Canada and the interior of North America, as well as its trading posts in India and the islands of the Caribbean. Britain's triumph had been fueled by a sophisticated fiscal-military bureaucracy that funded its forces by means of deficit spending. With the war's end in 1763, these debts began to come due. The British ministry understandably believed these burdens could not be borne by the home islands' heavily taxed populations.

This conclusion, reached with no hostility toward British Americans, led to the Stamp Act crisis of 1764–66 and the subsequent eruption of a 10-year-long protest movement after Parliament attempted to tax the American colonies without their explicit consent. The political protest movement had intellectual, institutional, and popular elements to it. The ideological core of the protest has been described alternatively as being built around "country thought" (which warned of the dangers of strong central government and standing armies), libertarianism, a natural rights philosophy, or republicanism. It was, in fact, a fusion of a number of clearly identifiable strains of these radical political languages that warned of the danger of a strong central government and a standing army.

Initially, at the center of this thought lay the desire to restrict the central state's power to tax by demanding actual representation, meaning representatives voted into office by distinct and geographically definable electorates. Writers such as John Dickinson and John Adams established the intellectual justification for resisting arbitrary taxation, and newspapers, pamphlets, broadsides, sermons, and open-air meetings were used to politically mobilize the population of British America in support of their positions on taxation and the imperial relationship. Politically motivated mobs attacked officials who tried to implement British policies, destroying their homes and even using tar and feathers to torture them.

The appearance of committees and congresses, operating outside the law and the empire's established political boundaries, amplified the importance of the people in politics. It was not just that these bodies were formed by different types of popular appointment—sometimes involving town meetings or colonial assemblies, and other times based on popular acclaim or even individual initiative. Rather, resistance was based on the idea that the committees and congresses defended the people, who were the sole source of their authority. These extralegal bodies became major political players, attempting at once to unify colonial political resistance and to broker a new relationship between the colonies and the mother country.

This process began in 1765 with the appearance of the committee known as "the Loyal Nine" in Boston, and with the Stamp Act Congress that met in New York in 1765 to petition George III for redress and beg for an equitable solution to the crisis. Eventually, committees of correspondence, observation, and safety would appear in every town and colony, numbering eventually in the hundreds, if not thousands. All would appeal to the people for support, and they would base their authority to act on that support. In January 1775, for example, the freeholders of Elizabeth County, Virginia, "pursuant to notice given by advertisements, met at the courthouse of the said county, to elect a committee," in much the same way they elected local officials and assemblymen. Those seeking a place in the increasingly important committee structure had to appeal to the freeholders in a setting much like that of a regular election day.

The British Empire's deteriorating political situation after the Boston Tea Party of December 1773, the resulting "Intolerable" Acts, designed to punish Boston and Massachusetts for being centers of opposition to Britain's imperial policies, and the Quebec Act of 1774, which recognized the Catholic religion in Quebec and seemed to establish arbitrary government in Britain's new Canadian colony, led to fundamental political shifts in the ideological structure of provincial thinking. The old family-based and faction-based politics gave way to a primary split between those who supported radical measures in defiance of British authority and those who wished to remain in the empire. The former came to be known as Whigs, while the latter came to be called Tories or Loyalists, and their political divisions would soon become part of a bloodletting.

What had begun as an effort to preserve the British Constitution, as provincials understood it, became in 1775 a movement for the establishment of an independent republic or republics. With this republicanism came universalist views of human rights and human nature that profoundly challenged the assumptions of monarchical Europe and, for that matter, the slaveholding patricians of the American provinces themselves. Deference and patriarchy were attacked, at least as conscious assumptions, and all politics became based on the premise that authority derived from the people, and that all political actions had to be for the common good of the emerging nation.

The republican state governments that appeared between 1776 and the 1780s reflected this republican utopianism and amounted to a radical experiment in self-government. Three of the states, Pennsylvania, Georgia, and what became Vermont, adopted unicameral constitutions that proclaimed a radical egalitarian vision of republican citizenry. Upper chambers like the colonial councils or senates were deemed unnecessary, as were governors as they had existed in the empire. The designers of the unicameral governments threw down institutional hierarchy because it would have allowed the sort of interested men who had sat in the colonial councils to affect social distinction and block the collective will of a free republican citizenry. All, or at least all white property holders, were now considered brother citizens, and thus equal.

Even those new states that adopted a bicameral governing structure accepted the idea that political power now rested with the mass of the population. The new constitutions weakened the governors and upper houses; established annual elections in many cases, thereby making all or most officials dependent on immediate popular pressure and thus forced to appeal to voters constantly; began to do away with multiple office holdings, the practice of one man being able to hold several legal or government positions simultaneously; initiated the process of the abolition of slavery in the North; and proclaimed the sovereignty of a republican people free from historical restraints of royal patriarchy and deferential traditions.

As the new order took shape, political celebrations changed. Gone were the king's birthday and other political holidays associated with the British royal family. In their place came the Fourth of July, Washington's Birthday, the anniversaries of the Boston Massacre and the Lexington and Concord battles, the anniversary of the evacuation of Boston by the British in March 1776, and later the anniversary of the evacuation of New York by British forces in 1783, all of which became part of a new calendar of political celebrations. The processions and feasting and toasting remained a part of this, and leading men remained keen to participate. But they now carefully acknowledged the people, rather than the monarch, as supreme sovereign and (sometimes) supremely wise, and they proclaimed the values of republicanism and the events of the Revolution as central to their political views. Ominously, though, they could not always agree on what those values were, or on what sort of political future the Revolution promised.

Faction and the First Party System

The Continental Congress provided leadership during the war, and the Articles of Confederation passed in 1781 provided for a continuing, but weak, central government. The states were the primary location of political action, and politics became notably more modern in some respects. "Tickets" appeared in some states, and politicians engaged in endless appeals to the people in order to gain authority. The lower houses of the state legislatures became the centers of political power, while the states retained control of their militias and courts and continued to print their own money. Laws governing debtor-creditor relationships, often of a most arbitrary nature, were passed by legislatures, resulting in near anarchy in the political economy of the states.

Even as factions struggled over the new state governments, the breakdown in legal, political, and economic relationships encouraged some gentlemen to advocate the creation of a stronger government. The struggle to create the federal government in 1787–88 encouraged new factions, namely the Federalists, meaning those who supported the new constitution and a strong central government, and the Anti-Federalists, who wanted power to remain in the states and feared strong central governments. At the core, this was really a disagreement over what the Revolution had been fought for, and what it would mean for future generations of Americans to be a free, republican people.

Their struggle, bitter and protracted, further politicized vast portions of the population as the Constitution was debated in special state conventions, in assemblies, and in the towns and the smallest villages. Heated political debates filled the pamphlets and newspapers as preachers addressed political questions from the pulpit and politicians lectured crowds about the consequences of defeat and the fruits of victory for their respective factions. Although the Federalists triumphed and the debates subsided, the bitter division over the Constitution eventually led to the nation's first political party system, when the spread of republican ideology and the idea of popular sovereignty beyond American borders again raised the question of how strong the central government should be.

The utopian impulses evident in republicanism and the American Revolution generally gave them tremendous transatlantic appeal. Political and intellectual shock waves originating from the Atlantic's western shore soon spread everywhere. The spread of revolutionary republicanism to France greatly amplified the ideology's impact in the Atlantic world and northern Europe. The republican explosion that was the French Revolution of 1789 had a profound impact on all Western societies, and indeed beyond them. The French themselves had been heavily influenced by the American Revolution and American politics. Large numbers of French subjects had participated in the American cause on their own account, and hundreds of French officers and tens of thousands of men fought with the formal French expeditionary force that aided the American cause after 1778. French intellectuals studied American republicanism in reading clubs, Masonic lodges, and salons. These became major conduits through which knowledge of American developments and republicanism passed into French society. As Thomas Paine wrote, "the New World" might by its example "regenerate the old."

In America, initial near-universal support for the French Revolution eventually gave way to acrimony and disagreement leading to what came to be known as the First Party System. The radical turn of that revolution signaled by the execution of America's former ally Louis XVI and the outbreak of war in Europe between Revolutionary France and the monarchical powers fractured the American body politic severely enough to lead to the rise of two main, competing parties. These were not the modern parties we know today, but they were tightly organized, institutionalized political organizations that vied for power.

The bitter struggle between these two parties, known as the Democratic-Republicans (or Republicans) and the Federalists, dominated American society in the latter half of the 1790s and was in large part driven by the question of the degree to which, if at all, the American republic should support Revolutionary France. Jefferson and his supporters among the Democratic-Republicans urged assistance to a sister republic as part of a broader goal of global republicanization, a revolution that would spread to Africa and Asia as well as through Europe. The more conservative revolutionaries, such as Washington, Hamilton, and Adams, formed the backbone of the Federalist Party and urged strict neutrality in the European wars. They leaned diplomatically toward Great Britain in terms of commercial policy, as manifested in the Jay Treaty of 1794, which heavily favored the British. They blamed the French example for much disorder in America, including the Whiskey Rebellion, a popular uprising in the interior over taxation and representation, and the appearance of the party system itself, still seen as an undesirable development in a republican society.

Worse yet, the two parties disagreed over the power of the central government and the meaning of the Revolution. The Democratic-Republicans argued that political power should reside in the states, and indeed that the Revolution had been fought to stop overreaching central authority. The Federalists believed in a strong central government with extensive taxing power and a standing army. They argued this was the only way independence could be preserved in a hostile world.

The resulting controversies almost led to civil war in America in the late 1790s. Beginning in President Washington's second term, the tone of politics changed dramatically. Adherents to the rival parties founded newspapers with political agendas, and these papers carried vicious attacks on opposing political figures. Even the president himself was attacked in print and speeches, albeit indirectly. The election of 1796 saw Thomas Jefferson

The American Revolution exerted a powerful influence on the French Revolution, which led to a fracturing of the American body politic that in turn led to the first American party system, one largely driven by the question of the degree to which, if at all, the American republic should support Revolutionary France. Democratic-Republicans like Thomas Jefferson (left) urged support for France, while Federalists, who idolized George Washington (right), urged strict neutrality in the European wars. ***(Library of Congress)***

put forward as a candidate to challenge Vice President John Adams, and the supporters of each ran rival tickets on the state and local level. Neither group was a party in the modern sense, but they were both self-aware groups bitterly opposed to one another. It became so bitter that the different parties held rival celebrations of the Fourth of July, Washington's Birthday, and other political holidays of the republic. By 1798 and 1799, men who had fought side by side in the Revolutionary War were no longer speaking, and it seemed that civil war was possible.

The election of 1800 was as irregular as any in American history, but in the end it signaled an astonishing transformation. Jefferson again ran against Adams, the incumbent, but the election was so close it was thrown into the House of Representatives, because none of the candidates had an electoral majority. After many ballots, Jefferson was proclaimed the winner. Only the peaceful transfer of power from the Federalists, who had been in power since 1789, to the Democratic-Republicans led by Jefferson, defused the tensions, and indeed this event marked a watershed in politics, as one group handed over power to another with a very different political agenda. It was left to Jefferson to call for unity in his inaugural speech: "We are," he declared, "all republicans, we are all federalists," and indeed his election led eventually to the decline of the First Party System.

The continuation of republican revolutions in the 19th century in Haiti, Latin America, and Europe saw the actors in those dramas repeatedly invoke the American example to justify their own actions, which speaks to the profound alteration in world politics that began in the 1770s. From this period forward, movements proclaiming the ultimate sovereignty and welfare of a disembodied "people" were seen as legitimate challengers to the monarchical and oligarchic orders that dominated Western society. In a century, America had changed from a colonial backwater with crude, traditional politics to the standard-bearer of republican political order.

—Brendan McConville

Further Reading

Bailyn, Bernard. *The Ideological Origins of the American Revolution.* Enlarged ed. Cambridge, Mass.: Belknap Press of Harvard University Press, 1992.

Beeman, Richard. *Plain, Honest Men: The Making of the American Constitution*. New York: Random House, 2009.

———. *The Varieties of Political Experience in Eighteenth-Century America*. Philadelphia: University of Pennsylvania Press, 2004.

Bonomi, Patricia. *A Factious People: Politics and Society in Colonial New York*. New York: Columbia University Press, 1973.

Breen, T. H. *American Insurgents, American Patriots: The Revolution of the People before Independence.* New York: Hill & Wang, 2010.

Bushman, Richard L. *King and People in Provincial Massachusetts*. Chapel Hill: University of North Carolina Press, 1992.

Elkins, Stanley M., and Eric McKitrick. *The Age of Federalism: The Early American Republic, 1788–1800*. New York: Oxford University Press, 1995.

Holton, Woody. *Forced Founders: Indians, Debtors, Slaves, and the Making of the American Revolution in Virginia*. Chapel Hill: University of North Carolina Press, 1999.

McConville, Brendan. *The King's Three Faces: The Rise and Fall of Royal America, 1688–1776*. Chapel Hill: University of North Carolina Press, 2006.

Nash, Gary B. *The Unknown American Revolution: The Unruly Birth of Democracy and the Struggle to Create America.* New York: Penguin, 2006.

Wood, Gordon S. *Creation of The American Republic, 1776–1787*. Chapel Hill: University of North Carolina Press, 1969. Reprint, 1998.

———. *The Radicalism of the American Revolution*. New York: Alfred A. Knopf, 1992.

18th Century POPULAR AND FOLK CULTURE

Little distinction can be made between popular culture and folk culture at the outset of the 18th century. Folk culture is identifiable in a cultural artifact's degree of localism, informality, and collective participation. Popular culture, on the other hand, is explicitly created for mass consumption, and it attempts to cater to the tastes of a range of people. As the century progressed, aspects of American culture slowly began to take on popular attributes. This development happened more quickly in colonial America's cities than in rural places. The American Revolution, by creating a sense of national identity that had not previously existed, put in place the conditions amenable to the growth of popular culture. At the end of the century, the separation of folk and popular cultures had developed enough to be recognizable, though popular culture was still in its rudimentary stage.

At the outset of the 18th century, the separate colonies still shared elements of a largely English culture. Literacy rates were higher in some places, such as Massachusetts, than others, particularly in the South. Nevertheless, the shortage of printed material meant that the transmission of stories, legends, and news was primarily oral. Stories, music, poems, dance, and religious ideas spread and were perpetuated largely by word of mouth and direct example. As British subjects, Americans—and particularly the elite of coastal cities—generally emulated English culture or looked to it for inspiration, at least through roughly 1760. Culture everywhere was influenced greatly by church services and other communal activities such as barn raisings and harvest festivals.

Despite common elements, different regions of British North America were culturally distinct. Religious practices—while important in virtually all areas—varied from place to place. The nature of leisure, games, and other pastimes also varied. And the presence of slavery shaped the development of culture in every colony, though differently, based on factors such as the concentration of slaves.

Culture in Early 18th-Century New England

New England culture revolved around religion in a host of ways. Religion not only supplied the region with its most-read book, the Bible, but with the religious tracts that constituted a significant portion of what else there was available to read. Church services provided an important spiritual experience for the devoted, but they were also a crucial ritual of public solidarity and an essential source of information to be shared by the congregation. Early in the century, most New Englanders disdained the making of music in church settings. However, the singing of psalms gradually became more common in Congregational churches throughout New England, and music in church received a boost beginning in the 1720s through the spread of the Englishman Isaac Watts's collection of *Hymns and Spiritual Songs*.

As in their church services, New Englanders were ambivalent about the making of music anywhere. Similarly, dancing was generally looked down upon. There was regional variation, however. Dancing was much more socially acceptable in Connecticut than in Massachusetts, for example. In both colonies widespread fears remained that dancing would lead to licentious behavior. Despite dancing's negative associations, however, people throughout the region continued to perform traditional English folk dances.

The original Puritans who settled New England had been opposed to England's festive culture, but they embraced many of the folk games associated with that culture. Eighteenth-century New Englanders continued to play various games, but only provided that the games were considered moral or, in their words, "lawful." Sports and games should merely be a diversion that did not interfere with important responsibilities and should be pursued in a spirit of restraint that disdained such vices as deceit, gambling, and drunkenness. Activities that lent themselves to such misbehavior—for example, horse racing—were strictly proscribed. With that ethic in mind, New Englanders pursued a host of activities such as swimming, skating, various rudimentary versions of football, and bat-and-ball games.

Culture in the Early 18th-Century Middle Colonies

The cultural landscape of the middle colonies—including New York, New Jersey, and Pennsylvania—was more diverse and less restricted by religion and morals than that of their Puritan neighbors to the north. The English had conquered New York in 1664, but much of the culture of that colony remained significantly Dutch in orientation well into the 18th century. This was particularly true of communities up the Hudson Valley, where food, dress, house construction, and pastimes such as bowling and ice-skating reflected Dutch origins. Closer to the coast the population was more heterogeneous, and a larger variety of pastimes were popular. Colonial New Yorkers bowled, raced boats and horses, watched cockfights, and engaged in the tavern culture of drinking with greater gusto than was the case in New England. Dance was also more popular and respectable among white New Yorkers, with the French minuet a popular addition to the traditional folk dances of English, Dutch, and German origin.

The middle colonies were as diverse denominationally as they were ethnically. Virtually all the different denominations incorporated some form of music into their services. While some churches had organs, the most popular musical instruments in churches as well as outside them were various kinds of fiddles and violins, and woodwind instruments such as flutes. Literacy rates were lower than in New England, but Bibles and religious tracts circulated widely, along with diaries and collections of poems. The laws of Pennsylvania, shaped by Quakers, were if anything stricter than New England's concerning the proscription of cultural activities such the making of music and dancing, but by the beginning of the century Quaker hegemony was under threat, and the culture of the colony in the Philadelphia area was becoming more open.

There were more slaves in the middle colonies than in New England, both in terms of raw numbers and as a percentage of the overall population. Consequently, the culture of African Americans was better developed, and more distinct from the culture around it, than in New England. The two regions had their similarities, however: Slaves in both places engaged in a variety of festivals that involved ritual role reversals of the sort that were common in both Africa and Europe. In New England, slaves generally called their main festival "Negro Election Day," whereas in New York and New Jersey it was named "Pinkster Day." These festivals were scenes of great merrymaking, during which slaves dressed in extravagantly ornamented clothing, played and danced to music of mixed African and European origin, and elected "kings" or "governors" from their midst who were elaborately celebrated and who then adjudicated minor disputes.

Culture in the Early 18th-Century South

Southern culture was also religiously oriented but was more boisterous than that of either New England or the middle colonies. Whereas horse racing was outlawed in many of the colonies to the north, the residents of Virginia, North Carolina, South Carolina, and Georgia embraced it as a favorite leisure-time pursuit. White southerners favored games that either lent themselves to gambling, such as cards, or games like wrestling and cudgeling that put participants in danger of bodily harm. Plantation culture virtually demanded that its members extravagantly display their wealth and hospitality, and balls featuring music and dancing were a frequent occurrence. Compared to the other colonial regions, religion was more of a private matter in the colonial South, and many slave owners attended church out of social obligation to do so. Music played an important role in the services of the Anglican church, the dominant religion in the region, complementing a culture in which music occupied a central place in essentially every part of life.

The cultures of southern slave communities varied enormously. Slaves in a relatively urban environment such as Richmond, Virginia, tended to be less distinctly African in cultural behavior than the Gullah communities along the South Carolina coast, where slaves were a larger percentage of the population and lived in greater isolation from whites. Universally, though to varying extents, slave culture was composed of a mixture of African and European traditions; indeed, many newly transported slaves had encountered some European culture in Africa. Early in the century, nevertheless, the culture of slave communities was largely African influenced, even though many masters discouraged African customs and languages. The domestic slave population was continuously supplemented by increasing numbers of African-born slaves, and in language, dress, child-rearing practices, diet, music, dancing, religion, and festivals, slaves clung to their heritage. Adherence to African culture was a form of resistance to slavery. For example, many imported slaves clandestinely maintained their African names rather than accept the name bestowed on them by their master. In some places, such as in the Seminole homeland in northern Florida or in the numerous maroon communities founded by runaway slaves, culture evolved into a mix of African and Native American customs and traditions. By the 1740s in the Chesapeake region of Virginia, however, the majority of slaves were native born. By the end of the century, that would be the case throughout the South. Young black Americans were increasingly raised by native parents, and a distinctly African American culture began to emerge.

Folk Culture on the Frontier

As on the coast, there was great variety among the cultures that populated the western areas of settlement early in the 18th century. To a greater extent than on the coast, rural isolation allowed various transplanted European communities to retain their traditional folkways. In western Pennsylvania and the Shenandoah region of Virginia, for example, traditional folkways of dress, food, storytelling, games, celebrations, dancing, and music persisted more purely in their original form. Scots-Irish Presbyterians clung fiercely to the habit of gathering in religious "field meetings," as they had done in the old country. Southern backcountry speech likewise retained a vocabulary drawn from Scotland that distinguished itself from coastal dialect. When a backcountry resident died, an elaborate set of rituals commenced, including a lengthy wake during which attendees solemnly read from the Bible, followed by the consumption of alcohol. Any dog or cat that passed over the body was immediately killed, for fear that it would transmit the fatal sickness to humans, and a plate of salt was usually placed on the corpse. These customs were practiced in Northern Ireland and Scotland and would continue in the highland South for centuries afterward.

The Great Awakening

Beginning in the 1720s and lasting until the 1750s, colonial America experienced a series of religious revivals that historians refer to as the Great Awakening. These revivals took place in every colony, though their causes, characteristics, and consequences varied from region to region. Taken together, however, they represented the awakening of a pan-colonial culture that was popular, more than folk, in its orientation. In New England the Congregational church split into Old Lights and New Lights, the latter tending to reject dense sermonizing and strict denominational orthodoxy in favor of a religious experience that spoke more directly to adherents' emotions. The middle colonies and western Virginia experienced the spread of greater denominational diversity, as the ideas of multiple denominations, and the words of itinerant ministers who advocated them, competed for the minds of residents. The most famous of these ministers, the Englishman George Whitefield, preached in every colony, attracting large crowds and extensive media coverage. At the apex of his career, Whitefield was one of the best-known public figures in the colonies. The level of renown he accumulated over such a large portion of the colonies attests to the emergence of an American culture that was not specific to locales, or even whole colonies. The Great Awakening also produced an increase in colonists' appetite for religious tracts, sermons, and hymnals. The more widely these circulated, the more Americans consumed the same cultural artifacts. The mass nature of the Great Awakening suggests it was a precursor to the rise of popular culture, but that argument is diminished by the degree to which it differed so dramatically from region to region and the extent to which participants often used revivals as a means to reinvigorate communal solidarity and consensus.

The waning years of the Great Awakening witnessed the opening of the French and Indian War. Waged on a scale and geographic breadth unprecedented in American history, the war further allowed colonists to develop the kind of pan-colonial consciousness that would make popular culture possible. The war required that America's coastal elites cooperate more than in the past, and settlers on the frontier encountered dangers and other war-related experiences similar to those of the coastal elites. Nevertheless, as the 1760s began, colonial America remained a region of many folk cultures, differing dramatically from one place to another in musical and dance styles, emphasis on literacy, dress, dietary preferences, oral traditions, sports and other pastimes, and religious traditions.

The American Revolution

The years of the American Revolution were the great watershed in the development of an American popular culture that was consumed on a mass scale and that could be commercialized for profit. In the decade preceding the outbreak of fighting, opposition by many colonists to British policies reinforced the sense that the colonies had common interests and that greater cooperation between them was necessary. The start of the Revolution itself in 1775 touched off a print revolution, as official government documents such as state constitutions and the Declaration of Independence circulated widely and were discussed and debated extensively. Other documents written to support or criticize the Revolution, notably Thomas Paine's *Common Sense*, were read throughout the colonies. This taste for political literature continued into the post-Revolutionary era, as the published writings of both Federalists and anti-Federalists competed for the public mind.

The Revolution imprinted itself on other aspects of a growing popular American culture. It created in many Americans a taste for popular patriotic poetry by such authors as Philip Freneau and Phillis Wheatley. Americans in every colony learned and sang such patriotic songs as "Yankee Doodle," "The Liberty Song," and "American Taxation." The Revolution even produced new ideas about fashion among urban Americans, who increasingly disdained the elaborate clothing and powdered wigs they had previously embraced in emulation of European aristocrats in favor of simpler clothing and hairstyles. During and after the Revolution, Americans began to forge a new identity, aided not just by political ideas, but by cultural artifacts embraced by many.

CHARLOTTE TEMPLE,
A TALE OF TRUTH
BY MRS. ROWSON,
LATE OF THE NEW THEATRE, PHILADELPHIA;
AUTHOR OF VICTORIA, INQUISITOR, FILLE DE CHAMBRE, &c.
NEW-YORK:
PUBLISHED BY EVERT DUYCKINCK,
NO 102 PEARL-STREET.
George Long, Printer.
1814.

The novel *Charlotte Temple, A Tale of Truth* (1791), written by the British-American novelist Susanna Rowson, was the most popular best seller in America at the end of the 18th century. Above is the title page of an 1814 edition of the book. *(Open Library)*

The Late 18th Century

In the wake of the Revolution, Americans remained a largely rural, relatively isolated people who clung to their folk traditions and experimented with new cultural forms based on their local interests. Americans would never again, however, be as free of the influence of popular culture as they had been before the Revolutionary War. Increasingly, Americans exhibited a collective sense of nationhood that was heavily dependent on such cultural artifacts as music, poetry, and stories that had arisen during the war. Americans read widely circulated publications more than ever, and the end of the century witnessed the rise of new kinds of publications. Among these were popular novels: William H. Brown's 1789 novel *The Power of Sympathy* is usually identified as the first novel written by an American, and the novel *Charlotte Temple*, first published in England in 1791, was widely read among literate Americans at the end of the century—some credit it as the first best-selling novel in America. Sheet music was also printed at much greater rates than before. Theatrical performances proliferated and included the increased presence of women on stage. Such early forms of popular culture, consumed by many of diverse backgrounds and locales, arose despite widespread reservations about their effect on the popular mind: Elite Americans in particular often expressed fears that the spread of commercialized culture endangered the American spirit of a moral, egalitarian republicanism by distracting the public with cheap, degrading amusements.

Despite the rise of a truly popular culture, and regardless of opposition to it, the great mass of Americans remained overwhelmingly attached to their local folk customs and traditions at the end of the 18th century. It would not be until the next century that a mature popular culture would begin to compete with and to replace folk culture in most of America.

—Paul M. Searls

Further Reading

Berlin, Ira. *Many Thousands Gone: The First Two Centuries of Slavery in North America*. Cambridge, Mass.: Harvard University Press, 1998.

Ellis, Joseph. *After the Revolution: Profiles of Early American Culture*. New York: W. W. Norton, 2002.

Fisher, David Hackett. *Albion's Seed: Four British Folkways in America*. New York: Oxford University Press, 1989.

Huff, Randall. *The Revolutionary War Era*. Westport, Conn.: Greenwood Press, 2004.

Kornfeld, Eve. *Creating an American Culture: 1775–1800*. New York: Palgrave Macmillan, 2001.

Lambert, Frank *"Pedlar in Divinity": George Whitefield and the Transatlantic Revivals, 1737–1770*. Princeton, N.J.: Princeton University Press, 2002.

Landsman, Ned C. *From Colonials to Provincials: American Thought and Culture, 1680–1760*. Ithaca, N.Y.: Cornell University Press, 2000.

Levine, Lawrence W. *Black Culture and Black Consciousness: Afro-American Folk Thought from Slavery to Freedom*. New York: Oxford University Press, 1967.

Smith-Rosenberg, Carroll. *This Violent Empire: The Birth of an American National Identity*. Chapel Hill: University of North Carolina Press, 2010.

Struna, Nancy. *People of Prowess: Sport, Leisure, and Labor in Early Anglo-America*. Champaign: University of Illinois Press, 1996.

18th Century PRESS

During the early 18th century, the first American newspapers appeared in New England. After 1725, newspapers could be found throughout the colonies, and they went on to play a paramount role in the colonists' struggles against British rule. By the time of the American Revolution, newspapers had evolved to reflect the different political perspectives that had emerged—Patriot, Tory, and Whig—and exercised considerable power in changing public opinion. After the Revolution, in the early Federal period, the press continued to flourish as a political force in the prevailing public debates about the direction of the new United States.

The First New England Newspapers

It is not surprising that the first American newspapers appeared on New England soil. A combination of factors made Boston, the largest colonial city, a natural site for the birth of the American newspaper, including its citizens' economic prosperity, which presented a strong base to support advertising; a high literacy rate; and a keen interest in community issues and culture. By 1638 the comparatively well-educated colonists of Massachusetts Bay had already opened the first press in the English colonies, in Cambridge, and they had also developed a postal system that could be harnessed to distribute newspapers.

North America's first newspaper was a short-lived venture launched in Boston by Benjamin Harris, a former London bookseller. The four-page *Publick Occurrences Both Forreign and Domestick*, which appeared on September 25, 1690, offered both foreign and local news. The fourth page was left blank so that readers could pen their own news items before passing the newspaper on. However, Harris's publication of unflattering news about the colonial government's allies, the Indians, as well as a story about the French king's seduction of the prince's wife, displeased the colonial government. Furthermore, Harris had violated Massachusetts licensing restrictions, first established in 1662, and colonial authorities shut down the paper after only one issue.

Fourteen years elapsed before John Campbell established what became the first continuously printed newspaper in the colonies. The *Boston News-Letter*, founded on April 24, 1704, contained information that Campbell gleaned through his official position as the Crown-appointed postmaster. As had long been the tradition in Europe, the colonial postal service was closely tied to journalism. A postmaster such as Campbell had access to important news dispatches and the latest local gossip—in short, nearly all the intelligence available to the community. Campbell's *Boston News-Letter* printed commercial and government news, legal notices, news of meetings and actions in court, and the like. As was typical at the time, Campbell clipped news from weeks-old London papers that had just arrived by ship and, as space allowed, presented it as foreign dispatches. The remaining one-third or so of the paper was devoted to news items detailing the arriving of ships and their cargoes; sermons; weather, especially storms; maritime news; society news, such as marriage and death notices; conflict with Native Americans; fires; sports; and other items of interest. In some ways, Campbell's conception of what qualified as "newsworthy" seems rather modern. But timeliness did not figure much in his definition. He often printed news (especially from London) that was many weeks old, apparently thinking it more important to publish in chronological order than to give space to the most recently occurring events.

Cautioned by the example of Benjamin Harris, Campbell cleared his copy with the colonial governor's office and thus avoided any major conflicts with the authorities. The result was a humdrum, semiofficial government organ. The *News-Letter* did not prosper, however. In fact, Campbell had to suspend it twice during its first six years, for periods of two and eight months, respectively. As Frank Mott notes in his *American Journalism*, "It was an open question for a time as to whether the people

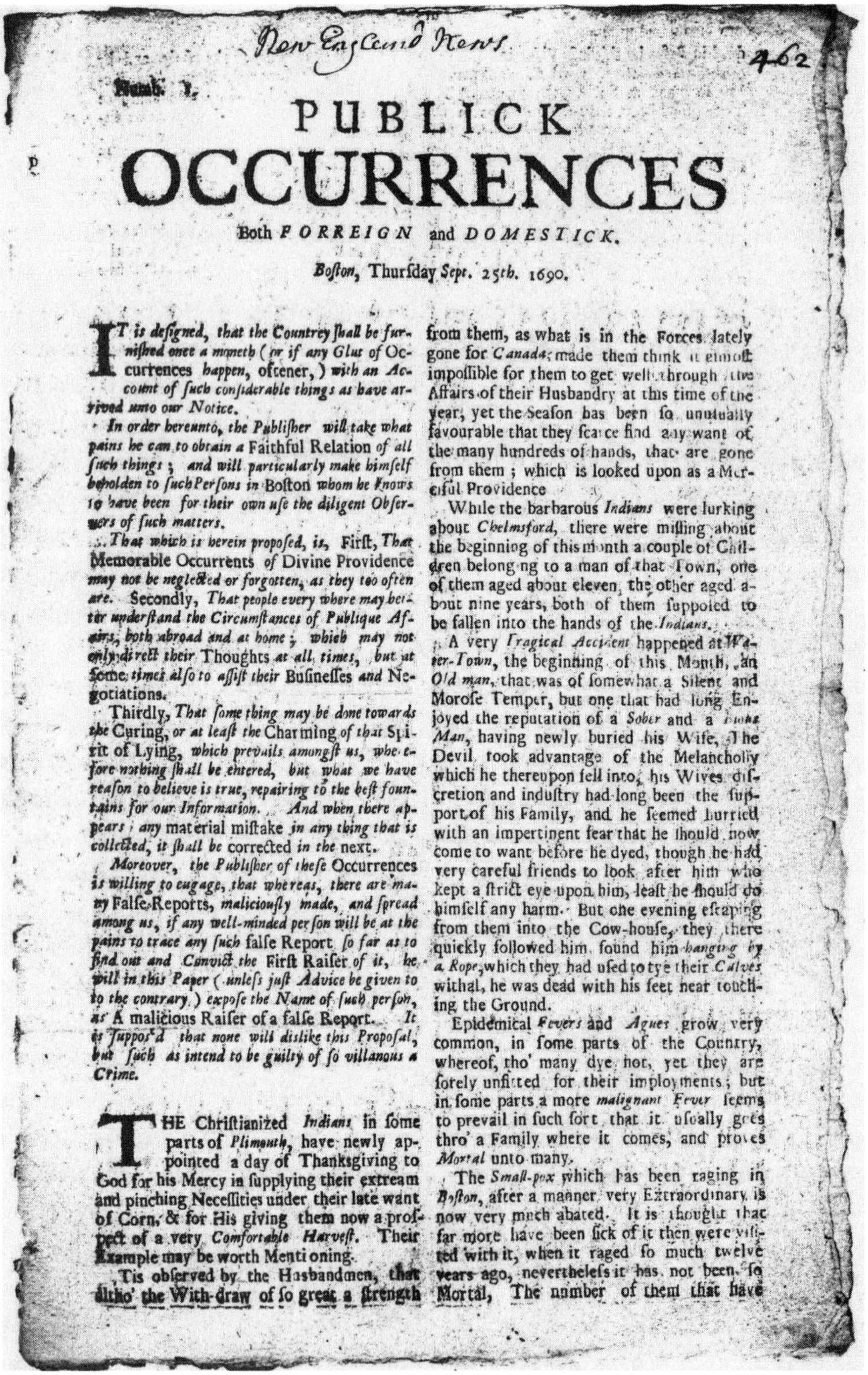

New England News 462

Numb. 1.

PUBLICK
OCCURRENCES
Both *FORREIGN* and *DOMESTICK*.

Boston, Thursday *Sept.* 25*th*. 1690.

IT *is designed, that the Countrey shall be furnished once a moneth (or if any Glut of* Occurrences *happen*, oftener,) *with an Account of such considerable things as have arrived unto our Notice.*

In order hereunto, the Publisher will take what pains he can to obtain a Faithful Relation *of all such things; and will particularly make himself beholden to such Persons in* Boston *whom he knows to have been for their own use the diligent Observers of such matters.*

That which is herein proposed, is, First, *That* Memorable Occurrents *of* Divine Providence *may not be neglected or forgotten, as they too often are.* Secondly, *That people every where may better understand the Circumstances of Publique Affairs, both abroad and at home; which may not only direct their* Thoughts *at all times, but at some times also to assist their* Businesses *and* Negotiations.

Thirdly, *That some thing may be done towards the* Curing, *or at least the* Charming *of that* Spirit of Lying, *which prevails amongst us, wherefore nothing shall be entered, but what we have reason to believe is true, repairing to the best fountains for our Information. And when there appears any* material mistake *in any thing that is collected, it shall be* corrected *in the next.*

Moreover, the Publisher of these Occurrences *is willing to engage, that whereas, there are many* False Reports, *maliciously made, and spread among us, if any well-minded person will be at the pains to trace any such* false Report *so far as to find out and Convict the* First Raiser *of it, he will in this Paper (unless just Advice be given to the contrary) expose the Name of such person, as* A malicious Raiser of a false Report. *It is suppos'd that none will dislike this Proposal, but such as intend to be guilty of so villanous a Crime.*

THE Christianized *Indians* in some parts of *Plimouth*, have newly appointed a day of Thanksgiving to God for his Mercy in supplying their extream and pinching Necessities under their late want of Corn, & for His giving them now a prospect of a very *Comfortable Harvest*. Their Example may be worth Mentioning.

Tis observed by the Husbandmen, that altho' the With-draw of so great a strength from them, as what is in the Forces lately gone for *Canada*; made them think it almost impossible for them to get well through the Affairs of their Husbandry at this time of the year, yet the Season has been so unusually favourable that they scarce find any want of the many hundreds of hands, that are gone from them; which is looked upon as a Merciful Providence.

While the barbarous *Indians* were lurking about *Chelmsford*, there were missing about the beginning of this month a couple of Children belonging to a man of that Town, one of them aged about eleven, the other aged about nine years, both of them supposed to be fallen into the hands of the *Indians*.

A very *Tragical Accident* happened at *Water-Town*, the beginning of this Month, an *Old man*, that was of somewhat a Silent and Morose Temper, but one that had long Enjoyed the reputation of a *Sober* and a *Pious Man*, having newly buried his Wife, The Devil took advantage of the Melancholly which he thereupon fell into, his Wives discretion and industry had long been the support of his Family, and he seemed hurried with an impertinent fear that he should now come to want before he dyed, though he had very careful friends to look after him who kept a strict eye upon him, least he should do himself any harm. But one evening escaping from them into the Cow-house, they there quickly followed him, found him *hanging by a Rope*, which they had used to tye their *Calves* withal, he was dead with his feet near touching the Ground.

Epidemical *Fevers* and *Agues* grow very common, in some parts of the Country, whereof, tho' many dye not, yet they are sorely unfitted for their imployments; but in some parts a more *malignant Fever* seems to prevail in such sort that it usually goes thro' a Family where it comes, and proves *Mortal* unto many.

The *Small-pox* which has been raging in *Boston*, after a manner very Extraordinary, is now very much abated. It is thought that far more have been sick of it then were visited with it, when it raged so much twelve years ago, nevertheless it has not been so Mortal, The number of them that have

Publick Occurrences Both Forreign and Domestick was North America's first newspaper. Published in Boston, *Publick Occurrences* consisted of three pages of information and a blank fourth page, supposedly offered so that people with more news or more accurate information could add it and then pass the paper on. Above is page one of the first and only issue. *(Massachusetts Historical Society)*

of Boston cared to supplant the old rumor-proclamation-broadside way of newsmongering with the more expensive newspaper or not."

In 1719, after 15 years as America's only newspaper, the *Boston News-Letter* faced its first competition. This was the *Boston Gazette*, founded by the new Boston postmaster, William Brooker, after the retiring Campbell refused to turn over the *News-Letter* to him as a perquisite of his office. The *Gazette*'s only real innovation was a market page, and it too was submitted for official government review before publication. When Brooker left the postal service less than a year later, he relinquished the *Gazette* to his replacement. All in all, five postmasters, including Brooker, edited it.

This safe, stodgy world of newspaper publishing was shaken up by the emergence of the spirited *New England Courant* in 1721. It was published without authority—or perhaps, in spite of it—by James Franklin, the elder brother of Benjamin Franklin. Unlike the establishment papers the *News-Letter* and the *Gazette,* the *Courant* practiced rebellious journalism with literary élan. It was bold and brilliant, independent and assertive, and it was guaranteed, from the start, to run afoul of the colonial government. Among Franklin's innovations was the "crusade" device, whereby an editor creates public interest in an issue through a campaign of news coverage. Inspired by the examples of the *Tatler* and the *Spectator*, the popular English essay papers of Joseph Addison and Richard Steele, Franklin also sought to bring witty cultural commentary to his readers. But historians judge Franklin's most important contribution to be his championing of a press freed from government control. The independent-minded and outspoken Franklin easily got on the wrong side of two powerful Puritan clergymen, Increase and Cotton Mather, over his paper's coverage of the issue of smallpox inoculation in 1721, which the Mathers supported. Franklin dared to undermine the Puritan theocracy by crusading against the new inoculation treatment in the *Courant*'s pages, while the Mathers and their supporters criticized the *Courant* in the *Gazette* and the *News-Letter*, as well as in pamphlets and a broadside, the *Anti-Courant.* But it was during the following year, when the *New England Courant* criticized the authorities for not doing enough to protect citizens from piracy, that Franklin found himself called before the Governor's Council (composed of the senior advisers to the governor in the Massachusetts Bay Colony) on contempt charges and jailed for a month. Released from prison, Franklin only continued his criticisms of the government. He ingeniously evaded the General Court's declaration that forbade him to print anything without official prepublication review by making his brother Benjamin the official publisher of the *New England Courant*. But the paper's tone became tamer, and it lost influence and circulation. While it ultimately lasted only five and a half years, Franklin made a strong stand for the newspaper's right to be published "without authority."

Newspapers Spread in New England and Beyond

Meanwhile, Philadelphia, the second-largest colonial city, saw its first newspaper established by Andrew Bradford, another postmaster, in 1719. The *American Weekly Mercury* was bolder than its earlier Boston counterparts, the semiofficial postmaster papers the *News-Letter* and the *Gazette*. It defended James Franklin when the *New England Courant* editor was thrown in jail, and it printed the English "Cato's Letters," which championed civil and religious liberties. Still, like all of the newspapers of this period, it was not very political, in stark contrast to the Revolutionary-era newspapers to come. And while widely circulated and often quoted, the *American Weekly Mercury* was soon to be overshadowed in Philadelphia by the journalism of Benjamin Franklin.

In 1729, Benjamin Franklin took over the *Pennsylvania Gazette*, started the previous year by Samuel Keimer. Under Franklin's direction, it became the most interesting and widely read paper in the colonies, as well as the one with the highest advertising revenue. Witty, bold, and innovative, Franklin was never one to avoid political controversy, though his common sense helped him to avoid trouble with the colonial authorities. Franklin's unqualified success with the *Pennsylvania Gazette* demonstrated for the first time that journalism could be a respectable and profitable occupation.

After 1725, newspapers sprang up all over the colonies. Increasing populations, economic growth, improved transportation and communication facilities, more and better schools, and rising political tensions all helped spur this development. Samuel Kneeland started the *New-England Weekly Journal* in 1727, along with the practice of using community correspondents to gather local news. That same year, Maryland became the fourth colony to have a newspaper when Annapolis's *Maryland Gazette* appeared. By 1750, at least 12 newspapers were being published in the colonies, in Maryland, Virginia, South Carolina, Massachusetts, New York, and Pennsylvania. By 1775, as David Copeland notes in his article on the colonial press, "40 papers appeared in . . . all colonies except New Jersey and Delaware." By the mid-18th century, most newspapers were issued semiweekly, or even triweekly. Many young newspapers failed after only a short time, however, usually because of financial difficulties. More than half of the approximately 20 newspapers started between 1690 and 1820 did not reach their second birthday, according to Clarence Brigham's *History and Bibliography of American Newspapers*. But the ones that survived commanded strong interest from the growing commercial class they served with essential news about trade and commerce as well as advertising. Typically, their publishers survived economically by printing many other documents besides the newspaper.

The ranks of colonial newspaper printers included at least 17 women. Before the Industrial Revolution, which separated home and workplace, women could naturally come to learn the printing business from their male relatives. Often succeeding their printer husbands who had died, these women included Elizabeth Timothy of South Carolina, who printed the *South Carolina Gazette* from 1738 to 1746. When the printer William Goddard founded a print shop and the *Providence Gazette* in 1762, his mother and sister, Sarah and Mary Katherine Goddard, joined him in the venture. As noted in *The Press and America*, the colonial publisher and press historian Isaiah Thomas referred to Mary Katherine as an "expert and correct compositor."

Colonial printers used a laborious process of setting type by hand in an iron frame, individual letter by individual letter. A pressure plate, or "platen," then pressed the inked lead type against the paper, printing the image. The paper needed to dry before the reverse side could be printed. At this rate, a printer (often assisted by an apprentice called a "printer's devil") could produce about 250 single-printed sheets an hour. The typical newspaper was printed on four pages of rough foolscap, each measuring about 10 by 15 inches. Headlines were uncommon, although they appeared more often after the mid-18th century. The only illustrations used were occasional woodcuts and, of course, the paper's masthead and the printer's colophon.

Advertising was limited in the first newspapers, but by the mid-18th century the more prosperous papers were able to fill three to five pages with advertisements from all manner of merchants. These took the form of small announcements, usually not taking up more than 10 lines, with the occasional woodcut to break up the expanse of type. The overall appearance was not unlike the classified ad section of the modern newspaper.

Much social and economic history can be discerned from these pages of 18th-century newspaper ads. Ads for runaway slaves and apprentices were common, as were ads for slaves for sale. Colonial newspapers frequently advertised commodities such as rum, molasses, sugar, and fabric of all kinds, as well as livestock, books, building supplies, millinery, houses to be let, and even lotteries.

Early Magazines

Compared to newspapers, magazines were in their infancy in the 18th century. But the few that existed did exert some influence, particularly during the Revolutionary period. The first efforts appeared in Philadelphia in January 1741, with Andrew Bradford's *American Magazine* and Benjamin Franklin's *General Magazine.* Franklin's lasted longer, but it survived only a total of six months. By 1800, nearly 100 magazines had been published (half in the years 1774–1800). Their average longevity was 14 months, and just two lasted as long as eight years. They faced many challenges, including small subscriptions (500 on average), nonpayment of subscriptions, and difficulties obtaining adequate printing equipment and supplies. Yet they had a "substantial" impact, according to the historian

Karen List, who notes that "they were read and considered by more people than their low circulation figures [averaging about 500] might indicate, and they were models for more financially successful publications to come."

American magazines, modeled on the English essay papers that also inspired early newspapers' content, included essays, commentaries, poetry, literary fiction, and at least some political and economic subject matter. These collections of "miscellany" usually were printed on rag paper that measured five to six by eight to nine inches. During the American Revolution, the *Pennsylvania Magazine* printed much of Thomas Paine's writings. Isaiah Thomas's *Royal American*, founded in 1774, was a repository for Patriot writings and the engravings of Paul Revere, a member of the Sons of Liberty.

The Press and the American Revolution

During the American Revolution, Patriot, Tory, and Whig editors harnessed the press as a means to express their ideas about government and other weighty issues. This was a departure from the earlier tradition of newspaper editors as artisan-printers, men who were often public printers for the official colonial government. Now, editors were not "not mere 'mechanics' but men of independent intellect and principle," as Bernard Bailyn and John B. Hench put it in *The Press and the American Revolution*.

The political tensions that led to the Revolution greatly spurred the development of the press. After all, in times of crisis, people seek information. And during the political conflicts that culminated in the American Revolution, colonists eagerly turned to newspapers as well as pamphlets. The following circulation figures, taken from Frank Mott's *American Journalism*, attest to this development: Before 1765, newspaper circulations typically ranged from a few hundred to 1,000 or more. By the mid-1770s, some newspapers in Boston and New York commanded circulations of more than 3,500. Granted, the total circulation for all newspapers in the colonies at the start of the Revolution was "less than 40,000 homes." But the audience was probably much larger, because copies were passed on to neighbors and acquaintances. They were also frequently read aloud or left in public gathering places, such as inns and taverns.

Among many causes of friction between Great Britain and its colonies, the Stamp Act of 1765 particularly angered colonial editors, ultimately galvanizing them to join the Patriot side. It aroused such ire because it placed a high tax on the paper used to print newspapers, as well as the advertisements they included. In the agitation following the Stamp Act's establishment, some editors suspended publication or refused to use stamped paper. Some papers, such as the *Pennsylvania Journal and Weekly Advertiser*, turned to satire. Its October 31, 1765, issue displayed thick black column margins (a symbol of mourning) to form a tombstone, with a woodcut of a skull and crossbones placed atop the page. Directly underneath the masthead, a headline proclaimed, "Expiring: In Hopes of a Resurrection to Life again." As a whole, the newspapers' protests helped rally the colonists against British rule.

Indeed, the Stamp Act crisis helped transform the press into a key element in the political debate. As tensions mounted, moderates with strong business and property interests, sometimes called "colonial Whigs," turned to newspapers and pamphlets to argue against "taxation without representation." Their most articulate spokesman was John Dickinson, whose 12 "Letters from a Farmer in Pennsylvania" were first printed in the *Pennsylvania Chronicle* in 1767–78, and then widely reproduced in other colonies. Read across America and in Europe, they called for colonial unity and urged peaceful resistance to British oppression.

As war approached, the press divided into two main camps: Patriot and Loyalist. Boston soon emerged as the locus of Patriot fervor. The Sons of Liberty, a group of radicals headed by Samuel Adams, wrote frequent columns for the *Boston Gazette*, which was edited by Benjamin Edes and John Gill. This passionate, radical journalism helped prepare the minds of the public for the concept of independence from Great Britain.

A brilliant propagandist, Adams made expert use of the colonial newspaper as a tool to build Patriot sentiment. Among his innovations was a campaign to chronicle and publish news of alleged British mistreatment of the

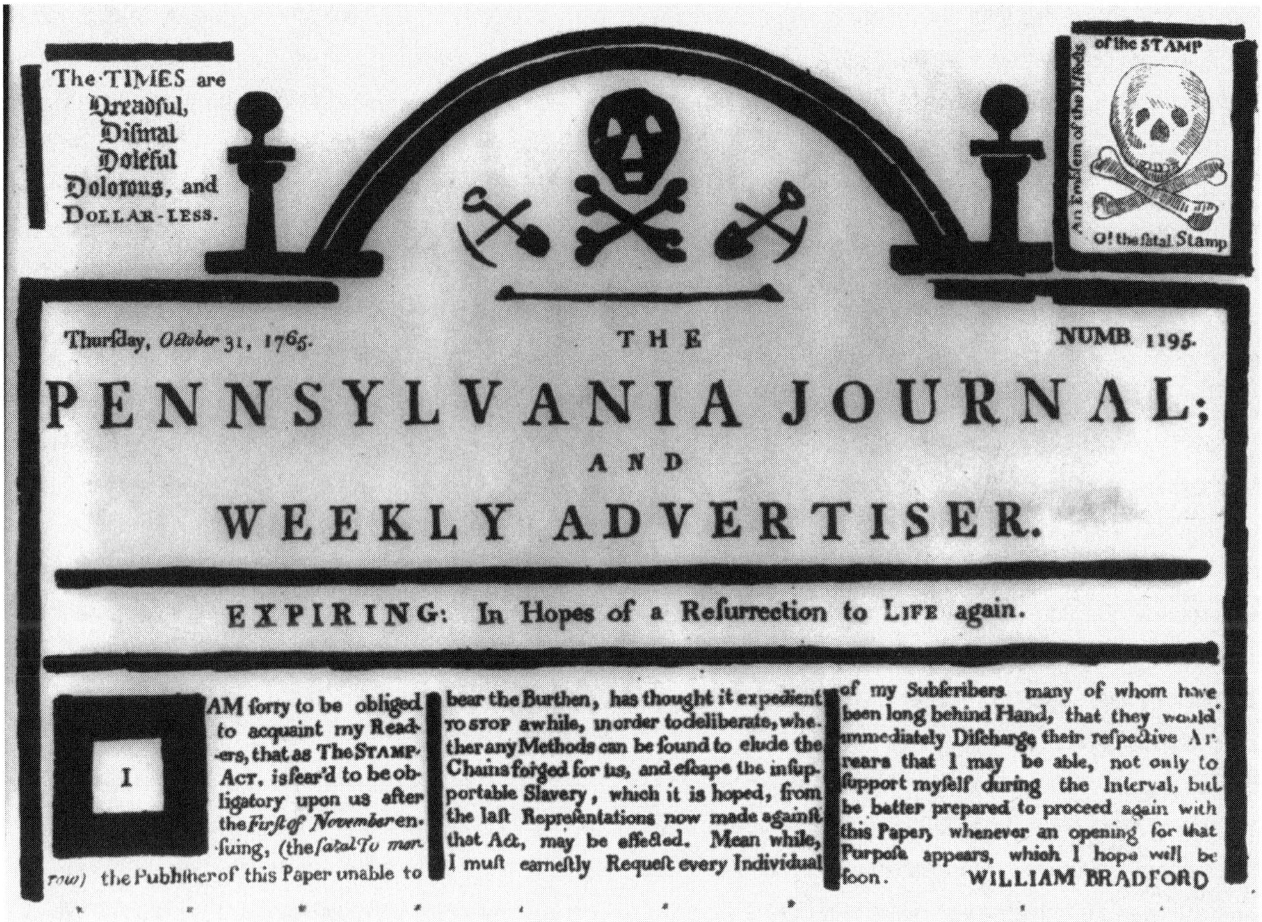

The·TIMES are
Dreadful,
Dismal
Doleful
Dolorous, and
DOLLAR-LESS.

An Emblem of the Effects of the STAMP
O! the fatal Stamp

Thursday, October 31, 1765. THE NUMB. 1195.

PENNSYLVANIA JOURNAL;
AND
WEEKLY ADVERTISER.

EXPIRING: In Hopes of a Resurrection to LIFE again.

I AM sorry to be obliged to acquaint my Readers, that as The STAMP-ACT, is fear'd to be obligatory upon us after the First of November ensuing, (the fatal To-morrow) the Publisher of this Paper unable to bear the Burthen, has thought it expedient TO STOP awhile, in order to deliberate, whether any Methods can be found to elude the Chains forged for us, and escape the insupportable Slavery, which it is hoped, from the last Representations now made against that Act, may be effected. Mean while, I must earnestly Request every Individual of my Subscribers many of whom have been long behind Hand, that they would immediately Discharge their respective Arrears that I may be able, not only to support myself during the Interval, but be better prepared to proceed again with this Paper, whenever an opening for that Purpose appears, which I hope will be soon. WILLIAM BRADFORD

The Pennsylvania Journal and Weekly Advertiser* and its publisher William Bradford turned to satire in response to the Stamp Act's establishment in 1765. Bradford printed an issue with a skull and crossbones representing the official stamp required by the act and suspended publication "In Hopes of a Resurrection to Life again." *(Library of Congress)

colonists (from insults to assault), culled by members of the Sons of Liberty from their contacts throughout the colonies. This early intercolonial communication network produced the "Journal of Occurrences" of 1768 to 1769, which was published in John Holt's *New York Journal* and in other papers from New England to Georgia. Although some reported incidents were probably falsified, the net result was to sway public opinion against the British occupiers.

Another Patriot paper that figured importantly in arousing Revolutionary spirit and maintaining morale was Isaiah Thomas's *Massachusetts Spy.* Begun in Boston in 1770, the *Spy* was moved to Worcester in 1775. Thomas published his eyewitness account of the fighting at Lexington and Concord in its pages. Hardly objective, Thomas's accounts still stir passions, including his dramatic description of a British officer who accosted the colonial militia while shouting, "Disperse, you damn'd rebels—Damn you disperse."

Pamphlets such as Thomas Paine's *Common Sense* (1776) also helped the Patriots turn public opinion against the British and prepare Americans for war. Indeed, *Common Sense* commanded sales of 120,000 copies during its first three months and was widely reprinted in colonial newspapers. It was the first American best seller, with its popularity superseded only by the Bible. When fighting broke out, Paine's *American Crisis* papers, widely republished in newspapers, helped rally public opinion with resonant words, including: "These are the times that try men's souls."

On the Tory, or Loyalist, side, the leading publisher was James ("Jemmy") Rivington, who founded *Rivington's New York Gazetteer* in 1773. Uncharacteristically neutral for the time, the paper at first tried to discuss all sides of the prevailing political issues. But this still aroused the ire of the firebrand Samuel Adams and the Radicals (Patriots) who were agitating for all-out support of their cause. After the fighting at Lexington and Concord, however, Rivington abandoned all objectivity. During the war, he renamed his paper the *Royal Gazette* and hewed unabashedly to Tory ideals. His newspaper was as partisan on one side as the Patriots' papers were on the other. Eventually, a mob burned Rivington in effigy and sacked his press. In 1781, after he heard the news of the British surrender at Yorktown, Rivington's *Royal Gazette* became much more moderate. But in 1783, the Radicals returned and ran him out of town. A similar fate befell other Loyalist papers that did not mute their opinions. Indeed, as the press became increasingly partisan, on both sides there was a concomitant decline of tolerance for differences in points of view.

It is hard to imagine the American Revolution succeeding without benefit of the extensive public forum and propaganda outlet that newspapers and pamphlets offered. At the end of the conflict, only 20 of the 35 prewar newspapers remained, though 35 new papers were founded during the fighting. All of these new papers were weeklies, and most were on the Patriot side. Their editors overcame political pressures, a lack of proper printing equipment and paper supplies, and other wartime constraints, including having to keep ahead of invading armies. Most important, newspapers and pamphlets proved their value as sources of essential information and a means with which to change public opinion and inspire unified citizen action. The value placed on the press was shown in the press freedoms the Founders included in the 1791 Bill of Rights to the Constitution, as stated in the First Amendment.

Journalism in the Early Republic

In the founding years of the new republic of the United States, the press played an active role in the debate over the Constitution and in the development of the new republic's first party system. Factional differences about the future of the United States were reflected directly in the press. Both those who supported and those who opposed ratification of the Constitution conducted their debates in pamphlets and in the pages of newspapers. Alexander Hamilton, James Madison, and John Jay wrote essays under the pen name "Publius" to form a collection of 85 articles known as the Federalist Papers. These superbly written political pieces strongly advocated the ratification of the Constitution, and between October 1787 and April 1788, 75 of them were published serially in the semiweekly *New York Independent Journal.* They were then reprinted in newspapers across the country and later published, in pamphlet and book form, with six additional essays, as *The Federalist*. Although they had limited influence on the ratification in New York, in the years following the adoption of the Constitution they were recognized as classic texts of constitutional government and political theory

As political parties evolved in the 1790s, each political faction enjoyed the support of a sponsored party newspaper. The Federalists, led by Alexander Hamilton and advocating a strong central government and loose construction, or interpretation, of the Constitution, made the *Gazette of the United States* a powerful voice. Founded in New York on April 15, 1789, it was edited by John Fenno. Other editors who backed the Federalists were Noah Webster, who edited the daily *Minerva* in New York starting in 1793, and William Cobbett, the editor of *Porcupine's Gazette and Daily Advertiser* in Philadelphia (starting in 1797).

Thomas Jefferson, the leader of the Democratic-Republicans, who believed in a strict construction of the Constitution and thought that power resided with the states, found an able spokesman in Philip Freneau, who founded and edited the *National Gazette* in 1791. Another strong Republican supporter was Benjamin Franklin Bache, the grandson of Benjamin Franklin, who founded the *Philadelphia General Advertiser* (later known as the *Aurora*) in 1790 at the age of 21.

Some historians have lamented this period's unalloyed vituperation and violent acts. Personal attacks were common, such as Bache's on George Washington: "If ever a nation was debauched by a man, the American nation has been debauched by Washington," the editor wrote in the *Aurora* on December 12, 1796. For this, Federalists, who idolized Washington, wrecked the *Aurora* office and beat Bache, whom Fenno caned in the street. William Cobbett also became famous for his vituperation, delivered under his pseudonym "Peter Porcupine." Many thought he went too far, however, when he attacked the memory of Benjamin Franklin as a way to lampoon Bache of the *Aurora*. Writing of Bache in *Porcupine's Gazette* on July 31, 1797, he referred to "his crafty and lecherous old hypocrite of a grandfather, whose very statue seems to gloat on the wenches as they walk the State House yard."

Another view is that this was a transitional period, during which the press sought to adapt to the stresses and strains of launching the new nation. After the Revolutionary experience, during which newspapers had developed into quite partisan political organs, perhaps this was a natural progression. At this time, when the political system of the new republic was being developed, most people viewed the press as an intentionally partisan institution.

Ironically, perhaps a measure of the press's growth as an institution to be reckoned with can be seen in the passing by the Federalist-dominated Congress of the Alien and Sedition Acts in 1798 (they would remain in force for the next two years). Essentially, the Sedition Act mandated a substantial fine and imprisonment for anyone who criticized the government. However, this bald attempt to suppress the perceived power of Republican journalists was above all a reflection of the vicious politics of the time. Overall, by 1800 the press had emerged as a major force in society, taking a dynamic role in shaping ideas and policy about the key issues of the day, particularly political issues.

—Nancy L. Roberts

Further Reading

Bailyn, Bernard, and John B. Hench, eds. *The Press and the American Revolution*. Boston: Northeastern University Press, 1981.

Baker, Ira L. "Elizabeth Timothy: America's First Woman Editor," *Journalism Quarterly* 54 (1977): 284–285.

Botein, Stephen. "'Meer Mechanics' and an Open Press: The Business and Political Strategies of Colonial American Printers." In *Perspectives in American History,* vol. 9, edited by Donald Fleming and Bernard Bailyn, 127–228. Cambridge, Mass.: Harvard University Press, 1975.

Brigham, Clarence S. *History and Bibliography of American Newspapers, 1690–1820.* Worcester, Mass.: American Antiquarian Society, 1947.

Copeland, David A. "Colonial Press." In *History of the Mass Media in the United States: An Encyclopedia*, edited by Margaret A. Blanchard, 147–149. Chicago: Fitzroy Dearborn, 1998.

———. *Debating the Issues in Colonial Newspapers: Primary Documents on Events of the Period*. Westport, Conn.: Greenwood Press, 2000.

Davidson, Philip Grant. *Propaganda and the American Revolution, 1763–1783*. Chapel Hill: University of North Carolina Press, 1941.

Emery, Michael, Edwin Emery, and Nancy L. Roberts. *The Press and America: An Interpretive History of the Mass Media*. 9th ed. Boston: Allyn & Bacon, 2000.

"The *E Pluribus Unum* Project: America in the 1770s." Available online. URL: http://www1.assumption.edu/ahc/1770s/default.html. Accessed May 12, 2004.

Humphrey, Carol Sue. "American Revolution and the Press." In *History of the Mass Media in the United States: An Encyclopedia,* edited by Margaret A. Blanchard, 37–38. Chicago: Fitzroy Dearborn, 1998.

———. *The Press of the Young Republic, 1783–1833*. Westport, Conn.: Greenwood Press, 1996.

———. *"This Popular Engine": New England Newspapers during the American Revolution, 1775–1789.* Newark: University of Delaware Press; London: Associated University Presses, 1992.

List, Karen K. "Magazines in the Eighteenth Century." In *History of the Mass Media in the United States: An Encyclopedia*, edited by Margaret A. Blanchard, 335–336. Chicago: Fitzroy Dearborn, 1998.

Monaghan, E. Jennifer. "The Uses of Literacy by Girls in Colonial America." In *Girls and Literacy in America: Historical Perspectives to the Present Moment*, edited by Jane Greer. Santa Barbara, Calif.: ABC-CLIO, 2003.

Mott, Frank Luther. *American Journalism: A History: 1690–1960*. New York: Macmillan, 1962.

Nord, David Paul. "A Republican Literature: A Study of Magazine Reading and Readers in Late Eighteenth-Century New York." *American Quarterly* 40, no. 1 (March 1988): 42–64.

Schlesinger, Arthur M. *Prelude to Independence: The Newspaper War on Britain, 1764–1776*. New York: Alfred A. Knopf, 1958.

Sloan, W. David. "'Purse and Pen': Party-Press Relationships, 1789–1816." *American Journalism* 6 (1989): 103–127.

Sloan, W. David, and Julie Hedgepeth Williams. *The Early American Press, 1690–1783*. Westport, Conn.: Greenwood, 1994.

Thomas, Isaiah. *The History of Printing in America*. 2 vols. Worcester, Mass., 1810.

Williams, Julie Hedgepeth. "Newspapers in the Eighteenth Century." In *History of the Mass Media in the United States: An Encyclopedia*, edited by Margaret A. Blanchard, 450–453. Chicago: Fitzroy Dearborn, 1998.

18th Century PROTEST AND REBELLION

Protest and rebellion are collective actions that seek to communicate grievances or reshape existing political, social, and economic conditions. Though existing outside the realm of formal political institutions and procedures, they constitute a form of political action. An analysis of protest and rebellion in 18th-century Anglo-America speaks volumes about early American social norms, social tensions, and attitudes toward authority. Social unrest during this period also intersected with the American Revolution, and placing the Revolution in the context of broader patterns of protest sheds light on both.

The pattern of protest and rebellion in the 18th century can best be understood by analyzing how it varied over time and space. Chronologically, this history of unrest can be divided into three periods: a pre-Revolutionary era (1700–63), a Revolutionary era embracing the years of the anti-imperial protest against Britain and the Revolutionary War (1764–83), and a post-independence era (1784–99). This division into periods helps to identify how patterns of protest evolved over time and relates them to the larger contours of the Revolution. Spatially, a distinction must be drawn between rural and urban unrest. The motives for and methods of protest varied greatly between the cities and the countryside, as did the relationship between protestors and government authority.

Pre-Revolutionary Era, 1700–1763

A friend of order living in British America in the 1750s could look back upon the previous half century with a good deal of satisfaction. Though there was a pulse of unrest in the colonies' major urban centers and even some outbreaks of protest in the hinterlands, most of this tumult was limited in scope and, with a few exceptions, did not challenge government authority. Though the first of the periods identified in this study was the least active, it still offers significant insights into the motives and cultural origins of 18th-century protest and rebellion.

Urban Patterns

Episodes of urban unrest during the first half of the 18th century exhibit a set of common features. First, urban protest was synonymous with mobs—with hundreds of people taking to the streets to voice grievances or impose their will. Second, these crowds were "extralegal" rather than simply anti-authoritarian. Mobs often functioned to support laws and social codes that government and judicial officials were unable or unwilling to enforce. In carrying out this extralegal function, mobs presented themselves as embodiments of the community's will. Finally, these extralegal crowds often represented a cross-section of urban society and acted purposefully and with restraint.

Crowd actions formed the spearhead of urban protest. Boston, New York, Philadelphia, and other 18th-century urban centers possessed the population needed to mobilize large-scale street protests. The prevalence of mob activity was not just a function of population density. Urban protestors drew upon popular traditions of protest and festive misrule that were communal and public. For instance, Boston's and New York's Pope's Day celebrations provided models for mob action in those cities. An annual celebration that roughly paralleled England's Guy Fawkes Day, Pope's Day became an occasion for anti-Catholic rhetoric and rowdy street processions by costumed crowds. It was also a manifestation of a much older European tradition of festive misrule: occasions on which ordinary folk, often with the tacit consent of their superiors, ritually suspended social norms. Ironically, urban folk evoked these traditions of festive misrule in episodes of protest designed to maintain the social order. Though the forms and rituals employed by crowds mirrored raucous occasions like Pope's Day, their intent was far different.

The purposeful, extralegal nature of mobs is one of the distinguishing features of 18th-century urban protest. This dimension of crowd activity is best illustrated by examining the motives and behavior of urban mobs.

Townspeople took to the streets in response to perceived threats to community norms and interests. This pattern of extralegal rioting can be seen in the various sorts of issues that ignited urban protest in the first half of the 18th century. City inhabitants rioted during periods of food shortage, sometimes to protest rising food prices and, more often, to forcibly keep foodstuffs from being exported overseas and, thus, increase local food supplies. Such was the case in Boston in 1710, 1711, 1713, and 1729. Boston was also the scene of mob actions against brothels in 1734 and 1737; crowds targeted houses of ill fame because they perceived them as corrosive to community morality. In addition, protest in seaport towns formed in response to impressment—a form of legally countenanced kidnapping carried out by the Royal Navy to assure that its ships were sufficiently manned. The arrival of navy "press gangs" who swept up involuntary recruits sparked riots in Boston in 1741, 1745, and 1747. Urban folk held this practice as a mortal threat because it robbed families of loved ones and wage earners and stripped coastal towns of workers.

Rural Patterns

Rural protest in the first half of the 18th century does have some features in common with urban unrest. Both urban and rural rioters were purposeful and discriminating; both also looked back to European traditions of rebellion and festive misrule in weaving together methods and rituals of protest. However, there are also significant differences between the two that demonstrate that rural unrest ultimately followed a distinct trajectory.

The first half of the 18th century witnessed outbreaks of unrest along the Pennsylvania-Maryland border (1730s and 1740s), in northern New Jersey (1740s and 1750s), the Hudson Valley (1750s and early 1760s), northeast Pennsylvania's Wyoming Valley (starting in the late 1750s), South Carolina's Rocky Mount district (1750s to early 1760s), and North Carolina's Granville district (1750s to early 1760s). In these various episodes of conflict, ordinary farmers fought landlords, and each other, over land or the terms under which it was held. Competing claims to property lay at the heart of this contention. Frequently one group of claimants held titles obtained from the Crown, colonial governments, land speculators, or even Indian nations, that overlapped the grants of another group. Adding to this discord were squatters—people who occupied land without any legal title—who justified their claim to property simply by right of occupancy. In several cases territorial disputes between colonies intersected with and intensified this struggle for property. Hudson Valley farmers hoping to escape the grasp of powerful manor lords took advantage of a boundary dispute between New York and Massachusetts to obtain land from the latter colony. Likewise, border disputes between Pennsylvania and Connecticut and Pennsylvania and Maryland fueled unrest in northeast and southern Pennsylvania respectively. In all these regions, provincial governments issued deeds that overlapped claims held by settlers from rival colonies, creating conflicts over soil and jurisdictional rights.

These outbreaks of unrest had a number of common features that distinguish them from episodes of urban protest. Unlike urban riots, rural unrest revolved around issues of land ownership or the terms under which soil rights could be secured. More important, while urban protest did not directly challenge the legitimacy of government or established social hierarchies, rural rebellions did. This was certainly the case in land riots that intersected with intercolony territorial disputes and where contestants inevitably challenged the legitimacy of the opposing jurisdiction. In addition, episodes of rural protest that pitted ordinary farmers against wealthy landlords raised the specter of class conflict. Finally, whereas urban protest flourished in situations where mobs appeared to embody a unified community will, rural protest emerged where authority and communities were divided.

That episodes of rural protest were generated by powerful social tensions and possessed anti-authoritarian features also helps to explain the different texture of agrarian unrest. While urban protest was collective and public, rural unrest was often small-scale and clandestine. Rural rioters commonly attacked their targets in disguise and sometimes even under cover of darkness. Considering that agrarian protest involved direct challenges to established social and political authorities, such practices were necessary to avoid prosecution. Moreover, while the behavior of many urban mobs was ritualistic in nature, rural mob tactics were more instrumental and practical. In addition to employing the effigy burnings and riotous processions that were the stock-in-trade of urban mobs, rural rioters knocked down fences, destroyed crops, drove off livestock, and destroyed homes. All these tactics were linked to battles over soil rights: By destroying the property of their opponents, rioters sought to undermine their legal claims and ability to occupy the land. Finally, rural unrest was sustained rather than episodic. Unlike the cities, where outbreaks of protest were intermittent and ad hoc, the countryside saw the emergence of distinct protest movements that endured over time and developed coordination and leadership.

The Revolutionary Era, 1764–1783

The period between the conclusion of the Seven Years' War (1756–63) and the end of the Revolutionary War saw changes in patterns of urban and rural unrest. In early America's towns and cities, the goals of protest changed and its level grew as the colonies became embroiled in their dispute with Britain over taxes, imperial regulations, and authority. Though the aims of rural rioters remained the same, the scale and intensity of disturbances also increased in the countryside. Besides the Revolution, the primary catalyst behind this rising tide of unrest was a surge of frontier expansion in the second half of the 18th century.

Urban Patterns

During this period urban protest intersected with the struggle between the colonies and Great Britain. Starting with riots against Britain's Stamp Act (one of many laws passed by Parliament to raise revenue in the colonies) in 1765, mobs aimed their ire at imperial officials in an effort to thwart Britain's efforts to impose new economic regulations. In Boston on the evening of August 14, a crowd tore down a building built by the newly appointed stamp distributor, Andrew Oliver. The mob then moved on and ransacked Oliver's home. This event set a pattern of protest for roughly a decade and produced some of the most famous events of the American Revolution, such as the Boston Tea Party in 1773 when colonists—some of them dressed as Indians—dumped three shiploads of taxed British tea into Boston Harbor. Boston was not the only city to experience anti-imperial protest. In New York, crowds protesting the Stamp Act repeatedly took to the streets in the fall of 1765. To these disturbances New York added a violent confrontation between the city's inhabitants and British soldiers known as the "Battle of Golden Hill" on January 19, 1770, and its own tea party on April 22, 1774. A mob in Charleston, South Carolina, followed the path blazed by their northern counterparts and held another anti-imperial tea party in December 1774.

Though the anti-imperial crisis had a significant impact on the nature of urban protest, it did not produce a radical break with older patterns. Revolutionary-era mobs were firmly rooted in long-standing patterns of urban unrest, and there was significant continuity in their methods, rituals, and motives. Anti-imperial mobs' practices of parading and burning effigies and their habit of donning costumes—most famously enacted by the Indian-clad colonists who perpetrated the Boston Tea Party—all clearly point to deeply rooted traditions of protest. As was also the case with their forebears, Revolutionary-era urban mobs were purposeful, discriminating in their targets, and cross-class in their composition.

Crowds continued to take to the streets in response to issues that had sparked protest in the pre-Revolutionary era. Anti-impressment riots took place in New York in July 1764 and 1765; Newport, Rhode Island, also experienced impressment riots in July 1764 and again in June 1765. Likewise, the twin issues of impressments and imperial customs regulations sparked Boston's "*Liberty* Riot" of June 10, 1768. On this occasion several thousand Bostonians took to the streets when sailors from the HMS *Romney* (who were also "running a press" in the city) attempted to impound John Hancock's sloop *Liberty* for customs violations. The mob battled the British

„BOSTON TEA-PARTY."
Three cargoes of tea destroyed. Dec. 16. 1773.
A number of the inhabitants, disguised as Indians, boarded the ships in the night, broke open all the chests of tea, and emptied the contents into the sea.
No. 8.

The Boston Tea Party of December 16, 1773, in which colonists dumped three shiploads of taxed British tea into Boston Harbor, is one of the most famous events leading up to the American Revolution. This protest, however, was just one among many collective actions taken by colonists in the run-up to war with Britain—actions such as Stamp Act riots in Boston, the Battle of Golden Hill in New York City, and the anti-imperial tea party in Charleston, South Carolina. ***(Library of Congress)***

sailors and attacked customs officials and their homes. The persistence of food riots also linked urban rioting in the pre-Revolutionary and Revolutionary eras. Indeed, the economic instability caused by the Revolutionary War increased the prevalence of this type of disturbance. New York experienced food riots in 1775 and 1776; Boston in 1777, 1778, and 1779; Providence, Rhode Island, in 1775; Salem, Massachusetts, in 1777; and Philadelphia in 1779.

The extralegal function of colonial-era mobs also carried on into the Revolutionary era. Indeed, the ability of mobs to police and enforce community norms was much in demand. When imperial authority collapsed in the 1770s, Revolutionary committees moved in to fill the power vacuum. These committees, which were very much extralegal institutions themselves, often relied upon mobs to enforce their authority. For example, on August 22, 1775, a crowd of New Yorkers tarred and feathered a shoemaker named Tweedy after he spoke out against the city's committee. The urban food riots mentioned above were also often tied to the committees' efforts to control food prices and regulate the importation of banned goods such as tea.

Rural Patterns

As in the cities, levels of unrest increased across the countryside during the 1760s, 1770s, and 1780s. The colonies' rebellion against British rule created an atmosphere conducive to instability. Frontier expansion also fueled rural protest. Anglo-American colonists occupied hundreds of thousands of acres during the Revolutionary era. This process was not orderly and peaceful but contentious and conflict-ridden. As was also the case with urban protest, there was much continuity between this period and the previous one. Several pre-Revolutionary episodes of agrarian unrest carried over into the Revolutionary era, and the motives and tactics of rural rebels largely remained the same.

Disputes over soil and jurisdictional rights continued to be a source of conflict. This pattern only grew as European American settlers moved into uncharted regions where land claims were blurry at best. Massachusetts's District of Maine saw the outbreak of violence between squatters and landlords in the 1760s. Maine's rural insurgents, who came to be known as "Liberty Men," sustained their resistance throughout the Revolutionary period. Likewise, conflict erupted in the Hampshire Grants (Vermont) when settlers and land speculators from New York came to blows over property with New England settlers, known as "Green Mountain Boys," who held deeds issued by New Hampshire. The battle between tenant farmers and the Hudson Valley's manor lords reached a climax with an uprising in 1766 led by William Prendergast. British troops stationed in New York helped to quell this disturbance. Resistance did not end here, however, but continued on into the following decades. The dispute over the Wyoming Valley intensified during the 1770s and 1780s as settlers from both Connecticut and Pennsylvania flooded into the region and came into conflict. Finally, Pennsylvania became embroiled in another territorial dispute with Virginia over present-day southwestern Pennsylvania in the 1770s. As with the Wyoming region, settlers and land developers holding competing provincial land grants battled one another for property and power.

The social and economic dislocation of the Revolutionary era also contributed to rural unrest. Contention over debt, taxes, Indian policy, and political power sparked protest because these issues impinged upon the ability of farmers to obtain and secure property. Unrest in northern New Jersey between farmers and elites carried into the late 1760s as "Liberty Boys" protested against county courts. Pennsylvania experienced unrest during the Paxton Boys riots of 1763–64 when what started as bloodthirsty vigilantism against Indians bloomed into a protest against Pennsylvania's provincial government and ended with a march by armed rioters on Philadelphia. Only the timely arrival of royal troops and the hasty formation of a city militia turned back the rioters. Farther south, both North Carolina and South Carolina experienced major episodes of backcountry unrest. In the South Carolina Regulation of the late 1760s, frontier vigilantes battled bandits and vagrants and clamored for a more effective frontier judicial system. In the North Carolina War of Regulation of the late 1760s and early 1770s, the complaint among frontier insurgents was not about a lack of government but government corruption. The rebels' response was to forcefully shut down the county court system. In the end, provincial authorities violently put down the rebellion at the Battle of Alamance in 1771. The inhabitants of western Massachusetts who styled themselves as the "Berkshire Constitutionalists" challenged perceived injustices by suspending county courts between 1774 and 1780. Western Massachusetts and Connecticut also saw farmers rise in protest against taxes and debt during Ely's Rebellion in 1782.

The motives behind agrarian protest were not the only commonality with the pre-Revolutionary era: The tactics and methods used by rural rioters also remained consistent. Moreover, rural rebels' habit of forming coordinated, long-term movements became even more pronounced during the Revolutionary era. Maine's Liberty Men, Vermont's Green Mountain Boys, New Jersey's Liberty Boys, and North Carolina's and South Carolina's Regulators all created organized protest movements. The level of structure and organization achieved by many rural protest movements was linked to the fact that several of these disputes involved jurisdictional conflicts between colonies and, later, states. This situation often enabled rioters in places like southeastern Pennsylvania, Pennsylvania's Wyoming Valley, and Vermont to associate themselves with one of the contesting jurisdictions.

The Post-Independence Era, 1784–1799

Protest and rebellion in the years after America won its independence from Great Britain saw older trends blend with contention over the nature of America's post-independence social order. Specifically, urban and rural unrest intersected with debates over the legitimacy of popular protest and how to balance community and individual interests in a republican society.

Urban Patterns

There was continuity in urban protest after American independence. Crowds in the 1780s and 1790s took action against food shortages, whorehouses, and other perceived threats to community interests and norms, just as their colonial-era forebears had. For example, in 1793 and 1799 New Yorkers mobbed bawdy houses. Likewise, the city's inhabitants rose up in moral outrage during the "Doctors' Riot" of April 1788. On this occasion, a crowd attacked the city's medical school after rumors spread that grave robbers supplied the bodies of deceased city residents to medical students for dissection.

At first glance it seems that older traditions of rioting remained alive and well in America's towns and cities. However, changes in the landscape of urban unrest also came into focus during this period. In particular, urban elites and officials were increasingly intolerant of urban unrest. New York officials called out the militia from the surrounding countryside against rioters during the Doctors' Riot. Violence ensued when the mob confronted the troops, and in the resulting fracas the militia shot and killed three rioters. The mob assault on New York bawdy houses in 1799 also required the militia to restore order.

New trends in urban unrest also concerned the motives behind protest. Crowd actions increasingly intersected with the rise of partisan politics as the political battles that took place between Federalists, anti-Federalists, and Democratic-Republicans spilled into the streets. In Carlisle, Pennsylvania; Albany, New York; and New York City in the 1780s, street processions by anti-Federalists and Federalists devolved into violence. By the 1790s such politically motivated crowd actions had become a feature of urban partisan politics. For example, in July 1798, singing matches between pro-Federalist and pro-Democratic-Republican crowds in New York devolved into violent street battles. Moreover, in a foreshadowing of 19th-century patterns of urban disorder, ethnic tensions started to contribute to unrest. On Saint Patrick's Day 1799 an anti-Irish street parade in New York resulted in violence when the city's Irish inhabitants attacked the procession.

The changing nature of urban unrest, combined with a growing intolerance among elites and government officials for popular disturbances, marked the unraveling of colonial-era traditions of urban protest. America's cities were becoming larger and more heterogeneous; lines of class, political affiliation, ethnicity, and race increasingly divided urban populations at century's end. In this context it was more difficult for urban mobs to appear as a legitimate expression of the will of the people, because the people themselves were often not of one mind. The merging of mob activity and partisan politics was especially corrosive to colonial-era traditions of protest. Political mobs were by their very nature factional, and it was very difficult to pass off their activities as expressions of the common good. Time and time again one faction accused the other of using crowds to achieve narrow, partisan goals. The ultimate casualty of such rhetoric was the idea of the mob as an extralegal embodiment of the community. America's post-independence republican social order also delegitimized popular crowd activity. In a nation where political power theoretically rested in the hands of the people, any challenge to government authority and order was in itself a threat to the commonwealth.

Rural Patterns

The peak of rural unrest in 18th-century America came in the decades after the colonies gained their independence from Britain. This period witnessed the climax of a number of agrarian insurgencies that predated the Revolution and the outbreak of several large-scale rebellions.

Struggles over property continued to contribute to disorder in the countryside. In Maine, settlers carried on their battle against land speculators for possession of frontier lands. In Vermont, New Englanders were still fighting settlers and landlords from New York. The Hudson Valley saw fresh outbreaks of violence between tenant farmers and the valley's manor lords. Conflict also erupted between settlers and speculators over control of northwest Pennsylvania's "Donation Lands"—grants issued to Revolutionary War veterans by the state of Pennsylvania that had in many cases fallen into the hands of powerful land developers. Finally, in the 1780s, squatters occupying lands west of the Ohio River battled against federal troops who sought to impose the national government's authority and soil rights on the frontier.

Rural folk also continued to battle it out over issues of taxation, debt, and government policy. In central and western Massachusetts, farmers rose up in rebellion against the state of Massachusetts during Shays's Rebellion in 1786–87. The rebels shut down the county courts in order to halt prosecution for debt and challenged the very authority of the state. Massachusetts responded by raising a militia army that eventually dispersed rebel forces at an engagement at Petersham on February 4, 1787. Farmers also rebelled against the federal government's whiskey excise tax in the early 1790s. The uprising gained the most momentum in western Pennsylvania. As with Shays's Rebellion, the Pennsylvania Regulation—better known as the Whiskey Rebellion—ended when the federal government sent a militia army of 13,000 troops into western Pennsylvania to restore order. Pennsylvania experienced another bout of protest when farmers in the eastern part of the state challenged federal authority and taxes during Fries's Rebellion in 1799. The federal government again quelled this outburst of protest with troops.

In keeping with previous patterns of rural unrest, most of these rebellions generated substantial protest movements. Shays's Rebellion, the Whiskey Rebellion, and Fries's Rebellion all saw the emergence of coherent campaigns that orchestrated resistance to government authority and created rebel militias that required the intervention of state and federal forces to put down. The insurgencies that land rioters maintained in Maine, Pennsylvania, Vermont, and the Hudson Valley, though less spectacular, were no less sophisticated. Northeast Pennsylvania's "Wild Yankees," Vermont's Green Mountain Boys, and Maine's insurgents—who came to be dubbed "White Indians"—all constructed durable resistance movements.

Also in keeping with pre-independence episodes of agrarian conflict, all these rebellions and insurgencies produced bloodshed. While Shays's Rebellion, the Whiskey Rebellion, and Fries's Rebellion certainly led to deaths and serious injuries, what is most striking is the pattern of violence that emerged out of the post-independence era's land disputes. Agrarian insurgents in Maine, Pennsylvania, and New York stepped up the level of violence against their opponents and even engaged in the cold-blooded murder of surveyors, land agents, and law officers.

This woodcut from 1787, originally published in *Bickerstaff's Boston Almanack of 1787*, shows Daniel Shays and Job Shattuck of the Massachusetts "Regulators," who led the farmers' revolt against Massachusetts's burdensome tax policy that was putting many farmers and landowners deep into debt. The revolt came to be known as Shays's Rebellion. *(Smithsonian Institution)*

What the highly organized nature and violence of agrarian unrest again points to is the critical importance of the issues out of which it grew. Whether disputes emerged over soil rights, taxes, or debt policies, all these episodes ultimately touched upon the ability of ordinary folk to achieve independence. Independence here does not refer to an amorphous concept of individual freedom but to a more specific 18th-century understanding of the term: the possession of property and the economic security and political rights that came along with it.

These rural protest movements also intersected with powerful debates over the nature of America's post-independence social order. During the 1780s and 1790s Americans argued over whether political power should be dispersed and local or centralized and national. They also battled over whether the Revolution was essentially a constitutional event that aimed to simply replace imperial authority with rule by local elites, or if it should go beyond this limited goal and attempt to institute a new social order in which common folk obtained a greater share of power. America's post-independence agrarian disturbances connected with these larger themes.

Though government forces crushed Shays's Rebellion, the Whiskey Rebellion, and Fries's Rebellion, long-standing property disputes that generated agrarian resistance in Maine, New York, Pennsylvania, and Vermont endured and in some cases even ground on into the 19th century. Though state officials called out the militia against land rioters when they crossed the line from protest to murder, the use of force is not what ended these insurgencies. Instead, compromise ultimately brought this contention to a close. Pennsylvania's Compromise Act (1799) and Massachusetts's Betterment Act (1808) made provisions to provide northeast Pennsylvania's and Maine's agrarian insurgents with land at prices they could afford and eventually undermined resistance in these regions. The concessions made to Vermont's rural rebels were far more significant. When the federal government admitted Vermont to the Union in 1791, it consummated the Green Mountain Boys' bid for independence from New York.

—Paul B. Moyer

Further Reading

Bellesiles, Michael A. *Revolutionary Outlaws: Ethan Allen and the Struggle for Independence on the Early American Frontier*. Charlottesville: University Press of Virginia, 1993.

Bouton, Terry. "A Road Closed: Rural Insurgency in Post-Independence Pennsylvania." *Journal of American History* 87 (December 2000): 855–887.

Dutrizac, Charles D. "Local Identity and Authority in a Disputed Hinterland: The Pennsylvania-Maryland Border in the 1730s." *Pennsylvania Magazine of History and Biography* 115 (January 1991): 35–61.

Gilje, Paul A. *The Road to Mobocracy: Popular Disorder in New York City, 1763–1834*. Chapel Hill: North Carolina University Press, for the Institute of Early American History and Culture 1987.

Henderson, Elizabeth. "The Northwestern Lands of Pennsylvania, 1790–1812." *Pennsylvania Magazine of History and Biography* 60 (1936): 131–160.

Humphrey, Thomas J. *Land and Liberty: Hudson Valley Riots in the Age of Revolution*. DeKalb: Northern Illinois University Press, 2004.

Kars, Marjoline. *Breaking Loose Together: The Regulator Rebellion in Pre-Revolutionary North Carolina*. Chapel Hill: North Carolina University Press, 2002.

Kinney, Kevin. *Peaceable Kingdom Lost: The Paxton Boys and the Destruction of William Penn's Holy Experiment*. New York: Oxford University Press, 2009.

Klein, Rachel N. "Ordering the Backcountry: The South Carolina Regulation." *William and Mary Quarterly* 38 (October 1981): 661–680.

Maier, Pauline. "Popular Uprisings and Civil Authority in Eighteenth-Century America." *William and Mary Quarterly* 27 (January 1970): 4–35.

McConville, Brendan J. *Those Daring Disturbers of the Public Peace: The Struggle for Property and Power in Early New Jersey*. Ithaca, N.Y.: Cornell University Press, 1999.

Moyer, Paul. *Wild Yankees: The Struggle for Independence along Pennsylvania's Revolutionary Frontier*. Ithaca, N.Y.: Cornell University Press, 2007.

Nash, Gary B. *The Urban Crucible: Social Change, Political Consciousness, and the Origins of the American Revolution*. Cambridge, Mass.: Harvard University Press, 1979.

Newman, Paul Douglas. *Fries's Rebellion: The Enduring Struggle for the American Revolution*. Philadelphia: University of Pennsylvania Press, 2004.

Pencak, William, Matthew Dennis, and Simon P. Newman, eds. *Riot and Revelry in Early America*. University Park: Penn State University Press, 2002.

Richards, Leonard L. *Shays's Rebellion: The American Revolution's Final Battle.* Philadelphia: University of Pennsylvania Press, 2002.

Slaughter, Thomas P. *The Whiskey Rebellion: Frontier Epilogue to the American Revolution*. New York: Oxford University Press, 1986.

Smith, Barbara Clark. "Food Rioters and the American Revolution." *William and Mary Quarterly* 51 (January 1994): 3–38.

Szatmary, David P. *Shays' Rebellion: The Making of an Agrarian Insurrection*. Amherst: University of Massachusetts Press, 1986.

Taylor, Alan. *Liberty Men and Great Proprietors: The Revolutionary Settlement on the Maine Frontier, 1760–1820*. Chapel Hill: University of North Carolina Press, for the Omohundro Institute of Early American History and Culture, 1990.

Young, Alfred F. *The American Revolution: Explorations in the History of American Radicalism*. DeKalb: Northern Illinois University Press, 1976.

18th Century RACE RELATIONS AND CONFLICT

Racial discrimination and slavery played important roles in 18th-century America. White Americans developed various arguments to justify racial discrimination, slavery, and expansion into Native American lands. In particular, they deemed Africans and Native Americans uncivilized, childlike, animal-like, or cursed by God. While efforts to institutionalize racial discrimination and slavery marked race relations in the early 18th century, the First Great Awakening and the American Revolution challenged these trends by introducing notions of universal equality based on Christian and Enlightenment beliefs.

Racial Theory and Racial Identity

From the opening of the 18th century, European Americans claimed that their ways of life were superior to those of African and Native Americans. In part, American Natives and Africans were considered uncivilized because they did not appear to cultivate the lands on which they lived or produce goods at a European standard. As such, their civilizations seemed less advanced than those of Europe. According to white Americans, African and Native American cultures had no respect for women, lacked intellectual development, and had no economic prosperity. Europeans commonly drew on religion to further validate racial discrimination and slavery, claiming that because most Africans and Native Americans were not Christians, they were inferior beings. For example, based on interpretations of scripture, Europeans argued that enslavement of Africans was justified because they supposedly descended from Ham (Cham), who according to the book of Genesis had been cursed by Ham's father, Noah.

Prior to the 18th century, the peoples from the European, American, and African continents that met in the so-called New World connected through specific ethnic, religious, and social commonalities. By the 18th century, however, American colonial society had been organized by skin color or racial background, and African, European, and Native Americans began to identify themselves along these lines. These forged identities sustained and reinforced racial divisions while bringing about new loyalties among peoples of European, Native, or African descent. Native Americans united more frequently to battle white expansion into their lands as they came to understand that they had a common enemy in the European settlers. In the 1760s, for example, the Lenni Lenape spiritual leader Neolin recognized the need for a pan-Indian collaboration that would enable Native Americans to preserve their cultures and lands.

Racism and slavery, meanwhile, served as a common experience for African descendants of various ethnic backgrounds, through which they began to identify as African Americans. People of Wolof, Bakongo, Akan, and Igbo ancestry, among others, now worked together to build communities and cultures that helped them endure oppression and in some cases resist slavery. On the other hand, whites of all social and ethnic backgrounds collaborated as the ruling race. Through institutionalized racism and slavery, those of European descent maintained privileged positions in society regardless of their social status or ethnic background. White elites benefited the most from slavery, but they secured support for the institution from poor and working-class whites, who wanted to protect their racial preeminence in colonial society.

Codifying Racism and Slavery in the Early 18th Century

Continuing the trend that had begun in the late 17th century, American slavery and racism became increasingly institutionalized in the 18th century. Planters from the West Indies who relocated in the North American colonies first introduced slave codes that had been used in the English Caribbean. Colonies across North America adopted codes that institutionalized slavery, controlled the movements of free and enslaved blacks, regulated manumissions, limited African Americans' legal rights, and forbade interracial marriages. Though these laws mostly affected African descendants, they generally pertained to both African and Native Americans.

Slave codes generally deemed slaves to be capital or property, and they usually barred slaves from owning property themselves. Other laws limited the movement and rights of enslaved Africans. In most colonies, slaves needed permission from their master to leave the plantation, and neither enslaved nor free blacks could testify in court against whites. In fact, slaves had hardly any protection from the law, while slaveholders had the right to punish or discipline their slaves at their own discretion. As early as 1700, New York's governing council instituted a curfew for enslaved blacks and prohibited more than three African American slaves from congregating together. A 1735 South Carolina act even determined what slaves could wear. To avoid having slaves demand manumission if they converted to Christianity (based on the New Testament assertion that all are equal in Christ), colonies implemented laws stipulating that slaves who converted did not automatically become free. In Virginia, for instance, "An act concerning Servants and Slaves" of 1705 determined that slavery and Christianity did not conflict, and New York implemented a similar law in 1706.

Colonial governments also passed laws regulating the lives of free blacks. South Carolina and Georgia, in 1740 and 1755, respectively, determined that blacks were considered slaves unless they could prove otherwise. Because free blacks were often considered instigators, slaveholders tried to limit the number of free blacks in their communities. New York City began to restrict manumissions in 1712 when it determined that a slaveholder who chose to manumit a slave had to post a bond of 200 pounds and guarantee that the manumitted person could take care of her- or himself. A 1735 South Carolina act determined that privately manumitted slaves had to leave the colony within six months of their manumission, and they were not allowed to return to the colony for at least seven years. If a slave did not abide by these restrictions, he or she risked being reenslaved by the public treasurer. Pennsylvania's 1725–26 "Act for Better Regulation of Negroes" implemented restrictions on manumissions, and free blacks who appeared to spend their time loitering risked temporary or lifelong enslavement.

Laws circumscribed the lives and movements of free African Americans in other ways as well. Statutes prevented free blacks from holding real estate, voting, and holding political office. Colonies also restricted free blacks from certain occupations: New York City, for example, prohibited blacks from selling oysters in a 1715 act. Moreover, most colonies kept African Americans from carrying arms and entering military service. When African Americans were allowed to join local militias, they were often assigned the lowest-level tasks.

Race relations in the French and Spanish colonies developed differently than they did in the British colonies due to the French and Spanish cultures and laws, and because these colonies did not develop a plantation economy until the latter part of the 18th century. In these colonies, African descendants had more opportunities to obtain their freedom and advance socially and economically. Free people of African descent in both Louisiana and Florida were allowed to hold property and testify in courts. Spanish authorities at times encouraged manumission and often depended on free people of color to settle their colonies. The French Black Code, or *Code noir*, required slaveholders to baptize slaves and give them time off on Sundays and religious holidays; moreover, slaves could marry each other, an act that English planters often prohibited, and husband, wife, and young children could not be separated through sale.

American racial inequality and slavery were predominantly maintained through force, the threat of violence, and legal codes, but European descendants also sustained racial divisions and racial supremacy in other cultural and social ways. For example, celebrations such as Election Day, most commonly celebrated in the English colonies, and the Dutch-American Pinkster celebration helped secure the hierarchical societies. In particular, the practice of role reversal or inversion, in which those who were in power allowed those in lower social positions to have absolute authority for a short period, had an important function in these New

World traditions. Giving temporary freedom and symbolic power to enslaved men and women secured order and stability because slaves would be careful not to jeopardize this temporary freedom. White Americans also maintained their hierarchical societies through ideas of paternalism. As part of their efforts to "civilize" African descendants, white men took on the role of patriarch, exercising autocratic control over an extended family that included their children, wives, and black slaves. Paternalism allowed a slaveholder to feel like a benevolent patriarch, caring for his slaves by feeding, housing, and disciplining them, all for the good of the slaves who allegedly were not able to take care of themselves.

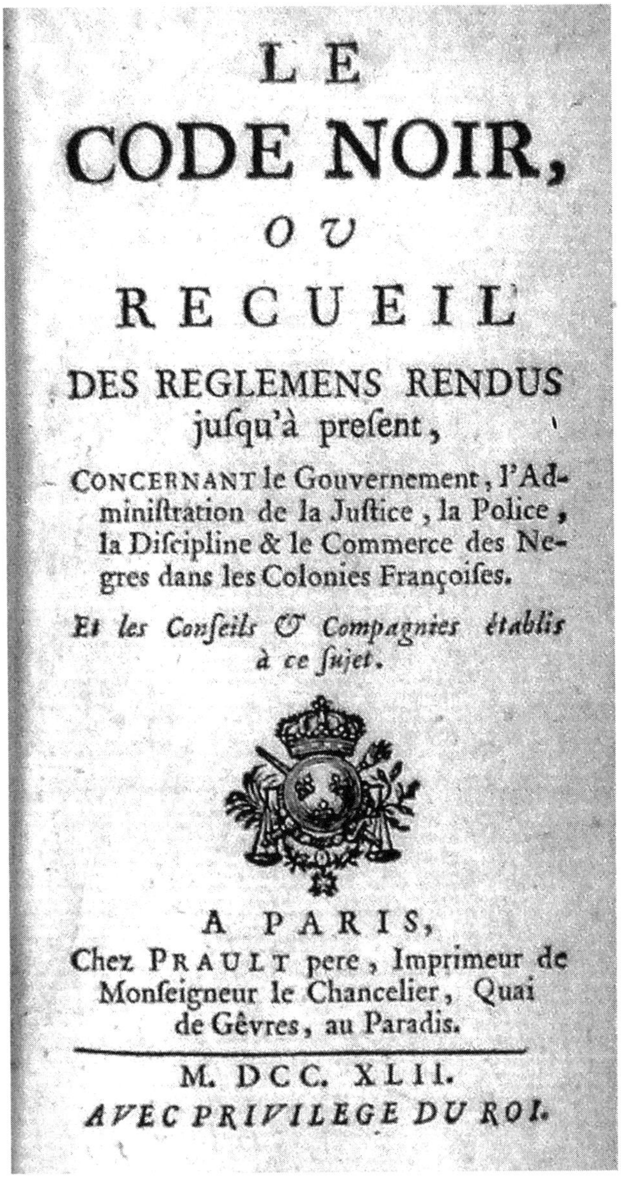

LE

CODE NOIR,

OU

RECUEIL

DES REGLEMENS RENDUS
juſqu'à preſent,

CONCERNANT le Gouvernement, l'Adminiſtration de la Juſtice, la Police, la Diſcipline & le Commerce des Negres dans les Colonies Françoiſes.

Et les Conſeils & Compagnies établis à ce ſujet.

A PARIS,
Chez PRAULT pere, Imprimeur de Monſeigneur le Chancelier, Quai de Gêvres, au Paradis.

M. DCC. XLII.
AVEC PRIVILEGE DU ROI.

Race relations in the French and Spanish colonies were markedly different from practices in the British colonies due to cultural, legal, and economic differences. Although the *Code noir*, or Black Code—a decree passed by the French king Louis XIV defining the conditions of slavery in the French colonial empire—placed restrictions upon free blacks, it also required slaveholders to baptize their slaves and give them Sundays and religious holidays off. Above is the 1742 edition of the *Code noir*. *(Palais du Luxembourg exhibit)*

Interracial Relationships

In North America's British colonies, interracial sexual relationships were often considered scandalous, and in many places they were outlawed. Virginia prohibited interracial marriages in 1705, Pennsylvania deemed interracial relationships illegal in a 1725–26 law, and Georgia proscribed such marriages in 1750. Nevertheless, sexual relations between Americans of all ethnic backgrounds occurred regularly. Although many of these unions were voluntary, black women often endured sexual intimidation or outright sexual abuse from their white masters or overseers. Because children inherited the slave status of their mother, relationships with enslaved women proved particularly beneficial to slaveholders, who would hold the legal rights to any children that came out of such sexual exploitation.

In most British colonies, a white-black racial binary created a situation in which African descendants, regardless of any European ancestry, were always considered black. Such a racial dichotomy did not exist in the Spanish and French colonies, where children of partial European descent often held privileged positions over people of full African or Native American parentage. In fact, miscegenation was not uncommon and generally accepted in Spanish and French colonies, where white fathers of mixed-race children more commonly acknowledged their offspring. Moreover, French and Spanish settlers frequently intermarried with Native American women to establish close connections with local Native tribes, or as a way to resolve the sexual imbalance that generally existed in the early European settlements of Florida and Louisiana.

Relations between Native and African Americans were as complex and diverse as those between Europeans and nonwhites. Some runaway slaves found refuge among American Indians, and some Native people were enslaved alongside Africans. In both these situations, close relationships existed among the two groups, sometimes leading to intermarriage. On the other hand, certain Native American nations agreed to return runaway slaves that entered Native lands to their white masters. The Five (and later Six) Nation Iroquois, for example, signed treaties with English colonial authorities in which they promised to return any refugee slaves they encountered in their territory.

Conflict

Slavery and racism were not accepted without resistance from Native and African Americans. Individuals challenged these institutions and America's racially organized society through arson, larceny, judicial activism, or outright revolt. The New York Slave Revolt of 1712 and the Stono Rebellion in South Carolina in 1739 were the most threatening to the slave system. In both of these rebellions, enslaved Africans killed whites, but neither of the revolts led to a successful escape from slavery or an overthrowing of the institution. In fact, these rebellions led authorities to impose stricter slave codes and to respond aggressively to any rumor of slave conspiracy.

Native Americans reacted to European expansion rather than racial discrimination. When Native American nations united, like the Five Nation Iroquois, they had greater power to negotiate and trade with whites and resist European expansion into their lands. The Ottawa leader Pontiac, for example, led a pan-Indian resistance movement against British expansion, generally known as Pontiac's Rebellion (1763–66). While this revolt proved that a combined Native American effort could challenge colonial forces, Pontiac did eventually sign a peace treaty with his opponents.

Midcentury Challenges to Racial Inequality

In the mid-18th century, religious revivals began to spread throughout the British colonies. Inspirational preachers such as Theodore Frelinghuysen, Gilbert Tennent, Jonathan Edwards, and George Whitefield led this religious awakening, known as the First Great Awakening. Through emotional and energetic preaching, these evangelists touched hundreds of thousands of Americans, whether they were of European, African, or Native American descent. The religious awakening centered on the message of equality and pluralism, which resonated in particular with poor whites and African and Native Americans. Revivals were open to people of all social and racial backgrounds, and anyone could experience a religious awakening. Consequently, numerous African and Native Americans converted to Christianity during this period, and Native and African American preachers like Samson Occom, David George, and Harry Hosier ("Black Harry") became well-respected preachers for both black and white audiences.

Although the evangelical message of equality before God held great significance during the awakening, black and Native converts were not necessarily treated as equals by their white Christian brothers and sisters. Black men and women attending sermons often had to listen from the church gallery or even from outside the church. In fact, many of the key figures of the Great Awakening never spoke out against slavery, and several owned slaves. While evangelism did not end racism and slavery in the American colonies, the growing inclusion of African and Native Americans in Christian churches did have significant effects on American race relations. Articulate Christian converts such as Phillis Wheatley, James Albert Ukawsaw Gronniosaw, Jupiter Hammon, and Samson Occom demonstrated to white Americans that Native and African Americans were not necessarily heathens or unintelligent. At the same time, some religious groups began to openly challenge slavery and racism. American Quakers, for example, sought to end both slavery and warfare against Indians because these practices conflicted with their religious beliefs. The majority of the Quakers saw the abolition of slavery as a Christian obligation, and at their annual meeting in 1758, the Pennsylvania Quakers decided to prohibit its members from owning slaves.

The religious revivals did not reach the Catholic Spanish and French colonies. Moreover, it was not until the Second Great Awakening in the late 18th and early 19th centuries that enslaved blacks turned to Christianity in great numbers. Southern white elites, who greatly benefited from slavery, were reluctant to endorse a religious movement that preached equality. Initially, many of these slaveholders resisted the evangelical spirit and tried to keep their slaves from the revivals out of fears that Christian slaves would be more likely to challenge their enslavement.

Race Relations in the Late 18th Century

In the years leading up to the American Revolution, republicanism began to dominate the American political discourse. Increasingly, American thinkers and politicians emphasized values such as liberty and rights for all people. The principles that all people had unalienable rights and the legitimacy to fight tyranny, as expressed in the Declaration of Independence, not only spurred American resistance to British colonial rule but also challenged American race relations. Inspired by the Revolutionary spirit, several African American slaves in Massachusetts requested manumission. A number of slaves in Boston petitioned for their freedom in 1773, and several years later Mum Bett (1781) and Quock Walker (1783) challenged their enslavement in court, citing Article 1 of the new Massachusetts constitution: "All men are born free and equal, and have certain natural, essential, and unalienable rights." Their efforts helped bring slavery to an end in Massachusetts in 1783, making it the first state to abolish slavery.

The claim in the Declaration of Independence that "all men are created equal" also motivated free African Americans to resist racial discrimination. In 1787, for example, a group of black Bostonians demanded education equal to that of whites. That same year, black Freemasons under the leadership of Prince Hall received permission from a British lodge to establish their own African Masonic lodge, a request that had been denied by white American Masons. Evidently, the republican ideals did not permeate all parts of society, and African American men and women still encountered racial discrimination on a daily basis, regardless of the Revolutionary rhetoric. In fact, one of the key revolutionary figures, Thomas Jefferson, who himself held slaves, wrote in *Notes on the State of Virginia* (1787) that descendants of Africans were inferior to whites.

The Second Great Awakening

Like the First Great Awakening, revivals of the Second Great Awakening, which began in the 1790s, attracted people of all social and ethnic backgrounds. This time, however, Christian churches admitted black Americans in far greater numbers than was the case in the earlier awakening. Baptist and Methodist denominations repealed their antislavery decrees in the late 18th century, eliminating the main objections that kept southern slaveholders and their slaves from joining these denominations. Slaveholders now often used slave baptisms to justify slavery, using scripture to validate slavery and convince their slaves that they should be faithful to their masters. In some instances, white Americans converted their slaves to Christianity as a way to defend slavery: By giving them access to the Christian religion, these Africans received spiritual liberation in return for their physical enslavement. Though American churches now more commonly included African Americans, most denominations condoned slavery and racism, and churches usually separated black churchgoers from the rest of the congregation.

Still, while Massachusetts abolished slavery, and other northern states, such as Pennsylvania, New York, and New Jersey, passed gradual emancipation laws, slavery in most southern states actually hardened in the late 18th century. In fact, the federal Constitution of 1787 further reinforced slavery with the "three-fifths compromise," which determined that slaves counted toward a state's population as three-fifths of a person. Moreover, slavery expanded in many of the southern states because new developments in sugar and cotton production, such as Eli Whitney's 1793 invention of an improved cotton gin, made the use of slave labor even more lucrative for white planters. The expansion of plantation economies into Florida and Louisiana caused a greater dependence on slave labor in these regions, and race relations in these regions consequently deteriorated.

In slaveholding states, tensions in race relations intensified as a result of the Haitian Revolution (1791–1804), which was the first slave revolt to successfully overthrow a government. Slaveholders always feared the possibility of slave rebellion, and the Haitian Revolution demonstrated that this fear could become a reality. Thus, planters in North America became increasingly worried that news of the rebellion might inspire their slaves to imitate the Haitians and revolt. In Louisiana, where many refugees from Haiti (French Saint-Domingue) settled with their slaves after the revolt broke out, planters suspected that the Pointe Coupee slave conspiracy of 1795 had been inspired by the Haitian Revolution. Such stories of Caribbean instigators led many slaveholding states to become careful in admitting slaves from the West Indies.

A Century of Racial Intolerance

Race relations in 18th-century America were marked by racial discrimination, slavery, and European expansionism, though the Great Awakenings and the American Revolution challenged notions of racial inequality. As a result of these changes in American thought, religion, and society, African and Native American conditions temporarily improved, but by the late 18th century it became clear that white Americans were not ready to accept nonwhites as their equals. Economic as well as social motives led white Americans to maintain racial discrimination in America's laws and society well into the 20th century.

—Andrea C. Mosterman

Further Reading

Berlin, Ira. *Many Thousands Gone: The First Two Centuries of Slavery in North America.* Cambridge, Mass.: Belknap Press of Harvard University Press, 1998.

Brown, Kathleen. *Good Wives, Nasty Wenches, and Anxious Patriarchs: Gender, Race, and Power in Colonial Virginia.* Chapel Hill: University of North Carolina Press, 1996.

Colburn, David R., and Jane L. Landers, eds. *The African American Heritage of Florida.* Gainesville: University Press of Florida, 1995.

Dowd, Gregory Evans. *War under Heaven: Pontiac, the Indian Nations, and the British Empire.* Baltimore, Md.: Johns Hopkins University Press, 2002.

Durant, Thomas J., Jr., and J. David Knottnerus, eds. *Plantation Society and Race Relations: The Origins of Inequality.* Westport, Conn.: Praeger, 1999.

Fischer, Kirsten. *Suspect Relations: Sex, Race, and Resistance in Colonial North Carolina.* Ithaca, N.Y.: Cornell University Press, 2002.

Foote, Thelma Wills. *Black and White Manhattan: The History of Racial Formation in Colonial New York City.* New York: Oxford University Press, 2004.

Gellman, David N. *Emancipating New York: The Politics of Slavery and Freedom, 1777–1827.* Baton Rouge: Louisiana State University Press, 2006.

Gomez, Michael A. *Exchanging Our Country Marks: The Transformation of African Identities in the Colonial and Antebellum South.* Chapel Hill: University of North Carolina Press, 1998.

Higginbotham, A. Leon, Jr. *In the Matter of Color: Race and the American Legal Process; The Colonial Period.* New York: Oxford University Press, 1978.

Isaac, Rhys. *The Transformation of Virginia, 1740–1790.* Chapel Hill: University of North Carolina Press, 1982.

Jordan, Winthrop D. *White over Black: American Attitudes toward the Negro, 1550–1812.* Chapel Hill: University of North Carolina Press, 1968.

Nash, Gary B., and Graham Russell Gao Hodges. *Friends of Liberty: Thomas Jefferson, Tadeusz Kociuszko, and Agrippa Hull; A Tale of Three Patriots, Two Revolutions, and a Tragic Betrayal of Freedom.* New York: Basic Books, 2008.

Parent, Anthony S., Jr. *Foul Means: The Formation of a Slave Society in Virginia, 1660–1740.* Chapel Hill: University of North Carolina Press, 2003.

Richter, Daniel K. *Facing East from Indian Country: A Native History of Early America.* Cambridge, Mass.: Harvard University Press, 2003.

Saeger, James Schofield, ed. *Essays on Eighteenth-Century Race Relations in the Americas.* Bethlehem, Pa.: Lawrence Henry Gipson Institute, 1987.

Spear, Jennifer M. *Race, Sex, and Social Order in Early New Orleans.* Baltimore, Md.: Johns Hopkins University Press, 2009.

Sweet, John Wood. *Bodies Politic: Negotiating Race in the American North, 1730–1830.* Baltimore, Md.: Johns Hopkins University Press, 2003.

White, Richard. *The Middle Ground: Indians, Empires, and Republics in the Great Lakes Region, 1650–1815.* Cambridge, U.K.: Cambridge University Press, 1991.

18th Century RELIGION

During the 18th century, American religious beliefs and practices underwent significant change, as the continent witnessed dramatic population growth, the development of new theologies, and the founding of the United States. In 1700, religion in North America reflected the preceding century's settlement patterns. Most Euro-Americans worshipped in state-supported churches, with religious affiliation largely mirroring ethnic identity. Along the Eastern Seaboard, English Congregationalists, the descendants of 17th-century Puritans, inhabited New England and eastern Long Island. Dutch Reformed and English Anglican residents of New York and East Jersey shared territory with a variety of other smaller communities. English and Welsh Quakers dominated West Jersey, Pennsylvania, and Delaware, alongside some Swedish Lutherans. The Anglican church claimed the largest number of adherents in the colonies from Maryland south to South Carolina, though populations of dissenting (i.e., non-Anglican) Protestants and Catholics were also present. Catholic empires bracketed the English coastal establishments. The Spanish to the south and the French to the north and west stirred English North Americans with a sense of fear and unified them around the idea that they were part of a Protestant empire.

The continent's African residents, nearly all enslaved, practiced the faiths they had brought with them from their homelands. More than a century of enslavement and close contact with Europeans had brought relatively few conversions to Christianity, as masters were wary that baptisms of those they held in bondage might compromise slavery both legally and ethically. Most Africans, for their part, had little to gain from conversion to Christianity. Native Americans, on the other hand, had been the targets of significant missionary efforts during the 17th century, most notably French Jesuits in Canada and the Great Lakes region and Spanish Franciscans in the Southwest. Protestant efforts had been largely unsuccessful, though small numbers of Indians had become Christian, particularly in New England. In 1700, more than a century into the European colonial project and despite deep and sustained contact among diverse peoples, most North Americans practiced the faiths of their ancestors in ways that would have been familiar to those progenitors.

By 1800, the religious culture of the new United States had changed considerably. The 18th century saw the development of four major American religious trends, all of which had consequences for religion in the United States for centuries to come. First, Protestant Christianity, the faith of the vast majority of British North American colonists, developed more-effective institutional structures as denominational communities increased their presence and effectiveness along the Eastern Seaboard. Second, two new and related religious movements, evangelicalism and the Enlightenment, fractured the Protestant community so that religious diversity existed not only where it was fostered by ever-growing ethnic diversity, such as in the Mid-Atlantic region, but also within communities dominated by British Americans, such as New England and the Chesapeake. Third, Protestant missionaries to enslaved African Americans in British America and the Caribbean saw the beginnings of Afro-Protestantism take root. Finally, some American Indian communities experienced a wave of Nativist revivals that responded to Europeans' incursions, even as others who had become part of Christian communities developed new, Native Christianities. Last, the American Revolution and the subsequent adoption of the U.S. Constitution in 1789 fundamentally reshaped the relationship between religion and government that had existed in the colonial era.

Building Religious Institutions

The 18th century witnessed what the scholar Jon Butler has called a process of "Christianization." Beginning at the end of the 17th century and in the first quarter of the 18th century, British North Americans embarked on a sustained project of religious building. This process included both laying literal foundations for houses of worship and building up a ministerial and denominational establishment that in many places had been quite sparse. In Virginia, for example, Anglican church buildings increased from around 35 in 1680 to 61 in 1724. In 1702, Maryland legally established the Church of England, as did North and South Carolina (in forms that gave a variety of rights to Protestants who dissented from the Anglican church). New York, too, moved toward state sponsorship of religion, though it tolerated a greater variety of faiths.

In New England, the Congregational heritage of 17th-century Puritanism ensured that each jurisdiction had an established Protestant church. An early sign that religious unity was dissolving, however, came in the form of greater Anglican presence. Boston saw its first Anglican congregation in 1686, and over the next 90 years its small but well-connected congregation grew steadily. A second Anglican church was founded in the old Puritan capital in 1723, and a third in 1735. More dramatic growth for the Church of England occurred in New Haven in 1722, when the "Yale Apostasy" saw the conversion of Yale College's rector, Timothy Cutler, and several other divines from New England's Calvinist orthodoxy to the Church of England and to Arminianism, a more liberal theology in which humans, rather than God, play a dominant role in their own salvation. The event, which had a powerful effect on a young Jonathan Edwards (1703–58), the 18th-century's most important American theologian, signaled the growth of liberal and cosmopolitan views within erstwhile Puritan communities.

As New England and the southern colonies witnessed institutional growth and establishment within the Church of England, the increasing immigration of Scottish Presbyterians and Continental Protestants led to the gradual development of new denominational structures, generally centered in the Mid-Atlantic region. The first American Presbyterian organization was formed in Philadelphia in 1706, although it drew member congregations from as far away as Long Island, incorporating former Puritans as well as Scottish colonists. As more Scottish and Scots-Irish migrated to the Mid-Atlantic, however, the denomination expanded rapidly. By 1716 there were three presbyteries. Over the next decades the Presbyterian church continued to grow in structure and numbers, if not often in harmony. Divisions arose within the new polities over approving ministers and subscription to the Westminster Confession.

Immigration of foreign Protestants increased the continent's diversity in other ways as well. German sectarians had begun moving to Pennsylvania in response to William Penn's welcome in the late 17th century. Germantown, founded in 1683 just outside Philadelphia, included Mennonites as well as German Pietists, who emphasized personal piety and a strong devotional life. These early migrations were dwarfed, however, by the large numbers of German Lutherans and German Reformed who migrated to the region beginning in the 1720s. The European state churches were slow to organize ministerial oversight for these migrants, many of whom arrived as indentured servants. Only in the 1730s and 1740s did leaders such as John Philip Boehm and Michael Schlatter (German Reformed) and Henry Melchior Muhlenberg (German Lutheran) successfully bring some measure of institutional order to these communities.

As Euro-Americans used institutional means to lend structure to their religious lives in new and rapidly evolving colonial situations, African Americans faced similar challenges, but with far fewer tools in their control. In the first decades of the 18th century, the African slave trade brought tens of thousands of new slaves to the Chesapeake and Lower South. The percentage of enslaved workers born in Africa, as opposed to the Caribbean or North America, soared, so that in 1700 the newly arrived accounted for 90 percent of the Chesapeake's African population. Africans, of course, came from diverse backgrounds and possessed a wide variety of religious customs. Some were Muslims; others had little prior contact with Abrahamic faiths. In North America, enslaved Africans faced the same difficulties as other migrants, such as the loss of a coherent religious community and the difficulty or impossibility of performing certain vital rituals in a foreign environment, but widespread Christianization did not begin until the end of the 18th century. Euro-Americans and newly arrived Africans shared little in terms of cultural context, and because Christianization might be seen as grounds for emancipation, missionary work among slaves was infrequent and discouraged throughout most of the century.

Great Awakening and Revival

The pivot point of 18th-century religion in North America was the Great Awakening. Beginning in the late 1720s and reaching its peak in the 1740s, this series of revivals, conversions, and religious controversies over issues such as the rights of itinerant preachers and emotion (or "enthusiasm") in religious experience marked a high point in religious energy in colonial America. The movement found deep resonance in New England, where the gradual flagging of Puritanism had left a feeling of spiritual malaise. Cycles of religious renewal in the region, sometimes linked to external events, such as the earthquake of 1727, prepared believers for the theology of the "new birth," in which individuals experienced a moment of conversion or awakening and felt they had been "born again" in Christ, and the practice of revivalism. A strong emphasis on these elements of religious experience would later form the basis for "evangelical" Protestantism.

The Puritan tradition in New England provided one cultural context for the revivalism of the Great Awakening, but equally important were Continental Pietists who sought to reinvigorate religious experience throughout the Protestant world. Many German Pietists in particular found fertile territory among the Mid-Atlantic's German speakers. Following the theologian Philipp Jakob Spener's emphasis on small prayer groups, or conventicles, in which an individual would strive for a deeper religious experience culminating in the "new birth," religious activists began striving for a general awakening. Highly mobile communities, particularly the Halle Pietists and the Renewed Moravian Church, led by Count Nikolaus Ludwig von Zinzendorf, connected fellow believers in Europe, Great Britain, and North America.

At the height of the revivals, itinerant preachers, adept in bringing great crowds to a crescendo of spiritual excitement and emotion, traveled throughout the countryside, often preaching outdoors when no traditional meeting place was available or sufficient. The most memorable of these preachers, George Whitefield, journeyed tirelessly throughout both Great Britain and British North America. Great crowds appeared wherever Whitefield preached, helped in no small measure by an active publishing and publicity agenda. Equally important to the long-term development of American religion was the preaching and writing of Jonathan Edwards, whose 1734–35 revival in Northampton, Massachusetts, is often seen as an early high point of the Great Awakening in America. Edwards's deep and thoughtful Calvinism ran counter to the Arminianism he saw evident in the Yale Apostasy and on the rise more generally in the Protestant world. Yet he believed in the value of emotional preaching and revivalism as a part of religious experience, and as the revivals

Itinerant preachers played a large part in propagating the revivalist spirit, traveling from town to town, visiting small communities, and often preaching outdoors. George Whitefield (above) was an evangelist who did missionary work in the colony of Georgia in 1738 and spent his career traveling and evangelizing throughout the American colonies as well as in Scotland, Ireland, Wales, and England. ***(Library of Congress)***

became more and more controversial, he was one of the revivalists' most effective polemicists. On the opposite side, Boston's Charles Chauncy, a Congregationalist, argued that revivalism led to spiritual lawlessness (antinomianism) and dangerous enthusiasm.

Revivalism was equally popular, and equally controversial, within the Presbyterian community. Scottish communion fairs formed a third major antecedent for the revivals, alongside Continental Pietism and the heritage of Puritanism in New England, and Scottish immigrants therefore arrived with a cultural context for the awakening, including experience with emotional, outdoor preaching. Revivalists found some of their greatest successes in regions where there were large numbers of Scottish settlers, especially New Jersey's Raritan Valley. The Dutch Reformed minister Theodore Jacob Frelinghuysen spread the teaching of European Pietism there beginning in the 1720s. In 1726 the Presbyterian minister William Tennent founded a school known as the Log College, in Bucks County, Pennsylvania, where he trained ministers, including his sons, in an "experimental" religion that was conducive to revival. His son Gilbert became a prominent revivalist and leader of the "New Side" faction of Presbyterians, who were sympathetic to the revivals and to itinerant preaching. "Old Side" Presbyterians resisted these innovations, as had many congregations and divines in Congregationalist New England, and though the Presbyterian polity reunited in 1758, an underlying tension between revivalist (or evangelical) and conservative Presbyterians remained.

By the mid-1750s, much of the early revivalist fervor had abated. Jonathan Edwards was dismissed from his pastorate in Northampton in 1750 after a conflict with congregants. George Whitefield continued to travel and preach until his death in 1770, but the dramatic gatherings that marked his 1740 trip were replaced by a quieter trend of denominational growth among evangelicals that foreshadowed the more striking growth of the Methodists and Baptists in the century's final decade. Nonetheless, the Great Awakening, influenced by the Calvinist Edwards and, in subsequent decades, the teachings of the Arminian and Methodist John Wesley, ushered in significant shifts in the theologies and religious practices of British North America's Christians. The movement's long-term outcome, the rise of American evangelicalism, makes it among the most significant of 18th-century cultural developments.

Native Americans embarked on a parallel movement of revival during the mid-18th century, as Native communities coped with the consequences of prolonged engagement with Europeans, including steep demographic decline, persistent warfare, sporadic missionary efforts, and economic dislocation. A new form of religious teaching developed, particularly in those areas that were home to multiethnic Indian communities, the result of dislocation in earlier tribal settlement patterns. A series of prophets, most notably the Delaware Neolin in Pennsylvania's Susquehanna Valley, taught that Europeans and Indians came from separate creations, and that Indians needed to end their dependence on Europeans and return to their native ways. This theology found wide acceptance among many Indian groups, and it formed a basis for efforts at unified resistance to whites, such as that led by the Shawnee prophet, Tenskwatawa, and his brother Tecumseh, in the Great Lakes region in the beginning of the 19th century. Meanwhile, renewed Protestant missionary work among Indians, led by the Moravians in the Mid-Atlantic and also including the work of David Brainerd and Jonathan Edwards, encouraged the growth of Christian Indian communities.

The Enlightenment and Religion

The second half of the 18th century also saw the influence of liberal and Enlightenment thinking in American religious circles, particularly in New England and among the social elite. Characterized by faith in human reason, moral sensibility, and a belief in the importance of natural (as opposed to scriptural) revelation, these trends manifested in the formation of Unitarian and Deist circles, while even the strict Calvinist Jonathan Edwards found himself strongly influenced by the writings of some of the Enlightenment's principle British thinkers: John Locke and David Hume. Theological liberals in North America drew strength from anti-revivalism, rejecting "enthusiasm" in religion and placing a rational approach to faith and Christian living at the center of their theology. Many also challenged the traditional Calvinist conception of a wrathful and supremely powerful God, emphasizing instead human moral agency, God's benevolence, and, for some, universal salvation of humanity. Gradually, challenges to traditional conceptions of the Trinity also emerged, centered at the Anglican King's Chapel in Boston and at Harvard University. By the end of the century, these hearths had formed the basis for a much wider Unitarian movement and, eventually, denomination in New England.

The religious perspective most closely associated with the era of the American Revolution is Deism, though it may be understood more properly as a philosophy than a religion. Deists took the position that human reason was sufficient for understanding the world and for understanding God, therefore removing the need for scriptural revelation. Deism's life span was shorter than that of its liberal cousin, Unitarianism, but its influence on some of the nation's founders has led to its lasting impact. Nonetheless, although such key figures as Benjamin Franklin and Thomas Jefferson were Deists in intellectual outlook, the appellation never referred to an effective denominational organization, and neither man claimed it as a religious identity. By the end of the century, Deism's rationalism had been linked to antireligion, not least through the writings of Thomas Paine, and also to the radicalism of the French Revolution, bringing it into disfavor in American religious circles.

Deism was a philosophy that held that religious knowledge exists in every person and can be accessed through the use of reason, not through scriptural revelation or church teaching. The avowed Deist Thomas Paine (above), who wrote that Christianity was "a fable," believed in a supreme being but as his tract *The Age of Reason* makes clear, he strongly opposed organized religion. *(Library of Congress)*

Religion and the Revolution

The majority of Euro-Americans worshipped in congregations that received some sort of government support in the late colonial period. During the era of the American Revolution, however, issues surrounding the relationship between state and church became increasingly important to the political troubles brewing between the British North American colonies and England. After the Seven Years' War, controversy over the potential appointment of an Anglican bishop for the British North American colonies made North Americans jealously protective of their religious freedoms, particularly from encroachment by the Crown. In the preceding decades, the Anglican hierarchy had grown frustrated with the ecclesiastical disorder in the American provinces that had resulted from the absence of a local bishop in so large a region. Some clergy and members of the Church of England in the colonies wearied of having to send candidates for ordination to England. Moreover, as the Anglican church increased its presence in the colonies, this disability became more cumbersome, though some Anglicans, particularly in the South, enjoyed the privileges that came with a local lay-led church establishment.

The potential for an Anglican bishop met with the greatest opposition in New England, however, where the established Congregationalists worried that a greater Anglican establishment would curtail their freedoms. The Revolutionary War ultimately eliminated the possibility of a bishop who reported to Canterbury, but while it raged, the storm served to heighten Americans' worries over their religious freedoms and to increase their distrust of the larger British imperial structure. Those worries surfaced again with the passage of the Quebec Act in 1774, a provision that allowed Catholics in recently conquered French Canada to continue to worship as they had before the war. For Protestants in those colonies that were on the verge of rebellion, the act joined the "popish" menace with the specter of British imperial tyranny, spurring on the Revolutionary cause.

Issues of church and state played a role in the Revolutionary crises, and the most important innovation of the Revolutionary era for American religion came in that arena as well. The reality of religious diversity, which existed in all of the new United States, made the establishment of a single religion at the federal level a near impossibility in practical terms. For pragmatic and philosophical reasons, the federal Constitution of 1787 was intentionally mute on nearly all religious issues (save for barring religious tests for office holding), and the First Amendment stated, "Congress shall make no law respecting an establishment of religion, or prohibiting the free exercise thereof." These 16 words transformed the environment in which Americans of all religious traditions built their lives. Although it would be several decades before all of the individual states eliminated their religious establishments, the ratification of the Constitution and the Bill of Rights accelerated the trend toward disestablishing religion at all levels.

The idea that church and state ought to be separated had a long heritage in British North America before 1787. In the 17th century, as the colonies were being founded, New England's Puritans had prohibited ministers from holding public office, Rhode Island's Roger Williams had established freedom of religion in order to keep churches pure of the taint of state meddling, and William Penn's "Holy Experiment" had explicitly embraced religious freedom and welcomed immigrants, leading to a cacophonous diversity. A century later, in the 1760s and 1770s, the establishment of religion in Anglican Virginia had become a source of political strife. Evangelicals (principally Baptists and Presbyterians) sought freedom from the burdens of the colony's taxes and vestries, which they believed were linked to a sinful and dissolute elite culture, while committed Anglicans argued for the religious establishment as the basis for a community's shared morality. Although legislation passed in 1776 eliminated the requirement that dissenting Protestants (Protestants who dissented from the Anglican establishment) pay to support the Anglican church, dissenters were still required to pay for schools. This requirement led to a lengthy legal battle, the outcome of which was an alliance between evangelicals—who wanted the state out of religious matters—and elites who were sympathetic to the Enlightenment position that religion ought to be kept apart from state matters. The resulting 1786 Statute for Religious Freedom, written by Jefferson and guided through the Virginia legislature by James Madison, provided a model for the Constitution's framers.

Evangelical Growth

In the last decades of the 18th century and the first decades of the 19th, American religious demography was transformed by two related developments: the dramatic growth of the evangelical denominations (Methodists and Baptists) and the beginnings of widespread Christianization among African Americans. The first trend, the spread of evangelical denominations, reflected the denominational maturation of the revival movements of the first half of the century. Southerners, in particular, were drawn into new Baptist, Methodist, and, to a lesser degree, Presbyterian organizations, in large part because of the collapse of the established Anglican church in that region after the end of the Revolutionary War. These denominations also proved particularly mobile, and they spread rapidly into frontier regions to the west of colonial settlements. The Methodists provide the best example. Francis Asbury, the leader of that church in America during the final decades of the 18th century, presided over a system that was at once flexible and organized. He assigned traveling ministers called "circuit riders" to rural congregations, enabling a relatively small number of pastors to serve large numbers of congregants. In 1771, there were about 300 Methodists in British North America. In 1816, when Asbury died, the denomination claimed more than 200,000 adherents in the United States.

The Baptist story was less organized and more decentralized. Baptist missionaries from New England began working in the South during the 1750s. By the era of the

Revolution, Baptists had become a significant voice in the southern religious landscape, a development that accelerated with the end of the Revolution and the movement of southerners westward into the Appalachian Mountains. The historian Christine Leigh Heyrman has calculated that the white membership of the three largest evangelical denominations in the South—the Methodists, Baptists, and Presbyterians—leapt from 36,378 in 1776 to 95,343 in 1790, and then to 238,255 in 1813.

As evangelicalism was spreading rapidly among whites, Christianity also began to take hold among African Americans. Afro-Protestantism developed as a result of missionary endeavors from whites, and also through leadership within the black community, as Christianity began to provide a venue for organized community life within slave society. But Christianity developed slowly among blacks. Evangelical religion, with its emphasis on the unifying experience of the new birth, contained an egalitarian and leveling impulse, and this had motivated some evangelists to direct their attentions to the enslaved as early as the 1730s. Preaching to slaves was unpopular among many masters, however, and enslaved Africans, many of whom were newly arrived from Africa, resisted the foreign tradition in favor of African religious practices throughout much of the 18th century. By 1785 the expanding evangelical denominations were seeking new adherents, and they turned again to African Americans. Some masters were now receptive to their efforts, and in 1790, 28 percent of Virginia Baptists and 21 percent of Virginia Methodists were black. These souls sometimes took positions of leadership within integrated churches, even occasionally ministering to whites. White denominational leaders, however, moved carefully between supporting a theology of spiritual equality, accepting the reality of slaveholding, and maintaining integrated communities.

By the end of the century, the white-led denominations had defined slavery as a political rather than a religious issue, and they therefore declined to mount a protest to the institution. Although southern evangelical denominations continued to count blacks as members throughout the antebellum period, African American Christians also founded new, separate congregations. Notable among these was the Bethel Church for Negro Methodists, founded in Philadelphia in 1793 by Richard Allen. This church later became a founding part of the African Methodist Episcopal (AME) Church. In the slave South, Christianization also continued among African Americans outside of the churches. African Americans developed a distinctive Christian practice beyond the control of the white community, incorporating many elements of African culture. The religious culture that developed among slaves had a lasting impact on the practice of American Christianity broadly, particularly in the South.

In August 1801, tens of thousands of evangelical Christians, representing many denominations, gathered at Cane Ridge, Kentucky, for an outdoor revival. The event signaled the start of 19th-century revivalism, but it also serves to mark how much American religion had evolved during the 18th century. Kentucky, a new member of the United States, had no religious establishment, and those places in the nation that still maintained tax-sponsored religious institutions (such as Massachusetts) were dwindling in number. The Anglican (now Episcopalian) church and the Congregationalists, so dominant among Euro-Americans in 1700, were barely present west of the Appalachians in 1800, outpaced by the more nimble Baptists, Methodists, and Presbyterians. The region's rapidly growing population was therefore predominantly evangelical, embracing the changes in Protestant religious practice that had occurred in the preceding century. While whites moved aggressively into new regions of the continent, Indians turned again to Nativist religious movements, such as those led by Tenskwatawa, the Shawnee prophet, and Handsome Lake, among the Seneca. Religion at the end of the 18th century was, if anything, a more powerful social force than it had been at the beginning, and it continued to play a pivotal and multifaceted role in the lives of Americans.

—Katherine Carté Engel

Further Reading

Ahlstrom, Sydney E. *A Religious History of the American People.* New Haven, Conn.: Yale University Press, 1972.

Andrews, Dee E. *The Methodists and Revolutionary America, 1760–1800: The Shaping of an Evangelical Culture.* Princeton, N.J.: Princeton University Press, 2000.

Bloch, Ruth H. *Visionary Republic: Millennial Themes in American Thought, 1756–1800*. Cambridge, U.K.: Cambridge University Press, 1985.

Bonomi, Patricia U. *Under the Cope of Heaven: Religion, Society, and Politics in Colonial America.* New York: Oxford University Press, 1986.

Bridenbaugh, Carl. *Mitre and Sceptre: Transatlantic Faiths, Ideas, Personalities, and Politics, 1689–1775.* New York: Oxford University Press, 1962.

Butler, Jon. *Awash in a Sea of Faith: Christianizing the American People*. Cambridge, Mass.: Harvard University Press, 1990.

Curry, Thomas J. *The First Freedoms: Church and State in America to the Passage of the First Amendment.* New York: Oxford University Press, 1986.

Dowd, Gregory Evans. *A Spirited Resistance: The North American Indian Struggle for Unity, 1745–1815.* Baltimore, Md.: Johns Hopkins University Press, 1992.

Frey, Sylvia R., and Betty Wood. *Come Shouting to Zion: African-American Protestantism in the American South and British Caribbean to 1830*. Chapel Hill: University of North Carolina Press, 1998.

Hatch, Nathan O. *The Democratization of American Christianity.* New Haven, Conn.: Yale University Press, 1989.

Heyrman, Christine Leigh. *Southern Cross: The Beginnings of the Bible Belt.* Chapel Hill: University of North Carolina Press, 1997.

Holifield, E. Brooks. *Theology in America: Christian Thought from the Age of the Puritans to the Civil War.* New Haven, Conn.: Yale University Press, 2003.

Hutson, James H. *Church and State in America: The First Two Centuries.* Cambridge, U.K.: Cambridge University Press, 2008.

Irons, Charles F. *The Origins of Proslavery Christianity: White and Black Evangelicals in Colonial and Antebellum Virginia.* Chapel Hill: University of North Carolina Press, 2008.

Isaac, Rhys. *The Transformation of Virginia, 1740–1790*. Chapel Hill: University of North Carolina Press, 1982.

Juster, Susan. *Doomsayers: Anglo-American Prophecy in the Age of Revolution*. Philadelphia: University of Pennsylvania Press, 2003.

Kidd, Thomas S. *The Great Awakening: The Roots of Evangelical Christianity in Colonial America*. New Haven, Conn.: Yale University Press, 2007.

Lambert, Frank. *Inventing the "Great Awakening."* Princeton, N.J.: Princeton University Press, 1999.

Marsden, George M. *Jonathan Edwards: A Life*. New Haven, Conn.: Yale University Press, 2003.

Noll, Mark A. *America's God: From Jonathan Edwards to Abraham Lincoln*. New York: Oxford University Press, 2002.

Schmidt, Leigh Eric. *Holy Fairs: Scotland and the Making of American Revivalism.* 2d ed. Grand Rapids, Mich.: Eerdmans, 2001.

Sobel, Mechal. *The World They Made Together: Black and White Values in Eighteenth-Century Virginia.* Princeton, N.J.: Princeton University Press, 1989.

Ward, W. R. *The Protestant Evangelical Awakening.* Cambridge, U.K.: Cambridge University Press, 1992.

Westerkamp, Marilyn J. *Triumph of the Laity: Scots-Irish Piety and the Great Awakening*, 1625–1760. New York: Oxford University Press, 1987.

Wheeler, Rachel M. *To Live upon Hope: Mohicans and Missionaries in the Eighteenth-Century Northeast.* Ithaca, N.Y.: Cornell University Press, 2008.

18th Century RIGHTS AND LIBERTIES

Eighteenth-century British Americans conceived of rights very differently than contemporary Americans do. In the early 21st century, Americans think of rights in a broad, dual sense: as both a freedom from government and as a guarantee to government-provided benefits. They also think of equality differently. They understand equality to mean not only an equal treatment under the law, but also an effort to seek equal conditions and outcomes, often using the law to achieve these goals. By contrast, 18th-century British Americans construed rights and equality much more narrowly. They considered equality in terms of an equal application of the law as subjects of colonial and imperial governments, but rarely would equality of condition have been considered a political right.

Background: The Sources of Colonists' Rights and Liberties

In British North America in the 18th century, the sources of rights and liberties were tied to English common law, as well as to political events in 17th-century England. English common law (judge-made law) provided liberties acknowledged and protected through court decisions and rights recognized since the Middle Ages, such as those articulated in the 1215 Magna Carta. In the 17th century, imperial officials had, in most cases, allowed colonial courts to develop their own procedures and make their own decisions without review by English courts. Thus, the colonies developed their own common law system. The rights were partially derived from English cases, but other precedents were created entirely by the colonial courts. One particularly important institution, established in England and brought over to the colonies, was the jury trial. By the 18th century the jury trial had become so ingrained in American law that imperial attempts to eliminate it in the 1760s contributed to the American Revolution.

The other sources of American claims of rights and liberties were political and constitutional events in the British Isles in the 17th century. Prior to the English Civil War (1642–51), Parliament had been a weak body, largely responsible for raising tax revenue and advising the king regarding legislation. After the Restoration of the monarchy in 1660, Charles II sometimes ruled without Parliament, but Parliament exercised greater power in the creation of legislation and displayed a diligent suspicion of the king's exercise of power.

The Glorious Revolution of 1688–89 saw a further assertion of Parliament's rights. In 1688, Parliament forced James II, a Catholic king despised by many, to flee the throne, which was declared vacant. Parliament offered the crown to James II's daughter, Mary, and her Protestant husband, the Dutch stadtholder William III of Orange, provided they acquiesce to a Declaration of Rights that firmly placed sovereignty with Parliament and, by extension, with the people. The new king and queen acquiesced, and Parliament made the declaration into statutory law by enacting the Bill of Rights in 1689. That act provided for a limited monarchy and restricted royal power regarding the suspension of Parliament, the levying of taxes, and power over the army in time of peace. Parliament gained such extensive power relative to the Crown that the English constitutional government was fundamentally changed.

The English Civil War and the Glorious Revolution had long-term consequences in the colonies, shaping Americans' conceptions of rights and liberties in the 18th century. The tradition of legislative suspicion of royal claims to prerogative power, inherited from the Civil War, the increase in legislative power, and the new rights asserted by Parliament for all Englishmen after the Glorious Revolution resonated for American colonists and, later, patriots down to the American Revolution.

Intellectual and Political Influences on the Colonies

British Americans were also influenced in their understanding of rights by Enlightenment thinkers such as John Locke and Algernon Sydney, who argued it was necessary for the law of the state to be harmonious with natural law. "Natural law" was the law of permanent moral principles deduced through rational thought. Locke argued that a natural order existed and that the purpose of government was to protect it. Government was the product of an agreement—popularly referred to as the "social compact"—created between rulers and ruled, wherein the people surrendered some of their liberty in order to be collectively protected by the rulers. If the government, either through corruption or tyranny, violated this agreement, the people were justified in overthrowing the government through rebellion.

British Americans' understanding of rights was greatly influenced by Enlightenment thinker John Locke (above), who argued that a natural order existed and that government, which was a product of an agreement between the governing and the governed, existed to protect it. Locke's philosophy was read by many throughout the colonies in the years leading up to the Revolution in essays published in newspapers and pamphlets. *(Library of Congress)*

Responses to political practices in England from the 1720s to the 1740s also helped to shape British Americans' understandings of rights. During much of this period, Parliament was led by Robert Walpole, the leader of the Whigs, who opponents charged had betrayed the principles of the Glorious Revolution by making ministerial appointments to corrupt favorites, thereby creating a large, lethargic bureaucracy and increasing taxes. Reacting to Walpole's leadership, the English writers Thomas Gordon and John Trenchard published a series of essays, titled *Cato's Letters*, warning the British public that Walpole's patronage system threatened the liberties gained in the Glorious Revolution. On the other side of the Atlantic, Gordon and Trenchard's writings encouraged British Americans to view their own royal governors with greater scrutiny.

Imperial Control and Conflict

The British Empire's concentration on the commercial development of its colonies in the early 18th century resulted in a loose oversight of the colonies' internal affairs. This period of what the British politician Edmund Burke termed "salutary neglect" enabled the colonial assemblies to increase their powers vis-à-vis the colonial governors. The assemblies saw themselves as analogous to Parliament, and the governors as analogous to the king. As Parliament had tamed the Crown, the colonial assemblies sought to tame their governors by periodically resisting paying their salaries and gaining the power to appoint local officials. The assemblies' powers over finance were important. The assemblies initiated revenue bills and oversaw the expenditure of funds, including governors' salaries. This "power of the purse" was a key element in the colonies' sense of self-government until the American Revolution.

This period of neglect ended in the aftermath of the Seven Years' War (1756–63), with the inauguration of new imperial policies that would ultimately lead to revolution. The war had made Britain the dominant colonial power in North America, but it had also left the nation with a heavy burden of debt. To help fund that debt, and to provide for the increased number of troops stationed in America to protect the empire, Britain turned to the colonies for revenue. After a period of salutary neglect, Parliament also was anxious to tighten its control over the colonies.

Parliament increased enforcement of existing customs laws, and beginning in 1764 it levied a series of taxes designed to raise revenue and assert parliamentary supremacy. In 1764 it introduced levies on sugar, coffee, and molasses, and those accused of violating the law were to be tried in vice-admiralty courts before British naval officers, not juries. The following year Parliament imposed a new stamp tax on many printed documents, including legal documents and newspapers. The taxes were modest, but the colonies resisted them on the grounds that colonists could be taxed only through their elected representatives. They saw the taxes as a direct challenge by Parliament to the authority of colonial legislatures and a dangerous precedent that threatened home rule. In defending their position, the colonists turned to both intellectual tradition and common law. Prior to Parliament's move to tax the colonies, the colonists' prime use of English political writers was to resist the powers of royal governors and preserve individual liberty. Now colonists returned to these arguments to resist what they saw as new and powerful threats to their liberties by Parliament. Locke's philosophy was read by many throughout the colonies in essays published in newspapers and pamphlets. Meanwhile, the colonial lawyers who led the intellectual resistance appealed to the traditions of English common law, asserting that the denial of jury trials was a violation of English constitutional rights dating back to the Middle Ages.

In the fall of 1765, representatives of nine colonies assembled the Stamp Act Congress. They issued the Declaration of Rights and Grievances, which condemned the Stamp Act and claimed for the colonists the inherent rights of all natural-born Englishmen. These included the right to trial by jury and the right of people to be taxed only through their elected representatives. Protests, led by the self-styled "Sons of Liberty," followed throughout the colonies. Parliament eventually repealed the Stamp Act in

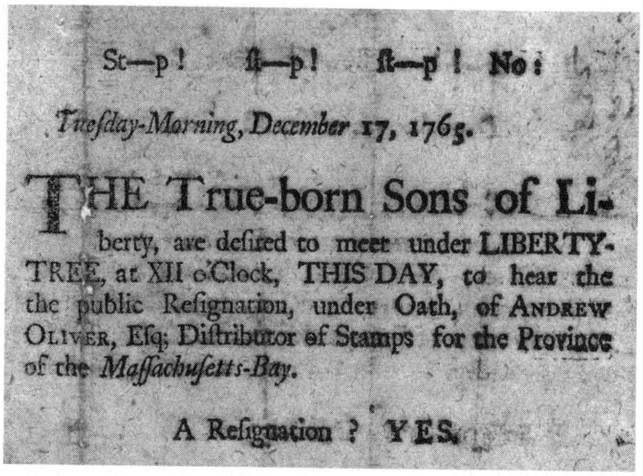

St—p! ſt—p! ſt—p! No:

Tueſday-Morning, December 17, 1765.

THE True-born Sons of Liberty, are deſired to meet under LIBERTY-TREE, at XII o'Clock, THIS DAY, to hear the the public Reſignation, under Oath, of ANDREW OLIVER, Eſq; Diſtributor of Stamps for the Province of the *Maſſachuſetts-Bay.*

A Reſignation? YES.

The Sons of Liberty were made up of various groups of colonists—artisans, merchants, and intellectuals from all 13 colonies—who organized protests against Great Britain starting in 1765 during the Stamp Act crisis. Above is a broadside from 1765 announcing a gathering to witness the resignation of Andrew Oliver, the Massachusetts official charged with administering the act. ***(Massachusetts Historical Society)***

1766 in the face of massive noncompliance and threats of mob violence, but it also passed the Declaratory Act, stating that Parliament's authority was the same in America as in Britain, and that it retained lawmaking power over the colonies "in all cases whatsoever."

This claim of power was put to the test in 1767, when Parliament enacted the Townshend Acts, a series of five acts primarily designed to assert parliamentary supremacy while raising revenue from the colonies for their own administration. Some of the money would be used to allow independent salaries for imperial officials in the colonies, which would strengthen the imperial hand by freeing it from the assemblies' control of the purse. Once again, the colonists protested, not only in pamphlets arguing for political rights, but also by well-organized trade boycotts of British-made imports. A conciliatory Parliament, fearing rebellion, again repealed the taxes, except a tax on tea. Nevertheless, the underlying issues regarding parliamentary supremacy and the right to tax remained unresolved, and the Townshend Acts united American resistance against Parliament's actions.

To Revolution

Parliament's efforts to extend its power into areas of governance previously controlled by the colonists led to a widespread suspicion of any British imperial acts in the colonies. The furor over the Townshend Acts had subsided by 1773, but when Parliament passed the Tea Act of 1773, which exempted the East India Company from paying tariffs on shipments of tea to America, the colonists again saw their rights threatened. Colonials denounced the act as a devious effort to get them to pay the Townshend tea duty, and thus concede Parliament's right to tax them. Widespread protests climaxed in the Boston Tea Party, during which colonists, some dressed as Mohawk Indians, dumped 90,000 pounds of tea into Boston Harbor.

The Tea Party convinced British officials that they had to react strongly to assert imperial control, and Parliament enacted a series of punitive laws against Massachusetts known as the Intolerable Acts. These measures closed the port of Boston, unilaterally altered Massachusetts's charter so that provincial councilors would no longer be elected but appointed by the Crown, gave sheriffs appointed by the Crown the role of selecting juries, and strengthened the powers of the royal governor while weakening those of town meetings. The acts raised the fear that Parliament would gut charters in other colonies and destroy traditional rights.

By this point the colonists' understanding of their rights had evolved. At the beginning of the imperial crisis, they had claimed they were entitled to the rights of Englishmen that Parliament had won from the king at the time of the Glorious Revolution. If Parliament were to exercise general governmental powers, especially taxation, then the colonists needed to be included among the elected representatives serving in Parliament. Taxation without representation was tyranny. By 1774, however, the more radical colonists were asserting that Parliament had no right to legislate for the colonies at all. They contended the king ruled in the dominion (the colonies) and Parliament ruled in the realm (the land of England). Parliament, therefore, had overstepped its authority. Yet a "social compact" bound the king and his subjects; if the king failed to observe the traditional rights of Englishmen, the colonists had a right to resist and, if pressed, rebel.

Accordingly, the colonies, acting in concert (except for Georgia) through delegates to the First Continental Congress, which met in Philadelphia in 1774, passed the Declaration of Rights and Resolves. This declaration condemned Britain's imperial policy since 1763 and rejected Parliament's claims of sovereignty within the colonies, contending that Parliament could only regulate "external" trade, or commercial relations, rather than legislate on matters within the colonies. The resolves were the last efforts to seek reform within the empire. The actions of the Congress precipitated a showdown with Parliament, which determined to use troops in a show of strength. Tensions came to a head in April 1775, when British troops clashed with colonial militia at Lexington and Concord. The first shots of the Revolution had been fired.

By 1776, with the issuance of the Declaration of Independence, the colonies presented a united claim to rights that had been violated by the king. Although the laws of Parliament had provoked the war, the Declaration—written primarily by Virginia's Thomas Jefferson—proclaimed that it was the king that had transgressed the colonists' "unalienable rights" (those that could not be taken or given away) to "life, liberty, and the pursuit of happiness." The Declaration referenced Locke's idea of the right of revolution, contending that government was legitimate only with the "consent of the governed."

The Post-Revolutionary and Confederation Period

The governments established after independence reflected the colonial experience and Americans' understanding of rights. Early state constitutions were short, since the powers of government were to be limited. Constitutions opened with philosophical statements on the origin and principles of government, and with a lengthy bill of rights, so as to make the purpose and limitations of government clear. Because power resided with the people and their representatives, legislatures dominated and executives were weak.

The national government established under the Articles of Confederation was also weak. Sovereignty resided with the states as the governments closest to the people. The Articles established a unicameral legislature with no separate judiciary. The executive was an annually elected president who presided over Congress but had no powers. Congress did not have the power to raise an army, regulate foreign or interstate commerce, or levy and collect taxes. It could only request that the states pay their fair share of federal expenses—and many did not.

The U.S. Constitution, Its Ratification, and the Bill of Rights

The states' authority led to the perception of an overabundance and abuse of liberty. The states in the 1780s acted like independent nations, in some cases making their own foreign policies, forming navies, enacting discriminatory economic legislation against other states, and printing their own currency. The Confederation constitution's inability to prevent such practices led to the drafting of a new constitution, after a meeting of all colonies (excepting Rhode Island) in Philadelphia in the summer of 1787.

The proposed United States Constitution sought to increase national governmental power. Yet these new powers—such as taxation, regulation of interstate commerce, and a more powerful executive—reminded many Americans of the British imperial powers that led to the Revolution. Therefore, a large body of political leaders demanded that any new Constitution formally recognize express limits on national governmental power through a bill of rights. The Constitution's supporters initially argued that no bill was necessary because, under the Constitution, the national government lacked any power to curb individual liberties. Yet the enthusiasts for a bill of rights made its inclusion a condition of their votes to ratify the Constitution. Proponents of the Constitution, led by James Madison, acquiesced, and the Bill of Rights was unopposed in the first Congress and became part of the Constitution by 1791.

The protections of the Bill of Rights, such as freedom of political speech and the right to not be forced to testify against oneself in court, were seldom the subject of court cases in the 18th century. They became important rights only in the 20th century. Yet the Bill of Rights was not only instrumental in obtaining ratification of the Constitution—it also reflected Americans' fears of consolidated, powerful government. The Bill of Rights functions at a constitutional level as a limit upon the power of the federal and state governments. Those fears of oppressive state power reflected in the Bill of Rights were born out of the colonial experience and have remained a part of American politics ever since.

—Ian J. Drake

Further Reading

Anderson, Fred. *Crucible of War: The Seven Years' War and the Fate of Empire in British North America, 1754–1766.* New York: Vintage, 2001.

Bailyn, Bernard. *The Ideological Origins of the American Revolution*. Cambridge, Mass.: Belknap Press of Harvard University Press, 1967.

———. *The Origins of American Politics*. New York: Vintage, 1970.

Breen, T. H. *The Marketplace of Revolution: How Consumer Politics Shaped American Independence*. New York: Oxford University Press, 2005.

Davis, David Brion. *Inhuman Bondage: The Rise and Fall of Slavery in the New World*. New York: Oxford University Press, 2006.

Ellis, Joseph J. *Founding Brothers: The Revolutionary Generation.* New York: Alfred A. Knopf, 2000.

Fischer, David Hackett. *Liberty and Freedom: A Visual History of America's Founding Ideas*. New York: Oxford University Press, 2004.

Friedman, Lawrence M. *A History of American Law*. 3d ed. New York: Simon & Schuster, 2005.

Gillespie, Michael Allen, and Michael Lienesch, eds. *Ratifying the Constitution*. Lawrence: University Press of Kansas, 1989.

Haskins, George Lee. *Law and Authority in Colonial Massachusetts: A Study in Tradition and Design*. 1960. Reprint, Lanham, Md.: University Press of America, 1985.

Henretta, James A., David Brody, and Lynn Dumenil. *America: A Concise History.* Vol. 1, *To 1877*. 3d ed. Boston: Bedford/St. Martin's, 2005.

Hoffer, Peter Charles. *Law and People in Colonial America*. Rev. ed. Baltimore, Md.: Johns Hopkins University Press, 1998.

Holton, Woody. *Forced Founders: Indians, Debtors, Slaves, and the Making of the American Revolution in Virginia*. Chapel Hill: University of North Carolina Press, 1999.

———. *Unruly Americans and the Origins of the Constitution.* New York: Hill & Wang, 2007.

Kelly, Alfred H., Winfred A. Harbison, and Herman Belz. *The American Constitution: Its Origins and Development.* Vol. 1. 7th ed. New York: W. W. Norton, 1991.

Nelson, William E. *Americanization of the Common Law: The Impact of Legal Change on Massachusetts Society, 1760–1830*. Athens: University of Georgia Press, 1994.

Taylor, Alan. *American Colonies*. New York: Viking, 2001.

Wood, Gordon S. *The Creation of the American Republic, 1776–1787*. 1972. Reprint, Chapel Hill: University of North Carolina Press, 1998.

———. *The Radicalism of the American Revolution*. New York: Alfred A. Knopf, 1992.

18th Century SCIENCE AND TECHNOLOGY

The development of science and technology in 18th-century America was characterized by the growth of independence among colonial-born scientists, a transition that was made complete after the American Revolution. Supported by their counterparts in Britain and Europe, colonial scientists focused their attention on the new and rich natural environment of North America while trying to establish ties to the European scientific community. In port cities of New England and the Mid-Atlantic region, where access to trade goods from Britain and university-led educational opportunities were prevalent, centers of scientific investigation emerged and networks grew, connecting scientists with other scientists in the colonies and with their British and European sponsors. As the century progressed, these networks of natural historians, as scientists studying the natural world were then called, fully engaged with the North American landscape, weather, and night sky, and with its geography, flora, and fauna—all of which offered a vast laboratory for scientific investigation. This growing knowledge of a uniquely American natural history transformed the work of American scientists into a pursuit of full intellectual autonomy, taken up as a national call following the acquisition of political independence from Britain.

Transatlantic Ties in Pre-Revolutionary Days

Though there were few if any professional scientists in America prior to the Revolutionary period, gentlemen scientists, often without any real training, tried to stay abreast of developments in theory and technology in Europe. Circumstances made this a great challenge. Virtually all books on new theories in science, like Newton's *Optics*, were printed and imported from Britain or Europe. Most scientific apparatus and instruction manuals also were imported from across the Atlantic. Due to the scarcity of both expertise and tools for creating finely honed original instruments, mechanically minded innovators, mostly in urban areas with access to ports, studied imported scientific instruments and attempted to reproduce them. And most practitioners of science looked across the Atlantic—especially to London—for intellectual guidance and support.

London was one of the foremost scientific centers in Europe. Its scientific community was moderated by the Royal Society of London for the Improvement of Natural Knowledge, founded in 1660, and indeed, many of the most important scientists in colonial America were fellows of the Royal Society. North American Royal Society members, however, occupied a second-class status. According to British thinking, they lived on the periphery of civilization. The climate, flora, and fauna of North America were poorly understood in this period, and many British natural historians speculated that the environment in the Americas was inferior and would physically and morally stunt anything that lived there. Americans spent a lot of energy arguing against this prejudice.

Regardless of their status, colonial members of the Royal Society studied North American natural phenomena, collected species, wrote reports, and tabulated scientific observations of the weather, the planet, and natural occurrences, and members of the Royal Society in Britain acted as patrons for these activities. These patrons mailed instructions on what kinds of specimens to collect and send back to London, and supplied their American contacts with manuals on the newest experiments in optics, electricity, or physics. Some American practitioners of science were more independent of their British counterparts, however, especially as the century progressed. Benjamin Franklin, who among his other accomplishments investigated electricity, and John Mitchell, a physician from Virginia who performed anatomical experiments to determine the cause of yellow fever, rarely sought or received instructions from their British patrons.

Before becoming a Founding Father of the United States, Benjamin Franklin was one of the most important American scientists of the 18th century, respected on both sides of the Atlantic for his activities in various areas of science and technology. The above engraving shows Franklin engaged in his famous kite experiment, which he undertook as part of his investigations into electricity. ***(Jupiter Images)***

Natural History, Exploration, and New Worlds

Observing the natural world and mining it for interesting specimens, new species, and medicinal substances constituted the major enterprise of natural historians in the century. Indeed, the 18th century was dominated by the science of taxonomy—the systematic classification of living things—and the exploration of new lands by European powers helped fuel the growth of this burgeoning endeavor. Famous botanists such as Carolus Linnaeus from Sweden and Georges-Louis Leclerc, Comte de Buffon, from France looked to collect, study, organize, and order all known specimens of life, and European expeditions fanning out across the world often included natural historians on board to catalog new species.

With Linnaeus's new system of binomial nomenclature to name living creatures, introduced in 1751, the work of natural historians became much easier, and eager American scientists joined the feverish drive to explore, identify, and name new species. They sent their samples of new plants for inclusion in natural histories of various colonies or settlements, which were often written by visitors—often from abroad—who traveled and lived in their area of observation for several years. In fact, despite the prejudicial perspective through which "Old World" natural historians viewed North America, many came to the Americas to find a wealth of new species to discover, name, and describe, including Pehr Kalm, a student of Linnaeus, who traveled throughout North America from 1748 to 1751 in search of new species. And natural historians living and practicing in the Americas—including perhaps the most well-known of all, the Philadelphia-based botanist John Bartram—encountered a wealth of new natural material to explore.

Science throughout the Colonies

Pronounced geographical, religious, and economic differences existed among the 13 colonies, and these variations helped determine the types of scientific activity practiced in specific locales and where the centers of scientific investigation would emerge. The New England colonies were dominated by a merchant-based economy and import activity generated in port cities, including Boston and Newport. The region also established the first universities in British North America. Originally founded as theological schools, Harvard College, the nation's oldest college, established in 1636, and Yale College, established in 1701, became central locations for the discussion, teaching, and practice of scientific experiments copied from those being carried out in England and Europe.

Boston—with nearby Harvard as an educational wellspring, its port as a conduit for information and goods, and its urban makeup as a network for the exchange of ideas—was a center of scientific activity. Because of the close-knit family connections encouraged by the Puritan ethic, dynasties of families educated at Harvard helped lead the development of science in the North. As a major port city, Boston was often first to receive shipments of valuable materials for scientific apparatus such as glass, metal parts, and textiles. Many of the merchants directly involved in British trade were associated with Harvard College and Boston politics and determined the state of learning among the interested elite.

Cotton Mather was one such figure. A minister and avid student of both theology and the sciences, Mather was a member of the Royal Society, for whom he wrote prolifically. He studied the medicinal properties of plants and collected curiosities and accounts of "prodigies," a term applied to wonders of the natural world. Along with Zabdiel Boylston, another Boston physician and collector of natural curiosities, Mather, at the urging of his slave Onesimus, engaged in the first smallpox inoculation trial in the American colonies during the epidemic of 1721–22. The Harvard-Boston connection nurtured an experimentally based scientific culture, collections of books and instruments, and public lectures, such as those delivered by Isaac Greenwood on mathematics, physics, experimental philosophy, and astronomy. Interesting natural specimens in the form of plants, animals, and geological objects were collected from New England, either for private use or for submission to the Royal Society.

Like New England, the mid-Atlantic colonies were home to large port cities, such as New York, Philadelphia, and Baltimore, and therefore had access to materials arriving on merchant vessels that could be used to construct scientific apparatus. In time, Philadelphia rivaled Boston and became the center of science in North America. This leadership was due in large part to Benjamin Franklin (1706–90), who before becoming a Founding Father of the United States was a pioneer of scientific thought and experimentation in British North America. Franklin was instrumental in establishing in 1751 what would become the University of Pennsylvania, as the first college in the colonies to focus on liberal arts, not on the preparation of clergy. In 1743, under Franklin's direction, the American Philosophical Society was founded in Philadelphia; it brought together countless scientists, tradesmen, artisans, and inventors, as well as statesmen, politicians, lawyers, clergymen, and others, as a way of organizing and enhancing learning and serving the public sphere. The American Philosophical Society would provide the model for future scientific societies, including the Boston-based American Academy of Arts and Sciences, founded in 1779 by John Adams, John Hancock, Samuel Adams, and James Bowdoin, and numerous other scientific organizations of the 19th century that would help to professionalize scientific endeavor. This nexus of learning and scientific enterprise—with Franklin as a leader, Philadelphia at its core, and the American Philosophical Society at its epicenter—connected much of the activities of practitioners of science throughout the colonies—northward to Boston and southward to the southern colonies.

Science in the southern colonies was relatively limited, lacking many of the advantages of the urban-based scientific activities typical of New England and the Mid-Atlantic. Because practitioners of science lived far from one another and often had plantations to run or other agricultural economic concerns to occupy their time, they relied on networks of correspondence and the generosity of urban friends for new books imported from Europe or printed in Boston and Philadelphia, as well as for the material they needed to perform medical procedures, create scientific apparatus, and record data. Nevertheless, scientists in the southern colonies managed to remain connected with the Royal Society in London, mainly through the apothecary and botanical cataloger James Petiver of London, some even positioning themselves as valuable collectors of specimens on an international stage.

Most new and interesting botanical specimens that were collected in the southern colonies—and strange and curious specimens of flora and fauna abounded in these regions—were sent to the Royal Society, rather than to colonies in the Mid-Atlantic region and New England.

Alexander Garden, a physician in Charleston, South Carolina, attempted to use his powerful transatlantic ties to create an educational botanical garden of all known species of plants in America. (Garden relied on Benjamin Franklin and his circle of correspondents as a secondary resource.) William Byrd II, a Virginia planter, not only surveyed the frontier to the south and west but also avidly collected—with the aid of his slaves—specimens of seeds, insects, plants, and animals to send to the Royal Society. His attachment to London and to his British identity was typical of southern botanical collectors, who cultivated relationships with long-term visitors such as Mark Catesby of London, whose *Natural History of Carolina, Florida and the Bahamas* (1731) enlivened interest in the scientific potential of the southern colonies.

Again, science became more firmly established in the Mid-Atlantic and northern colonies because of the advantages of urban networks. Material goods—including books, almanacs predicting the weather and natural disasters, scientific instruments, and publications about experiments—accumulated and remained in urban areas of the Mid-Atlantic and Northeast. Scientific activities in the South were more dispersed, and specimens were constantly being sent away; as a result, scientific communities were slower to develop.

American Scientists Stake Their Claim

As the century progressed, native-born scientists gained further independence from their transatlantic patrons. Perhaps the most important American scientist was Benjamin Franklin, who staked his claim to scientific fame and autonomy by midcentury, before he would turn much of his intellect and energy to the national project of political independence. Not only the leading force behind the American Philosophical Society, Franklin was a polymath active in many areas of science and technology and respected on both sides of the Atlantic. In 1726 he started a printing company in Philadelphia, which would make him rich and put in his hands some of the most important technologies of the modern period. In 1744 he developed a safer, more efficient heating stove, known as the Franklin stove. In the late 1740s and 1750s he experimented with electricity—developing a lightning rod and describing in his notes the now-famous experiment with a kite in a lightning storm—hoping to unlock the secrets of static electricity. These studies led him to a new theory of electricity—that it was not composed of two separate fluids but resulted from the positive and negative charges repelling each other in a single fluid—and would lead to groundbreaking developments in the next century, such as the electric battery and current electricity. His findings were published in 1751 in *Experiments and Observations on Electricity*, and this work was eventually translated into French, German, and Italian. The publication brought Franklin international recognition.

John Bartram (1699–1777), one of Franklin's partners in the founding of the American Philosophical Society, also gained international acclaim. He became the most accomplished plant collector in the colonies and was lauded by Linnaeus—to whom Bartram sent many specimens—as one of the greatest botanists in the world. While Bartram remained closely linked to his British sponsors—in 1765 he was awarded the position of king's botanist of North America—his work helped to establish the validity and study of the natural history of North America. He researched extensively throughout eastern North America, including a trip in 1765–66 to the Southeast, after which he published the influential *Diary of a Journey through the Carolinas, Georgia, and Florida.* His family homestead, outside Philadelphia, hosted the first botanical garden in North America, and his sons, John and William Bartram, carried on the tradition after the Revolution.

The American Revolution put many scientific activities throughout the colonies on hiatus, and they did not resume fully until early in the 1780s. When they did, a new scientific agenda was being established by political figures who were also actively engaged in creating a national program of scientific knowledge that would better the republic and challenge the European Enlightenment with an American one. Suspended throughout most of the Revolutionary years, the American Philosophical Society was rejuvenated in the early days of the republic by Franklin, Jefferson, and a network of prominent community members and

John Bartram was the most accomplished plant collector in the colonies and is considered one of the greatest botanists of the 18th century. The above wood engraving from 1884 shows his home outside Philadelphia, which hosted the first botanical garden in North America. ***(Jupiter Images)***

curious investigators who drove the goals of the nascent "Republic of Science."

After Franklin's death in 1790, Jefferson assumed the position of the foremost natural philosopher in the United States. His scientific circle of collaborators included David Rittenhouse (1732–96), an astronomer who had built the first "orrery," or planetarium, in America and succeeded Franklin as president of the American Philosophical Society. Rittenhouse was an inventor who also undertook geographical surveys of the colonies and, through his efforts to systematize American weights and measures, was appointed the first director of the American mint. Benjamin Rush (1745–1813), a prominent Philadelphia physician, was another prolific contributor to knowledge in the early republic. Exerting intellectual and philanthropic efforts in abolition, prison reform, the treatment of insanity, and republican and humanitarian causes, Rush was best known for his uniform medical treatment program of administering bleeding and purging, a program that came under scrutiny during the 1793 yellow fever epidemic in Philadelphia.

Joining Rush and Rittenhouse in the American program to tabulate indigenous natural knowledge was Benjamin Smith Barton (1766–1815), Rittenhouse's nephew and devoted botanist, who used his efforts to survey lands and collect specimens for an American *materia medica*, a catalog of plants with medicinal healing properties found on the continent. William Bartram (1739–1823) contributed as well; he would equal his father, John, in fame as a botanist, authoring *Travels through North and South Carolina, East and West Florida, the Cherokee Country, the Extensive Territories of the Muscolgulges, or Creek Confederacy, and the Country of the Chactaws* (1791), which was considered an indispensable source for detailed information on the flora and fauna of the Southeast; he also became a well-known ornithologist.

Jefferson—at the forefront of these efforts to explore and catalog indigenous natural history—engaged in a lengthy debate with Buffon, the French natural historian, over the superiority of the size of American species in comparison to those discovered in Europe. Hoping to claim a place in the world for the United States, Jefferson insisted that American species were larger than any other species yet discovered and began a campaign to provide evidence of the American "mammoth." For this, Jefferson found his proof, though in an extinct species: Bones of at least two mastodons were discovered near Newburgh, New York, in 1801, and one grand specimen was assembled and displayed in Charles Willson Peale's museum in Philadelphia. One of the country's most famous artists, Peale founded his museum of natural history in 1784 after receiving a series of gifts from his colleagues in Philadelphia. It would be the nation's first major museum, and at the turn of the century its most celebrated exhibit set the record straight—at least in the minds of the public—about the ability of the North American continent to support grand-sized specimens of natural life.

The exchange of natural specimens and curiosities—ethnographic, mechanical, and natural—was the basis for professional relationships between natural philosophers and historians. Derived from a long tradition of exchange between the colonies and their European patrons, exchange of specimens established a community of credible gentlemen in the new republic who proved their worth through the circulation of objects and ideas. The patronage and gift system that initially made collections and museums possible would become increasingly government-supported in the 19th century. At the end of the century, Americans no longer relied on Europeans for guidance in the sciences, and the establishment of a government designed to unite diverse peoples with radically varying histories influenced the use of current and former scientific investigation as an emblem of national prowess. Electricity became an American phenomenon under the investigations of Ben Franklin; botany was reappropriated by Jefferson, the Bartrams, Peale, and Barton for local, American repositories to be used in future systems of classification; and the stars over the Western Hemisphere were observed by American astronomers such as David Rittenhouse, the data intended for describing the physical features of the United States. During the colonial era, science in the American context was closely related to British projects, and specimens were used to further the power of the British Empire. After the establishment of the United States as a country, American science came to be lauded as an example of how the new nation was equal to its vanquished colonizers.

—Kristen Keerma

Further Reading

Berkeley, Edmund, and Dorothy Smith Berkeley. *Dr. John Mitchell: The Man Who Made the Map of North America.* Chapel Hill: University of North Carolina Press, 1974.

Boorstin, Daniel J. *The Lost World of Thomas Jefferson.* 1948. Reprint, Chicago: University of Chicago Press, 1993.

Chaplin, Joyce. *The First Scientific American: Benjamin Franklin and the Pursuit of Genius.* New York: Basic Books, 2006.

Conniff, Richard. *The Species Seekers: Heroes, Fools, and the Mad Pursuit of Life on Earth*. New York: W. W. Norton, 2010.

Dain, Bruce. *A Hideous Monster of the Mind: American Race Theory in the Early Republic*. Cambridge, Mass.: Harvard University Press, 2002.

Daniels, George. *Science in American Society: A Social History*. New York: Alfred A. Knopf, 1971.

Delbourgo, James. *A Most Amazing Scene of Wonders: Electricity and Enlightenment in Early America.* Cambridge, Mass.: Harvard University Press, 2006.

Gerbi, Antonello. *The Dispute of the New World: The History of a Polemic, 1750–1900*. Translated by Jeremy Moyle. Pittsburgh, Pa.: University of Pittsburgh Press, 1973.

Hindle, Brooke, ed. *Early American Science.* New York: Science History Publications, 1976.

Leventhal, Herbert. *In the Shadow of Enlightenment: Occultism and Renaissance Science in Eighteenth-Century America*. New York: New York University Press, 1976.

Lindeman, Janet Moore, and Michele Lise Tarter, eds. *A Centre of Wonders: The Body in Early America.* Ithaca, N.Y.: Cornell University Press, 2001.

McGaw, Judith A., ed. *Early American Technology: Making and Doing Things from the Colonial Era to 1850.* Chapel Hill: University of North Carolina Press, 1994.

Parrish, Susan Scott. *American Curiosity: Cultures of Natural History in the Colonial British Atlantic World.* Chapel Hill: University of North Carolina Press, 2006.

Stearns, Raymond Phineas. *Science in the British Colonies of America.* Chicago: University of Illinois Press, 1970.

St. George, Robert Blair. *Conversing by Signs: Poetics of Implication in New England Culture.* Chapel Hill: University of North Carolina Press, 1998.

18th Century SECTIONS AND REGIONS

Eighteenth-century British North America was defined by regional variation. By 1700, England's American colonies could be divided into at least four distinct cultural regions on the continent—New England, the Mid-Atlantic or middle colonies, the Chesapeake, and the Lower South—in addition to the Caribbean colonies of the West Indies and the Atlantic islands of Bermuda and the Bahamas. By 1800, the early national United States added the trans-Appalachian West to this regional array; it would soon purchase the vast Louisiana Territory beyond the Mississippi River. While a broad process of social and cultural convergence muted local and regional variations over the course of the 18th century, these variations persisted into the 19th century, setting the stage for continued sectional conflict and eventual civil war.

Regional Diversity

The haphazard experience of planting European colonies in the New World left a patchwork of settlements along the North Atlantic seaboard. As a consequence, 18th-century English colonists inhabited provincial societies marked by contrast and variation. Neighboring colonies—for instance, Massachusetts and Connecticut or South Carolina and Georgia—often shared similarities in colonial experience, but differences among settlements generally multiplied along a north-south continuum stretching from the Caribbean to the Canadian Maritimes. Much of this regional variation was rooted in fundamental differences in local economy, society, and history. Colonies south of Pennsylvania were largely organized around intensive, New World staple-crop agriculture performed by unfree labor. Colonies north of this district tended to cultivate European livestock and crops (plus maize) in family units.

Key demographic differences could be mapped onto this basic north-south axis. In the more southerly climes, colonists encountered higher rates of death and disease, imbalanced sex ratios, and lower birth rates. Populations in the more northerly latitudes, by contrast, generally enjoyed a longer life expectancy, a higher percentage of women and children, and a greater rate of population growth by natural increase. This difference had important implications for migration patterns and population diversity. On the northern end of the regional spectrum, New England's population was unusually homogeneous, descended for the most part from its original English Puritan stock. To the south, Chesapeake society was also largely Anglo-American, though replenished by continuing bouts of immigration from England and increasingly supplemented by slave importations from Africa. The rest of colonial British America experienced much higher rates of immigration. The Lower South and Caribbean colonies imported vast numbers of African slaves to tend to their staple crops; even with inhumane mortality rates, blacks outnumbered whites in many rural parishes. Northwestern European settlers came in sizable numbers to the middle colonies; together, these Welsh, Scots-Irish, German, Dutch, and other European immigrants often constituted a majority over their resident English populations.

Other important social and cultural differences aligned along the north-south spectrum. Economic and social inequity was more pronounced in southern plantation regimes, where elites concentrated land, slaves, wealth, and authority, than in northern farming communities geared toward family agriculture. Politics and religion also followed this regional pattern. In the northern reaches of British America, New Englanders practiced the social covenant in town meetings and corporate governments; they institutionalized their Puritan principles in established Congregational churches. Proprietary and royal forms of government predominated in the middle and southern colonies, respectively, and these colonial polities tended to be organized by county or parish instead of town.

The Anglican church held sway in large sections of the Chesapeake and Lower South, at least in the first half of the 18th century, while an assortment of Protestants, including Presbyterians, Quakers, Lutherans, Baptists, and Calvinist Huguenots, competed for adherents for their denominations in the ethnically diverse and religiously pluralistic middle colonies. Though generalizations are difficult, religious devotion tended to increase as one traveled north along the Atlantic seaboard, as did community literacy rates and investments in education.

Of course, some commonalities existed across colonial British America. Most colonists spoke English as their first language, though other European, African, Indian, and creole languages predominated in places. Most colonists professed the Protestant faith, though in different forms; local regimes favored Anglicanism in the tidewater South, Congregationalism in orthodox New England, and religious toleration in between. Over time, more and more colonists engaged in individualistic, acquisitive behavior, and many more enjoyed access to land ownership than comparable populations in Europe. At midcentury, virtually all colonists considered themselves loyal subjects of the king; they all lived under representative regimes governed in accordance with Anglo-American political and legal traditions. Yet even these shared English (or after 1707, British) traits of colonization were often overshadowed by regional patterns of settlement that shaped societies along the north-south spectrum.

New England

For reasons of cultural as much as physical geography, New England occupied one extreme along this spectrum of regional settlements. Long assumed by historians to represent the typical model of Anglo-American colonial development, New England's experience may be more fairly characterized as exceptional. Unlike other English ventures in North America, New England was founded as a religious experiment rather than a profitable enterprise. The region's 17th-century Puritan founders planted intensely religious, corporate settlements from north of Massachusetts Bay to well west of New Haven. This unique pattern of Puritan colonization, centered on the family, town, and congregation and reproduced in succeeding generations, established the long-term basis for New England's regional peculiarity.

However promising at the outset, this orthodox Puritan vision of society began to unravel in the century after 1660. In the process, 18th-century New England gradually shed some—though certainly not all—of its regional distinctiveness. Rapid natural population growth and territorial expansion opened the region to new ways of life. Between 1710 and 1770, New England's population nearly quadrupled to over 700,000 inhabitants. From a cluster of isolated settlements around Massachusetts Bay, the Connecticut River Valley, and along the shores of Long Island Sound, New Englanders swelled into the hills, valleys, and lowlands between the Hudson and Penobscot rivers. As the region's young and mobile generations dispersed across the landscape, traditional ties of family, community, and church loosened.

At the same time, the regional economy evolved from localized, family-based agriculture to surplus commercial production of cereals and livestock and specialized fishing, whaling, and timber industries, largely intended for overseas export. As goods increasingly headed to market, New England merchants solidified domestic networks between town and country and accelerated foreign trade with the rest of the Atlantic world economy. At the same time, New England's urban centers—including cities such as Boston and Newport, seaports such as Portsmouth and Salem, and interior towns such as Springfield and Hartford—grew in size and stature. Commercialization and urbanization brought in turn greater economic mobility, professional specialization, and social stratification. The resulting rise in individualism surfaced in politics, where discord and factionalism, instead of harmony and consensus, became the rule of the day. This creeping worldliness was even more pronounced in the religious sphere: Doctrinal divisions increased, rates of church membership declined, and evangelical denominations made greater inroads on the Congregational establishment, especially after the Great Awakening of the 1740s. To the dismay of many traditional authorities, the pious Puritan of the 17th century seemed more and more the enterprising Yankee of the 18th.

Throughout this transformation, New England remained the most cohesive region in colonial British America, largely a testament to its deep-seated corporate identity. Massachusetts and Connecticut, the initial outposts of Puritan colonization, formed the region's core area of settlement all the way through the American Revolution. Yet even 18th-century New England was far from uniform. Sandwiched between its stalwart neighbors, tiny Rhode Island had long been anomalous. A traditional enclave of religious toleration for Baptists, Quakers, and Jews, Rhode Island developed a thriving livestock and mercantile economy in the 18th century. With commercial wealth came slavery; an estimated 5,000 of New England's 13,000 blacks lived in Rhode Island. Farther from the region's orthodox core, the frontier settlements of New Hampshire and Maine epitomized New England's expansion into the putative wilderness. Though both areas were administrative satellites of Massachusetts—New Hampshire did not enjoy formal independence until 1741 and Maine until 1820—these frontier communities proved even less beholden to the old ways and more receptive to timber and fishing industries, outside migration, and evangelical religion. Aggressively expansive in spirit, New England's Yankee population continually pressed up against its neighbors. Over time, the region's sphere of influence extended as far south as New York, Long Island, and eastern New Jersey and as far east as Nova Scotia (acquired from the French in 1713) and Newfoundland, setting a trend of New England expansion that would continue long after independence.

Chesapeake

If New England was the most exceptional region in 18th-century British America, then the Chesapeake settlements of Virginia and Maryland in many ways represented the mainstream of Anglo-American colonial development. Unlike Puritan New England, 17th-century Chesapeake society was—like much else in colonial English America—unsettled and improvisational. Largely committed to the intensive, profitable cultivation of tobacco for European markets, early colonial Virginia and Maryland did not develop the strong sense of community more familiar to the north. Yet this initial trend toward social incoherence did not hold for the century after 1660. While 18th-century New England appeared to be coming apart at the seams, Chesapeake society at the same time appeared to be coming together and achieving a new sense of stability. In this way, the Chesapeake region exemplified a developmental trend across much of 18th-century British America toward greater complexity, cohesion, and order.

After surviving their initial growing pains, the English settlements on the Chesapeake Bay experienced a remarkable demographic, economic, and territorial expansion in the 18th century. Population growth drove much of this transformation. From about 121,000 inhabitants in 1710, Virginia and Maryland's combined population increased more than fivefold to nearly 650,000 inhabitants by 1770. This growth encompassed a monumental transition in the region's primary labor force, roughly between 1680 and 1720, from white servitude to black slavery. Blacks, who constituted but 1 in 10 Chesapeake inhabitants in 1700, represented approximately 40 percent of the population after 1760.

This racially segregated labor force enabled a dramatic midcentury rise in the production of tobacco, the Chesapeake's trademark agricultural staple, as well as a mature diversification of the economy into corn and wheat cultivation and flour, iron, timber, and shipbuilding industries. As it had since the early 17th century, tobacco culture prevailed in the rich soils of the coastal tidewater zone, which had been largely settled by 1700. Tobacco's heavy land requirements impelled its westward spread along the region's many rivers into the upland Piedmont, which swelled in new plantations between 1700 and 1750. By midcentury, the thirst for land among Chesapeake residents had resulted in a thinly dispersed but largely contiguous zone of rural settlement from the head of the Chesapeake Bay in the north to the Albemarle Sound (technically North Carolina) in the south to the Shenandoah Valley and Allegheny Mountains in the west.

A profound transformation in Chesapeake society and culture accompanied this 18th-century expansion. The transition from white servitude to black slavery in the region created a racial caste system distinguished by white solidarity, black subjugation, and sharp class differentiations. A growing population of black slaves, the result of forced immigration and (for the first time in colonial American history) natural increase, occupied the bottom rungs of the Chesapeake social ladder. Increasingly congregated on large plantations, blacks managed, despite the hardships of plantation labor, to create some semblance of family life and common slave culture by the middle decades of the 18th century.

Poor and middling whites occupied the intermediary position in Chesapeake society. The vast majority of white Virginians and Marylanders were small agricultural producers who raised tobacco, grain, and livestock, occasionally with the aid of unfree labor. A small minority of whites constituted a rising class of artisans, merchants, and professionals. These groups largely deferred to a landed gentry class of native-born elites, who commanded the top position in the regional social hierarchy. Bound by intermarriage and common interests, these elite planters asserted patriarchal control over wives, children, and slaves and monopolized authority over the region's civil and religious institutions. From their Georgian manor houses, Chesapeake planters supplied political stewardship in the genteel republican style and sought the polite refinement, or "improvement," of their rude provincial societies. Nominally Anglican, Chesapeake planter society nonetheless encouraged a general social permissiveness and libertarian mentality that aimed to maximize personal freedom, wealth, and happiness. A new wave of evangelical religion challenged this liberal, permissive ethos after the Great Awakening of the 1740s, but it remained the dominant streak in Chesapeake regional culture well into the 19th century.

Middle Colonies

Situated midway between New England and the Chesapeake, the Mid-Atlantic colonies of New York, New Jersey, Pennsylvania, and Delaware comprised no simple amalgam of these two older, neighboring regions, but their own unique historical and geographical product. Indeed, the middle colonies encompassed at least two distinct subregions: a Hudson Valley settlement concentrated on New York City and its hinterlands in New York, Long Island, and eastern New Jersey; and a Delaware River settlement concentrated on Philadelphia and its breadbasket in Pennsylvania, Delaware, and western New Jersey. Both areas were characterized by unusual linguistic, ethnic, and religious diversity, in stark contrast to the Puritan uniformity of New England or the dominant tobacco culture of the Chesapeake.

Seized from the Dutch in 1664, the English colonies of New York and East Jersey received a stream of northwestern European dissenters, imported Africans, and neighboring New Englanders to their shores. Greater Pennsylvania—encompassing William Penn's proprietary Quaker commonwealth and the remnants of New Sweden along the Delaware—welcomed a host of Quakers and Welsh, German, and Scots-Irish immigrants to its lands farther south. Thanks to regular immigration and steady natural increase, the population of the middle colonies grew nearly eightfold, from just under 70,000 to around 556,000, in the six decades after 1710. The colonies' population explosion drove sweeping territorial expansion in the region, such that most of the Hudson Valley (bordering on Iroquois country in New York's interior) and nearly all of the Pennsylvania Piedmont and Great Valley had been settled by midcentury. These booming settlements left a mosaic of vibrant localities, from Dutch Albany and Huguenot New Rochelle to German Lancaster County, across the better part of the Mid-Atlantic countryside.

For all this undeniable heterogeneity, the middle colonies also proved a melting pot of sorts for a hybrid regional culture. Over the course of the 18th century, a moderately affluent and relatively tolerant commercial society developed in the Hudson Valley and Philadelphia hinterland. On countless family farms, freeholders and tenants in these "bread colonies" produced impressive quantities of grain, flaxseed, livestock, and garden produce for home consumption and export to the Atlantic market. Flour, meatpacking, food-processing, timber, iron, and shipbuilding industries developed around this mixed agricultural economy, and merchants, artisans, and professionals serviced this dynamic commercial activity, especially in the growing urban centers of New York and Philadelphia. Though free labor predominated in Mid-Atlantic workplaces, servitude and slavery were not unknown in the region. Servants accounted for about 5 percent of Philadelphia's labor force, while slaves made up roughly 15 percent of the Hudson Valley's population in the late colonial period. Such impoverished laborers contrasted markedly with a rising urban mercantile and professional elite, whose affluence spurred increased consumption of English imports and local investments in cultural institutions. For most inhabitants, widespread prosperity promoted flexibility and tolerance in social relations and spread the region's reputation as the "best poor man's country." Although locals may have hailed from different backgrounds and disagreed about politics and religion, they generally shared a strong commitment to possessive individualism and the pursuit of individual and family happiness. Like many of their contemporaries in 18th-century British America, the inhabitants of the middle colonies eventually discovered social coherence in the pluralism, materialism, and individualism that had long characterized the region.

Lower South

Diversity of a different sort marked the colonies of the Lower South. Settled a half century or more after the New England and Chesapeake colonies, the Carolinas and Georgia shared as much in common with Britain's Caribbean possessions as with their continental neighbors. Colonized originally by Barbadians in 1670, the coastal Carolina lowcountry soon developed its own variant of the tropical, plantation-based slave society practiced in the West Indies. As in the Caribbean islands, a small landed gentry of white planters commandeered large numbers of subordinate African laborers for the purpose of cultivating agricultural staples, in this case rice and indigo. The region's unusual demographics supported this arrangement. By 1740, blacks accounted for over 40 percent of the Lower South's population; blacks outnumbered whites by more than two to one in South Carolina (after 1720) and Georgia (after 1755). In some of the most intensive rice-growing districts around Charles Town, the black-white ratio stretched as high as nine to one, testifying to conspicuous black majorities comparable in size only to 18th-century Jamaica. Thanks to heavy forced importations of slaves from the West Indies and Africa (particularly Angola) and the successive arrival of English, Scots, Scots-Irish, and German immigrants, the region's population soared from just over 25,000 inhabitants in 1710 to just under 350,000 in 1770, a remarkable 14-fold increase in only six decades.

Not all of this rapid population increase went to the Carolina lowcountry. A portion of it settled in the Albemarle district south of the James River, a virtual outgrowth of Chesapeake tobacco society that was culturally and geographically separate from the rest of Carolina—a geopolitical situation codified in 1712 with the formal division of the colony into North and South Carolina. Another segment, largely overflow from the Pennsylvania and Virginia frontiers, ventured deep into the Carolina interior. This backcountry population cultivated grains, tended to livestock in "cowpens," and engaged in the profitable trade in Indian slaves and goods.

Nonetheless, Carolina's lowcountry slave society, clustered around Charles Town, contained over 90 percent of the Lower South's population and set the dominant pattern for the region, so much so that it quickly subsumed James Oglethorpe's humanitarian scheme in neighboring Georgia. Founded in 1732 as a non-slaveholding refuge for convicts and religious dissenters, Georgia soon came under South Carolina's sway and eventually replicated its lowcountry social form. Characterized by a high degree of stratification, Carolina plantation society relied on the labor of its majority slave population to favor a commercial gentry of planters, merchants, and lawyers that was the wealthiest in colonial British North America. This lavish wealth enabled lowcountry grandees to import massive quantities of European consumer goods and transform Charles Town, the fourth-largest city in British North America, into an elegant provincial center of culture and the arts. Lowcountry luxury and indulgence also spelled social permissiveness; compared to their northern neighbors, Carolinian attitudes toward religion, law enforcement, and education were relatively lax. Such latitude even extended to the region's slave population, which (despite the indignities of a draconian slave code) managed to preserve some aspects of its African culture and foster an African American regional

Estimated Population of the New England, Mid-Atlantic, Chesapeake, and Lower South Colonies, 1710 and 1770

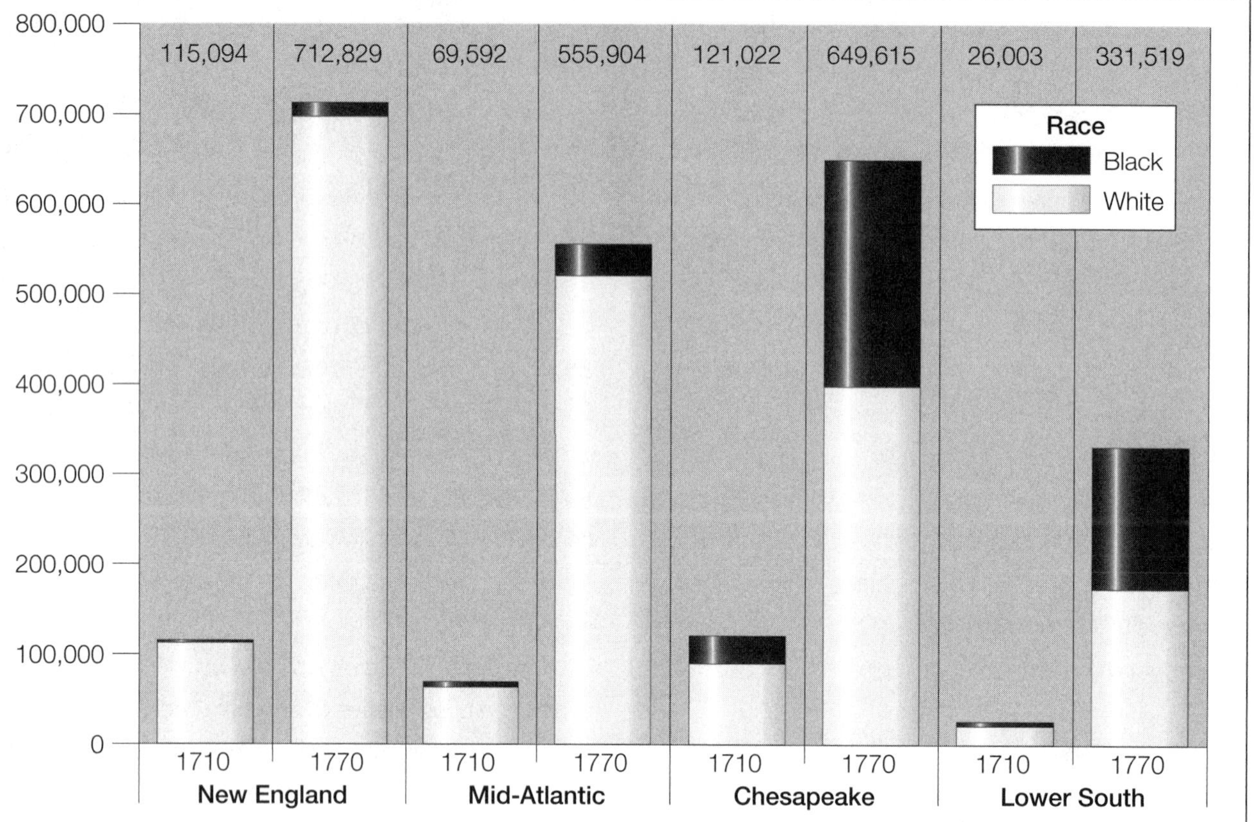

Source: U.S. Department of Commerce, Bureau of the Census, *Historical Statistics of the United States: Colonial Times to 1970*, 1168 (Washington, D.C.: Bureau of the Census, 1975).

Between 1710 and 1770, New England's population grew more than sixfold to over 700,000 inhabitants; the Chesapeake region's population increased more than fivefold from about 121,000 inhabitants in 1710 to nearly 650,000 inhabitants by 1770; the middle colonies' numbers grew nearly eightfold, from just under 70,000 to around 556,000; and the Lower South's population soared from just over 26,000 inhabitants in 1710 to more than 331,000 in 1770.

dialect, or pidgin, known as Gullah. Generally assigned a daily task rather than hours of gang labor, Carolina slaves enjoyed a considerable degree of autonomy in the day-to-day operations of plantation life.

Convergence

By the middle of the 18th century, New England, the middle colonies, the Chesapeake, and the Lower South represented four distinct cultural regions on the North American continent. Yet, just as rapid development had reshaped these various regions, it also drove a common social and cultural convergence that brought the American colonies more in line with one another and their common reference point in metropolitan Britain. For all their unmistakable variation, Britain's North American colonies were considerably more alike in 1750 or 1760 than they had been a half or full century earlier. Each of them experienced high rates of population growth, territorial expansion, and economic development in the 18th century, resulting in provincial societies that were noticeably more complex, differentiated, prosperous, and similar to one another than their 17th-century predecessors had been.

As America's colonial societies matured, they increasingly came to resemble their parent across the ocean. Like metropolitan Britons, American colonists bought prodigious quantities of British and European tea, sugar, textiles, pottery, and other consumer goods, thereby participating in a worldwide consumer revolution that transcended regional and national boundaries. Elite Americans of the 18th century also mimicked genteel British styles of dress, speech, and custom in a bid to refine, or "improve," their provincial lives along metropolitan lines. As American colonists integrated their local and regional economies with Atlantic and global markets, they encountered more news and information from the metropolis and increasingly emulated British political culture. By the close of the Seven Years' War (1756–63), colonial Americans considered themselves by right loyal subjects of George III and full-fledged members of the expanding British Empire. Over the course of the 18th century, this broad process of convergence and metropolitanization served to mute much of America's interregional variation, even if it could never entirely erase it.

Confederation

Convergence, however, did not necessarily translate into confederation. Since political life in early America was organized by colony instead of region, Britain's North American colonies shared few common political experiences before the American Revolution. As Benjamin Franklin explained in a 1760 pamphlet, the 14 maritime colonies from Nova Scotia to Georgia "are not only under different governors, but have different forms of government, different laws, different interests, and some of them different religious persuasions and different manners." Franklin understood the difficulties of confederation among America's mutually jealous colonies all too well; his own proposed plan of defensive union at Albany in 1754 did not secure ratification by a single colonial assembly.

Pre-Revolutionary Americans, in short, showed little interest in forming an enduring union. During the imperial crisis of the 1760s and 1770s, many colonists did rally in support of ad hoc intercolonial associations such as the Stamp Act Congress (1765) and the First Continental Congress (1774), but these temporary bodies merely sought the repeal of odious parliamentary legislation. Not until November 1777, a full 16 months after declaring independence from Britain, did the Second Continental Congress manage to agree on a final draft of Articles of Confederation among the former colonies; it took an additional 39 months (until March 1781) for all 13 state legislatures to ratify them. In the meantime, Britain's guiding military strategy in the Revolutionary War (1775–83) sought to capitalize on the self-evident weakness of the American confederation and divide and conquer it along regional lines. British imperial forces aimed to isolate rebellious Massachusetts from its sister colonies in the war's opening phase; they later endeavored to splinter the wartime confederacy in massive northern and southern campaigns focused on the strategic pivots of New York City and Charles Town, respectively.

Though the American rebels ultimately managed to fight imperial forces to a draw, many contemporaries questioned whether America's embryonic union, encompassing such diverse regions, could survive the labors of independence. A looming sectional crisis in 1786 over the contested navigation of the Mississippi River exposed several structural deficiencies in the weak Articles and provoked public suggestions that the United States might naturally devolve into a set of separate regional republics or confederacies. Such bold talk added momentum to the movement for federal constitutional reform, just as sectional tensions complicated long-term political solutions to the enduring dilemma of American regional diversity. As citizens of different states and regions with clashing economic interests and divergent cultural values, Americans in the 1780s were, in the words of the Massachusetts delegate Elbridge Gerry, "neither the same Nation nor different Nations."

At the Philadelphia Convention in the summer of 1787, Gerry's fellow delegates drafted a new federal constitution to accommodate these manifold differences within a revised frame of government. Most famously, the 1787 Constitution contained two key sectional compromises: It instituted a bicameral Congress elected on the dual basis of equal and proportional representation; and it counted three-fifths of a state's slave population for the purposes of apportioning representatives and direct taxes. Perhaps most significantly, the new Constitution remained committed to the American governing principle of federalism, or the division of sovereignty between state and central governments. Confronted with administering a composite polity of diverse states and regions, America's Founders relied on a revised form of federalism to balance local prerogatives and general needs.

Old Northwest and Southwest

While the 1787 Constitution settled relations among America's older seaboard regions, newer regions of American settlement were taking shape in the continent's interior. The immense trans-Appalachian territory, formally acquired from Britain in the Treaty of Paris (1783) ending the Revolutionary War, more than doubled the size of the newly independent United States and extended its jurisdiction to the Mississippi River. Even before this territory could be organized, eastern settlers rushed in, oftentimes infringing on Indian land reserves and sparking volatile controversies between states with competing territorial claims. The Northwest Ordinance of 1787, one of the final acts of the Confederation Congress, brought some semblance of order to this process. This landmark legislation organized the territory northwest of the Ohio River into one district, established rules for its interim governance by Congress, and outlined a three-stage process by which it could transition from territorial status to full statehood. Not long afterward, the Southwest Ordinance (1790) performed the same service for the territory southwest of the Ohio River, with one critical exception—it permitted the introduction of slavery into the region, while the Northwest Ordinance had nominally banned it.

Following these ordinances, American settlers poured into the trans-Appalachian West in even greater numbers. They formed an advancing wedge of white settlement along a frontier stretching from Vermont and New York in the north to Kentucky and Tennessee in the west to Georgia in the south. Three distinct zones of settlement began to emerge in this expansive western region. On the northern frontier between Lake Champlain and the Cuyahoga River, New Englanders left the strongest imprint, especially in the new state of Vermont (1791), although these Yankee pioneers intermingled with settlers from the Hudson Valley and Pennsylvania. In the Ohio River Valley, regional migrations from New England, the Mid-Atlantic, and Virginia converged in more equal proportions, creating a vibrant western mix of eastern regional cultures. Farther south, in the new states of Kentucky (1792) and Tennessee (1796), traditional southern settlement patterns and ways of life predominated, as Virginia and Carolina pioneer families left the Piedmont and Great Valley for available lands to the west. In the process, white settlers made rapid conquest of Indian lands, overwhelming and displacing the Iroquois in New York, the Algonquian tribes in the Ohio country, and the Cherokees, Creeks, and Choctaws in the Southwest.

Expansion and Tension

The confluence of regional settlement streams in the trans-Appalachian West followed a general pattern toward convergence in 18th-century America. To contemporaries in the last quarter of the century, this blending of regional societies in the West had the potential to serve as a nationalizing force for the early United States. But the trend toward national consolidation was not inevitable. In America's federal republic, loyalties to the emerging nation often intersected and competed with loyalties to an established locale, state, region, or section. In the end, the western territory proved as much the seedbed of American nationalism as of its dissolution. As 19th-century Americans discovered, sectional conflicts over western expansion only intensified after the purchase of the vast Louisiana Territory from Napoleonic France in 1803. By the mid-19th century, the contested fate of slavery in these western territories sparked sectional crisis and civil war. Early America's distinctive regions may have converged over the course of the 18th century, but they never entirely congealed. Like sand in an hourglass, they diverged again in the 19th century, leaving the enduring problem of American regional diversity for future generations to solve.

—Daniel C. Wewers

Further Reading

Anderson, Fred. *A People's Army: Massachusetts Soldiers and Society in the Seven Years' War*. Chapel Hill: University of North Carolina Press, 1984.

Ayers, Edward L., Patricia Nelson Limerick, Stephen Nissenbaum, and Peter S. Onuf. *All Over the Map: Rethinking American Regions*. Baltimore, Md.: Johns Hopkins University Press, 1996.

Bailyn, Bernard. *The Ideological Origins of the American Revolution*. Cambridge, Mass.: Harvard University Press, 1967.

Beeman, Richard R. *The Varieties of Political Experience in Eighteenth-Century America*. Philadelphia: University of Pennsylvania Press, 2004.

Breen, T. H. "An Empire of Goods: The Anglicization of Colonial America, 1690–1776." *Journal of British Studies* 25, no. 4 (1986): 467–499.

Bushman, Richard L. *The Refinement of America: Persons, Houses, Cities*. New York: Alfred A. Knopf, 1992.

Butler, Jon. *Becoming America: The Revolution before 1776*. Cambridge, Mass.: Harvard University Press, 2000.

Fischer, David Hackett. *Albion's Seed: Four British Folkways in America*. New York: Oxford University Press, 1989.

Grasso, Christopher. *A Speaking Aristocracy: Transforming Public Discourse in Eighteenth-Century Connecticut*. Chapel Hill: University of North Carolina Press, 1999.

Greene, Jack P. *Pursuits of Happiness: The Social Development of Early Modern British Colonies and the Formation of American Culture*. Chapel Hill: University of North Carolina Press, 1988.

Hatch, Nathan O. *The Sacred Cause of Liberty: Republican Thought and the Millennium in Revolutionary New England*. New Haven, Conn.: Yale University Press, 1977.

Hendrickson, David C. *Peace Pact: The Lost World of the American Founding*. Lawrence: University Press of Kansas, 2003.

LaCroix, Alison L. *The Ideological Origins of American Federalism*. Cambridge, Mass.: Harvard University Press, 2010.

Loughran, Trish. *The Republic in Print: Print Culture in the Age of U.S. Nation Building, 1770–1870*. New York: Columbia University Press, 2007.

Meinig, D. W. *The Shaping of America: A Geographical Perspective on 500 Years of History*. Vol. 1, *Atlantic America, 1492–1800*. New Haven, Conn.: Yale University Press, 1986.

Murrin, John M. "A Roof without Walls: The Dilemma of American National Identity." In *Beyond Confederation: Origins of the Constitution and American National Identity*, edited by Richard Beeman, Stephen Botein, and Edward C. Carter II, 333–348. Chapel Hill: University of North Carolina Press, 1987.

Onuf, Peter S. *The Origins of the Federal Republic: Jurisdictional Controversies in the United States, 1775–1787*. Philadelphia: University of Pennsylvania Press, 1983.

Riordan, Liam. *Many Identities, One Nation: The Revolution and Its Legacy in the Mid-Atlantic*. Philadelphia: University of Pennsylvania Press, 2007.

Taylor, Alan. *American Colonies*. New York: Viking, 2001.

White, Richard. *The Middle Ground: Indians, Empires, and Republics in the Great Lakes Region, 1650–1815*. New York: Cambridge University Press, 1991.

Wood, Peter H. *Black Majority: Negroes in Colonial South Carolina from 1670 through the Stono Rebellion*. New York: Alfred A. Knopf, 1974.

18th Century TRADE

Overseas trade was the most dynamic component of the 18th-century American economy. Atlantic commerce unleashed the wealth-producing capacity of British America—Great Britain's North American and West Indian colonies—and later that of the newborn United States of America. Colonial commerce had been structured by the British Parliament to serve the interests of the mother country, and American participants largely conformed to British rules governing trade—when it was in their interest to do so. In the 1760s and 1770s, merchants and mariners in colonial ports challenged British authority to regulate commerce and set in motion the opening phase of the American Revolution. In the immediate postwar years, the overseas trade of the new American nation was fragmented and tentative. Ratification of the Constitution (1789) established a basis for coherent commercial policy, and the declaration of war between Great Britain and France (1793) provided unprecedented opportunities for American trade that led to the most rapid commercial expansion in the nation's history.

Regulation

Colonial commerce functioned within a broad set of principles that dominated western European economic thought and policy from the 16th to the late 18th centuries. Mercantilism, as it has been known since the publication of Adam Smith's *The Wealth of Nations* (1776), was an expression of economic nationalism that sought to enrich a state by restraining imports and encouraging exports. The goal of mercantilist policies—which had the effect of pitting one trading nation against another—was to strengthen the state by achieving a "favorable" balance of trade that would bring gold and silver into the country, maintain domestic employment, and maximize government revenue through tariffs on trade.

The English Acts of Trade and Navigation, better known as the Navigation Acts, were consistent with basic mercantilist principles. The first of the English statutes governing colonial commerce, passed by the Commonwealth Parliament in 1651 and reenacted by the Restoration Parliament in 1660, required that commodities imported into England be carried in English ships manned largely by English sailors. The act of 1660 stipulated that certain colonial goods (such as tobacco and sugar) be exported only to England or another English colony. An act of 1663 stipulated that European goods could be imported into the colonies only from England. An act of 1673—and numerous subsequent acts—refined the system of duties and strengthened enforcement. Trading with nations at peace with the Crown was allowed, as long as it conformed to the Navigation Acts.

Colonial commerce was also governed by a tangle of British, Irish, and colonial statutes, ordinances, and regulations that reflected local conditions, interests, and aspirations. Some of these enforced standards of quality (such as a New York law requiring the inspection of flour); others dealt with weights and measures (such as a Philadelphia ordinance specifying the length of barrel staves); still others attempted to steer the direction of trade (such as the Irish parliament's bounty on North American flaxseed shipped directly to Ireland). In addition, individual ports had regulations designed to ensure the efficient loading and unloading of ships and the orderly movement of goods through city streets.

The customs service was responsible for enforcement of the Navigation Acts and the collection of revenue on behalf of the British treasury. By the beginning of the 18th century, the American colonies had been broken up into customs districts, in each of which officials monitored the coming and going of ships, oversaw compliance with trade regulations, collected duties, and initiated the seizure of ships and cargoes found in violation of the Navigation Acts. The London government authorized establishment of a system of admiralty courts in America to adjudicate violations of the Navigation Acts and other types of maritime-related claims.

In spite of these efforts, smuggling and other forms of illicit commerce thrived in colonial America. Broadly speaking, illegal trade took three forms: (1) the importation of manufactured goods and Asian luxuries, such as tea, spices, and certain fine fabrics, from Amsterdam, Rotterdam, and other northern European ports; (2) the North American importation of "foreign" (mostly French) sugar and sugar products disguised as British West Indian produce; and (3) trading with the (French and Spanish) enemy, an activity that reached its peak during the Seven Years' War (1756–63).

Structure

The structure of colonial commerce was, for the most part, consistent with the intent of the Navigation Acts. A significant share of this trade consisted of bilateral exchanges with ports in England, Scotland, and, in some instances, Ireland. North American and West Indian plantation produce (such as tobacco, sugar, rum, indigo, and rice) and a short list of other goods (such as flaxseed, specialty hardwoods, and pig iron) were carried to the British Isles, where they were exchanged for a vast array of manufactures (ranging from linens, nails, and window glass to carriages, furniture, and musical instruments), as well as foodstuffs such as beer, cheese, and salted beef.

Colonial vessels also engaged in complex multilateral patterns of trade, some involving northern Europe, the Iberian Peninsula, and the Atlantic islands (important as a source of popular wines). The best known of these multilateral patterns was the so-called triangular trade, various permutations of which linked the British Isles, the West Coast of Africa, and ports in the West Indies and North America in the Atlantic slave trade, the most notorious component of colonial commerce.

Most of the activities that constituted colonial commerce—but not all—were conducted within the confines of the law. Situated far from the center of British authority, the western Atlantic—particularly the Caribbean region—provided enticing opportunities for North American and British West Indian vessels to call at the ports of Great Britain's Dutch, French, and Spanish rivals. Officials in the free-trading Dutch (St. Eustatius and Curaçao) and Danish (St. Thomas, St. John, and St. Croix) islands encouraged such exchanges. Policymakers in Versailles and Madrid struggled ineffectively to maintain the exclusivity of their Atlantic trading systems consistent with their national and mercantilist goals.

Until late in the colonial period, Atlantic commerce owed its vitality to the European demand for sugar—from whatever source. By 1700, the near exclusive cultivation of sugar and other West Indian produce in the English and French Caribbean had led to overdependence upon external sources of supply for the provisions, building materials, and other goods necessary to support slave-driven plantation agriculture. North America's West Indian trade—most highly developed in New England and the Middle Atlantic colonies—was a powerful stimulant to the emerging American economy, creating demand for labor and fueling immigration. By the middle decades of the 18th century, however, American economic expansion was as much the result of growth within the North American economy itself as it was of the demands of markets in the British and foreign West Indies.

The structure of colonial trade was dependent on the availability of accurate and timely information, some of it public and some private. From early in the 18th century, newspapers on both sides of the Atlantic published detailed information on market conditions, commodity prices, exchange rates, natural disasters, and political circumstances affecting trade. Such information (such as news of harvest failure in Ireland) could shift the course of trade. As important—from the perspective of individual merchants widely dispersed throughout the Atlantic region—was the reliability of private shipping and the British postal service for the conveyance of mercantile correspondence.

Merchants and Merchant Communities

In British America, to be an overseas merchant implied doing business with correspondents abroad and involvement is some aspect of importing and exporting, whether as a factor or agent, or as a merchant trading on his (or, occasionally, her) own account. Overseas traders were prominent figures in colonial America, where the term "merchant" was broader and more inclusive than in the British Isles. Besides applying to substantial businessmen engaged in overseas trade primarily at the wholesale level, the term was adopted by all manner of traders and shopkeepers involved in the collection, exchange, and distribution of goods.

In 18th-century Atlantic trade, overseas merchants were responsible for purchasing goods for export; ordering, and later distributing, incoming cargoes; negotiating bills of exchange; securing and overseeing ships, officers, and crews; hiring additional shipping space; arranging for marine insurance; keeping the company books; representing the firm's interests in court; supervising employees, including bookkeepers, clerks, day laborers, and slaves; maintaining all correspondence; and—if there was one—managing a retail store. Critical to the success of an overseas merchant were reputation and personal relationships, often between correspondents who had never met face to face.

Finance

Atlantic trade depended on capital, credit, and efficient payment mechanisms, as well as the availability of marine insurance. Land and other natural resources were abundant in colonial America, but capital and credit were persistently scarce. London, the financial center of the British Empire, was the principal source of the financial resources that underpinned Atlantic commerce. Of primary importance was access to capital in an age when long trading voyages and slow remittances tied up the resources of a merchant for extended periods.

Easy credit fueled the overseas trade of the British Empire. Before the development of commercial banks, merchants on both sides of the Atlantic offered some form of credit. The most significant providers were large London wholesalers moving vast quantities of English manufactured goods to markets in British North America and beyond. One year's credit on export sales was commonplace by the middle of the 18th century, and credit of up to two years was not unknown.

Bills of exchange—the most important financial instruments—allowed the orderly movement of wealth over great distances. The highly negotiable bills enjoyed many of the features of modern checks, except that funds were drawn from accounts in private hands rather than at banks. The most sought-after bills were those drawn against reputable firms in London, and their widespread use solidified London as the financial center of the British Empire. Even so, specie (gold and silver coins from a variety of nations) continued to play a role throughout the 18th century, particularly in international exchanges.

Managing risk was a pressing concern of businessmen in overseas trade. Just as partnerships allowed the pooling of capital (and the sharing of profits and losses), marine insurance offered protection against the loss of a ship and its cargo. For a fee (the premium), a syndicate of insurance underwriters bound themselves to cover potential losses for a particular voyage. By the mid-18th century, London had displaced Amsterdam in providing safe and reliable marine insurance. Pockets of maritime underwriting appeared elsewhere as well, such as in New York and Philadelphia, where insurance offices were a feature of port life in the decades before the Revolution.

Exports

Colonial trade in the 18th century was driven by demand in the British Isles and on the European continent for the produce and natural resources of the New World. North America's West Indian trade—accounting for about a quarter of exports—grew in tandem with the expansion of sugar production in the Caribbean. However, Atlantic trade was about much more than sugar, tobacco, and the other plantation articles. The array of goods offered by each of the five regional economies of British America reflected the diversity of local resources and conditions.

The exports of New England (Massachusetts, Connecticut, Rhode Island, and New Hampshire) and maritime Canada (Newfoundland, Nova Scotia, and, after 1763, Quebec) were the most varied. Fish accounted for about a third of New England's exports and dominated those of Maritime Canada. Fish found large and expansive markets in the Caribbean and southern Europe. Livestock and salted meat, along with an array of wooden products (from ax handles to framed buildings), were also important in New England trade. A typical New England cargo included modest quantities of a wide range of goods—from apples and beeswax to potash and whale oil. Although Boston and Newport were the region's most important trading centers, there was a lively export trade at smaller ports such as Portsmouth (New Hampshire), Salem (Massachusetts), Providence (Rhode Island), and New London (Connecticut).

The middle colonies of New York, New Jersey, Pennsylvania, and Delaware could boast the fast-growing cities of Philadelphia and New York and the best-developed agricultural hinterland in British America. By the 1770s, wheat and flour—nearly all of it sent to the West Indies and southern Europe—accounted for roughly three-quarters of the exports of the "breadbasket colonies." There was as well a lively flaxseed export to Ireland (the region's most important wintertime trade), as well as significant shipments of pig iron, potash, and grain to the British Isles.

Exports from the Upper South (Maryland and Virginia) were dominated by tobacco, the most valuable North American export. As much as 85 percent of tobacco exports to Great Britain were reexported to the European continent. By the Revolution, wheat and flour accounted for about 20 percent of exports. The Upper South was not a region of thriving port towns. A notable exception late in the colonial period was the emergence of Baltimore, Maryland, gateway to the rich agriculture of the Shenandoah Valley.

The trade of the Lower South—the Carolinas, Georgia, and, late in the colonial period, East and West Florida—was dominated by large-scale plantation agriculture. Rice accounted for more than half the value of exports, and roughly two-thirds of rice shipments went to Great Britain. Indigo—all of which went to Great Britain—accounted for about 20 percent of exports. The Lower South was also a source of naval stores (pitch, tar, and turpentine), though never in the quantities demanded by the government in London, which hoped to break the Royal Navy's dependence on northern Europe. Charleston, South Carolina, was among the most important ports in North America.

The exports of the British West Indies—principally Barbados, Antigua, St. Christopher, Nevis, Montserrat, and Jamaica—were the most valuable of any region in British America. Roughly 94 percent of shipments consisted of sugar and sugar products, about 86 percent of which was sent to Great Britain, with the remainder (mostly molasses and rum) going to British North America. Exports in this slave-based plantation economy were largely managed by factors and "town agents" in places such as Bridgetown (Barbados), St. Johns (Antigua), and Kingston (Jamaica), where trade was more narrowly focused than anywhere in North America.

In addition to the commodity exports, colonial merchants provided a wide array of "invisible exports," that is, goods and services not recorded in customs ledgers. Notable among these were exports of ships and shipping services. A significant share of invisible exports related to financial and legal services. These included representation for clients abroad in debt collection and in the resolution of disputes.

Imports

Imports to America experienced impressive growth in the 18th century. The share of total English exports sent to the protected markets of British America increased from about 6 percent in 1700 to over 25 percent by the mid-1770s. This growth was driven by an expanding population, rising income, and shifts in behavior—encouraged by newspaper advertising and easy credit that laid the foundation of the consumer society. Imports were also encouraged by economies of scale that reduced the cost of English manufactured goods for American consumers and by surplus shipping capacity—especially in eastbound vessels—that lowered transfer charges.

By the Revolution, colonial markets were taking better than half of Britain's exports of wrought iron and copper, nails, cordage, beaver hats, linens, silks, and printed cottons. There were, in addition, significant imports of foodstuffs, among them English beer, salted beef and butter from Ireland, and Asian teas and spices. Such goods found their way into the colonial backcountry by means of a rudimentary distribution system in which barter played a large role.

Because imports exceeded exports, 18th-century America struggled under a persistent trade imbalance. Easy credit terms led to dangerous levels of debt and periodic financial crises, notably in 1772 when the entire system appeared on the verge of unraveling. Conspicuous

Exports to and Imports from England by the American Colonies and States, 1700 to 1790

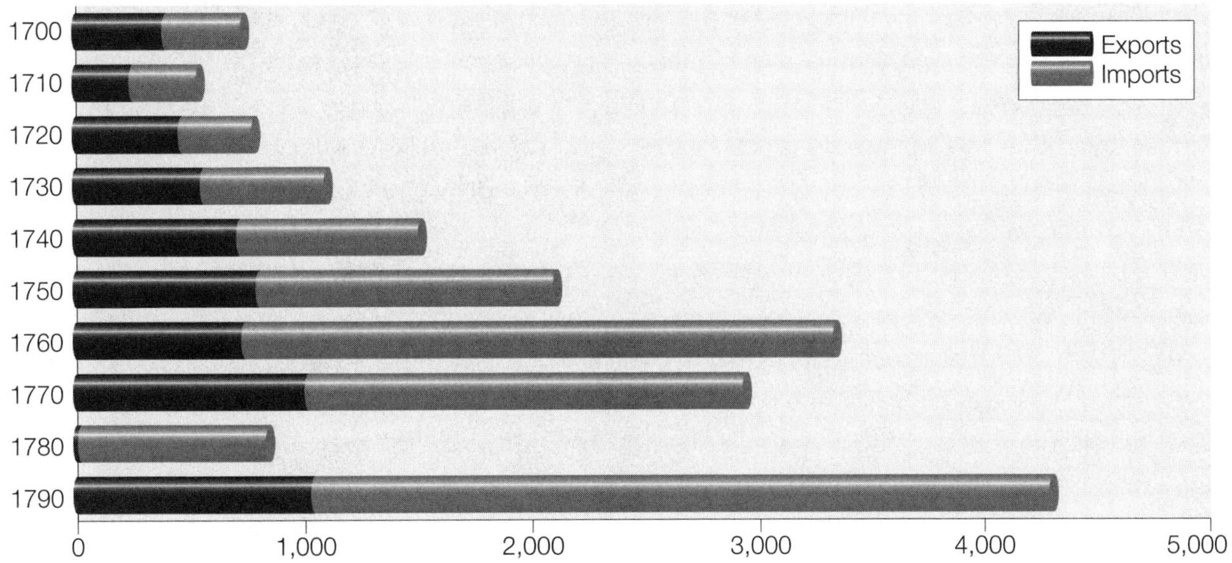

Year	Exports (thousand pounds sterling)	Imports (thousand pounds sterling)	Year	Exports (thousand pounds sterling)	Imports (thousand pounds sterling)
1700	395	344	1750	815	1,313
1710	250	294	1760	761	2,612
1720	468	320	1770	1,016	1,926
1730	573	537	1780	19	825
1740	718	813	1790	1,043	3,258

Source: U.S. Department of Commerce, Bureau of the Census, *Historical Statistics of the United States: Colonial Times to 1970*, 1176–1177 (Washington, D.C.: Bureau of the Census, 1975).
Note: Includes data for the following colonies, and the states that succeeded them: Massachusetts, Connecticut, Rhode Island, New Hampshire, New York, Pennsylvania, Virginia, Maryland, and Carolina. Data for Georgia is included in the figures from 1740, except for the import figure for 1760.

Across the 18th century, the balance of trade—the difference between imports and exports—between Britain's North American colonies and England came to strongly favor English imports, representing in part the exclusionary trade policies enforced by Britain on the colonies. Growing demand in the colonies, however, was also a major factor in this import growth, caused by increasing population, rising incomes, and a commensurate growth in interest in consumer goods in the colonies. Even at the time of the Revolution, English imports still moved into British North America, despite a sharp decline in the amount.

consumption among members of the planter class—many already deeply in debt—added disproportionately to the problem and led to the mortgaging of crops not yet in the ground. Exporters contributed to this imbalance as well. Overcapacity in British workshops flooded the colonies with imports and occasionally led to dumping (sales below the cost of production) through discount auction houses in urban centers.

Human Cargoes

Fee-paying passengers, indentured servants, and enslaved Africans all found their way to British America within the context of colonial commerce. Most unbound men and women traveling to and from colonial America did so as paying passengers aboard merchant vessels. This "invisible" trade moved large numbers of emigrants to the colonies and contributed to social mobility in the Atlantic economy. Nearly every incoming and outgoing trading vessel carried at least a few passengers to supplement freight earnings.

The large and well-established trade in indentured servants is better known. Not to be confused with slavery, voluntary indentured servitude involved the legal bonding of a servant to his or her employer for a predetermined period, typically four years. The indenture (a contract that entitled the holder to a servant's labor) was made freely before a magistrate in Great Britain or Ireland in return for passage across the Atlantic. Upon arrival in America, the captain of a servant-carrying vessel sold the indentures to the highest bidder. Indenture contracts were negotiable instruments and could be resold, the price reflecting the value of the labor remaining to the purchaser. No fewer than half of all white persons who immigrated to British America came as indentured servants.

The slave trade—the trafficking in human beings as legal property—was linked, directly or indirectly, to every aspect of colonial commerce. Merchant houses in London and Liverpool dominated the trade, but there was significant North American involvement as well, notably in Rhode Island. British slaving vessels, larger than those from colonial ports, carried an impressive variety of manufactured goods to the west coast of Africa. The smaller North American slavers were more likely to carry mixed cargoes of rum and other colonial produce. The slave trade typically employed purpose-built vessels designed to maximize carrying capacity and the control of enslaved Africans.

Assembling a slave cargo at a West African slaving station could take months and often involved complex negotiations with African and European intermediaries. At the conclusion of the westbound voyage (the notorious Middle Passage) most enslaved Africans were landed in the British West Indies, with lesser numbers sent to the Carolina Low Country, the Chesapeake region, or farther north. Sales were typically conducted through specialized auction houses, some of which offered credit to their most substantial customers. The West Indian and North American merchants involved in slave trading typically represented principals in Great Britain or the "northward" colonial ports. In addition to the primary slave trade, there was a thriving secondary trade by means of which enslaved Africans already in British America were resold and dispersed throughout the colonies.

Trade and Revolution

The reconfiguration of British trade policy in the 1760s figured prominently in the imperial crisis that led to the American Revolution. Until then, the 18th century had been a period of lax enforcement of the Navigation Acts. In this period of "salutary neglect," policymakers in London were reluctant to interfere with the thriving Atlantic economy. In the colonies, customs officials were underpaid and left to fulfill their duties with little support from above. Significant numbers of them accepted gratuities (bribes) to look the other way when faced with violations of laws governing trade.

The staggering national debt incurred during the Seven Years' War and colonial America's brazen wartime trade with the French enemy led the London government to rethink its policies governing trade. An act of 1763—passed in the throes of a severe postwar recession—called for the deputizing of British naval officers as customs enforcement agents with broad powers of search and seizure. The American Revenue Act of 1764 (better known as the Sugar Act) reduced duties on certain goods (foreign rum and molasses, for example) while increasing duties on others. But the Sugar Act contained harsh enforcement provisions that threatened to undermine the structure of colonial commerce. In 1765, reaction to the Stamp Act and its burdensome indirect taxes on commerce led to an effective boycott of trade with Great Britain, lifted only after repeal of the Stamp Act in 1766.

In 1767, still determined to exert firm control over colonial trade, Parliament passed a series of measures known as the Townshend Acts. They required the collection of duties in American ports on British paper, painters' colors, red and white lead, glass, and tea. The Townshend Acts also established an American customs board and empowered colonial courts to issue writs of assistance, essentially open-ended search warrants. An effective boycott of British trade was in place by March 1769, and a year later Parliament removed all the Townshend duties except that on tea.

The reopening of colonial ports led to a period of vigorous commercial activity, as well as glutted markets and a credit crisis that threatened the stability of trade. Trouble erupted once again when Parliament came to the rescue of the East India Company in 1773. The Tea Act of that year gave the company an unassailable competitive advantage in American markets, putting the livelihoods of both fair traders and smugglers at risk. Parliament's arbitrary interference in the colonial economy brought immediate reaction—best exemplified by the Boston Tea Party. The British response took the form of the Coercive, or "Intolerable," Acts of 1774. London's punitive legislation rekindled discontent, led the Continental Congress to shut off trade with Great Britain and Ireland, and precipitated armed skirmishes that evolved into full-scale revolutionary war.

Revolution did not bring an end to American commerce, however. Against daunting odds, the Patriots maintained a fragile wartime trade through agents in France and the Netherlands. This activity took many forms but centered on the tiny Dutch island of St. Eustatius in the Lesser Antilles, where goods vital to the war effort were gathered for shipment to North America aboard fast blockade-runners. The British—forced to import a large share of their military and civilian supplies—were involved in Atlantic trade throughout the war.

Overseas Trade and the New American Nation

The Treaty of Paris (1783) confirmed American independence and removed commercial grievances that figured in the run-up to Revolution. Independence also brought restrictions. From the vantage of Great Britain, the United States was now a foreign country whose trade deserved no preferential treatment. Financial services were still available in London, but they were more costly and less convenient, and the British legal system no longer guaranteed the "rights of Englishmen" to citizens of the new American nation. On the high seas, the protection of the Royal Navy was not available to American vessels, rendering trade precarious, especially in the Mediterranean, where commerce-raiding by Algerine corsairs was endemic.

For the new United States of America—whose economy had so long benefited from Atlantic commerce—this was a brave new world. Serious challenges faced the nation as it struggled to establish a presence in foreign markets. Trade with France began during the war (1778), and selected French West Indian islands became legal destinations for American shipping. However, both Great Britain and Spain (partially) closed their New World colonies to vessels and goods from the United States. Even so, trade with the British West Indies continued, but it was indirect and often clandestine, and far less profitable than it had been before 1775. In this period of adjustment, American merchants sought out new opportunities in the Netherlands, Germany, Scandinavia, and elsewhere in Europe, and in the mid-1780s opened trade with China.

The newly independent American states were too weak and too loosely allied to compete on an equal footing with Europe's commercial powers. Congress, under the Articles of Confederation (1781–89), had no authority to regulate commerce and aid shipping. Ratification of the Constitution (1789) introduced a coherent national policy with respect to trade and navigation and gave the federal courts exclusive jurisdiction over admiralty and maritime affairs. In July 1789 Congress established the United States Customs Service, and President George Washington signed the nation's first tariff act—authorizing the collection of duties on imported goods. Tariffs accounted for about 90 percent of government revenue between 1789 and the Civil War.

American trade benefited from high prices abroad for agriculture produce and strong domestic demand for European manufactured goods. Flour displaced tobacco as the leading export. Breadstuffs, tobacco, rice, and lumber made up over three-fourths of the value of American exports in 1790—breadstuffs accounting for about 40 percent and tobacco 20 percent of the total. In 1790 about a third of all U.S. exports were sent to the West Indies. The value of American exports to Saint-Domingue (modern Haiti) exceeded those to all other West Indian islands combined.

The outbreak of war between Great Britain and France in 1793 presented American merchants with unparalleled opportunities. Both sides resorted to neutral shipping and authorized importations from the United States on a vast scale. During the wars of the French Revolution (1792–1802) and the beginning phase of the subsequent Napoleonic Wars, earnings from exports and shipping services reached about 13 percent of national income. War also led to the abandonment of commercial monopolies by the European powers and opened promising new markets, especially in Spain's continental colonies. By the end of the 18th century the United States had effective control of the world's carrying trade.

American neutrality was fraught with danger, however. Great Britain refused to enter into a commercial treaty with the United States, preferring instead to regulate trade with its former colonies by executive decree. By 1794 the British navy had captured hundreds of American merchant ships doing business with the French. That year Congress responded with a two-month embargo on all shipping in American ports and entered into comprehensive negotiations with the London government that led to the Jay Treaty (ratified in 1794 but not in effect until 1796). The agreement required Great Britain to compensate American shipowners for their losses and resolved a number of long-standing political and territorial issues. For its part, the United States gave "most favored nation" trading status to Great Britain and acquiesced in British anti-French maritime policies. Incensed by the Jay Treaty, the French began seizing American vessels and precipitated an undeclared war between the United States and France (1798–1800).

In spite of the risks, the carrying and reexport trade of the United States in the closing decade of the 18th century invigorated the domestic economy. Exports in 1800 stood at about four and a half times their level of 1790. A similar rise in imports was driven by earnings from overseas trade. The nation's thriving commerce encouraged the development of American cities and towns, fostered agricultural expansion, and advanced a myriad of activities, from insurance underwriting to shipbuilding. Although the opening decade of the 19th century brought a contraction of trade, the war years had established American commerce on a global scale.

—Thomas M. Truxes

Further Reading

Andrews, Charles M. *England's Commercial and Colonial Policy*. Vol. 4, *The Colonial Period of American History*. New Haven, Conn.: Yale University Press, 1964.

Breen, T. H. *The Marketplace of Revolution: How Consumer Politics Shaped American Independence*. New York: Oxford University Press, 2004.

———. *Tobacco Culture: The Mentality of the Great Tidewater Planters on the Eve of Revolution*. Princeton, N.J.: Princeton University Press, 1985.

Davis, Ralph. *The Rise of the English Shipping Industry in the Seventeenth and Eighteenth Centuries*. Newton Abbot, Devon, U.K.: David & Charles, 1962.

Doerflinger, Thomas M. *A Vigorous Spirit of Enterprise: Merchants and Economic Development in Revolutionary Philadelphia*. Chapel Hill: University of North Carolina Press, for the Omohundro Institute of Early American History and Culture, 1986.

Earle, Peter. *Sailors: English Merchant Seamen, 1650–1775*. London: Methuen, 1998.

Egnal, Marc. "The Economic Development of the Thirteen Continental Colonies, 1720–1775." *William and Mary Quarterly*, 32 (April 1975): 191–222.

Estes, Todd. *The Jay Treaty Debate, Public Opinion, and the Evolution of Early American Political Culture*. Amherst: University of Massachusetts Press, 2006.

Hancock, David. *Citizens of the World: London Merchants and the Integration of the British Atlantic Community, 1735–1785*. Cambridge, U.K.: Cambridge University Press, 1995.

Harper, Lawrence A. *The English Navigation Laws: A Seventeenth-Century Experiment in Social Engineering*. New York: Columbia University Press, 1939.

Johnson, Emory R., et al. *History of Domestic and Foreign Commerce of the United States*. 2 vols. Washington, D.C.: Carnegie Institution of Washington, 1915.

Klein, Herbert S. *The Atlantic Slave Trade*. Cambridge, U.K.: Cambridge University Press, 1999.

McCusker, John J., and Russell R. Menard. *The Economy of British America, 1607–1789*. Chapel Hill: University of North Carolina Press, for the Omohundro Institute of Early American History and Culture, 1985.

Morgan, Kenneth. *Slavery, Atlantic Trade and the British Economy, 1660–1800*. Cambridge, U.K.: Cambridge University Press, 2000.

Nash, R. C. "The Organization of Trade and Finance in the British Atlantic Economy, 1600–1830." In *The Atlantic Economy during the Seventeenth and Eighteenth Centuries: Organization, Operation, Practice, and Personnel*, edited by Peter C. Coclanis, 95–151. Columbia: University of South Carolina Press, 2005.

Pares, Richard. "The London Sugar Market, 1740–1769." *Economic History Review* 9 (December 1956), 254–270.

———. *Yankees and Creoles: The Trade between North America and the West Indies before the American Revolution*. Cambridge, Mass.: Harvard University Press, 1956.

Price, Jacob M. *Capital and Credit in British Overseas Trade: The View from the Chesapeake, 1700–1776*. Cambridge, Mass.: Harvard University Press, 1980.

———. "Economic Function and the Growth of American Port Towns in the Eighteenth Century." *Perspectives in American History* 8 (1974): 121–174.

———. "What Did Merchants Do? Reflections on British Overseas Trade, 1660–1790." *Journal of Economic History* 49 (June 1989): 267–284.

Shepherd, James F., and Gary M. Walton. *Shipping, Maritime Trade, and the Economic Development of Colonial North America*. Cambridge, U.K.: Cambridge University Press, 1972.

Sheridan, Richard B. "The British Credit Crisis of 1772 and the American Colonies." *Journal of Economic History* 20 (June 1960): 161–186.

———. *Sugar and Slavery: An Economic History of the British West Indies, 1623–1775.* Aylesbury, Buckinghamshire, U.K.: Ginn and Company, for the Department of History at the University of the West Indies, 1974.

Smith, Abbot Emerson. *Colonists in Bondage: White Servitude and Convict Labor in America, 1607–1776*. New York: W. W. Norton, 1971.

Smith, Simon D. "Gedney Clarke of Salem and Barbados: Transatlantic Super-Merchant." *New England Quarterly* 76 (December 2003): 499–549.

Steele, Ian K. *The English Atlantic, 1675–1740: An Exploration of Communication and Community.* New York: Oxford University Press, 1986.

Truxes, Thomas M. *Defying Empire: Trading with the Enemy in Colonial New York*. New Haven, Conn.: Yale University Press. 2008.

———. *Irish-American Trade, 1660–1783*. Cambridge, U.K.: Cambridge University Press, 1988.

18th Century TRANSPORTATION

Methods of transportation in the American colonies at the outset of the 18th century were little changed from those of previous centuries. The dominant—and really the only reasonably convenient—form of transportation was waterborne, and for that reason most colonial cities were clustered along shorelines or navigable waterways. When forced to travel by land, most people walked from city to city, following old Native American trails and newly cut roads. The wealthy bought horses for individual travel, and in rare cases carts, wagons, and coaches were used for moving freight and passengers. Though waterborne transportation would remain the easiest, most efficient, and preferred mode of travel throughout 18th-century America, the road network would expand continuously throughout the century, making travel by land easier. By the end of the century, a web of stagecoach lines was beginning to spread across ever-larger parts of the country. So while travel in America remained difficult and challenging for some, physical mobility was becoming a fact of life for a growing number of Americans.

Distribution of Settlements

Understanding travel in 18th-century America begins with understanding its geographical context. Early settlement in North America had been shaped by the same geographical factors that would come to dominate transportation concerns in the 18th century, namely, the availability of waterways. St. Augustine (1565), Jamestown (1607), and Plymouth (1620)—the first settlements in Florida, the Carolinas, the Chesapeake region, and New England, respectively—were all located on the open coast of the Atlantic Ocean. New Amsterdam (1625) was located on Manhattan Island because New York Harbor offered perhaps the best anchorage on the Eastern Seaboard, and Albany (1624) represented the farthest navigable northern reach of the Hudson River, and as such became a key trading point with the difficult-to-navigate backcountry.

Every major city in the 18th century was a port, whether on the ocean or on a river. Even among inland settlements, very few towns were located far from navigable rivers. In the Chesapeake region (Virginia, Maryland, and Delaware), the many tobacco-growing plantations generally clustered along rivers, where their private docks allowed them to load their crops directly onto Europe-bound sailing ships. And as Americans began to move farther away from the coast, they found that the only really practical ways to get past the barrier of the Appalachian Mountains followed waterways.

Transportation Technologies

Sailing ships were the backbone of American transportation in the 18th century. Methods of propulsion in the maritime world had changed little since ancient times, and seafarers still relied on the power of the wind in a cloth sail to push their ships along. Though ships had grown larger in the preceding centuries, and creativity with the arrangement of the sails had allowed them to attain, under certain conditions, somewhat higher speeds, 18th-century sailing ships remained vulnerable to calming (being unable to move if the wind died down), as well as to the violent storms common to the Atlantic Ocean.

Sailing ships of the era were divided into two classes: smaller coastal vessels that sailed up and down the Atlantic shoreline, and seagoing ships. Coastal vessels typically had a shallower draft, allowing them to sail up rivers and into shallow harbors to pick up cargo and passengers, but they could not withstand the storms of the Atlantic and were thus obliged to sail near shore. Seagoing vessels had a deeper draft and were thus restricted to ports with deeper harbors, but they could sail more safely out of sight of land. Fortunately for ocean-going ships, European explorers and navigators had long since discovered a set of natural ocean currents and prevailing winds running clockwise in a giant circle around the North Atlantic. These currents made the journey, while lengthy (sailing time was measured in weeks or months), relatively safe and, for merchants, quite profitable. Given the importance of maritime transportation and commerce, it is unsurprising that by the 18th century a large shipbuilding industry had developed in the colonies, making use of North America's vast stands of old, strong timber to build ships suitable for the physically taxing Atlantic trade.

Commerce with the interior was carried out on boats specifically designed for that purpose. Some rivers in America, notably the Hudson, Connecticut, Susquehanna, and Potomac, were open to large-ship traffic, but commerce traveled on smaller rivers and creeks as well. Traveling up a minor waterway often involved avoiding rapids or other obstructions by portaging (carrying) the boat around the obstacle, so the vehicle used had to be light enough to be carried, as well as small enough to have the necessary shallow draft. The Chesapeake Bay area was home to a class of flat-bottomed coastal vessels called Durham boats, and many other coastal areas developed similar varieties of shallow-draft inshore vessels.

The boat that dominated the fur trade was an adaptation of the canoe, a vessel that Native Americans had been using for thousands of years. The simplest canoes were made out of a single log, burned out in the middle so that it could hold people and cargo. These were sturdy and durable, but relatively heavy and with a limited cargo capacity. More complex canoes made by both Native Americans and colonists were composed of a wooden frame covered with bark from a white birch tree, making them both lighter and able to carry more cargo. The fur trade that became a prime user of the inland waterways adapted the basic design of these birch-bark canoes to carry even more cargo and the large number of men necessary to conduct a fur expedition, a design that came to be known as the voyageur canoe. Another style of light boat, the bateau, also became widely used in the 18th century. Originally brought to America by French explorers, and built with a flat bottom, bateaux were employed for moving cargo as well as troops and their supplies. Both classes of light craft, canoes and bateaux, were crucial to what limited transport capacity existed in the interior of the continent.

Land-Based Transportation

Transportation on land in 18th-century America was significantly more difficult than its waterborne equivalent. At

Flat-bottom boats called bateaux, like the one in the line drawing above, were originally brought to America by French explorers. These shallow-draft vessels were used extensively in the fur trade and to transport heavy cargo, as well as to carry troops and their supplies. *(Pearson Scott Foresman)*

the beginning of the 18th century, American roads—when they existed at all—generally represented little improvement over the Native American trails, whose paths they often followed. Roads were little more than rutted, muddy tracks cut haphazardly through the forest. The dense forest of the new land made road construction much more difficult than it was in England. Bridges over rivers were mostly nonexistent, and where travel by wagon was possible at all, it was difficult and unreliable.

Roads and Road Construction

The difficulty in overland travel began to ease, though slowly and in a very limited fashion, over the course of the 18th century. By 1750 the King's Highway connected all of the major coastal cities between Boston and Charleston. (Its name fell out of favor during the American Revolution, when it was changed to the present Boston Post Road.) Taverns and inns sprung up at regular intervals along the King's Highway and other important, well-established roads, allowing riders and travelers to change horses and rest for the night.

Though the King's Highway was originally constructed as a post road (a conduit for carrying the mail), there were other factors that drove road construction in 18th-century America. One such factor was the desire to support military operations of European-style armies, such as those of the North American colonial powers Britain and France. These armies required large amounts of supplies, which were carried by a supply train of wagons and noncombat personnel. The first major military road was built through southern Pennsylvania by the Braddock expedition in 1755, and though the expedition failed in its military goal of capturing French-held Fort Duquesne (Pittsburgh), it proved the feasibility of such a road. General John Forbes built a second road in his ultimately successful expedition against the same target three years later. The Braddock Road and the Forbes Road were significant not only for their military importance, but because they pointed the way west, across the foreboding barrier of the Appalachian Mountains. Braddock's road was the first to allow wagons to cross the Appalachians; indeed, his expedition saw the first widespread adoption of the durable, large, cargo-carrying Conestoga wagon, a creation of German settlers in southern Pennsylvania that would later become a hallmark of American westward expansion on the Great Plains.

The desire of Americans for westward expansion drove the construction of new roads in the latter half of the 18th century. Where narrow waterways and trails had previously sufficed for the limited needs of the fur trade and explorers, the movement of whole families and communities across the Appalachians required roads that could facilitate the passage of wagons and herds. The Wilderness Road, originally cut by Daniel Boone, provided access to the Kentucky country, making possible that state's inclusion into the Union in 1792. Though road travel remained difficult, slow, and often dangerous, it became more common as the century wore on, and it would explode in popularity in the century to come.

Methods of Overland Travel

To make use of this growing network of roadways (or what passed for them), Americans needed technologies that would both take advantage of the gift of the prepared road and withstand its remaining rigors. Some Americans, particularly the poorest, had no option other than to travel by foot. Yet walking, though invulnerable to bad roads, was naturally slow and miserable, so Americans sought other ways to travel. The answer, as it had been since the earliest years of European exploration, generally involved horsepower. Whenever they could, Americans acquired horses; when they could afford to do so, and where the roads and other necessary infrastructure existed, they acquired wagons and coaches for those horses to pull. Farmers got their produce to market by bringing together convoys of wagons such as the Conestoga type used by the Braddock expedition, and families heading out to settle in new areas packed their belongings into such durable conveyances. Wagons came in various sizes and might be pulled by one horse or several, depending on their intended use. England had already developed an extensive culture centered on various types of wagons and carriages (wheeled, horse-drawn vehicles designed for passengers rather than cargo), but the paucity of usable roads in the American colonies prevented the development of such a system in America in the 18th century.

As the century went on, rudiments of a carriage-and-wagon system and culture began to develop in America. As in England, a system of stagecoach transportation developed in 18th-century America, though it was greatly limited by the lack of passable roads. Logically, stagecoach transportation developed initially in New England, an area of old settlement with decent weather and relatively short distances to be covered. Sometime in the late 1710s or early 1720s, Jonathan Wardwell, a Boston tavern owner, advertised the first known stagecoach service in America, traveling to Rhode Island. Though stagecoach services remained crude and uncomfortable throughout the 18th century—the luxurious, decorated stagecoaches of the public imagination would not come into use in America until the 1800s—they gradually expanded throughout the colonies, and then the republic. The East Coast became crisscrossed with stage routes, traveling along major roads such as the King's Highway, but also into the hinterland. After the Revolution, the system continued to expand, and it took on the important function of carrying the mail on government contract. Stagecoach travel, though, remained arduous, uncomfortable, and slow, and the inns where stage passengers would stay overnight remained an important institution.

A Century of Slow Progress

Though travel in 18th-century America remained, as a whole, quite difficult, the increasing construction of roads and the introduction of the stagecoach made it somewhat easier over the latter half of the century. And the very end of the century saw the introduction of several technologies that portended easier transport in the future. Construction began on the first canals in America, such as the Santee Canal in South Carolina and the Schuylkill and Susquehanna Canal in Pennsylvania, in the last decade of the century, spreading the ease and convenience of waterborne transportation to areas where it had previously been unavailable. The year 1795 saw the opening of the Philadelphia and Lancaster Turnpike Road, the first major turnpike (an often privately improved, maintained, and, consequently, tolled road) in America, as well as the first advanced, planned, and artificially surfaced road in the country. Finally, in England, a technology that would eclipse both canal and turnpike—the steam engine—was coming into popular use, though not yet for transport. It would be steam power, on rails and at sea, that would provide the foundation for the next chapter in the history of American transportation.

—Sandy Johnston

Further Reading

Burns, William E. *Science and Technology in Colonial America.* Westport, Conn.: Greenwood Press, 2005.

Colonial Williamsburg Web site. URL: http://www.history.org/history/teaching/enewsletter/april03/iotm.cfm. Accessed October 12, 2010.

Dunbar, Seymour. *A History of Travel in America*. New York: Tudor, 1937.

Federal Highway Works Administration. "The Paintings of Car Rakeman: 1795—*The Philadelphia and Lancaster Turnpike Road*." Available online. URL: http://www.fhwa.dot.gov/rakeman/1795.htm. Accessed October 12, 2010.

Holmes, Oliver W. *Stagecoach East: Stagecoach Days in the East from the Colonial Period to the Civil War.* Washington, D.C.: Smithsonian Institution Press, 1983.

International Museum of the Horse Web site. URL: http://imh.org/legacy-of-the-horse. Accessed October 12, 2010.

Jones, Daniel P. *The Economic and Social Transformation of Rural Rhode Island, 1780–1850.* Boston: Northeastern University Press, 1992

Thompson, Peter. *Rum Punch and Revolution: Taverngoing and Public Life in Eighteenth-Century Philadelphia*. Philadelphia: University of Pennsylvania Press, 1999.

University of Virginia, Department of American Studies. "Canals." Available online. URL: http://xroads.virginia.edu/~HYPER/DETOC/transport/canal.html. Accessed October 12, 2010.

Van Hoesen, Walter Hamilton. *Early Taverns and Stagecoach Days in New Jersey.* Rutherford, N.J.: Fairleigh Dickinson University Press, 1976.

18th Century WAR

In the 18th century the focus of warfare in North America shifted. Wars between Europeans and Native Americans to prevent European settlement ended as Native Americans were increasingly pushed away from the Atlantic seaboard. Indian warfare shifted to attempts to contain European settlement east of the Appalachian Mountains. Wars fought between Europeans for dominance of the continent took on a new prominence, beginning with a series of intercolonial wars and ending with the American Revolution. Early in the century, intercolonial wars were loosely tied to European conflicts, and gains or losses in North America were used as bargaining chips in peace negotiations without reference to colonial concerns. Later, European powers came to see control over North America as a goal in its own right. During the French and Indian War (1754–63), North America became a central battlefront in a global conflict over empire between Britain and France. Colonial military power became apparent during the American Revolution with the creation of an American military able to defeat professional European armies. After the Revolution, the United States engaged in a series of conflicts with Native Americans to consolidate territorial acquisitions, and in the so-called Quasi-War with France to protect American commerce. These events marked the creation of a new military presence that would come to dominate the continent in the following century.

Weapons and Warfare

Warfare in 18th-century America was a hybrid of indigenous tactics and European logistical and strategic practices. Fighting combined the mobility of Native Americans and colonists with the organization and professionalism of European armies. Native Americans remained the masters of guerrilla-style raids, but after decades of conflict with Indians, colonists had adopted some indigenous practices, and by the Seven Years' War, colonies had formed ranger units of scouts and wilderness fighters akin to modern-day special forces. In this context, British Americans developed the Pennsylvania long rifle, which was accurate to up to 250 yards. Inappropriate for pitched European-style battles because of its slow reloading time and inability to accept a bayonet, the long rifle was the perfect weapon for the raids and counter-raids that characterized frontier warfare in the early years of the century.

General imperial neglect and British cultural unease about standing armies meant colonists relied on colonial militias, though in the imperial wars they also sought troops and munitions from Britain. British American communities were required to organize militias, typically of every able-bodied man in a town; militiamen received rudimentary military training and were counted on to act as a local defense force in the absence of imperial garrisons—of which, before 1755, there were only two on the mainland, in New York City and in South Carolina. Professional soldiers almost universally scorned these militias as unreliable at best. Provincial forces did most of the fighting until the French and Indian War. After 1754, provincial forces, often relegated to supply and support roles, supplemented large numbers of imperial troops, many of whom were American-born enlistees. During the American Revolution, American armies were often largely composed of militia units around a smaller core of professional soldiers.

In contrast to the colonies, Britain, France, and other European states were funding large and increasingly professional standing armies and navies, deployed worldwide in the service of empire. These armies generally fought in massed ranks of troops standing shoulder to shoulder, facing off across open fields at perhaps 50 yards apart. The primary weapon of the European infantryman was the muzzle-loading, smoothbore, flintlock musket. Inaccurate beyond 100 yards, the musket was relatively easy to use and load. Bayonet charges would often decide the battle as one side tried to smash the opposing lines. Colorful uniforms and martial music helped coordinate armies of tens of thousands in the smoke of battle.

In the 18th century, navies, not armies, often decided wars. Control of the seas meant control of supply lines, economies, and the ability to maneuver forces. By the 1750s Britain's Royal Navy emerged as the greatest naval power in the world and would dictate the terms of many land battles. By the opening of the French and Indian War in 1754, British commanders were learning that using European tactics was a disaster in wilderness fighting and had created specialized light infantry units based upon American rangers. These highly mobile infantry units combined tactical flexibility to operate in conventional battle lines or as wilderness scouts and shock troops. Many officers trained in these methods would return to fight in the American Revolution. Contrary to myths of dogmatic British reliance upon European tactics, British troops often proved more adept at hybrid American-style warfare than troops serving under George Washington. Victory in pitched battles often went to those armies that could best unite the logistical, professional, and strategic acumen of Europe with the tactical peculiarities of the American context.

The Wars

Queen Anne's War (1702–1713)

Queen Anne's War was the American component of the War of the Spanish Succession (1701–14). Following the death of King Charles II of Spain in 1700, Europe went to war over the rival claims to the Spanish throne of the French Bourbons and the Austrian Hapsburgs. Spain and France fought an alliance of Austria, England, the Netherlands, and most of the German principalities. In North America, colonists intensified their ongoing border raids as the primary military strategy of the war.

In the colonies, Queen Anne's War began on the already troubled border between Spanish Florida, which included modern Georgia, and the English colony of Carolina. In 1702, Carolina governor James Moore led an unsuccessful expedition against the Spanish stronghold of St. Augustine, besieging the fort there for four months before he was forced to withdraw. In 1703–4, Moore, no longer governor, led a private raiding expedition against the mission settlements of northwest Florida. Survivors of this and subsequent raids fled to St. Augustine or the French settlement at Mobile, leaving an uninhabited no-man's-land between the English and Spanish colonies. Neither the Spanish nor the French were able to mount meaningful counterattacks.

The greatest concentration of fighting was in New England and French Canada and Acadia (modern-day Quebec and the Maritime provinces). Beginning in 1703, New France encouraged its Native American allies to attack outlying settlements along the New England frontier. The most devastating of these attacks was the raid against Deerfield, Massachusetts, on February 29, 1704, in which about 50 inhabitants were killed and 100 taken captive. The purpose of these raids was to discourage the expansion of English settlements into the interior and to keep the New England militia from massing and invading Canada.

In response, Massachusetts raised troops to carry the war to New France. At first the New Englanders concentrated their forces in raids against Native American settlements along the border between Maine and Acadia. The real focus for Massachusetts was the Acadian capital, Port Royal, which was a haven for French privateers and a recruiting station for hostile Native Americans. After failed campaigns by colonial militias against Acadia in 1704 and 1707, a combined force of colonial militia and British regulars, supported by the Royal Navy, captured Port Royal in 1710. Encouraged by this success, New England urged a more aggressive campaign against New France. In 1711 Britain sent troops to help New England invade Canada with a two-pronged attack against Montreal and Quebec. The effort was abandoned after accidents on the St. Lawrence River caused heavy losses of ships and men.

Queen Anne's War ended with the Treaty of Utrecht in 1713. France retained most of Canada and Louisiana but made important concessions to Great Britain, recognizing British claims to the Hudson Bay area and ceding control of Acadia and Newfoundland. Settlers in Massachusetts, who had suffered heavy loses in the expeditions against Acadia, felt betrayed when Acadia was renamed Nova Scotia and established as a new colony. The benefits of closing the French privateering base in Port Royal were lost when the French established the fortress of Louisbourg on Île Royale (later Cape Breton Island).

Indian Wars (1715–1725)

The period between Queen Anne's War and the War of Jenkins' Ear saw relative stability and peace between European powers but was marked by brutal warfare between Native Americans and British colonists in South Carolina and on the New England frontier. The Yamasee War (1715–18) and Governor Dummer's War (1722–25) marked a crucial turning point in European/Native American struggles along the Atlantic seaboard. The Yamasee War was the final effort of Native Americans to reverse the establishment of a colony along the British Atlantic coast. A number of southern tribes, including the Yamasee, Creek, Cherokee, and Chickasaw, united to attack British colonists along the Carolina coast. The war, which initially threatened the survival of the South Carolina colony, proved extremely costly for all sides. Despite some success, Native Americans could not maintain their alliances, as some tribes made a separate peace with the British. The resulting political settlement established British South Carolina as the dominant power along the coast and transferred Native American power to more inland groups like the Cherokee and Catawba.

Governor Dummer's War, fought along the New England frontier from present-day Vermont to Maine, typified later European and Native American conflicts. Expanding colonial settlements met resistance from Native Americans who sought to contain British settlement to the Atlantic coastline. Allying with the French, who also opposed British claims to the land, Native Americans tried to roll back the British frontier in a strategic effort that would reappear in colonial warfare throughout the century. Rather than a full-scale attempt on the part of the Indians to drive Europeans back into the sea, Governor Dummer's War was a frontier war to establish boundaries of settlement between European powers and Native American allies.

The War of Jenkins' Ear (1739–1744)

The War of Jenkins' Ear was the first war between European powers to be fought primarily over colonial issues. Restrictions on British trade in the Spanish West Indies were a constant source of conflict between Britain and Spain. British merchants often violated the restrictions; Spanish colonial officials responded by boarding British vessels to search for contraband. In 1738, during a parliamentary debate on the freedom of the seas, British merchant captain Robert Jenkins supposedly waved his severed ear, claiming the Spanish cut it off during a boarding skirmish. To the British public, Jenkins's ear became a symbol of Spanish atrocities. When Spain refused to give up its right to search British vessels, Britain declared war in October 1739.

Britain attempted to seize Spanish territory in southeastern North America, the Caribbean, and Central America. In North America, British and Spanish colonists battled over the border between Spanish Florida and the new British colony of Georgia from 1740 to 1742, with neither side taking territory from the other. By the beginning of 1744 the war had disintegrated into a series of minor raids and privateering operations. This period did mark the emergence of the Royal Navy as one of the foremost European navies, rivaled only by those of France and Spain.

King George's War (1744–1748)

The War of Jenkins' Ear was swallowed up by the larger conflict known in Europe as the War of the Austrian Succession (1740–48) and in North America as King George's War. Triggered by the accession of Maria Theresa to the Austrian throne in 1740, the War of the Austrian Succession was essentially a struggle over the control of central Europe between France, Prussia, and Austria. When Britain entered the war against France and Prussia in 1744, the focus in North America shifted from the Spanish colonies to the French.

Hostilities began in North America in May 1744, when French forces from Louisbourg seized the fishing station of Canso in Nova Scotia. Louisbourg was an irritant to New England. Its port was home to both the French fishing vessels that competed in the fishing grounds of the Grand Banks and the French privateers that preyed on New England merchant vessels. The attack on Canso fueled fears that the French intended to take back Nova Scotia, which was still home to several thousand French-speaking Acadians.

Governor William Shirley of Massachusetts lobbied other British colonies to support an expedition against Louisbourg. In 1745 some 4,000 New England volunteers, neither equipped nor trained for siege warfare, attacked the fort with the help of a Royal Navy squadron. Louisbourg, the most formidable armed post in North America, surrendered in June after a two-month siege. The French government sent a fleet to retake Acadia, but the force arrived in such poor condition as a result of hurricanes and smallpox that the fleet never engaged in combat; its main impact on the war was infecting France's Native American allies with smallpox. The Louisbourg expedition was the last major campaign of the war, but the French and their Native American allies continued to raid British settlements along the frontier. Both sides engaged in privateering against merchant vessels and coastal villages. The war ended with the signing of the Treaty of Aix-la-Chapelle in 1748. When word of the treaty provisions reached the colonies, New Englanders were outraged to hear that Britain had exchanged Louisbourg for the return of Madras in India.

Before the French and Indian War: British, French, and Spanish Possessions, 1750

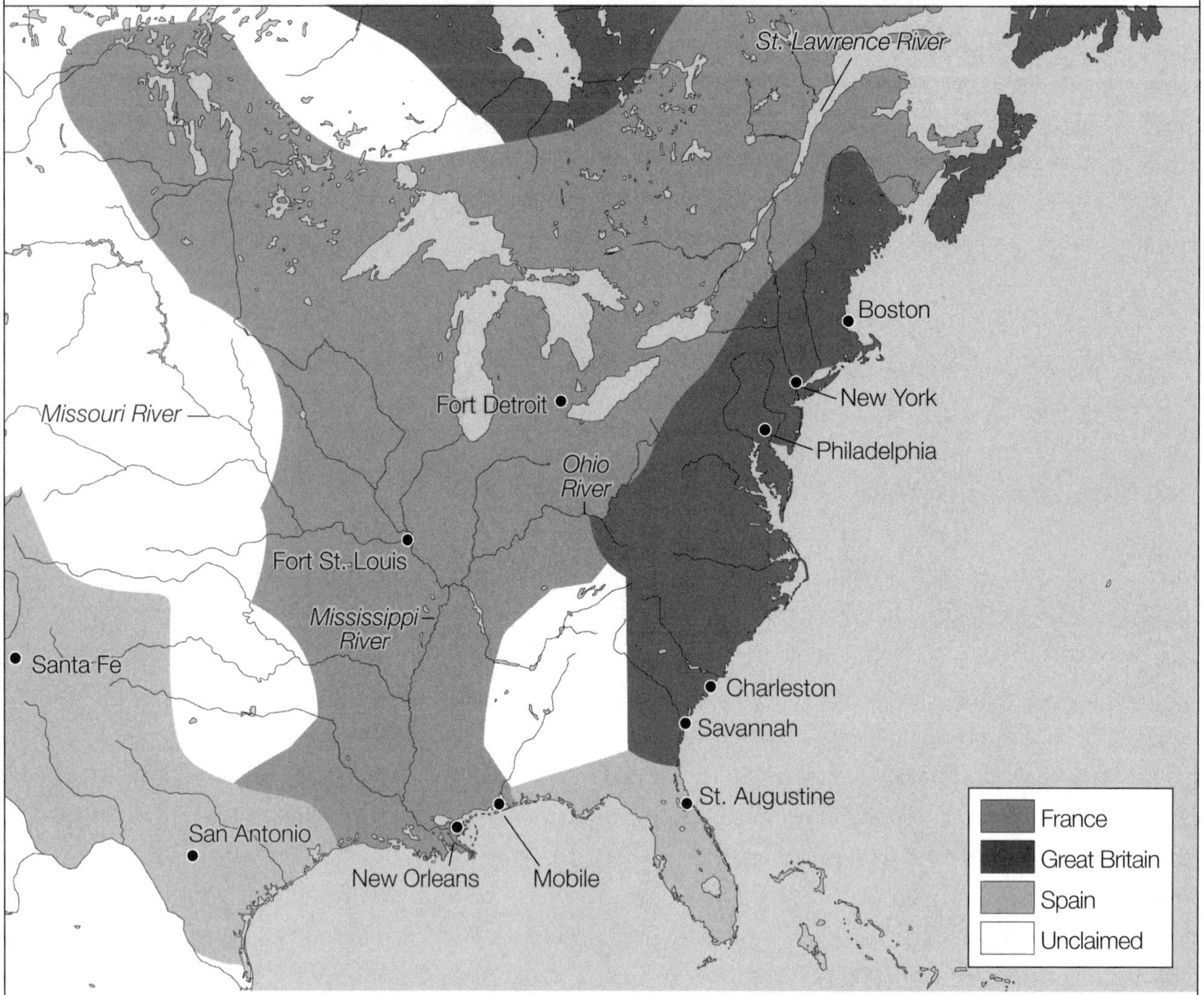

Source: adapted from "Map of the New-France about 1750" by Pinpin.

The French and Indian War, a worldwide struggle for empire between Britain and France known as the Seven Years' War in Europe, was the first truly global conflict. The above map shows the territorial holdings in North America in 1750.

French and Indian War (1754–1763)

Known in Europe as the Seven Years' War, the French and Indian War began in North America and spread into a worldwide struggle for empire between Britain and France. The two powers fought for control of the Ohio River Valley, the Great Lakes, and Canada in North America, over sugar islands in the West Indies, and over the slave and gum trades in West Africa. This conflict marked the first time that tens of thousands of British troops were present in North America, led by a coordinated military administration that urged greater colonial unity. It was the first truly global conflict, was fought on five continents, and killed over one million people.The conflict started on the frontier of the Ohio country. Settlers from Pennsylvania and Virginia had begun to move west of the Appalachians into territory claimed by France. In an attempt to block British expansion, the French built a series of forts along the frontier. Virginia demanded that they withdraw. Instead, a

After the French and Indian War: British and Spanish Territory, 1763

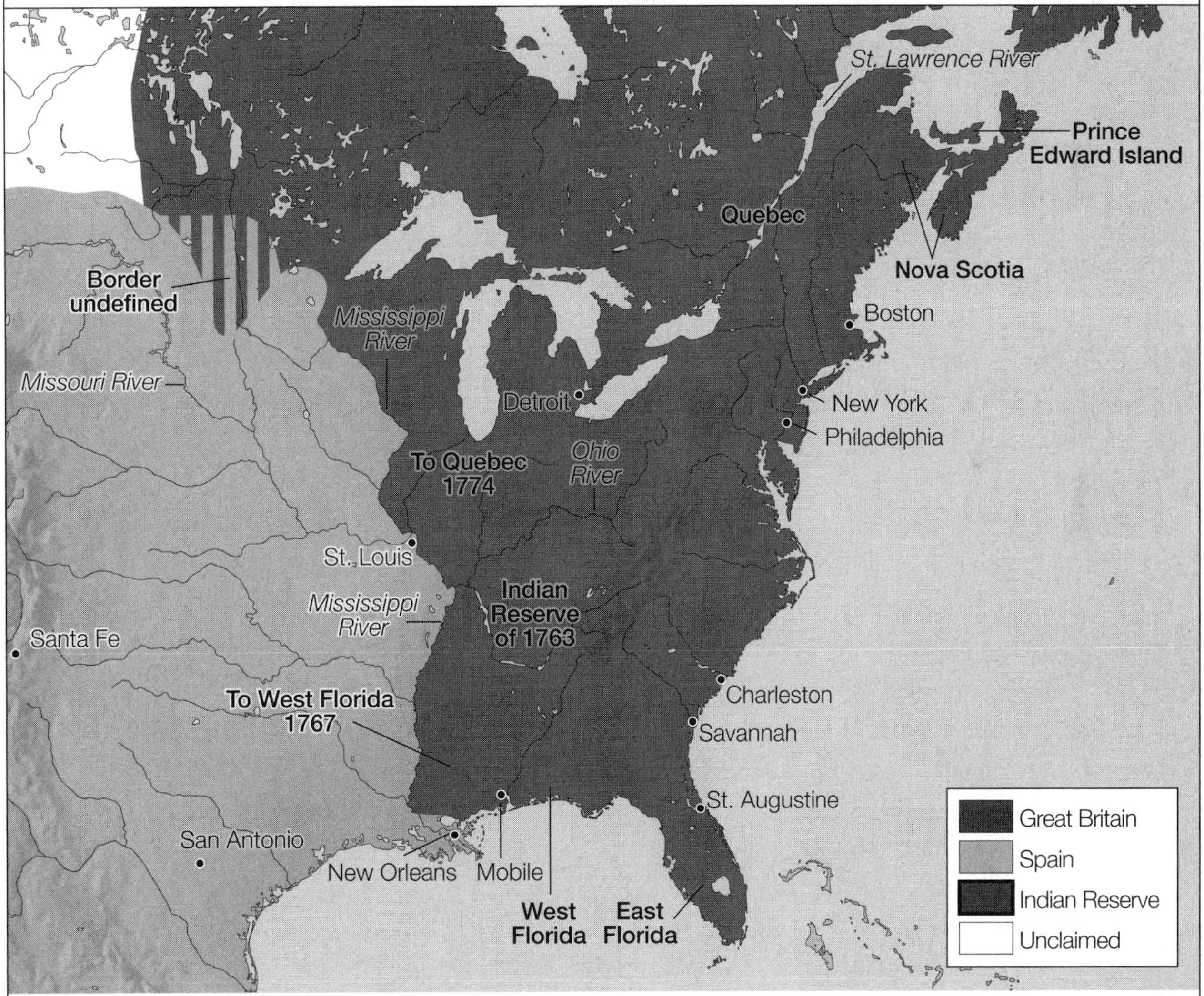

Source: adapted from "North America 1762–83" by Jon Platek.

The Treaty of Paris that officially ended the French and Indian War in 1763 redefined British, French, and Spanish colonial territories, leaving Britain as the dominant colonial power in North America. France ceded Canada and the French territory east of the Mississippi to Britain and—in a separate, secret treaty—the Louisiana territory west of the Mississippi to Spain; Spain relinquished Florida to Great Britain.

French force seized a fort Virginians had begun to erect at a British trading post at the Forks of the Ohio, the site of modern Pittsburgh, and built Fort Duquesne in its place. In 1754 a small Virginia militia detachment led by 22-year-old Major George Washington attempted to take back the site but was defeated by French troops at the makeshift fortification called Fort Necessity.

Both Britain and France saw the incidents in the Ohio country as an opportunity. With a larger navy but a smaller army than France, Britain hoped to avoid a land war in Europe. France wanted to divert British naval strength from French ports and vital targets in the Caribbean. Although technically still at peace in 1755, both European powers sent sizable professional forces to North America to reinforce their colonial militias.

The British planned a simultaneous campaign against the four French outposts that they felt were the most blatant violations of their territorial rights: Fort Duquesne, Fort Beauséjour in Nova Scotia, Fort St. Frédéric on Lake Champlain, and Fort Niagara. The goal was to take control of the Ohio country, though strategy eventually evolved into a quest for all of French Canada.

Fort Beauséjour fell after a two-week siege with little resistance, and the French-speaking Acadians of Nova Scotia were deported. Initial British efforts to take the other three forts failed. Provincial troops led by Major General William Johnson, the British Crown's superintendent of Indian affairs in the colonies, and William Shirley, the governor of Massachusetts, were stopped before they reached Forts St. Frédéric and Niagara. Johnson's campaign was partially successful both in capturing the French commander of North America and in establishing the northern outpost of Fort William Henry at the southern tip of Lake George along the vital waterway between Albany and Montreal. Unfortunately for the British, the Marquis de Montcalm, a highly skilled European veteran, took charge of French forces. More devastating from the British perspective, the new commander-in-chief of British forces in North America, Major General Edward Braddock, was defeated on the way to Duquesne by a much smaller group of French militia and Native Americans. Two-thirds of the British force were casualties in the battle, and Braddock himself and many of his officers were killed. The survivors, rallied by Braddock's aide George Washington, retreated to Fort Cumberland in Maryland.

Both London and Paris responded to the news of Braddock's defeat by sending more troops and new commanders. In May 1756 Britain and France finally declared war. The French maintained the offensive in 1756 and 1757, pushing back the British frontier with the capture of Forts Bull, Oswego, and finally William Henry. Colonial disunity and British commanders who did not understand the political realities of colonial government hampered British efforts. Colonial governments were unwilling to contribute money and resources for an already expensive war, and British officers could not order compliance.

By 1757, British losses in North America had forced a change of government in London. William Pitt the elder, leader of the House of Commons, took charge of the war effort. Pitt understood Britain's strengths—a large navy, millions of colonists, and a fiscal-military economy that could tolerate tremendous deficit spending on munitions, troops, and buying allies. Pitt also believed that permanently eliminating French Canada would finally secure British North America. Pitt increased the number of British regulars in North America and handpicked officers who were both aggressive and adaptable to the hybrid style of American warfare. He recruited substantial colonial forces by promising colonial legislatures that Britain would bear the cost, and began a slow but ultimately successful replay of the four-pronged strategy of 1755. At sea, the Royal Navy swept the oceans of French shipping and began a process of capturing French colonies cut off from European aid.

Pitt's strategy was implemented in the campaigns of 1758. Lieutenant General Jeffrey Amherst captured Louisbourg in July. The forts at Oswego and Duquesne fell in quick succession, cutting off New France's access to much of its interior. The Royal Navy blockaded French ports and prevented significant reinforcements from reaching the war zone.

A year later, British forces took control of Niagara and Ticonderoga. The British advance culminated with Major General James Wolfe's defeat of the French on the Plains of Abraham, outside Quebec, on September 13, 1759. The city surrendered five days later. Montreal, the capital of New France, was surrendered on September 8, 1760, effectively ending the war in North America. By 1762, Spain had joined the war on the French side, which precipitated the British campaigns in the Philippines and the capture of Havana.

The Treaty of Paris, signed in February 1763, redefined British, French, and Spanish colonial territories. France ceded Canada and the French territory east of the Mississippi to Britain in exchange for the return of several Caribbean islands, and, separately, had ceded the Louisiana territory west of the Mississippi to Spain. Spain relinquished Florida to Great Britain, in exchange for guaranteed control over Cuba. Britain was left as the dominant colonial power in North America.

Cherokee War and Pontiac's Rebellion (1760–1766)

The end of the war in North America in 1760 meant that Britain no longer had to compete with France to win Indian allies through gift giving and trade concessions. The suspension of ritual gifts was a political threat to tribal chiefs, who redistributed gifts to support their authority. British prohibitions on trading gunpowder and weapons caused economic hardship and, in some cases, near starvation for the tribes.

In April 1763 the Ottawa chief Pontiac took action. Believing that a united Native American force with French support could drive the British from the Great Lakes region, he organized a multitribal alliance against the British. Pontiac's efforts were reinforced by the teachings of the religious leader known as the Delaware Prophet, who preached the rejection of European trade goods and a return to traditional Native American customs.

On May 9, following a failed attempt to take Fort Detroit, Pontiac called for a simultaneous uprising against British outposts throughout the Great Lakes region. The Chippewa, Delaware, Huron, Illinois, Kickapoo, Miami, Potawatomi, Seneca, and Shawnee all responded. By late June 1763, Pontiac's forces had captured eight of the ten British forts west of Niagara, while two major posts, Forts Pitt and Detroit, remained under siege. British relief forces, the lack of French support, and dwindling supplies left Pontiac in an increasingly tenuous situation. He was eventually forced to negotiate a preliminary peace in 1765.

To the south, similar practices of limiting gifts to the Cherokee had caused a rebellion along the Carolina and Georgia frontiers in 1760–61. Denied their customary grants of gunpowder, Cherokee villages united against efforts to remake British-Indian relations. British forces eventually nullified initial Cherokee successes once the latter's supplies ran out and resistance became impossible to maintain.

In the short run, Pontiac and the Cherokee succeeded. Many Great Lakes Indian communities formed new ties with the British similar to those they had enjoyed with the French. More importantly, the Proclamation of 1763 prohibited settlement west of the Appalachians, and British colonists already in the area were ordered to leave. The proclamation soothed Native American fears, but the colonists resented London's interference in their affairs.

The American Revolution (1775–1783)

The relationship between Great Britain and its American colonies became increasingly strained after 1763, mostly because of two related issues: the imposition of new taxes and the permanent presence of British troops on American soil. Over time, British efforts to maintain greater economic and political control and American opposition to those efforts led to a military buildup as political discussions proved ineffective at resolving imperial differences.

The Revolutionary War began with a relatively minor skirmish between British regulars and American militiamen at Lexington and Concord on April 19, 1775. After driving the British back into Boston, militias from across New England laid siege to the city, while the Second Continental Congress met in Philadelphia. Recognizing that an assemblage of individual colonial militias could never win a war, Congress formed the Continental army, with George Washington as commander-in-chief.

The British were soon pressed on every front. Ethan Allen and Benedict Arnold captured Fort Ticonderoga and Crown Point. By the spring of 1776 Washington had occupied Dorchester Heights, overlooking Boston. On March 17 General William Howe evacuated his troops and set sail for Nova Scotia, leaving Boston in American hands. In the south, Lord Cornwallis and Sir Henry Clinton were repulsed in their attempt to seize Charleston.

The main theater of war then shifted from Massachusetts to New York, New Jersey, and Pennsylvania as Howe's forces joined with reinforcements from England in an effort to capture New York and separate Pennsylvania and the southern colonies from New England. Howe's troops, part of Britain's largest amphibious invasion force until the 20th century, forced Washington from one position to another, with grievous American losses. By the end of the year, Washington's troops had been pushed out of New York and New Jersey into Pennsylvania. The American army was at a low point, short on men, supplies, and confidence. On the evening of December 25, 1776, Washington led a daring raid across the Delaware River and took the Hessian garrison at Trenton, New Jersey. The battle at Trenton and a follow-up victory at Princeton forced the British to abandon New Jersey. The small victory had enormous psychological effects for both sides, bolstering American enthusiasm and undermining Howe's belief in British dominance. Importantly, Washington learned valuable strategic lessons and adopted a Fabian strategy of maneuver and evasion, fighting only when he had reasonable chances of success. As long as a Continental army remained in the field, the British could not claim victory.

In June 1777 the British tried once again to separate New England from the rest of the colonies. British troops under General John Burgoyne moved south from Quebec toward Albany, where he was supposed to meet up with Howe's forces from New York and a contingent from the west. None of the British forces reached Albany. Instead of marching north, Howe diverted his troops to Philadelphia. Burgoyne failed to understand the realities of troop movement in the American wilderness. His march was slowed by the logistical problems of obtaining supplies and transporting artillery through wilderness territory. He was about 25 miles north of Albany, near Saratoga, when Continentals and militia under Horatio Gates and Benedict Arnold blocked his path. Two bloody battles ensued in September and October. Burgoyne, out of supplies and faced with a superior force, tried to retreat but was forced to surrender on October 17 in what would be a turning point of the war.

France had provided the Americans with clandestine aid against its old enemy since the start of the war. Following Saratoga, France openly allied with the Americans, bringing the embattled colonies badly needed financial aid, troops, advisers, and, most importantly, a fleet able to combat the Royal Navy. Once France entered the war, Britain found itself in an increasingly global conflict rather than an American rebellion. Spain declared war against Britain in 1779, followed by Holland in 1780.

Despite Burgoyne's debacle, Howe's campaign against Philadelphia was a resounding success for the British, who outmaneuvered the Americans through creative uses of light infantry warfare. Howe took Philadelphia but again could not capture Washington's army and end the war. The British abandoned the city in 1778 in response to the French entry into the war. In the west, Virginian George Rogers Clark led a small force of frontiersmen to capture much of the Ohio country that would be ceded to America during the peace negotiations.

British strategic shifts toward the southern colonies increased the role of African Americans in the struggle. The Revolution was the first war in which the 500,000-member slave population of the 13 colonies featured prominently. While some 5,000 blacks, both slave and free, fought for the American cause, perhaps three times as many blacks, lured by promises of freedom upon British victory, fought for the king.

In 1778 the British captured Savannah, Georgia, in the initial phase of a southern strategy to capitalize on southern Loyalist support. In May 1780 British forces under Sir Henry Clinton captured Charleston, the most important city in the South, along with an entire Continental army, and easily swept up most of the Carolinas into British control. Shortly thereafter, Clinton sailed back to his headquarters in New York with more than half his troops, leaving Lord Charles Cornwallis a reduced force with which to defend an extended chain of posts against American guerrilla attacks. A Continental army under Horatio Gates was decimated at Camden, and Gates earned disgrace for abandoning his troops during the battle. Generals Nathanael Greene and Daniel Morgan reformulated American strategy and engaged Cornwallis in a chase across the Carolinas, exhausting the British. The Battle of Cowpens on January 17, 1781, was a major American victory and, combined with the inconclusive engagement at Guilford Courthouse on March 15, seriously bloodied Cornwallis.

Weakened by his losses, Cornwallis abandoned the lower South and led his exhausted army toward Virginia, expecting to join forces with the traitorous Benedict Arnold, now a British general. After rampaging through Virginia, Cornwallis received orders from Clinton to establish a naval base on the coast. Assuming the Royal Navy was in command of Chesapeake Bay, Cornwallis built a fortified base on the peninsula at Yorktown. It was a costly mistake.

A French fleet from the West Indies cut off the entrance to Chesapeake Bay. At the same time, Washington and the French general the Comte de Rochambeau left a decoy army facing Clinton's headquarters at New York and moved the majority of their forces south toward Cornwallis. Cut off by the French and Continental armies and blockaded from the sea, Cornwallis surrendered on October 19, 1781.

Thereafter, Britons generally lost the will to fight, and major land combat ceased. Cornwallis's surrender contributed to the fall of Lord North's government in favor of the peace faction led by Lord Rockingham. Peace negotiations began on March 5, 1782. The Treaty of Paris, which recognized the independence of the United States, was signed on September 3, 1783.

Post-Revolution Conflicts

American borders extended to the Mississippi River and included dozens of Native American tribes who had aligned with Britain to protect their homelands. From 1783 until after the War of 1812, the United States engaged in a series of military expeditions against indigenous resistance movements. The Old Northwest Territory was the center of much of this conflict, which was in part spurred by Britain.

On the high seas, American shipping, now removed from British protection, came under threat from pirates in the Barbary states of North Africa and, increasingly after the start of the French Revolutionary wars, from Britain and France. The nascent United States Navy, built around a core of frigates, such as the USS *Constitution*, that were larger and more heavily armed than normal frigates, engaged in an undeclared war with French ships, largely in the Caribbean, to protect American commerce. The Quasi-War, from 1798 to 1800, was the first test of the American navy and provided operational experience for the larger threats of the early 19th century, namely the Barbary Wars and the War of 1812.

Warfare in America during the 18th century spurred the transformation of a continent. From the early frontier raids to the largest British amphibious invasion until the 20th century, war increased in complexity, ferocity, and influence, touching nearly everyone in North America.

—Pamela D. Toler and Ethan R. Bennett

Further Reading

Anderson, Fred. *Crucible of War: The Seven Years' War and the Fate of Empire in British North America, 1754–1766*. New York: Alfred A. Knopf, 2000.

Black, Jeremy. *Warfare in the Eighteenth Century*. London: Cassell, 1999.

———. *The War for America: The Fight for Independence, 1775–1783*. New York: St. Martin's Press, 1991.

Brumwell, Stephen. *White Devil: A True Story of War, Savagery, and Vengeance in Colonial America*. Cambridge, Mass.: Da Capo Press, 2005.

Demos, John. *The Unredeemed Captive: A Family Story from Early America*. New York: Alfred A. Knopf, 1994.

Dixon, David. *Never Come to Peace Again: Pontiac's Uprising and the Fate of the British Empire in North America*. Norman: University of Oklahoma Press, 2005.

Dull, Jonathan R. *The Age of the Ship of the Line: The British and French Navies, 1650–1815*. Lincoln: University of Nebraska Press, 2009.

Egerton, Douglas. *Death or Liberty: African Americans and Revolutionary America*. New York: Oxford University Press, 2009.

Ferling, John. *Almost a Miracle: The American Victory in the War of Independence*. New York: Oxford University Press, 2007.

Fischer, David Hackett. *Washington's Crossing*. New York: Oxford University Press, 2004.

Graymont, Barbara. *The Iroquois Indians in the American Revolution*. Syracuse, N.Y.: Syracuse University Press, 1972.

Haefeli, Evan, and Kevin Sweeney. *Captors and Captives: The 1704 French and Indian Raid on Deerfield*. Amherst: University of Massachusetts Press, 2003.

Higginbotham, Don. *The War of American Independence: Military Attitudes, Policies, and Practice, 1763–1789*. Boston: Northeastern University Press, 1971.

Jennings, Francis. *Empire of Fortune: Crowns, Colonies, and Tribes in the Seven Years War in America*. New York: W. W. Norton, 1988.

Ketchum, Richard M. *Saratoga: Turning Point of America's Revolutionary War*. New York: Henry Holt, 1997.

———. *Victory at Yorktown: The Campaign That Won the Revolution.* New York: Henry Holt, 2004.

Leach, Douglas E. *Arms for Empire: A Military History of the British Colonies in North America, 1607–1763*. New York: Macmillan, 1973.

Little, Anne M. *Abraham in Arms: War and Gender in Colonial New England*. Philadelphia: University of Pennsylvania Press, 2007.

Marshall, P. J. *The Making and Unmaking of Empires: Britain, India, and America c. 1750–1783*. New York: Oxford University Press, 2005.

Middlekauff, Robert. *The Glorious Cause: The American Revolution, 1763–1789*. Revised and expanded edition. New York: Oxford University Press, 2005.

Middleton, Richard. *Pontiac's War: Its Causes, Course and Consequences*. New York: Routledge, 2007.

Palmer, Michael A. *Stoddert's War: Naval Operations during the Quasi-War with France, 1798–1801*. Columbia: University of South Carolina Press, 1987.

Peckham, Howard H. *The Colonial Wars, 1689–1762*. Chicago: University of Chicago Press, 1964.

Plank, Geoffrey. *An Unsettled Conquest: The British Campaign against the Peoples of Acadia*. Philadelphia: University of Pennsylvania Press, 2001.

Quarles, Benjamin. *The Negro in the American Revolution*. Chapel Hill: University of North Carolina Press, 1961.

Silver, Peter. *Our Savage Neighbors: How Indian War Transformed Early America*. New York: W. W. Norton, 2008.

Steele, Ian K. *Warpaths: Invasions of North America.* New York: Oxford University Press, 1995.

Urban, Mark. *Fusiliers: The Saga of a British Redcoat Regiment in the American Revolution*. New York: Walker and Co., 2007.

Weintraub, Stanley. *Iron Tears: America's Battle for Freedom, Britain's Quagmire, 1775–1783*. New York: Free Press, 2005.

White, Richard. *The Middle Ground: Indians, Empires, and Republics in the Great Lakes Region, 1650–1815*. New York: Cambridge University Press, 1991.

18th Century WOMEN

African American, European American, and Native American women in British North America shared many experiences, despite their enormous cultural, economic, and political diversity. Most important among the differences separating them was that European women and most Native American women were free, while some Native American women and most African American women were enslaved. Nevertheless, whatever their racial, ethnic, or class background, these women were almost always subordinated to the men in their societies, by virtue of law and custom. They also generally had fewer economic opportunities than men, and they were primarily responsible for children, a pattern that has kept women in poverty in many cultures. Another commonality among these women was their vulnerability to sexual abuse, although enslaved women were particularly vulnerable in this regard.

Native American Women

Native American women were perhaps the most diverse of these groups in 18th-century North America. Some of them lived in cultures that were sedentary and primarily agricultural, while others lived in more nomadic groups. Some had regular contact with Europeans, while others may not have seen or been affected as profoundly by the European presence until decades or even centuries later. New diseases, trade goods, religion, and plants and animals brought by Europeans significantly disrupted Native peoples' lives and traditions. The starkest changes had been wrought in earlier centuries, when Native populations were decimated in the wake of epidemics. By the 18th century, Native American women were helping their communities contend with the impact of those changes.

In some regions Native American women intermarried with European men, facilitating diplomatic and economic relationships. In fur trade societies in the Great Lakes regions, for example, women married French fur trappers and traders. Indian families incorporated these men, sometimes into life in the longhouses, and gained access to the European goods they traded. In turn, the work of these men was enhanced by the extensive knowledge provided by their wives and new kin—knowledge of the land, of trapping and hunting territories, as well as of equipment critical for success in that environment, such as the warm moccasins the women made.

Among Native Americans, as with other groups, women and men had different and complementary roles. In many groups, women were responsible for agricultural production, while men hunted. This division of labor had important economic, familial, and political repercussions. Women's work as farmers, as well as the fact that men often traveled away from settlements to hunt and sometimes to make war, meant that women had significant control over the village space and oversaw the distribution of food and other resources among families. They also exercised an important political voice. The Iroquois, for example, lived in longhouses, dwelling spaces that were headed by a matriarch. The matriarch's husband and daughters and their husbands lived there, too. Her sons would move into the longhouses of the women they married. The longhouse, while organized along kinship lines, also had political voice, and the matriarch was a key figure in how the views of the longhouse were expressed to the tribal leadership. During the American Revolution, for example, some of the Iroquois tribes who decided to ally with the British noted that "the mothers also consented to it."

Some Native women converted to Christianity. Their numbers were never very large, but they were important in terms of their role in the contact between cultures and because of the tensions that developed around the presence of Christian Indians in many communities, particularly during conflicts such as King Philip's War (1675–76) and the Seven Years' War (1756–63). Both Catholics and Protestants sent out missionaries and established missions, Catholics in areas of the continent claimed by France or Spain and Protestants in the British colonies. In New England the missionary efforts of Protestants were most robust in the 17th century, but "praying towns" where Native American converts lived, such as the best known of these, Natick, Massachusetts, survived into the 18th century. The Moravians established successful missionary towns in Pennsylvania where Native American converts, primarily from the Delaware (Leni Lenape), lived. Native American women were important to these conversion efforts, and among such communities of Christian Indians they may have greatly outnumbered male converts.

Native American women living among the Europeans could be subject to terrible poverty. Particularly by the 18th century, the dislocations of Indian communities and traditions, and the disappearance of their old territories, made traditional Native self-sufficiency all but impossible. Some Native people were made to adapt to European laws and customs, which could include working for wages and also recognizing European forms of property. A will, for example, written in an Algonquian dialect by a Wampanoag woman who had converted to Christianity shows how Indians could imitate European ways of describing and passing on the types of property that in the traditional tribal context they would never have owned or would have been distributed after their death, according to tribal customs. In 1749 Naomi Omaush bequeathed items including pewter dishes and spoons to a local minister, and a blanket, cloth, and specific items of clothing to her kin. "My soul," she expected, "shall . . . go to meet the Lord in Heaven." The adoption, willing or unwilling, of European traditions, was not all that unusual. But Naomi Omaush was unusual in several other respects, one being that she owned something that she could will away. Most Native people, especially women, were in no position to own or bequeath anything, in European terms. But even on their own terms, the collective well-being of Native peoples was terribly degraded by the effects of depopulation and war.

European American Women

European American women, like Native American or African American women, came from diverse ethnic and religious backgrounds, but on the whole were a more homogeneous group. This was mainly due to the fact that most Europeans in the British colonies came from Britain, even though there were also significant populations of Scots-Irish (along the backcountry), Germans (especially in Pennsylvania), and Dutch (in New York). Among Europeans in North America, the ratio of men to women changed from the 17th to the 18th centuries and differed from region to region. Among North American empires, the British had the highest proportion of European women; many fewer French or Spanish women, proportionally, came to the colonies of North America. While areas like New England, where migration was dominated by family groups, had fairly even sex ratios from early in the 17th century on and thus could expand their population quite quickly, other places like the Chesapeake colonies of Virginia and Maryland and the French and Spanish colonies had much higher ratios of male immigrants, and thus their European populations grew more slowly. Into the 18th century those unequal ratios in the southern British colonies began to balance out; more women began to migrate, marry, and have children. European populations in Virginia and South Carolina, for example, started to grow quickly—from 38,000 and 1,500, respectively, in 1700, to almost 280,000 and 80,000 on the eve of the American Revolution. In those same years, Native populations declined from the thousands to the mere hundreds of people. Whereas the increase in European populations came both from immigration and from the balancing of sex ratios, leavened by relative prosperity, Indians were dying from disease, dislocation, and warfare.

Still, most European women lived in rural subsistence households, where they produced, rather than purchased, most of what they needed, and they did not have the resources necessary to improve their economic condition. Farm duties were usually very gender-segregated. Women's labor consisted of basic household tasks, including food preparation, child care, and the time-consuming and backbreakingly difficult job of laundering bedding and clothing. Women did work in fields to help with bringing in crops such as corn, wheat, and tobacco, but they also tended vegetable gardens to produce food for the household. They were also responsible for dairying—milking and producing cheese and butter—which became an increasingly important source of extra cash for households in some regions.

A disproportionately high number of independent women lived in the few major cities of the Eastern Seaboard:

Boston, New York, Philadelphia, Baltimore, and Charles Town (Charleston). Most were widowed, most had children, but some were never married. Warfare and seafaring jobs claimed the lives of many men—or kept them absent from home. In 1765 there were 20 percent more women than men in Boston. Heading their own households was so financially difficult for these women that most lived in or near poverty. The partial records from these seaboard cities show that women who headed households tended to cluster together along particular streets or blocks. Perhaps they did so because those were cheaper areas to live, or perhaps they sought out like neighbors for moral and even economic mutual support.

Whether they were married or not, women found work in cities doing the sorts of jobs that their rural counterparts also performed: domestic labor, including caring for children. One difference was that in rural areas domestic servants were primarily young women who worked before marriage, while in cities there was much greater demand for hired domestics of all ages. Women servants played an important role in elite households, where they might have specific and consistent household assignments, and in the homes of artisans, where they might perform jobs associated with both the workshop and the household. The wages women earned for such jobs were very, very low. Women's wages were always lower than men's, and they had many fewer job opportunities.

A few urban women entered into trades, especially those related to clothing, such as dressmaking. They also worked in food and beverage service, as tavernkeepers or servers, or as boardinghouse keepers. Any of these occupations could include providing a variety of services; for example, a boardinghouse keeper might also provide laundry and mending services for her tenants. A few women worked as teachers in the small number of schools open to girls. Nursing and midwifery were also in demand. Retail was perhaps the occupation most open to women at all levels of wealth. Hucksters sold on the street secondhand or second-quality goods; a woman might devote a small corner of a room in her home to shop goods; and a few women had more extensive inventories of imported goods. In all these occupations the expanding Atlantic economy played a role, as the greater volume of transatlantic trade in the 18th century brought more goods into seaport cities, and more work associated with that trade.

African American Women

The vast majority of African American women in 18th-century America lived in slavery. Slavery defined their material conditions, confined their time, and constrained their family and other relationships and experiences. Because Britain had no legal tradition of slavery, the British colonies in North America and in the Caribbean created laws to determine enslaved status, to define slaves as property, and to control enslaved people.

Laws designed to make slavery a more strictly controlled institution often targeted women explicitly. The most important laws, such as one passed by Virginia in 1662, defined slavery as a lifetime status, inheritable through the mother. That made women's sexual behavior and reproduction a matter of intense economic, legal, and even political interest for slave owners. Virginia enacted a harsh ban on interracial relationships in 1691 and reiterated it in 1753 and 1765. These laws were not aimed at white men who had sex (often coerced) with enslaved black women; rather, they made sure that blacks and whites could not have relationships that would be accorded the protection and the respect of the law. Free white women (not servants themselves) who bore mixed-race children were punished, and their children were made servants until they reached adulthood.

Over the course of the 18th century an increasing majority of enslaved people were born not in Africa, but in slavery in America. More mothers were able to have healthy pregnancies and give birth to healthy children in areas such as the Chesapeake—Maryland and Virginia—where there were larger American-born slave populations, perhaps in part because those denser communities allowed for more social support among enslaved people. These communities may have had a higher proportion of females in part because male slaves were seen as more desirable workers and thus more vulnerable to sale.

Women who were enslaved faced the same risks in childbirth as other women in this era. In addition, enslaved women were expected to continue to work until they delivered, and the extremely harsh conditions in which most worked probably contributed to their higher rates of mortality and to the higher rates of infant mortality among slave children.

Toward the end of the 18th century, larger free black communities developed in northern cities, most prominently in Philadelphia. There women were key actors in building institutions that became the cornerstones of those communities, such as the African Methodist Episcopal Church, founded in 1794 by Richard Allen and supporters, including his wife, Sarah. Sarah Allen's experience drew her to community organizing for abolition and other social welfare causes. In the 19th century more African American women would take part in the burgeoning abolitionist and women's rights movements.

Most African American women (and men) did not have the opportunities that Sarah Allen did. Another exceptional African American woman was the famous Boston poet Phillis Wheatley, who was remarkable for her talent and erudition. Born in Africa in the early 1750s and sold into slavery at a young age, she was a slave in the home of the Bostonians John and Susanna Wheatley, wealthy merchants. They saw to her education, including in Latin, and she wrote poetry that was published beginning in the late 1760s. Wheatley's poems never addressed her own life, either in slavery or freedom (she gained her freedom in 1773), emphasizing instead Christian themes, so, though her work is important, it tells us little about the lives of free or enslaved women of color, other than that in one exceptional case education and opportunity was afforded this talented woman.

Wheatley lived in New England, where literacy rates among women were generally higher and educational opportunities, though few, were greater than in the South. In the Mid-Atlantic region, particularly around Philadelphia and in New Jersey and New York, schooling for girls was available, albeit on a very limited basis. Most girls learned only basic literacy skills at home, from their parents.

Law

Virtually all women in 18th-century America existed within a system of enforced legal dependence. Even Native American women, once within the jurisdictions of Anglo-American law, were assumed to live in households headed by men, in which those men should have particular and dominant privileges. The Anglo-American legal system gave men control over almost all their household's property. Except in extraordinary circumstances, once a woman married, her property became her husband's. The law distinguished between real estate—land and buildings—and personal property, which included money and "movables" such as home furnishings. Any real estate a woman owned became her husband's to manage and to keep any rents, while personal property became his outright. For the most part, sons inherited real estate from their father's estates, while daughters inherited personal property. These practices gave women little economic capacity.

In other ways, too, the law enforced women's dependence. Married women could not sign contracts, even for work, because they were not considered independent people under the law. The theory was that a husband owned everything, even his wife's services, and only he could approve of those services being offered to someone else. Nor could women appear in court—presumably their husbands could speak for them. Absolute divorce was nearly impossible; in some colonies only the legislature could approve a divorce. Some couples were able to make agreements to separate, but even this was rare and usually available only in cases of bigamy or extreme abuse. Courts and legislatures were rarely sympathetic to petitions for divorce based solely on charges of abuse. Similarly, a husband's sexual misconduct was rarely grounds for divorce; women's sexual infidelity, on the other hand, was more threatening to a husband's control over the household and his social position and was cited in successful divorce cases.

Children, too, were affected by the law's assumption of female dependence and male control of property. Children were called "orphans" when their father died, even if their mother lived. A father, as head of household, was the dominant figure in his children's life from the perspective of the law. When a man died, a court assessed the value of his property (most people owned very little) and how it would be divided among his widow and children.

A widow usually would receive one-third of a man's real estate, if he had any, to use during her lifetime. If a man died without making a will, the remaining property would be divided among his children. If those children were minors, the court would appoint an executor to manage their inheritance, and a guardian for the children's care. There was no regular presumption that the mother would be either the executor or the guardian. Poor orphaned children were often indentured to work as servants until they reached adulthood (an age that varied across regions).

Eighteenth-century women were vulnerable to sexual coercion. Ideas about sex and honor, and understandings of the body and of consent itself, were reflected in laws and legal procedures that defined coercion narrowly and with prejudice, and often discounted altogether women's testimony about rape. Two related factors played a particular role in cases of sexual violence: status and race. As heads of household, husbands and masters claimed authority over and legitimate access to the bodies of their female dependents. Sex within marriage was understood to be de facto consensual, whether or not a woman testified to or claimed the contrary. Enslaved women were not permitted to testify against whites, except in extraordinarily rare cases. The ways that women's character and biology were described also influenced perceptions of coerced sex. Eighteenth-century people assumed pregnancy could not occur in cases where women resisted sex, and thus a pregnancy was never evidence of rape. And a woman's own behavior and reputation, as is true in most historical contexts, was much more rigorously scrutinized than that of the accused assailant. The Pennsylvania lawyer William Bradford acknowledged that rape cases, even when they were reported and prosecuted, were usually decided by the "rank, situation and character of the victim." Women of higher status were clearly less vulnerable to rape than other women, and enslaved women were clearly very vulnerable indeed. A woman who was enslaved had virtually no protection from sexual violence. By the 18th century, laws in most places forbade blacks from testifying against whites in court, and few people openly questioned any slaveholder's right to have sex with a slave he owned. But no woman, slave or free, could depend on a culture or a law that would protect her from sexual violence, or ensure the fair prosecution of her attacker if she was raped.

Religion

During the 18th century, women acquired new outlets for their religious commitments and experiences. Women had opportunities for leadership in only a few religious groups, most prominently the Quakers, who preached a gospel of equality. Evidence suggests that women made up the majority of congregants in the Christian denominations most numerous in 18th-century America. They also participated vigorously in the revivals that swept through all regions—sometimes collectively called the "Great Awakening." An increasing emphasis among Protestants on the gentleness of God and on an emotional style of religious practice in the 18th century (called evangelicalism) might have had beneficial effects for women at home and in public. In some cases evangelicalism seemed to have offered women not only solace, but also a justification for contesting the authority of their husbands. Abigail Abbot Bailey, for example, a New England woman whose abusive husband beat her and raped their daughter, routinely defied his order that she give up churchgoing. After her death, her pastor published an account of her ordeal and her faith. Some Protestant groups seem to have been more open to women's active church leadership earlier in their history, and then became more resistant as they gained numbers and moved into the Protestant mainstream.

Revolution

Many scholars have written about the experiences of women during the American Revolution and have wondered whether the revolutionary movement provided women any enhanced legal, political, or public voice. Politics and femininity were not supposed to mix. A few women did speak openly about the politics of the Revolutionary era. But these women, primarily from elite families, expressed their political views carefully. Probably the most famous example of a female Revolutionary voice was that of Abigail Smith Adams, who questioned why the Revolutionary leadership would advocate greater rights and representation for men but not for women. She wrote that the Congress should

Women during the Revolutionary era did not talk publicly about politics, as it was considered unseemly and unfeminine. One exception to this rule was Abigail Adams, wife of John Adams, who wrote that the Revolutionary leadership should "remember the ladies" in their pursuit of greater rights and representation for men. *(Library of Congress)*

"remember the ladies, and be more generous and favorable to them than your ancestors. Do not put such unlimited power into the hands of the Husbands. Remember all Men would be tyrants if they could. If particular care and attention is not paid to the Ladies we are determined to foment a Rebellion, and will not hold ourselves bound by any Laws in which we have no voice, or Representation." Adams's husband, John, away from home during his service in the Continental Congress, seems not to have taken her concerns very seriously.

Other women expressed their views in the same fashion as the men in their families and communities: They joined boycotts of imported British goods, provided an audience for the political theater of protests, and supported the war effort. Many women participated in the food rioting that broke out in cities and towns all over the colonies, in which angry mobs confronted merchants and shopkeepers they thought were hoarding goods or unfairly raising prices during shortages.

The American Revolution brought few changes that directly concerned women's condition. The Revolution did not eradicate slavery, nor did it overturn Anglo-American legal traditions concerning marriage and household economies. Late in the 18th century, however, some new American states began adopting more liberal divorce laws, giving a few more women the opportunity to be released from difficult marriages.

Another trend in the post-Revolutionary era was not in the domain of government at all. Among white American women, the birth rate began to drop dramatically. Women began to limit the size of their families using techniques for prolonging the period between their pregnancies. Demographers have used many kinds of historical evidence to show that from the mid-18th century to the mid-19th century the average size of families was shrinking. Fewer pregnancies meant women could have longer lives and could spend time in other endeavors that supported their family.

—*Karin Wulf*

Further Reading

Brown, Kathleen. *Good Wives, Nasty Wenches, and Anxious Patriarchs: Gender, Race, and Power in Colonial Virginia.* Chapel Hill: University of North Carolina Press, 1996.

Clark, Emily. *Masterless Mistresses: The New Orleans Ursulines and the Development of a New World Society, 1727–1834.* Chapel Hill: University of North Carolina Press, 2007.

Crane, Elaine. *Ebb Tide in New England: Women, Seaports, and Social Change, 1630–1800.* Boston: Northeastern University Press, 1998.

DuBois, Ellen, and Lynn Dumenil. *Through Women's Eyes: An American History with Documents.* New York: Bedford / St. Martin's, 2005.

Fischer, Kristen. *Suspect Relations: Sex, Race, and Resistance in Colonial North Carolina.* Ithaca, N.Y.: Cornell University Press, 2001.

Gelles, Edith B. *Abigail Adams: A Writing Life.* New York: Routledge, 2002.

Greer, Allan. *Mohawk Saint: Catherine Tekakwitha and the Jesuits.* New York: Oxford University Press, 2006.

Gunderson, Joan R. "The Double Bonds of Race and Sex: Black and White Women in a Colonial Virginia Parish." *Journal of Southern History* 52 (3): 351–372.

Hartigan-O'Connor, Ellen. *The Ties That Buy: Women and Commerce in Revolutionary America.* Philadelphia: University of Pennsylvania Press, 2009.

Jensen, Joan. *Loosening the Bonds: Mid-Atlantic Farm Women, 1750–1850.* New Haven, Conn.: Yale University Press, 1988.

Juster, Susan. *Disorderly Women: Sexual Politics and Evangelicalism in Revolutionary New England*. Ithaca, N.Y.: Cornell University Press, 1996.

Kelley, Mary. *Learning to Stand and Speak: Women, Education, and Public Life in America's Republic*. Chapel Hill: University of North Carolina Press, 2006.

Klepp, Susan E. *Revolutionary Conceptions: Women, Fertility, and Family Limitation in America, 1760–1820.* Chapel Hill: University of North Carolina Press, 2009.

Morgan, Jennifer. *Laboring Women: Reproduction and Gender in New World Slavery.* Philadelphia: University of Pennsylvania Press, 2004.

Norton, Mary Beth. *Liberty's Daughters: The Revolutionary Experience of American Women, 1750–1800.* Boston: Little, Brown, 1980.

Salmon, Marylynn. *Women and the Law of Property in Early America*. Chapel Hill: University of North Carolina Press, 1986.

Smith, Barbara Clark. "Food Rioters and the American Revolution." *William and Mary Quarterly*, 3d series, vol. 51, no. 1 (January 1994): 3–38.

Smith, Susan Sleeper. *Indian Women and French Men.* Amherst: University of Massachusetts Press, 2001.

Sturtz, Linda. *Within Her Power: Propertied Women in Colonial Virginia*. New York: Routledge, 2002.

Taves, Ann, ed. *Religion and Domestic Violence in Early New England: The Memoirs of Abigail Abbot Bailey.* Bloomington: Indiana University Press, 1989.

Ulrich, Laurel. *A Midwife's Tale: The Life of Martha Ballard, Based on Her Diary, 1785–1812.* New York: Vintage, 1991.

Wulf, Karin. *Not All Wives: Women of Colonial Philadelphia.* Ithaca, N.Y.: Cornell University Press, 2000.

Zagarri, Rosemarie. *Revolutionary Backlash: Women and Politics in the Early American Republic.* Philadelphia: University of Pennsylvania Press, 2007.

CUMULATIVE INDEX

Page numbers in **boldface** type indicate article titles. Page numbers in *italic* type indicate illustrations or other graphics.